The Business of Sustainable T and Managen

C000234869

The Business of Sustainable Tourism Development and Ma...g.....m provides a comprehensive introduction to sustainable tourism, crucially combining both theoretical and practical approaches to equip students with the tools to successfully manage a sustainable tourism business or destination.

Covering a range of crucial topics such as mass tourism, alternative tourism, human capital management, and many more, this book incorporates a global curriculum that widens the sustainable tourism debate to include theoretical perspectives, applied research, best practice frameworks, business tools, and case studies, facilitating a more comprehensive sustainable tourism educational strategy. Information on how to effectively implement strategies that can be applied to business environments, entrepreneurship, and job skills to enhance career preparation is at the forefront of this textbook.

Highly illustrated and with an interactive companion website including bonus learning materials, this is the ideal textbook for students of tourism, hospitality, and events management at both undergraduate and postgraduate levels.

Susan L. Slocum is an Associate Professor in the Department of Tourism and Event Management at George Mason University, Manassas, Virginia. Sue has worked on regional planning and development for 15 years and worked with rural communities in Tanzania, the United Kingdom, Belarus, and various locations in the United States. Her primary focus is on rural sustainable development, policy implementation, and food tourism, specifically working with small businesses and communities in less advantaged areas. Sue received her doctoral education from Clemson University and has worked at the University of Bedfordshire, UK, and at Utah State University. She has published seven books, including textbooks, numerous academic articles, and has been conferred the prestigious Fulbright Research Scholar (2019–2020) award.

Abena Aidoo is an Associate Professor in the Tourism and Events Management Program at George Mason University, Fairfax, Virginia. Her primary focus is on sustainable tourism development as a socioeconomic development tool, with specific emphasis on tourism policymaking and implementation, heritage and cultural tourism development and management, issues surrounding women tourists and women tourism producers, as well as emerging areas such as film and medical tourism. Abena received her doctoral degree from the University of Delaware in Urban Affairs and Public Policy, with an emphasis on tourism development.

Kelly McMahon is a business professional with 18 years in the high-tech industry creating and leading high-performing global teams. She believes that by valuing the whole person, employees are able to bring their best selves to work each day. Kelly contracted at Microsoft for over ten years before choosing to pursue an MBA in Sustainable Business from Presidio Graduate School (formerly BGI). Upon graduating, she began her people-management career, first at Isilon, then EMC, and Dell through a series of acquisitions. She recently ended her tenure at F5 Networks as the Senior Manager of User Enablement, striving to provide a consistent and high-quality end-user experience. She prides herself on delivering programs that produce measurable business results, including long-term customer and employee satisfaction. She is a change agent, working to transform business for good, using the three pillars of sustainability: People, Planet, and Profit.

The Business of Sustainable Tourism Development and Management

Susan L. Slocum, Abena Aidoo, and Kelly McMahon

Routledge
Taylor & Francis Group

LONDON AND NEW YORK

First published 2020
by Routledge
2 Park Square, Milton Park, Abingdon, Oxon OX14 4RN

and by Routledge
52 Vanderbilt Avenue, New York, NY 10017

Routledge is an imprint of the Taylor & Francis Group, an informa business

© 2020 Susan L. Slocum, Abena Aidoo, and Kelly McMahon

British Library Cataloguing-in-Publication Data
A catalogue record for this book is available from the British Library

Library of Congress Cataloging-in-Publication Data
Names: Slocum, Susan L., author. | Aidoo, Abena, author. | McMahon,
   Kelly, 1969– author.
Title: The business of sustainable tourism development and management /
   Susan L. Slocum, Abena Aidoo, and Kelly McMahon.
Description: Abingdon, Oxon ; New York, NY : Routledge, 2020. | Includes
   bibliographical references and index.
Identifiers: LCCN 2019054160 (print) | LCCN 2019054161 (ebook)
Subjects: LCSH: Sustainable tourism. | Tourism—Management.
Classification: LCC G156.5.S87 S58 2020 (print) | LCC G156.5.S87
   (ebook) | DDC 910.68—dc23
LC record available at https://lccn.loc.gov/2019054160
LC ebook record available at https://lccn.loc.gov/2019054161

ISBN: 978-1-138-49214-1 (hbk)
ISBN: 978-1-138-49216-5 (pbk)
ISBN: 978-1-351-03106-6 (ebk)

Typeset in Iowan Old Style
by Apex CoVantage, LLC

Visit the companion website: www.routledge.com/cw/9781138492165

Contents

Figures

Tables

Images

Preface

This book provides a comprehensive introduction to sustainable tourism that includes the application of both theory and practice. Combining a strong focus on tourism theories, each chapter concludes with a business tool and case studies designed to help the reader apply the theories discussed to real-world scenarios. Sustainable tourism is a growing academic discipline, taught at both undergraduate and graduate levels. Currently, sustainable tourism textbooks are focused either on theory, rural development, and developing nations, or on providing industry best practice and business development for career preparation. There are no books that adequately combine both. What makes this book stand out is its attempt to incorporate a global curriculum that widens the sustainable tourism debate to include theoretical perspectives, applied research, best practice frameworks, business tools, and case studies (which document the broader challenges to all stakeholders in the tourism value chain), facilitating a more comprehensive sustainable tourism educational strategy. The textbook also has a companion interactive website that includes additional materials to support a deeper understanding of sustainable tourism issues. Quiz questions and PowerPoint slides broaden learning further.

There has never been a more exciting time to study travel and tourism!

Chapter 1 defines travel and tourism and provides the historical context that gave rise to tourism becoming the world's largest industry, and ultimately to its use as a development tool. By exploring development paradigms since World War II and situating Jafaj's Tourism Platform model within these paradigms, readers situate a variety of worldviews in relation to tourism by understanding how they support economic agendas. Both the positive and negative impacts of tourism are discussed, and sustainable tourism is introduced as a method for minimizing those impacts. In the practical tools section, students learn about the process and importance of writing a vision statement for grounding a sustainable tourism business in shared values and future goals.

Chapter 2 frames tourism as a form of capitalism. It explains the seven types of capital that support the generation of wealth for both businesses and communities and discusses how to turn resources into capital. Community capitals discussed include natural capital, cultural capital, human capital, social capital, political capital, financial capital, and built capital. The chapter provides key considerations to support sustainable management strategies to protect each type. In the tools section, five practical steps are given for determining access to capital, and how to use them in a responsible manner that contributes to the overall health of the community and long-term sustainability of the industry.

Chapter 3 focuses on the benefits and costs of globalization and the role of tourism, both as a cause and a result of globalization. Globalization is contrasted against localism in the context of sustainable tourism development and advocates for the combination of globalization and localism into what is known as globalization from below (policy) or glocalization (management). The chapter makes clear that the interconnection between globalization and localism to support global awareness must remain appropriate to local contexts. The chapter tool is a stakeholder analysis, which provides a strategy to engage both the local community and international tourism sector in collaborative sustainable tourism development processes.

Chapter 4 discusses the role of good governance and policy formation to ensure sustainability standards are maintained in the development and management of tourism. It helps to clarify the challenges that different stakeholder groups face in governance participation. From international governing bodies, to local politics, this chapter discusses the importance of getting involved and working together to choose among different policy options when making management and development decisions. The challenges facing politics in tourism development are also debated. The tool at the end of the chapter teaches how to perform a cost–benefit analysis, which is useful for ensuring that initiatives reap the highest reward for all stakeholders.

Chapter 5 explains the sustainable traveler. It discusses market segmentation using demographics, geographic, psychographic, and behavioral traits. Tourism typologies are introduced in relation to consumer demand for sustainable travel. Current consumer movements, including sustainable consumption, the LOHAS movement, localism, and slow travel, further support future consumption potential for sustainable tourism. The process of conducting customer feedback research to ensure that the tourism product being offered meets the expectations of the sustainable traveler is an important business practice. Various data collection methods for measuring customer satisfaction are taught in the tools section at the end of the chapter.

Chapter 6 introduces the different types of mass tourism and discusses many of the sustainability challenges that are specific to mass tourism. Using the Tourism Area Life Cycle model, destination challenges and sustainability are discussed, specifically economic dependency prevalent in mass tourism destinations. Green tourism is differentiated from sustainable tourism, and the concept of sustainable mass tourism is introduced. Using a systems perspective in relation to tourism impacts explains how decisions in one area can have negative impacts in other areas. Sustainability reporting, using the Global Reporting Standards, is covered in the tools section at the end of the chapter.

Chapter 7 discusses alternative tourism as a direct response to unsustainable mass tourism. It discusses the importance of capacity building and capacity development. With community involvement, through alternative tourism, the socioeconomic benefits from tourism can be achieved and shared at all levels. Specific types of alternative tourism, including community-based tourism, ecotourism, and cultural tourism are explored. Challenges within alternative tourism include managing carry capacity, the commodification of culture, and the empowerment of local community members. The tool at the end of the chapter provides a "how-to"; the step-by-step process of building community engagement.

Chapter 8 introduces basic marketing concepts for sustainable organizations and discusses the role of visitor expectations and motivations in relation to achieving customer satisfaction. The unique aspects of sustainable destination marketing and management are discussed, as well as the marketing mix (product, distribution, pricing, and promotion) as a means to improve competitive advantage. The tools section at the end of the chapter covers the process of writing business plans and marketing plans for building and growing a sustainable tourism business, including an explanation of SWOT (strengths, weaknesses, opportunities, and threats) analyses.

Chapter 9 talks about ways of reducing the negative impacts of tourism through careful supply chain and value chain management practices. It provides guidance on how to build value chain partnerships, both upstream and downstream, and for efficient horizontal and vertical collaboration aimed at achieving the goal of sustainability. Securing input supplies, developing tour packages, and reverse logistics, as well as the role of focal companies, are also explained. Finding effective ways of sharing knowledge along the value chain increases sustainability success. The tools section provides practical guidance on how to choose supply partners to support the overall success of the value chain.

Chapter 10 is all about certifications, with the goal of helping managers recognize the most reputable tourism certifications globally. It covers the value of certifications for highlighting sustainable accomplishments, the overall certification process, and the various bodies involved that help to ensure the integrity of the certification process. There is also discussion of greenwashing and how to recognize it. The tool at the end of the chapter walks through an example of the European Union Ecolabel Tourist Accommodation Criteria and the seven hotspots that are identified as challenges for the sustainability of the tourist accommodation sector.

Chapter 11 covers human capital management and highlights some best practices for recruiting, hiring, and retaining high performing tourism personnel. It discusses the importance of writing a thorough job description, removing unconscious bias from the interview process, onboarding training, and the types of benefits that are valued by employees. It highlights the value of training and development for personal and professional growth, employee motivation, and retention within the tourism industry as a means to maintain a high level of customer service. The tool section discusses ways to create a workplace culture that values and encourages sustainability.

Chapter 12 considers the importance of visitor management, or the process of influencing visitor behavior as a means to reduce negative impacts. It discusses the various visitor management strategies that can help conserve tourism resources. It also discusses how to adapt a resource through substitution, site hardening, and visitor/operator qualification as means of protecting a site. The goal is to help managers understand the importance of communication, interpretation, and education for the visitor to support lifelong learning and permanent changes in visitor behavior. The tools section introduces the Mindfulness model as one way to enhance the visitor experience while communicating the need for sustainable behavior.

Chapter 13 is forward-looking and talks about the future of sustainable tourism. It discusses emerging trends in both tourism and sustainability and provides an overview of the changing economic situations that are leading to the emergence of new destinations and new travel segments worldwide. Global economic challenges likely to have an impact on sustainable tourism include income disparity and rural to urban migration. Environmental implications include climate change, species extinction, and acid rain. Emerging social trends such as secularism, nationalism, and xenophobia are also discussed. The tool at the end of the chapter explains trend forecasting to help future tourism practitioners use historic data to effectively inform future sustainability decisions and choices that preserve and enhance the tourism industry.

Acknowledgments

Writing a textbook requires extensive research. The authors acknowledge that without past scholars bringing attention to the exciting field of sustainable tourism, this book could not have been written. Moreover, we owe our appreciation to the numerous contributors who provided valuable case studies, which explain complex sustainable tourism concepts through easily digestible applications.

Xiaotao Bai – Graduate Student, Beijing International Studies University, Beijing, China

Monica Bernardi – Post Doctoral Researcher, Department of Sociology and Social Research, University of Milano-Bicocca, Milan, Italy

Nancy J. Brest – Owner, Tahoe Functional Fitness, Tahoe Vista, California

Margaret J. Daniels – Professor in the Department of Tourism and Event Management, George Mason University, Fairfax, Virginia

E'lisha Vitoria Fogle – Graduate Instructor of Record, Clemson University, Clemson, South Carolina

Ronda J. Green – Chair, Wildlife Tourism Australia, Queensland, Australia

Carol Kline – Associate Professor, Appalachian State University, Boone, North Carolina

Kelly McMahon – Senior Manager of User Enablement for F5 Networks, Seattle, Washington

John Read – PhD Student, University of Waterloo, Waterloo, Ontario, Canada

Susan L. Slocum – Associate Professor in the Department of Tourism and Event Management, George Mason University, Fairfax, Virginia

Alesia Smiakhovich – Student, Belarussian State University

Melanie Smith – Associate Professor, Budapest Metropolitan University, Budapest, Hungary

Scott M. Turner – Entrepreneur

Qijing Wang – Professor, Beijing International Studies University, Beijing, China

Trish Wright – Supervisor, Silverwood Theme Park

Chapter **1**

Introducing sustainable tourism

Overview

This chapter provides a general introduction to tourism. It defines travel and tourism and provides the historical context that gave rise to the use of tourism as a development tool. It explains the different development paradigms and shows how tourism has historically been viewed from within each of these paradigms. The impacts of tourism are discussed, and sustainable tourism is introduced as a method for minimizing the negative impacts of tourism. The process for evaluating a company's environmental and social attitude towards sustainable tourism is presented, as are the steps for constructing a sustainably-minded vision statement aimed at encouraging organization-wide support of ongoing sustainability initiatives.

CHAPTER OBJECTIVES

At the completion of the chapter, students will be able to:

- Define travel and tourism and describe their differences;
- Recount historical trends giving rise to tourism;
- Explain the prominent development paradigms and associated tourism platforms;
- Critique the impacts of tourism on destinations;
- Differentiate sustainable tourism from other forms of tourism;
- Determine a company's (or destination's) environmental and social management and marketing practices; and
- Write a vision statement to ensure support for sustainability throughout an organization.

Introduction

There has never been a more exciting time to study travel and tourism. Tourism is recognized as the world's largest industry and reaches every corner of the earth, from the glaciers of Antarctica, to the savannahs of East Africa, to the tallest mountains in Asia, and to the ancient Inca cities of South America. With an estimated 1.24 billion international travelers, tourism generated $7.61 billion in economic impact in 2016 (United Nations World Tourism Organization [UNWTO], 2017). If we consider the number of domestic tourists (those traveling in their home country), scholars estimate that this number is six to ten times higher (Sharpley, 2009). For example, it is estimated that at any given moment, there are over 300,000 people flying above the United States on planes (Sheller & Urry, 2004), and Americans drive approximately 3.17 trillion miles each year (US Federal Highway Administration, 2016). It is not surprising that tourism is being used as an engine of economic growth. Tourism provides foreign exchange earnings, government revenue, infrastructure improvements, and is a source for job creation and small business development.

Before we discuss the history of travel and tourism, it is important to define these two concepts. **Travel** is the physical process of moving from one area to another and is often the mode through which tourism occurs, although not all travel is tourism. **Tourism** is defined as "a social, cultural, and economic phenomenon" (UNWTO, 2014, p. 1) that includes "the temporary movement of people to destinations outside their normal places of work and residence, the activities undertaken during their stay in those destinations, and the facilities created to cater to their needs" (Mathieson & Wall, 1982, p. 1). Figure 1.1 provides a breakdown of the tourism industry. Tourists seek experiences through cultural and natural

Figure 1.1 The tourism industry

settings, often looking to form an emotional connection to a region and its people. Tourists pursue relaxation, such as visiting the beaches of Cancun Mexico, thrilling experiences, such as those found at Disney World, or may explore an exotic destination, like the Amazon, to learn about traditional cultures. This book focuses primarily on the tourism industry as a means to understand its experiential nature, and to provide an understanding of tourists' needs and expectations in order to support the successful development of business opportunities in this field.

Job creation is the most visible strength to support tourism development as tourism is the leading employer worldwide. The World Travel and Tourism Council (2016) estimates that tourism provides 284 million jobs, equivalent to 1 in 11 jobs in the global economy. Because the tourism supply chain is linked to other industries, such as agriculture, the arts, construction, and outdoor recreation, tourism can support job creation for women, youth, migrant workers, rural communities, and indigenous peoples. Taleb Rifai, former Secretary General for the United Nations World Tourism Organisation (UNWTO), acknowledges that "the sector's wide reach also stimulates entrepreneurship and growth of micro-, small, and medium-sized enterprises (MSMEs). MSMEs are the sector's main innovators and sources of economic diversification, as well as being major job creators across sectors" (World Economic Forum, 2017, p. 1). However, the development potentials of tourism have not always been recognized, and even today, not all communities welcome the 'invasion' of millions of tourists.

A brief history of travel and tourism

From the onset of human existence, people have traveled. Primarily they moved in search of food, moderate climates, and other natural resources to ensure survival. Once civilizations were formed, people traveled for trade and military control.

Travel, specifically to see sites and to experience cultures, did not begin until the Greek Empire (500 BCE), when people sought out education and religious activities, and city-states, such as Greece and Rome, became attractions in their own right. These empires possessed a large middle class, and the use of a common language and currency around the Mediterranean Sea provided a system for relative ease of travel. The Romans were known for their engineering talent, building roads, aqueducts, and shrines across their empire, as well as rest houses to accommodate travelers. While travel eased during the Middle Ages, the Renaissance provided new opportunities for commerce and leisure travel. The Grand Tour era in the seventeenth and eighteenth centuries allowed the wealthy, elite class to increase their status in society by exposing them to the 'civilized' world of art, science, and culture around Europe.

Technology advancements during the Industrial Revolution increased modes and speed of travel, including trains, steamers, and eventually the automobile and aircraft. However, the concept of organized travel did not begin until 1841, when Thomas Cook conducted his first excursion from Leicester to Loughborough in England, which included a picnic lunch and a brass band. The advent of paid vacations in the early twentieth century, the development of mass air travel during World War II, and the number of service veterans exposed to foreign countries during the war led to an increase in the desire to travel, and also the avenues to accommodate a large number of early adventurers. Table 1.1 shows milestones that led to the rise of tourism.

Table 1.1 Elements that influenced travel

Date	Event
4000 BC	Sumerians invent money
600 BC	The rutway invented, a basic form of the railway
1613	Grand Tour becomes popular
1807	First steamboat service – Albany, New York
1825	First passenger train service – Darlington, England
1814	Thomas Cook's first excursion from Leicester to Loughborough, England
1844	First passenger cruise line – P&O sailing from Southampton to Gibraltar
1872	Thomas Cook's first round the world tour
1903	First major hotel company opens in London – Trust Houses
1914	First passenger air flight – St. Petersburg – Tampa Airboat Line
1945	International Association of Travel Agents is established
1958	The Boeing 707 introduced
1975	The United Nations World Tourism Organization established

Tourism as development

Mass tourism (defined further in Chapter 6) exploded after World War II, although the role of tourism as a development tool was not yet fully recognized. This section explains development paradigms since World War II and the role tourism has played in economic development, as well as the evolving understanding of both the positive and negative impacts of tourism over time.

A **paradigm** is a system of concepts, values, perceptions, and practices shared by a society, which forms a particular vision of reality or a worldview. As society changes, so does its sense of reality, and the way it makes decisions about knowledge. Paradigms determine what is important and unimportant, reasonable and unreasonable, legitimate and illegitimate, possible and impossible, and what needs attention and what society should choose to ignore. Jafari's (1990) Tourism Platform model identifies four tourism paradigms between the 1950s and 1990s as a way to show how tourism knowledge has been incorporated into society. It is important to note that these stages are not necessarily separate or chronological, as many of these paradigms still exist today. The goal is to help explain the changing values associated with tourism, which has led to the development of the global tourism industry.

Jafari's Tourism Platform model

1. Advocacy platform
2. Cautionary platform
3. Adaptancy platform
4. Knowledge-based platform

Advocacy platform

After World War II, the world was in a state of complete devastation. The ravages of war left their mark on almost every region of the world, with countries like Germany, Japan, England, France, China, and much of Southeast Asia and Northern Africa in ruins. Buildings, roads, communication systems, and food supply chains were gone, leaving in their wake millions of hungry, unemployed people struggling for survival. The international community quickly realized that a new world economy had to be established from the ground up.

The prominent paradigm at that time was one of economic growth. **Economic growth** is defined as the increase in the value of goods and services produced per person, or at an aggregate level, by an economy from one year to another. The goal is creating markets for the transfer of goods and services as a means to generate employment, increase incomes, and rebuild infrastructure. After World War II, not only did industry need rebuilding, but a consumer base for goods and services needed to be created. At this time, tourism was viewed as a regional development strategy because it is labor intensive and generates direct revenue in the form of tourism spending. Moreover, after World War II, many countries were viewed as the 'enemy' and social conflict threatened the rebuilding efforts. Tourism was seen as a means to promote peace and stability because it has the potential to support cross-cultural understanding. Jafari calls this era the **advocacy platform** of tourism, where support for tourism was high. Many national and local governments, as well as nongovernmental organizations (NGOs), still view tourism from the advocacy approach and support tourism because it leads to a 'greater good', including job creation and intercultural understanding. Many scholars argue that the end result of the advocacy platform is mass tourism (Weaver, 2000).

By the 1970s, development agencies began to question if the focus on job creation was enough to support the needs of society. Governments began to look at **economic development**, or the process by which a nation improves the economic, political, and social well-being of its people, which includes economic growth, but also incorporates quality of life issues, such as open space, recreational opportunities, and health and safety initiatives. The economic development paradigm directly addresses environmental issues, which are often ignored in economic growth philosophies. In addition, society began to see a dark side to tourism and moved into the cautionary platform.

Cautionary platform

The **cautionary platform** views tourism as a bad thing, because of its negative impacts. Tourism jobs are often low paying and seasonal, undermining the general poverty alleviation goals of tourism development. Tourism has high **economic leakages** meaning

Image 1.1 Anastasi village, Mesa Verde, Colorado

Source: Susan L. Slocum

that tourism revenue, in the form of payments to tour companies and hotels, do not necessarily stay in the economy where visitation occurs. Leakages primarily result when consumer goods and services are imported from abroad. For example, many souvenirs are produced in China, imported into tourism destinations around the world, and sold to tourists. Much of the profit generated from the sale of these souvenirs is transferred back to China and does not stay in the local economy. From a social perspective, tourism can create cross-cultural conflict when local impoverished residents see the extravagance inherent in tourism. For instance, just the cost of an airline ticket to a foreign country may be outside the reach of most locals in that destination. Many sociologists and environmentalists still see tourism through a cautionary lens.

Adaptancy platform

The concept of community development came into being in the late 1980s when societies recognized the unequal distribution of economic opportunities to certain minority groups within them. Unlike economic development, **community development** is described as a process where community members come together to take collective action and generate solutions to common problems. It enhances economic growth and economic development through increased equity to all members of society, the provision of social services to all citizens, poverty reduction, and increased self-reliance. It involves capacity building, empowerment, and participatory planning and decision-making. Around this same time, tourism professionals began to dismiss the one-size-fits-all practice of tourism development, and recognized the value in adapting tourism to suit individual destinations and activity types.

The **adaptancy platform** refers to low-impact tourism development that can reduce negative impacts and has led to new ventures such as ecotourism, alternative tourism, and community-based tourism. Here, the tourism product is customized around the needs of individual tourists and to the resources within the destination. The general premise is that local resources should be used, including sourcing local supplies, and incorporating unique cultural elements into the tourism experience. This helps mitigate economic leakages and instills self-reliance for tourism destinations. This perspective is commonly held today by certain NGOs and small businesses in tourism destinations.

Knowledge-based platform

Sustainable development as a concept originates from the 1987 Brundtland Report and is defined as meeting current human development goals while at the same time supporting the ability of natural systems to provide the natural resources and ecosystem services on which future generations will depend (Keeble, 1988). Sustainable development is controversial as many agencies still rooted in the economic growth and economic development paradigms believe that sustaining cultures and environments is counter-intuitive to growing the economy. From a tourism perspective, sustainable development aligns with Jafari's **knowledge-based platform**, which views tourism from a holistic perspective through the critical analysis of the way tourism is created and marketed as a commodity (such as mass tourism) rather than just its impacts.

The knowledge-based platform recognizes that the long-term success of tourism as an industry relies on the natural and cultural resources tourists choose to visit. If these resources are destroyed, tourism is threatened with extinction. The knowledge-based platform requires sound scientific methods to find appropriate types and levels of tourism development. While mass tourism sites cannot be easily returned to their original state as natural, unspoiled areas, scientific investigations – in the form of environmental and social science studies – can document and potentially interrupt negative impacts that jeopardize the future of tourism and the host communities that support tourism. Many academics and international development organizations, such as the UNWTO, are strong supporters of the sustainable development paradigm.

Impacts of tourism

While tourism has many advantages as a development tool, history has shown that mass tourism results in extensive degradation of environments and cultures unless strategies are in place to minimize these impacts. Sustainable development emphasizes the **triple bottom line** – an accounting framework that considers impacts to the economy, the environment, and the society. All these terms reflect the emphasis of growing the economic opportunities of a region and profitability of a company, while at the same time maintaining natural and social resources so that future generations have an opportunity to experience them. Other terms commonly used include the three pillars of sustainability or, from a business perspective, people, planet, profit, which also highlights the importance of business success and the ethical treatment of employees.

Economic impacts of tourism

From an economic perspective, tourists bring new money into an economy. This is called a **direct effect** of tourism, or the changes in local economic activity resulting from businesses selling directly to tourists. In turn, tourism businesses must buy goods and services from other businesses. This is called an **indirect effect**, defined as changes in sales, income, or employment within a region in industries that are supplying goods and services to tourism businesses. Tourism also hires workers who earn a salary and spend this income in the local economy. This is called an **induced effect** of tourism. For example, let us say that a tourist purchases a meal in a local restaurant. The total bill paid for food and service is the direct effect of tourism visitation. However, the restaurant needs to buy meat and vegetables to serve to the tourists. This is the indirect effect. The salary that the cooks and servers earn, which is spent on their living expenses in the home economy, is the induced effect. If the tourist had not purchased the meal, the supply would have not been needed and the workers might not have been scheduled to work. Direct, indirect, and induced effects combined form the **total economic impact** of tourism. What is unique about tourism is that the tourists must travel to the site of production, bringing their wallets and money with them (as well as their negative impacts). In other export industries, goods are shipped overseas and much of the profit remains with the wholesalers. Therefore, tourism has the potential to create extended income and business opportunities, tax revenue, and foreign currency exchange because the tourists come to the site of tourism production.

Foreign exchange is the money earned from the export of goods or services and the receipt of foreign currency. With tourism, foreign visitors bring money into a country, and local citizens take money out of a country when visiting foreign destinations as tourists. The difference between inbound tourism expenditure and outbound tourism expenditure is known as the **tourism trade balance** with the rest of the world. The primary advantage of foreign exchange earnings is diversity of income, so that a country or business is not dependent on one currency. In other words, foreign exchange earnings can spread the risk associated with fluctuating currency values. Many multinational firms generate a large percentage of their income from foreign exchange earnings. For fiscal year 2016–2017, Emirates Group, the world's largest airlines, earned AED 2.1 billion (US$572 million) by investing in a strong US dollar (Emirates Group, 2017). Many governments also use foreign exchange for earnings and to spread risk if the value of their home currency is unstable.

Many governments struggle to earn tax revenue, especially in developing countries or rural areas where residents earn low incomes or unemployment is high. Tourists pay taxes, often through entrance visas, hotel taxes, or sales tax, and tourism businesses pay income tax and property tax. This money helps governments to offer basic social services, such as health care, paying teachers, and supporting emergency services, such as police and fire. Moreover, not all governments have the funds to build new roads or supply adequate electricity and clean water. When tourism businesses move into an area, such as hotels and resorts, they may build roads and power lines to service the tourists through capital investment. Local communities often benefit from these expansions as well.

Tourism also has many negative economic impacts. Tourism can cause inflation because tourists are less sensitive to price increases than local residents. For example, if someone makes a hand-woven basket, locals may only pay $10 for the basket, but a tourist may pay $20. Over time, the price of hand-made baskets will rise to $20 for tourists and residents alike as vendors seek to maximize their revenue. There are also opportunity costs associated with tourism. **Opportunity costs** are the loss of potential gain from other alternatives when one alternative is chosen. For example, if a beach is dedicated to tourism then many local residents may lose access to their traditional fishing grounds and the income fishing provided. Other negative

Image 1.2 Hiking in Grindewald, Switzerland

Source: Susan L. Slocum

economic impacts include the seasonality of employment, low wages, and petty crime, such as pickpocketing.

Environmental impacts of tourism

Tourism can have positive impacts on the environment. As tourism allows people to connect with the natural environment and see certain flora and fauna species in their natural habitat, a growing appreciation for nature arises. Tourism is a primary funding mechanism for environmental preservation, allowing for revenue generation through direct spending on park entrance fees. Moreover, tourists may donate money to development agencies and parks to protect species that they have seen in the wild. Poaching has long been a problem for natural areas, when local residents kill animals as a means to earn income and feed their families. However, when locals begin working in the tourism industry, their jobs become dependent on the wild animal populations and people begin to see the value of protecting these species. Evidence suggests that when tourism employment of locals increases, incidents of poaching decrease (Weaver & Petersen, 2008).

At the same time, tourists are generally wasteful, resulting in the extravagant use of certain resources. Tourists consume up to eight times more water than local residents and five times more electricity. Tourists may not always respect traditional walking paths, causing disruption to native vegetation that supports an ecosystem. Litter is a common problem in tourism destinations, specifically the use of plastic water bottles. Many rural and remote areas do not have the facilities to support proper waste treatment, or landfills to accommodate the excess waste generated by tourists. Developing countries rarely have recycling centers, thus many plastic bottles are burned to prevent the accumulation of trash. The treatment of sewage is especially problematic, and raw sewage is often dumped into rivers or oceans causing extensive environmental damage.

Social impacts of tourism

Quality of life plays a key role in economic development policies, and quality of life indicators are reflective of community values and desires. They may be in the form of **social indicators** – direct and valid statistical measures which monitor levels and changes over time in some fundamental social concern. Objective social indicators are often valued by governments and include unemployment rates, living conditions (number of people with running water in their home), or infant mortality statistics. Subjective social indicators are harder to evaluate and include feelings associated with job satisfaction, class identification, and happiness measures. Tourism has the potential to promote better maintenance of public facilities, such as roads, parks, sporting facilities, and public transport, provide better shopping, dining, and recreational opportunities in the region, and showcase regions in a positive light, which helps to promote a better opinion of a region and encourage future tourism and/or business investment. Tourists value local cultures and traditions, instilling community pride and self-worth, as well as creating an economic incentive to continue or revive old traditions.

Tourism also creates negative social impacts. Sometimes local traditions need to be adapted so that they appeal to tourist markets. This is called **commodification** – the transformation of goods, services, ideas and people into commodities, or objects of trade to meet real or perceived demand of tourists (Weaver, 2010). Tourism can disrupt the lives of local residents and create inconveniences such as traffic congestion, parking difficulties, and excessive noise. Interaction with tourists can also lead to the erosion of traditional values, especially related to gender roles,

Image 1.3 Forbidden City, Beijing, China

Source: Susan L. Slocum

and to an increased interest in consumer goods. Tourism can cause overcrowding, preventing residents from accessing their local attractions and nature areas.

Sustainable tourism

Sustainable tourism is a direct byproduct of sustainable development and attempts to increase positive impacts of tourism while mitigating the negative. **Sustainable tourism** is defined as tourism development that meets the needs of present tourists and host regions while protecting and enhancing opportunities for the future. Tourism is dependent on a robust economy, and often it is the environment and/or the people that tourists travel to see. However, the role of the triple bottom line is often contested in development circles. For developing economies that experience severe poverty issues, the economy is often the priority. From a conservation perspective, preserving a natural resource may be the primary goal, and restricting traditional uses may be seen as necessary to preserve a park or nature area. Often residents in a community value traditional social constructions and cultural practices that may interfere with natural or economic sustainability. Balancing the needs of the people, planet, and profit is not an easy endeavor.

In sustainable tourism, there are two views to represent the triple bottom line. There is weak sustainability and strong sustainability. **Weak sustainability** originates from environmental economics and is the philosophy that man-made capital is more important than natural capital. It is based on the notion that humans will develop technologies to replace dependency on

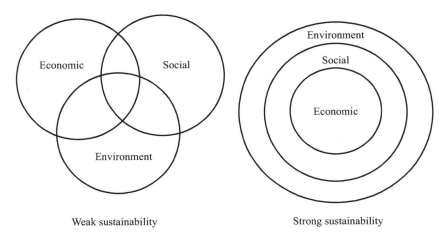

Figure 1.2 Weak versus strong sustainability

natural resources. **Strong sustainability** implies that technology and nature are complementary but not interchangeable, so that the existing stock of natural capital must be maintained and enhanced because the functions it performs cannot be duplicated through technological advancements. Slocum and Curtis (2017) write, "Strong sustainability is often associated with ecotourism or community-based tourism, where conservation or poverty reduction efforts are supported through tourism-generated revenue" (p. 28). Figure 1.2 shows the graphical representation of these concepts.

In tourism, weak sustainability places equal emphasis on maintaining the economy, environment, and society and is often viewed as 'greening' tourism through ethical supply chains (see Chapter 9). In areas already over developed, such as mass tourism destinations, weak sustainability provides an avenue to encourage sustainable behaviors and reduce the environmental and social impacts of tourism. Examples include energy and water reduction technologies, such as recycling and low flush toilets. Other examples include purchasing locally supplied food items or selling hand-crafted artworks in souvenir shops.

Strong sustainability is more common in ecotourism or community-based tourism where the needs of the environment and society are privileged above economic growth. Examples may include national parks, where protecting the resource maintains a higher priority than revenue generation. However, the reality is that often it is tourism revenue that provides the funding for national parks, thus the economy can take priority when a natural or cultural area faces funding challenges. As a manager of a sustainable tourism business, you will need to prioritize your revenue potential with the conservation of the environment and your community. We will discuss how to move your business towards a stronger form of sustainability throughout this book.

SUSTAINABILITY TOOL: WHERE ARE YOU NOW?

Building a culture of sustainability in an organization can be difficult and requires a commitment from both the top management and front-line employees. However, there are useful steps to help mangers establish a sustainability business (or destination) model. This textbook is designed to provide a number of tools to support the development of a sustainability culture in organizations, but often it is easiest to begin the transformation using

Table 1.2 Reasons to adopt sustainability

Reason	Strategy	For more information
Saving money and increasing profits	Saving money by using fewer resources and building ethical supply chains	Chapters 9 and 10
Improved brand value and reputation	Highlighting sustainability accomplishments that align with the business image	Chapter 8
Meeting customer demand	Understanding customer expectations in relation to sustainability and providing a quality and ethical product	Chapters 5 and 12
Providing a platform for innovation	As natural and social capital becomes scarcer and regulation regarding greenhouse gas emissions increases, innovation can help an organization adapt	Chapters 2 and 4
Business continuity and risk management	Long-term planning and forecasting allow organizations to monitor changes and emerging trends	Chapters 6, 7, and 13
Staff retention and attraction	Employees are increasingly seeking employment that is rewarding and demonstrates value to society	Chapter 11
Strengthening stakeholder relationships	Attract long-term investment partners, repeat customers, and build social capital with destination partners	Chapters 3 and 7

three initial steps: determining where an organization is, envisioning where it wants to be, and developing a clear set of steps that will get it there. This section will focus on where an organization is now.

Organizations have many reasons why they may want to be seen as environmentally and socially conscious (see Table 1.2). Not only does using fewer resources save the company money and improve profitability, but being seen as sustainable may attract new customers and can elicit support from nonprofit and government organizations in the form of new partnerships. First, an organization must understand its motivation to become sustainable, as that will guide which strategies it embraces. For some organizations, cost saving will be the motivation, for others, the value of altruism and giving back may guide their decisions. For others, it may be about attracting new customers or complying with government regulations. Often businesses may start a sustainability plan in order to save money or conform to new regulations, but may find that their success encourages a new motivation, such as being seen as an industry leader in sustainability, hence moving them towards altruism.

Many of the benefits of being sustainable come from marketing rather than actual sustainability management. Therefore, determining where an organization lies in relation to its marketing efforts versus management efforts is a good starting point to understand their commitment to sustainability. Moreover, knowing where a business lies today and where it strives to be in

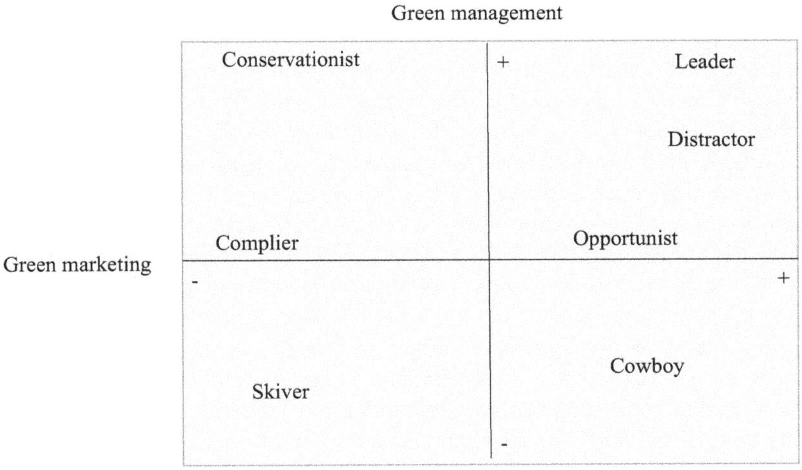

Green management

Conservationist	+	Leader
		Distractor
Complier		Opportunist

Green marketing

- ... Skiver ... Cowboy ... +

Figure 1.3 Corporate social and environmental attitudes

Source: Adapted from Font and Buckley (2001)

the future helps establish the path towards becoming more sustainable. Figure 1.3 shows how different environmental and social attitudes align with different marketing messages about sustainable practices (Font & Buckley, 2001).

Understanding how a company uses marketing and management to create its business (or destination) image is important, but also knowing where it wants to be as an organization is vital to building a sustainable tourism business.

- Conservationists – Focused on continuous improvement in sustainable operations. View marketing as increasing demand on the resource. Many consumers may not be aware of their commitment to sustainability.
- Leaders – Focus on competitive advantage through sustainability management by communicating their objectives to the public.
- Distractors – Want to be seen as sustainable and focus on tasks that are easily accomplishable, such as reduced consumption of water, waste, and energy.
- Compliers – Comply with regulation but sustainability is not a priority. They do not mention sustainability in their marketing.
- Opportunists – Use environmental and social claims for marketing and will comply with basic legislation, but only do what they have to in relation to sustainability management.
- Skivers – Focus on economic profit at the expense of the environment without drawing attention to themselves.
- Cowboys – Promote nature-based services and cultural opportunities, without respect for resources or people.

Therefore, as a business moves from, say, *cowboy* to *opportunist*, finding strategies that influence the overall operations of the company is important. On the other hand, when moving from *complier* to *distractor*, providing avenues for transparency that promote a company's achievements may be the appropriate strategy.

Writing a vision statement

One of the hardest aspects of moving towards sustainability is changing the minds of fellow employees, especially management, and communicating the benefits of responsible business practices. Therefore, it is important to clarify goals and develop a vision statement to build a culture that supports sustainability throughout the entire organization. It is important to understand the difference between a vision statement and a mission statement. A **mission statement** is a written statement of a company's purpose and values, which informs the company's decision-making and trade-offs to both members of the company and the external community. A **vision statement** is future-based and meant to inspire and give direction to employees of the company rather than customers. This statement should include what the company would look like as a sustainable organization. Employees need to understand how the **stakeholders**, entities or individuals that are significantly affected by the organization's activities, products, or services, will comprehend the new image and reputation that embraces sustainability without fearing that the change could jeopardize current successes. The goal is to sell the idea of sustainability to work colleagues to ensure that they value and adopt sustainability practices. Only with full commitment from all stakeholders can an organization be truly sustainable.

The first step in writing a vision statement is determining who will play a role in crafting it. It should be an inclusive process to ensure that a diversity of perspectives is considered. Conducting a series of workshops with key stakeholders who represent a cross-section of the organization, or interviewing a variety of employees from different departments allows for feedback from fellow team members. A vision statement should be concise, no longer than a few sentences, so that an organization is able to quickly repeat it and, more importantly, understand it. It should also be a reflection of the company's brand values. When crafting a vision statement, consider the following:

- Project five to ten years in the future;
- Dream big and focus on success;
- Use the present tense;
- Use clear, concise and jargon-free language;
- Infuse it with passion and emotion;
- Align it with business values and goals;
- Have a plan to communicate the vision statement to employees; and
- Be prepared to commit time and resources to the established vision.

Here are a few samples of vision statements from tourism companies.

> *We envision the development of our nation as a collection of diverse yet easily accessible islands, each of which is globally celebrated for the delightful experiences that it provides for visitors and for the sustainable economic and social benefits that it brings to our investors and residents.*
> *(The Bahamas Ministry of Tourism, 2020)*

> *Our vision is to accomplish our mission through: achieving and maintaining successful businesses, educating in true environmentalism and ecology, investing in children as an investment in our future, and showcasing the natural beauty of Costa Rica.*
> *(Blue River Resort and Hot Springs, Costa Rica, 2018)*

To unite event professionals, and together work towards increased attention to, and knowledge of, sustainability in event management.

(Sustainable Events Alliance, 2010)

Ocean Park Corporation, with focus on education, conservation and entertainment, will be the world's best Theme Park Resort, providing excellent guest experiences through the thrill of discovery, while connecting people with nature.

(Ocean Park Theme Park, Hong Kong, 2005)

Conclusion

This chapter has provided an overview of tourism using historical perspectives to highlight the need for sustainable tourism. By introducing a number of paradigms, all of which are still prevalent in tourism today, this chapter has shown the rise in tourism and its associated impacts. The chapter serves as a call to action for students to consider the need to support sustainable tourism and has provided two tools to support a company's journey into sustainable business management. By understanding where a company or destination is today and crafting a motivational vision statement to guide tomorrow, the first exciting steps into the realm of managing a sustainable tourism organization have begun.

CASE STUDY 1.1 LAKE TAHOE: JEWEL OF THE SIERRAS

NANCY J. BREST

Lake Tahoe has a long history as a popular tourist destination. Seeking tranquility and restoration, wealthy San Franciscans and Nevadans flocked to the lake for summer recreation in the mid-1800s. Elegant summer resorts began to pop up at the turn of the century. With reliable transportation provided by the railroad, resorts gambled on staying open during the winter months. The region hoped to capitalize on the

Image 1.4 Lake Tahoe in summer

Source: Nancy Brest

economic potential of winter sports, which was increasing in popularity in the late 1920s, building momentum in the 1930s, and culminating in the United States hosting the 1960 Olympic Winter Games in Squaw Valley. At that time, Hollywood's rich and famous, like the Rat Pack's Frank Sinatra and Dean Martin, came to Tahoe. The 1970s ushered in the Ski Bum culture, and today many technology billionaires and rock stars have laid roots in the region. This has brought a cascading effect of issues and opportunities.

Seasonality of the area

Peak summer season in Tahoe begins Memorial Day (May) and ends around Labor Day (September), while peak winter season is from late November (Thanksgiving) through mid-April. During these times, employment needs double at resorts and restaurants. These low-paying support jobs are difficult to staff locally, and seasonal workers are hired on international student visas. South Americans travel north during their summer break from December through March. Eastern Europeans come June through September. Although human resource departments help these students find housing, fewer resorts are providing on-site housing or transportation for these much-needed workers.

Housing

Beautiful weather, a cerulean blue lake, and deep powder snow draw people to Lake Tahoe year-round. Affordable housing is difficult to find for locals and seasonal workers alike. Scores of vacation houses remain unoccupied except during holidays and for a few weeks in the summer. Second homes that are offered for rent are increasingly being rented through the sharing economy to maximize profit, making long-term rentals hard to find and driving up prices. Some workers choose to live in the more affordable cities of Reno and Carson City in Nevada and commute to work.

Development

Many early settlers were drawn by the beauty of the lake and early developers purchased large parcels of lakefront land, while small resorts and summer cabins were built along the lake shore. Over a hundred years ago, conservationists had concerns about the impact of tourism, ranching, and logging on the environment surrounding Lake Tahoe. Rapid growth of casinos and resorts in the basin in the 1950s and 1960s caused concern again. Lawmakers from California and Nevada approved a bi-state compact creating the Tahoe Regional Planning Agency (TRPA) to oversee development in Lake Tahoe, which was ratified by Congress in 1969, creating the first bi-state planning agency in the country. The regional plan regulates the total additional development permitted in the region, categorized as residential, tourist accommodation, commercial, recreation, public service, and resource management. The TRPA adopted nine environmental threshold carrying capacities, which set environmental standards for the Lake Tahoe basin (TRPA, 2012) and indirectly defined the capacity of the region to accommodate additional land development.

Restraints on growth in the basin pushed development to the surrounding areas of Truckee and Squaw Valley. Truckee established one of the largest homeowner associations in the USA in the 1970s. Now multiple, exclusive gated communities exist, with more planned. These developments bring great potential to the area as well as spark controversy. The county government is located 70 miles away with only one out of five supervisors representing the Tahoe Truckee Area (Keep Tahoe Blue, 2016). Even though the Placer County Planning Commission recommended against it, the Board of Supervisors approved two large-scale developments; Martis Valley West adding 760 residential units and 34,000 square feet of commercial space on 670 acres, and the Village at Squaw Valley adding up to 900 residential units and 387,000 square feet of recreational and commercial space. These construction projects will generate over 500 jobs and approximately $22 million in tax revenue (Rockeman, 2018).

Claims have been filed in the California Court of Appeals. These projects add a significant number of cars on the road, increasing exhaust emissions in the air and decreasing water quality by sediment from sand used to maintain roads in winter. The primary concern with these developments is the gridlock that would ensue in the event of a natural disaster, as both projects are in areas with significant wildfire risk (Keep Tahoe Blue, 2016).

Transportation

New growth and development bring an influx of visitors to the area. In the high season, two-lane highways are stressed with bumper-to-bumper traffic. Winter highway closures from spinouts or whiteout conditions cause gridlock through town while motorists find a safe place to wait. Even though the county imparts a Traffic Impact fee on all land development to pay for a share of the future roadway system, improvement to the infrastructure is not currently being planned. Public transportation has improved, although it is still limited to the main routes and operate for limited hours, extending in the summer months. Although some resorts provide transportation, bus passes, or an employee shuttle, the sporadic bus schedule adds another layer of complexity to transportation for international students employed for seasonal work.

Climate of tourism

Lake Tahoe is an outdoor activity mecca. Locals and visitors alike are drawn to beautiful vistas for hiking, mountain biking, and climbing. Lake Tahoe's clear water and scenic shoreline attract many in the summer, and deep snow in the mountains from notorious winter storms draw visitors for snow sports in winter. Current and projected climate changes facing the area include increased air and lake temperatures, reduced winter snowpack, altered precipitation patterns, and more frequent and extreme storm events. These changes have the potential for a wide variety of environmental impacts, such as altered forest productivity, wildfire risk, water supply, public health, public safety, and ecosystem function. Resorts are mitigating the impact by installing state of the art snowmaking to draw skiers to their slopes, although they can only make snow if the temperatures are low enough. Smoke from wildfires in other parts of the state can blow into the basin and settle. Low snow and smoke can cause visitors to cancel their trips.

The tranquility and beauty of Lake Tahoe is loved by many. Spanning two states, two counties in California and two counties and an unincorporated city in Nevada, the 'Jewel of the sierras' continues to attract visitors from all over the world. Developers want to capitalize on its beauty, packaging it for the rich and famous technology moguls and retirees. But how much development can the region sustain?

Reflective questions

1. What can employers do to help international student workers temporarily settle into the region? Should employers be required to provide housing and transportation? What are some ways to balance long-term rental needs and share economy accommodations?

2. Some cities utilize System Development Charges (fees that are collected when new development occurs in the city that are used to fund a portion of infrastructure needs, such as new streets, sanitary sewers, parks, and water). Should developers be required pay SDCs in the Lake Tahoe region? What else could be done to mitigate the negative impacts of new development?

3. Summit County, Colorado provides free public transportation. Is this a good idea for resort areas to adopt, in general? Who should pay? Why or why not?

References

Keep Tahoe Blue (2016). *Martis Valley West Project In-Depth*. Retrieved from www.keep-tahoeblue.org/our-work/martis-valley-west-in-depth.

Rockeman, O. (2018). Squaw Valley redevelopment plan moves forward after series of lawsuits. *Sacramento Business Journal*, Aug 17, 2018. Retrieved from www.bizjournals.com/sacramento/news/2018/08/17/squaw-valley-redevelopment-plan-moves-forward.html.

Tahoe Regional Planning Agency (TRPA) (2012). *Regional Plan*. Retrieved from www.trpa.org/regional-plan/.

CASE STUDY 1.2 THE SHARING ECONOMY, TRAVEL, AND SUSTAINABILITY

MONICA BERNARDI

Introduction

The phenomenon of the sharing economy is gaining momentum. Started in the Silicon Valley in California in 2008 with Airbnb, it has spread nearly all over in the world. The basic concept is to share underutilized assets or services (idling capacities) between private individuals through internet innovative business models, reducing the need for the ownership of these assets (Botsman & Rogers, 2010). Advocates of the sharing economy consider it a complementary tool to favor local economic development, to reduce the social exclusion of local residents, and to decrease environmental impacts (Cohen & Kietzmann, 2014). At the same time, numerous experts point out the risks associated with the corporate form of this phenomenon, from the human impacts of the gig economy (a market system in which organizations contract with independent workers for short-term engagements), to housing shortages. This divide in public and academic opinion is related to the multifaceted nature of the sharing economy, which touches different fields – consumption, production, distribution and commerce – taking sometimes unexpected directions, far from the original concept of sharing (Martin, 2016).

This fast growth holds true, especially in travel: today it is nearly impossible to think about vacationing without using Airbnb, Uber, Lyft or one of the several platforms that propose experiences of authenticity with locals. Their success is closely tied to the agenda of the contemporary travelers, who have become more and more demanding and active, looking for emotions and experiences. As noted by Dredge and Gyimóthy (2015) "consuming travel is intimately bound to identity construction and narratives of authentic encounters with local culture" (p. 9). Also, the travelers' growing attention to environmental and social sustainability meets the core values of the sharing economy: platforms usually stress the idea of community, empowering people, local development, and sustainability as the basis of their activities.

Same business model, different outcomes

Airbnb is one of the most loved and, at the same time, hated, sharing economy platforms in the tourist sector, as well as one of the pioneers and leaders in the sharing economy. Although the company releases reports emphasizing its ability to support local communities and produce environmental benefits, research highlights the negative effects of the short-term rentals, especially on the historic cities (Sans & Quaglieri Domínguez, 2016). The presence of Airbnb indeed seems to reduce the affordable housing supply by distorting the housing market, and it activates the process of gentrification and segregation that pushes local people to move into other neighborhoods. One of the most famous cases is that of San Francisco, but many American cities, as well as European cities, are experiencing these processes, so much so that several local governments are trying to fix the situation by applying Airbnb regulations. At the same time, the so-called hotelization and Disneyfication effects occur, depriving neighborhoods and city centers of their original identity, and commodifying the local life to sell it as an added value of the apartment rent (i.e. transforming these areas into tourist spaces). Italian cities are some of the most significant examples: cities like Venice or Florence, already hyper touristic, register an alarming tendency to depopulate the city center with a huge loss of inhabitants in favor of tourists (Picascia et al., 2017); and locals are protesting to stop the tourist fluxes.

Nevertheless, the potential benefits generated by the sharing economy in the tourist sector, and even beyond, remain. There are indeed alternative ways in which platforms of home-sharing and experience-sharing (with local guides) can work for tourists and communities, becoming a real opportunity for locals and travelers by avoiding perverse externalities. The case of Seoul is quite illustrative. Here, the people-centered administration of Park Woo-Son is betting on the sharing economy as a complementary lever to favor economic development, strengthen social relations, and reduce environmental impacts. In 2012, the local government launched the *Sharing City, Seoul* project, through which to create a real ecosystem of sharing, building the required infrastructures, supporting local sharing organizations (to date 82 have been selected and involved), favoring the creation of a sharing offer, opening its public underutilized assets, empowering people, and socializing them in the use of sharing services (Bernardi & Diamantini, 2018). In addition, the local government is encouraging the birth of companies that reproduce the business model of the big players of the sharing economy, but on a local level, in order to avoid Silicon Valley cannibalization (Bernardi, 2015). The government is also supporting sharing solutions that are able to respond to urban problems (including isolation, and unemployment) seen in other destinations.

The sharing organizations cover different fields: goods, space, skills, experience, time, and content sharing. Among these, we focus on one in particular to show how a business model similar to that of Airbnb can have a completely different approach and impact: LetsPlayPlanet. It is a platform entirely based on the concept that everyone is a change-maker, including tourists. Its mission is to build a solid ground for responsible tourism in Asia, starting online to create offline social impact. The motto *Travel with Locals and Play for Social Change* depicts this attitude and aims to transform the travel experience into a human connection based on authenticity between travelers and local hosts. The founder, Sun Mi Seo, launched the platform in 2012 at the age of 27 after working in the sustainable tourism sector for the previous six years as co-founder of Traveller's Map, the first Korean social enterprise in the tourism industry. The strong orientation to social and environmental sustainability of this sharing organization depends on the desire to transform travel into an opportunity to make the world a better place through connections with locals. It can be considered a win–win approach since both travelers and hosts develop an intercultural understanding, take part in the local economy's development, become more aware, and begin new friendships. The staff of LetsPlayPlanet is mainly composed of millennials, a generation better able to make the most from information and communications technology spread, always connected, confident and open to change (Taylor & Keeter, 2010), and also a generation that knows the needs and desires of its peers and of the contemporary tourists. Therefore, they are able to conceive and offer more attractive solutions.

Among the platform's offer, we find different types of experiences with locals: some related to traditions and cultural and social life (e.g. the visit to the Seoul Fish Market or the Rooftop Chuseok cooking party with a Korean mother), with a recreational imprinting that favors the development of local activities. Others are more oriented to the environmental and naturalistic aspects (e.g. bird-watching with a local, and life experience like coconut wine making, seashell craft, and cassava cake making with the Olango Island Wildlife Sanctuary experience – Philippines; dolphin watching and snorkeling at Pamilacan island – Philippines; or wildlife photo-tours in Baluran National Park – Indonesia). Today the platform is a successful tourism marketplace, active in Korea, Japan, Indonesia, Malaysia, the Philippines, and Nepal.

Final reflections

The Korean case invites some reflections. The role of local government is a key element in the process of integration of the sharing practices in the community's life, avoiding perverse externalities. The creation of a sharing ecosystem allows product development, the spread of best practices, involves citizens, and makes a positive social impact locally. In general, tapping into the collaborative and sharing economy favors a better use of existing skills and assets, extracting value from what is already available in a destination. It could create many new business opportunities for the local population and, simultaneously, increase the local supply of services and activities that match contemporary tourist expectations.

The approach of platforms like LetsPlayPlanet differs by placing the attention on people and the planet. Traveling with local inhabitants allows the traveler to see the world through the eyes of local friends, and it is the best way of sustainable traveling which benefits local community, protects the environment, and conserves local culture, without activating the effects of hyper-tourism. This approach is working well in the Asian context, but it can be applied also to rural areas or less touristy destinations in Europe and the Americas.

Reflective questions

1. How has the sharing economy transformed tourism? Has it made tourism more or less sustainable? Why?

2. Is the sharing economy a form of weak or strong sustainability? Explain.

3. How can organizations, such as LetsPlayPlanet, ensure that they stay true to their values, yet provide growing opportunities to residents? Is there a point where a company can become too big to support sustainability?

References

Bernardi, M. (2015). Seoul rethinks sharing economy and proposes local solutions. *LabGov*. Retrieved from http://labgov.city/thecommonspost/seoul-rethinks-sharing-economy-and-proposes-local-solutions/.

Bernardi, M. & Diamantini, D. (2018). Shaping the sharing city: an exploratory study on Seoul and Milan. *Journal of Cleaner Production*, 203, 30–42.

Botsman R. & Rogers R. (2010). *What's Mine is Yours: How Collaborative Consumption is Changing the Way We Live*. Collins, London, UK.

Cohen, B. & Kietzmann, J. (2014). Ride on! Mobility business models for the sharing economy, *Organization & Environment*, 27(3), 279–296.

Dredge, D. & Gyimóthy, S. (2015). The collaborative economy and tourism: critical perspectives, questionable claims and silenced voices, *Tourism Recreation Research*, 40(3), 286–302.

Martin, C.J. (2016). The sharing economy: a pathway to sustainability or a nightmarish form of neoliberal capitalism? *Ecological Economics*, 121, 149–159.

Picascia, S., Romano, A., & Teobaldi, M. (2017). The airification of cities: making sense of the impact of peer to peer short term letting on urban functions and economy, Proceedings of the Annual Congress of the Association of European Schools of Planning, Lisbon 11–14 July 2017.

Sans, A.A. & Quaglieri Domínguez, A. (2016). Unravelling Airbnb: urban perspectives from Barcelona. In A.P. Russo and Richards, G. (Eds), *Reinventing the Local in Tourism: Producing, Consuming and Negotiating Place* (pp. 209–228). Channel View Publications, Bristol.

Taylor, P. & Keeter, S. (2010). *Millennials: A Portrait of Generation Next. Confident, Connected, Open to Change*. Pew Research Centre, Washington, DC.

STUDY QUESTIONS

1. Using Jafari's Tourism Platform model, place these scenarios into the appropriate paradigm.
   - A tourist that seeks out tour operators that are certified as fair trade.
   - A destination marketing organization that conducts a yearly economic impact study to increase tax support for the organization.
   - A city mayor that campaigns on a platform of improved schools and access to public parks.
   - A hotel manager that encourages his employees to volunteer at a local homeless shelter.
   - A fundraising campaign geared towards tourist donations to support a local orphanage.
   - A small farm that donates 10% of their revenue to a local conservation organization.
   - A policymaker that increases travel restrictions in order to protect against terrorism.
2. What is your local community doing to support sustainable development? List three examples.
3. Research a local destination marketing organization or tour operator. Do they promote sustainable tourism? Is it a form of weak or strong sustainability?
4. Which of the reasons to adopt sustainability discussed in Table 1.2 would motivate you the most to be a sustainable manager or business owner? Which would motivate you the least? Why?
5. Does your university consider itself sustainable? Where would it fall on the Corporate Environmental and Social Attitudes scale? Why?

DEFINITIONS

Adaptancy platform   promotes low-impact tourism development that can reduce negative impacts

Advocacy platform   sees tourism as a good thing and celebrates tourism's positive impacts on the economy and cross-cultural understandings

Cautionary platform   views tourism as a bad thing because of its negative impacts

Commodification   the transformation of goods, services, ideas, and people into commodities, or objects of trade

Community development   a process where community members come together to take collective action and generate solutions to common problems

Direct effect   a change in local economic activity resulting from businesses selling directly to tourists

Economic development   the process by which a nation improves the economic, political, and social well-being of its people

Economic growth   the increase in value of goods and services produced per person, or at an aggregate level, by an economy from one year to another

Economic leakage   revenue, in the form of payments to tour companies and hotels, that does not stay in the economy where visitation occurs

Foreign exchange   the money earned from the export of goods or services and the receipt of foreign currency

Indirect effect   a change in sales, income, or employment within a region in industries supplying goods and services to tourism businesses

Induced effect   a change in expenditures within a region as a result of household spending of the income earned in tourism and supporting industries

Knowledge-based platform   views tourism from a holistic perspective, through the critical analysis of the underlying structures of tourism rather than just its impacts

Mission statement   a written statement of a company's purpose and values, which informs the company's decision-making and trade-off to both members of the company and the external community

Opportunity cost   the loss of potential gain from other alternatives when one alternative is chosen

Paradigm   a system of concepts, values, perceptions, and practices shared by a society, which forms a particular vision of reality or a worldview

Social indicator   a direct and valid statistical measure which monitors levels and changes over time in a fundamental social concern

Stakeholder   an entity or individual that can reasonably be expected to be significantly affected by the organization's activities, products, or services

Strong sustainability   the idea that the existing stock of natural capital must be maintained and enhanced because the functions it performs cannot be duplicated through technological advancements

Sustainable development   meeting current human development goals while at the same time supporting the ability of natural systems to provide the natural resources and ecosystem services on which future generations will depend

Sustainable tourism   tourism development that meets the needs of present tourists and host regions while protecting and enhancing opportunities for the future

Total economic impact   the sum of the direct, indirect, and induced effects

Tourism   the temporary movement of people to destinations outside their normal places of work and residence, the activities undertaken during their stay in those destinations, and the facilities created to cater to their needs

Tourism trade balance   the difference between inbound tourism expenditure and outbound tourism expenditure

Triple bottom line   an accounting framework that considers impacts to the economy, the environment, and the society

Travel   the physical process of moving from one area to another

Vision statement   a future-based narrative meant to inspire and give direction to employees of the company rather than customers

Weak sustainability   the philosophy that man-made capital is more important than natural capital

Chapter **2**

Understanding capital

Overview

This chapter is an introduction to tourism as a form of capitalism. It highlights and explains the seven types of capital that support the generation of wealth for both businesses and communities. It details key considerations on how to turn resources into capital and how to encourage the sustainable management of different forms of capital. A tool to evaluate a company's access to capital is provided as the first step in becoming a sustainable business or destination.

At the completion of the chapter, students will be able to:

- Define capitalism;
- Explain the role of tourism in capitalism;
- Differentiate resources and assets from capital;
- Describe the seven types of capital and how they generate wealth for a business or community;
- Recount strategies to develop and maintain capital; and
- Recognize which forms of capital are available to enhance the tourism product.

Introduction

As discussed in Chapter 1, tourism provides a means to grow an economy, create jobs and government revenue, and is often considered the world's largest industry. Greenwood (1989) claims that tourism is the "largest scale movement of goods, services, and people that humanity has perhaps ever seen" (p. 171). Tourism is recognized as an export industry, in other words, tourism is produced in one region and purchased by people from outside that region. As an export industry, the economic goal of tourism is to grow over time as a means to continually improve the quality of life for residents (Jenkins, 1982).

Economic growth requires tourism destinations to grow so that they can accommodate an increasing number of visitors. Growth requires financial investment therefore; both the public sector and the private sector are key stakeholders when it comes to tourism development. The **public sector** is the part of an economy that is under government control, financed through tax revenue, and provides services for all members of society (public services), such as roads, transit, water, sewers, parks, and public safety. The **private sector** is typically the part of an economy that invests in profit-making businesses, such as hotel accommodations, restaurants, and entertainment. Thus, tourism plays a large role in **capitalism**, an economic and political system in which a country's trade and industry are controlled by private owners for profit, rather than by the public sector.

Capitalism is considered an efficient form of production and consumption for a number of reasons, primarily because it encourages innovation (as a means to generate more profit), consumers are free to choose the goods and service they want, producers will only produce what they can sell, and citizens are allowed economic freedom, preventing governments from becoming too powerful. The negative aspects of capitalism include: the potential for exploitation of workers; overuse of finite resources; and disparities between those who own factors of production and those who work for the owners. **Factors of production** are the inputs that are used in the production of goods or services in order to make an economic profit. The factors of production include land, labor, financial capital, and entrepreneurship (otherwise known as human capital). Individuals with access to the factors of production hold more power than those who work for them and are often the most influential when it comes to making sustainably-minded decisions.

Understanding capital

The development of tourism is dependent on a variety of resources, both tangible resources, such as natural areas and tourism infrastructure (hotels, transportation), and intangible resources, such as a destination's reputation (friendly, hospitable, attractive). These resources are considered forms of **capital**, or specific factors of production that generate wealth through investment. Capital is considered more durable than money (cash) because money can only be used to buy something, whereas capital can be used to generate new wealth. Capital has two distinctive characteristics that separate it from money: capital is not used up immediately in the process of production, unlike raw materials or intermediate goods; and capital can be created or increased, unlike land and non-renewable resources (Nitzan & Bichler, 2009). In other words, capital is what makes money, and capital can be used repeatedly to secure more money over time.

Capitalism requires the flow of capital, and successful entrepreneurs find ways to accumulate capital as a means to generate profit. Flora and Flora (2013) argue that entrepreneurial communities and individuals utilize seven different types of capital in order to establish new businesses and support economic development, as shown in Figure 2.1.

The goal within sustainable tourism is to ensure that we do not use up all the capital so future generations are not left without means to generate new wealth. However, it is important to understand the types of capital that can be used to develop a tourism business or destination. The remainder of this chapter will define these seven forms of capital and explain how they can be harnessed as a wealth generator for sustainable tourism businesses, and by extension, destinations.

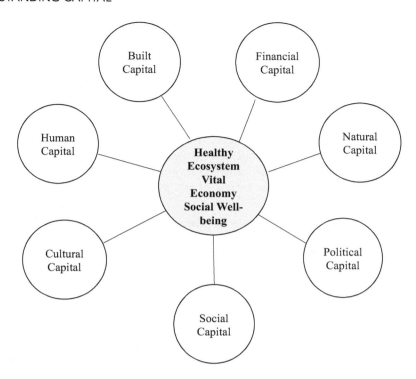

Figure 2.1 Seven types of capital

Source: Adapted from Flora and Flora (2013)

Natural capital

Natural capital is the world's stock of natural resources, which includes geology, soils, air, water, and all living organisms, and is a predominate feature in the environmental sphere of sustainability. It is important to realize that everything consumed started originally as a natural resource. For example, plastic is produced from oil, paper from trees, and metals from minerals. There are two types of natural resources, renewable resources and non-renewable resources. **Renewable resources** are those that are replenished naturally and can be used repeatedly, such as stream water that comes from rainfall or snowmelt, trees that are replanted or grow from seeds left after harvesting, or solar energy. **Non-renewable resources** are resources that take millions of years to form and cannot be renewed in a human lifetime. Examples include biofuels such as oil, coal, natural gas, as well as minerals, such as gold.

The environment becomes natural capital when it is used to make other goods and services or in some way generates wealth for a business or industry. Within the economic growth paradigm, natural resources are harvested to produce wealth, which in turn is left to future generations. For example, a person may want to build a redwood deck on the back of their home. By cutting down the redwood trees and building the deck, the value of the house increases. The house, in turn, can be inherited by the next generation. In the sustainability paradigm, the same homeowner would face the dilemma, "Does my child want the deck and increased house value or does she want to see redwood trees in their natural habitat?" From a sustainability perspective, the homeowner would preserve some of the trees and let the next generation decide how the trees should be used.

The environment can also be seen as natural capital when recognizing the inherent value of an entire ecosystem. In tourism, nature is one of the primary tourism products (Sharpley, 2009). Therefore, by keeping the ecosystem intact, wealth can be created through tourists' visitation and interaction with the natural environment. The difficulty lies in determining the value of the environment in its pristine form. Tourism receipts, such as park entrance fees, provide a basis for environmental evaluation, but do not take into account the extrinsic value that an environment provides. For example, the Amazon rainforest acts as a natural filter, removing many pollutants from the atmosphere. Plants take in carbon and release oxygen, helping to offset greenhouse gas emissions. Finding the economic value of clean air has proven difficult (Laurance, 1999). Therefore, natural capital has a larger value than tourism receipts alone would suggest.

Another prime example is the reintroduction of wolves into Yellowstone National Park in the USA, which has had profound impacts on the natural environment in Yellowstone. Wolves primarily eat elk and deer, which while causing a decrease in hunting revenue, has been important to the ecosystem because wolves generally cull weak or sick elk, and many species scavenge the remains of a wolf's meal. The lower elk population (and their need to be more aware of predators) has reduced overgrazing and spurred new growth of aspen trees. These trees, in turn, encourage beaver and songbird populations. It is estimated that the reintroduction of wolves increased tourism's economic impacts by $35 million in 2006 (Duffield, Neher, & Patterson, 2006). One could argue that wolves have become valuable natural capital for the states of Wyoming and Montana.

It is important to note that environmental capital and natural capital are different. **Environmental capital** includes natural capital but also comprises other assets, such as weather (sunshine, snow accumulation) as well as built capital, discussed later in this chapter. The bottom line is, if all of the natural capital at a given destination is used up or destroyed, leaving a barren and desolate environment with little aesthetic value, tourism ceases, and so does the economic capital that tourism revenue provides to the local community.

Cultural capital

Cultural capital can be defined as the stock of values, arts, crafts, cultural knowledge, performance, social practices, and access to heritage resources (McGehee, Lee, O'Bannon, & Perdue, 2010). Cultural capital involves the preservation of traditions, art forms, heritage sites, and traditional foods that can be harnessed to generate economic opportunities. Often tourists will travel in order

Image 2.1 Wild Kodiak bear, Alaska

Source: Susan L. Slocum

to experience traditional cultures that differ from their own. Culture may be classified as tangible or intangible. **Tangible culture** consists of physical artifacts, such as architecture or other built heritage. **Intangible culture** is the practices and representations of artifacts, objects, and cultural spaces. Examples include food, oral traditions, and performing arts. Chapters 6 and 7 highlight cultural tourism and some of the challenges of using culture to support economic opportunities.

Culture is ever changing and evolving. We have all experienced first-hand different cultural norms between ourselves and our parents or grandparents. Yet, we see many similarities as well. Culture is a general way of life and a worldview that is passed from generation to generation through stories, the arts, and religious or traditional practices. McGehee et al. (2010) write, "The strength of cultural capital requires ongoing learning and maintenance through cultural and language education and inter-generational sharing programs, and active programs of research, documentation, and storage of cultural resources" (p. 227). Much like built capital, cultural capital must be protected, preserved, and maintained to ensure its survival.

In tourism, culture can be transformed into cultural capital by harnessing the stories, practices, rituals, and physical assets of a region and communicating them in a way that forms the basis of the tourism product. Tangible cultural heritage must be physically maintained, through building repairs or the storage of museum artifacts, in order to be available for consumption by tourists. Sadly, countless culturally significant heritage sites and objects have been destroyed worldwide through wars, vandalism, and neglect. Similarly, poorly planned intangible cultural packages have damaged local communities. This is why it is important for communities to maintain levels of authenticity in the tourism product if culture is to be used as cultural capital.

Image 2.2 Squamish national culture, Capilano, British Columbia, Canada
Source: Susan L. Slocum

Intangible cultural packages must be presented in a way that can be consumed by visitors, such as by explaining food traditions and showcasing performing arts. Moreover, providing access to these resources is important to ensure visitors can use them, such as establishing walking trails, hosting cultural events, or teaching tourists local recipes.

Human capital

Human capital refers to the stock of knowledge, habits, social, and personality attributes, including creativity, embodied in the ability to perform labor so as to produce economic value (Goldin, 2016). **Human resources**, or the people who make up the workforce of an organization, business sector, or economy, can be converted into human capital through education, training, and supporting innovation. Zakaria and Yusoff (2011) write, "Pushing workers to the limits to maximize productivity and increased profits will end up creating robots or uncreative workers leading to a form of exploitation . . . leading to low productivity, low (work) quality, stress, no commitment, no motivation, and conflicts" (p. 53). Therefore, employers must understand the intrinsic value of each employee (what motivates them), so that any expenditure on employees is regarded as an investment rather than an expense. The importance of human resources and human capital management cannot be over emphasized and are discussed in more detail in Chapter 11.

Social capital

Relationships between people and organizations can be harnessed to create economic opportunities. **Social capital** is defined as the links, shared values, and understandings that enable individuals and groups in a society to trust one another and so work together (Keeley, 2007). Social capital consists of two primary elements: social networks (the people you know) and norms of reciprocity (people willing to help one another). Figure 2.2 shows the enabling conditions that must be in place to support social capital development and its ongoing maintenance.

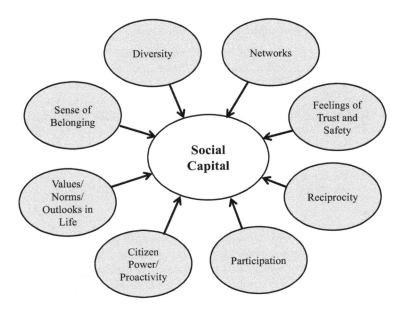

Figure 2.2 Elements of social capital

For social capital to be developed, all members of a community must *feel valued* and *trust* that their opinions matter. They must also believe that others will follow through on commitments and are genuinely concerned about the best interests of the group (Torell, 2002). *Participation* in local government can be viewed as creating a form of equity by allowing everyone to actively engage in the development of tourism policy. *Citizen power* refers to feelings of control over resources and business decisions. This form of economic involvement can foster a greater sense of local control over resources, encourage participation in decision-making and empower local people (Lele, 1991). Empowerment is generally tied to knowledge, as those with information can make better decisions (Coleman, 1988). As community members and businesses work together towards development goals, a common sense of values is created, and the benefits that any accomplishment will bring are shared. This creates a *sense of belonging*. A sense of belonging is often associated with basic human needs, like food and shelter, however, it can also be associated with the level of connectedness and involvement that a person has within a community. The concept of *reciprocity* implies that all members are working together towards a common goal, and that each member will offer their particular expertise and resources to fulfil the group's goal (Montgomery & Inkles, 2001). In other words, everyone involved must believe that they will receive some level of benefit (Hall, 2014) from participating in the community and sharing their strengths. *Diversity* of opinion and perspective ensures a variety of outcomes and development paths are considered, ensuring that everyone's perspectives are reflected. Lastly, in order for social capital to be developed, members of the community must believe that they can make a difference.

There are generally two types of social capital (Zahra & McGehee, 2013). **Bonding social capital** describes social networks made up of homogeneous groups of people. Examples of these networks include college fraternities and sororities, church youth groups, and street gangs. Industry associations, such as members of a local Convention and Visitors' Bureau, would also constitute bonding social capital. These are groups of people with common values and beliefs. **Bridging social capital** refers to social networks made up of socially heterogeneous groups that include people with different backgrounds, such as famers who may work with tourism companies to create a food-based destination, or conservation specialists who advise nature-based tourism development that supports conservation goals.

A combination of bridging social capital and government or industry leadership provides the most effective form of social capital building (Wilson, Fesenmaier, Fesenmaier, & Van Es, 2001), and "is where sound development, management, and promotion . . . can best be implemented" (Everett & Slocum, 2013, p. 796). Tourism organizations can unite restauranteurs, hoteliers, or event managers (bonding social capital) or it may bring together local community members, tourism businesses, and government officials (bridging social capital) to promote and enhance a destination. Social capital is linked with human capital and Chapter 11 discusses how to harness social capital within an organization by empowering employees and creating a work environment that supports sustainable tourism.

Political capital

Political capital has a variety of definitions, but according to the Sustainable Livelihoods Framework, it is the ability to use power in support of political or economic positions (Baumann & Sinha, 2001). In other words, it is how political decisions are made and the amount of influence a social group or industry has over the political process. Policies generally guide the economic system and allow businesses to convert assets into capital. For example, a person may own a large natural area, however certain environmental regulations may prohibit the owner from collecting revenue because of restrictions on its use. Political capital is closely related to social capital because it allows stakeholders the ability to self-determine how tourism is developed (Sharpley, 2009).

Tourism requires extensive involvement from the state through the development of other types of capital (specifically built capital, natural capital, and human capital). As a powerful economic and social force, tourism is often manipulated for political purposes and requires government intervention for the planning and governance of tourism resources. The political process of tourism is complex and is, therefore, covered in more detail in Chapter 4.

Financial capital

In relation to tourism development, **financial capital** is defined as financial wealth that is used to start or maintain a business (Koutra, 2008). Economic growth depends, to a large extent, on entrepreneurial activity, and entrepreneurs require start-up money and additional financial investments as they expand. Financial capital refers to the availability of financial instruments, such as loans or lines of credit, in order to provide investment opportunities for businesses. It can be argued that a lack of financial capital in developing countries is a primary deterrent for small business development, long-term economic growth, and a reason for high poverty levels (UNWTO, 2005).

Under financial capital, there are three general areas of focus: financial investment; micro finance/credit; and financial linkages/partnerships. Financial investment involves putting resources into the other forms of capital, such as social, human, and built capital. This investment generally comes from governments or large business enterprises, such as banks, but can also come from crowd sourcing platforms. Funding must be secured to build roads, educate people, and inform citizens of the political process through which tourism is developed. Koutra (2008) writes, "lack of investment in any of the forms of capital can be detrimental for the sustainability of tourism" (p. 1). For people without a credit history, or those who live in poor areas without street addresses, accessing loans can be very difficult. Banks generally do not trust poor people to be responsible with loans or to repay them in a timely manner (United Kingdom Department for International Development, 1999) and often require expensive collateral or charge high interest rates. The second area of focus, **micro finance**, or micro credit, is the lending of small amounts of money at low interest rates to new businesses, generally (but not exclusively) in the developing world. Third, financial linkages/partnerships involve either government and private partnerships that provide financial instruments to small business (such as micro finance) or partnerships between countries to create a larger financial market that warrants outside investment. A common example of financial linkages are non-governmental organizations that use donor funding to support loan and credit options for start-up businesses. There is also an increase in **crowd sourcing**, a financial model in which individuals or organizations solicit investment from a large, relatively open, and often rapidly-evolving, group of internet users.

Built capital

Built capital is any pre-existing or planned formation that is constructed or retrofitted to suit community needs, in other words, the man-made environment. Jacobs (2011) claims that built capital is the delivery system for all the other types of capital. Built capital includes infrastructure, such as roads, airports, and hotels, as well as the systems to deliver clean drinking water, process sewage, and transport waste away from human settlements. In tourism, built capital

Image 2.3 Kiev, Ukraine

Source: Susan L. Slocum

also comprises the attractions that tourists seek to visit, such as museums, theme parks, historic buildings, or battlefields. Built capital must be maintained and managed by a community or business in order to ensure the economic health and well-being of the resource.

Zekeri (2013) found evidence that built capital ranks second as the most influential form of capital to support growth in tourism (after natural capital). This is primarily because it links all other types of capital together. Built capital can only exist in relation to its use, such as transportation routes that deliver tourists to a destination. According to Coffey (2014), sewer and water treatment plants contribute to human capital through better environmental health for workers, and schools contribute to human capital through skills development. Building and maintaining infrastructure often requires diverse community input, which increases social capital and political capital. It also requires funding instruments, bringing new financial capital into a region. Moreover, built capital is often what provides access to natural capital in tourism, especially trails, campgrounds, and parks, which are visited by tourists.

SUSTAINABILITY TOOL: EVALUATING YOUR ACCESS TO CAPITAL

Part of understanding where a company or destination is in relation to sustainability is to recognize which forms of capital are available to enhance the tourism product, and which of these types of capital may need to be conserved if they are being overused. Employing each type of capital has both positive and negative impacts in a tourism destination. Therefore, finding ways to use capital in a way that harnesses positive change through tourism is important to the success of developing a sustainable business model. Table 2.1 highlights the positive and negative repercussions of using different forms of capital (Moscardo, 2012).

By utilizing a variety of capital, businesses can create a unique tourism product, while simultaneously being conscientious of the impacts that may arise. The Community Capitals Framework, developed by Flora and Flora (2013), is a great tool to help businesses support community development initiatives while simultaneously developing a sustainable tourism product. Mattos (2015) writes, "A community's capital approach allows us to view the various elements, resources, and relationships within a community and their contribution to the overall functioning of the community" (n.p.). First, a business must determine what assets are available, and then find a way to use them in a responsible manner. Below are steps a business can take in evaluating its access to capital:

Table 2.1 Links between tourism impacts and destination capitals

Capital	Positive tourism contributions	Negative tourism contributions
Natural	Resources and support are provided for the conservation and restoration of natural environments that serve as tourist attractions	Tourist population increase resource use. They consume greater amounts of water and energy and generate more waste
Cultural	Incentives from tourism for the preservation of cultural traditions and artifacts	Commodification of cultural traditions, and destruction of built heritage for the expansion of tourism facilities
Human	Provision of training and education for residents working in tourism	Tourists bring disease, globalized cultural influences, and non-traditional ideas with them creating health and/or social problems for residents
Social	Tourism can support traditional festivals that bring destination residents together and strengthen social connections	Controversial tourism development can create social conflict and break down social connections
Political	Tourist interest in ethnic minorities or marginalized indigenous populations can support greater political power for these groups	Transnational tour operators who control the flow of tourists can be given political power and advantage by elected officials
Financial	The creation of jobs and business opportunities that increase income opportunities for residents	Inflation and an increased cost of living for residents
Built	Building of transportation infrastructure to support tourism which provides greater opportunities for other economic sectors in the destination	Damage to infrastructure due to increased tourism use

Source: Adapted from Moscardo (2012)

Step 1: Is there a national or regional tourism policy that provides guidelines on how tourism should be developed?

The national strategy sets out clear priorities, goals, policies, objectives, interventions, and expected results that contribute to improving biodiversity protection, supporting community initiatives, and meeting local, national, and global commitments. These documents should provide an overview of political support for both tourism and sustainability. If sustainable tourism is valued in these documents, this implies that political capital exists and can be used as a resource to support a business. Moreover, it may imply that other businesses in an area are already engaging in sustainable tourism, allowing for increased social capital and the ability to develop a unified marketing message that encourages sustainably-minded tourism visitation.

However, you may find that tourism is highly regarded but sustainability is not, which means you have an opportunity to be a leader of sustainability in your region. This situation may also highlight the need for additional lobbying and community involvement in order to garnish increased support for the benefits of sustainable tourism development, which is a way to increase political and social capital in favor of your business ideas and vision. If political capital is lacking, highlighting the advantages of sourcing locally and cultural/environmental conservation may be needed, along with evidence that sustainability can support a larger economic impact without a need to increase the number of tourists visiting the area. In other words, let people know that they can host fewer tourists, and therefore have fewer disruptions throughout the community, while still reaping the same economic advantages of tourism development.

Step 2: What are the assets available and how can you utilize them in your product development?

Understanding the availability of natural, cultural, and built capital provides opportunities for you to market to your customers the reason to visit your area. Therefore, it is important to understand what your region offers that could be of interest to your customers, and to find unique opportunities that your competitors might not have considered. Not only should you consider actual sites of interest, but finding new and unique ways to engage tourists and create experiences within these sites is important. For example, if you choose to highlight traditional food, rather than just promoting a specific restaurant, consider ways to engage customers in cuisine-related experiences, such as offering cooking schools, demonstrations, or showcasing local farms that provide the ingredients, and then take them to a local restaurant as a way to package the culinary experience. If your area has a natural attraction, you can combine hiking, wildlife viewing, and an educational aspect that adds to the customer experience. How you package your product will depend on the human capital available, such as qualified guides that can connect what is being seen with aspects of history, heritage, or cultural understanding in a creative way for the tourist.

Step 3: Determine who can support your interest in sustainable tourism and what is already being done

Knowing what is currently being done to support sustainability is vital so that your efforts do not hinder other initiatives. It can also increase social capital in your community. For example, if a local hotel has a fund-raising campaign to support environmental conservation in your area, you may be able to collaborate with them and use a donation plan that is already successful. In addition, if the same hotel employs local dancers to offer an authentic experience for their guests, you may be able to do the same. You may choose to highlight cultural products from a different ethnic or social group as a way to spread the economic benefits throughout your region and promote the diversity found in your destination. Lastly, other organizations may have already established local supply networks that can benefit from an increase in distribution, which in turn can support an increase in local suppliers. All of these examples provide an opportunity to increase local networks, promote collaboration, and unite a community around tourism. It can also show your commitment to the local community, which may attract new customers.

Step 4: Determine what more is needed and what is not being done

Often businesses are started in areas where tourism is already established. However, how the assets in a destination are managed can jeopardize the future success of your investment. Therefore, it is important to be engaged in the management of your region's natural, cultural, and built resources. You may choose to serve on an advisory board or encourage your employees to volunteer in your community to ensure that your organization can spread your sustainability vision. Sometimes communities lack financial capital to make improvements to tourism resources, so backing a local organization in grant writing or fundraising campaigns can support an increase in social capital and ensure the long-term success of your investment. You can also engage your visitors in facilitating change in your community, especially where they express an interest in volunteering or donating to certain causes. Often there are more challenges than resources, so finding the appropriate avenue to support sustainability will vary depending on your assets, the type of business you operate, and your vision statement.

Step 5: Look at your internal operations to ensure you and your customers are operating in a way that supports your commitment to sustainability

Chapter 9 highlights specific tasks that can be used to encourage sustainable operations within your organization. These include reducing the use of resources, such as water and electricity, reducing the waste generated, and finding ways to source locally to provide more economic opportunities for residents. Moreover, there are ways to encourage your visitors to act in a more sustainable manner, such as encouraging them to use public transportation, respect the natural environment, and treat local residents with respect. These strategies are discussed in more detail in Chapter 12.

Conclusion

In theory, capitalism provides avenues for individuals to harness capital and generate profit or wealth. However, capitalism has many negative side effects inherent in the accumulation of capital by one person, one company, or one country. Capitalism is anti-humanistic when workers or community members are hindered in their ability to make more money and can be exploitive of the environment. Sustainability requires more than just the good will of business owners if it is to become the norm in tourism. It necessitates a governance system and policies that motivate businesses to act responsibly. Businesses have control over their choices and should find responsible ways of using resources in their tourism products. Sustainable tourism also needs businesses to educate consumers so tourists can make responsible choices in their consumption of resources while travelling. As a sustainable tourism business practitioner, it is important to have the tools to effect change in the future of the tourism industry. These topics are covered in more detail throughout the remainder of this book.

CASE STUDY 2.1 BEST PRACTICES IN ANIMAL-BASED TOURISM

CAROL KLINE

Appalachian State University

The tourism industry is full of examples where animals comprise the focus or a key part of the visitor experience. At the basest form, animal-based tourism (ABT) experiences are solely created to make money, and animals are treated purely as a revenue source. At its highest form, ABT can lead to further understanding of 'the other', including the tour operator, the animals, and the cultural context, which can lead to changed attitudes or behaviors, social bonding across cultures and species, and a deeper love for the natural world.

Best practices in ABT are very similar to best practices in all sustainable tourism ventures, with an added caveat that operators are responsible for the care of specific and individual animals and/or groups of animals, versus all animals included broadly within an ecosystem. ABT can be consumptive, whereby animals are killed and their body parts are used, or non-consumptive. A 2015 study examining wildlife tourism attractions divided ABT into four categories: wildlife-watching tourism, captive-wildlife tourism, hunting tourism, and fishing tourism (Moorhouse, Dahlsjö, Baker, D'Cruze, & Macdonald, 2015). This categorization would presumably not

Image 2.4 Elephant rides in Cambodia

Source: Susan L. Slocum

include ABT with tamed animals such as dogs, llamas, donkeys, yak, and other animals that have been 'domesticated' for human use such as the transportation of people or goods, or for entertainment and recreation such as dog racing, cock fighting, bull fighting, or rodeos. Likewise, it does not include animals raised for the sole purpose of being food, and aquatic animals of all types seem to be excluded from many ABT discussions.

The same 2015 study found that 80% of tourists to wildlife-watching experiences did not recognize and/or respond to signs of negative animal welfare. In the cases where animals are 'front and center' in the supply chain, the animal's welfare should be the utmost imperative for operators, and should be demanded by visitors, to support sustainability. In the cases where animals are sporadically or minimally visible, the tourist should still be a savvy and responsible consumer of ABT experiences.

Best practices in ABT for the visitor

Research, research, research . . .

There are dozens of organizations that strive to educate the traveling public, monitor operators, and develop policy toward creating better ABT. A solid hour of research on the web would make a traveler much more informed about the potential issues of virtually any destination. For example, the organization World Animal Protection puts out a list of 'elephant-friendly' travel companies. The International Fund for Animal Welfare has information on the best and worst countries for banning animals in circuses. The Global Federation of Animal Sanctuaries provides certification for animal sanctuaries, rescue centers, and rehabilitation centers. Tourism Concern has an Ethical Tour Operators Group, Responsible Travel publishes a list of attractions they denounce, and The Brooke have a code for responsible travel with horses and other equids . . . these are just a few examples of the many resources that exist.

Think about the supply chain

How did that animal get to be a part of the ABT experience? Could he/she have been plucked from the wild in order to become part of this attraction? Often, smaller animals are easier to transport, therefore other members of the family may be killed in order to more easily capture the offspring. Injuries and death of animals often occur during transportation, as well. In doing the research ahead, and thinking about the supply chain, you can avoid unethical facilities and businesses.

Follow the money

While you are doing your research, see if you can figure out if the revenue from the ABT benefits the community or conservation goals in general.

Refrain from getting a selfie

The organization World Animal Protection notes "If you can ride it, hug it, or have a selfie with the wild animal, the chances are it's a cruel venue." Animal selfies, while a hit on social media, can be extremely stressful for the animal. Wildlife selfie safaris are on the rise. *National Geographic* has done a wonderful job tackling this topic, and since late 2017 Instagram has acted responsibly by inserting pop-up warnings about potential hazards to wildlife (Daly, 2017).

Report suffering

There are places where animal suffering can be reported, including Born Free's website: www.bornfree.org.uk/report-animal-suffering.

Give back to animals

If you are going to volunteer at a shelter, sanctuary, or rehabilitation facility while you travel, make sure the facility, and the tourism operators that connect you with them, are reputable. Animal Experiences International is transparent in how they approach social responsibility and how visitors should approach ethical travel (see more at www.animalexperienceinternational.com/serious-1/). Additionally, reflect on your motives for volunteering to help animals to make sure the priority is providing aid and not for status reasons or to add to your resume. Some animal sanctuaries are overwhelmed with volunteers and media attention, to the detriment of other parks that may need more help, or where conditions are not as favorable to the animals (Taylor, 2018).

Best practices in ABT for the operator

Invest in quality interpretation

All conservation-based attractions need quality interpretation to impart influential messages to visitors about the value of the resources in question. Particularly if the resource is a sentient being, or group of sentient beings, care must be taken to present accurate and representative knowledge. By investing in the what, who, why, and how of interpretation, you will be maximizing your intended conservation goals. One resource in the United States is the National Association for Interpretation.

Invest in staff training

Not all employees are alike. Make sure that your staff not only are equipped with the proper training to interact with visitors but understand the inherent value of the sentient beings in your care. Refresher workshops on how to interact with wildlife are critical to staff understanding of wildlife instinct and behavior, as well as their own welfare and the welfare of the animal.

Leave human behavior to humans

Animals should never be 'trained' to ride bicycles, smoke cigarettes, dance, jump through hoops, or move in some way that is not innate to the species.

Join the experts

Just like visitors should do their research, operators also have a host of organizations to turn to, learn from, and join. Becoming a member of a reputable group, or becoming certified by them, demonstrates that you adhere to the ABT-related standards set out by that organization; find the one that best matches your tourism sector (e.g., tour operator, attraction management, transportation, lodging, marketing, etc.). Note that many organizations are still catching up when it comes to recommended ethical standards or codes, so align with an organization that has considered these matters deeply. As Fennell (2014) notes, even the United Nations World Tourism Organization's Global Code of Ethics for Tourism sets forth its ideal protocols from an anthropomorphic perspective.

Ensure the five freedoms

It goes without saying that attending to the five freedoms is the minimal standard of care: freedom from hunger and thirst; freedom from discomfort; freedom from pain, injury, and disease; freedom to behave normally; and freedom from fear and distress.

Don't use animals

A live animal is wonderful to see up close . . . for the human. Are there ways of getting the information across without having a captive animal in front of an audience? Are there animal substitutes that could be made? For example, some circuses are only displaying human feats of entertainment or providing life sized animal puppets to amuse audiences. If your attraction is conservation-based, are there other ways of exposing visitors to an ABT at a distance and in the animal's natural habitat?

Reflective questions

1. Where does eating animals fit within the realm of animal-based tourism? Should it be kept as separate since the animal is not alive anymore?

2. Some people feel that the five freedoms do not go far enough. What other welfare issues should be considered?

3. What should you do if you are at an attraction where wildlife is being fed by tourists or tourists are taking selfies?

References

Daly, N. (2017). Exclusive: Instagram fights animal abuse with new alert system. *National Geographic*. Retrieved from https://news.nationalgeographic.com/2017/12/wildlife-watch-instagram-selfie-tourism-animal-welfare-crime/.

Fennell, D.A. (2014). Exploring the boundaries of a new moral order for tourism's global code of ethics: an opinion piece on the position of animals in the tourism industry. *Journal of Sustainable Tourism*, 22(7), 983–996.

Moorhouse, T.P., Dahlsjö, C.A.L., Baker, S.E., D'Cruze, N.C., & Macdonald, D.W. (2015). The customer isn't always right – conservation and animal welfare implications of the increasing demand for wildlife tourism. *PLoS ONE*, 10(10), e0138939. https://doi.org/10.1371/journal.pone.0138939.

Taylor, M. (2018). *Elephant-based Volunteer Tourism: An Exploration of Participant Experiences and Reflections on Captive Elephant Welfare in Thailand* (Master's thesis, University of Waterloo).

CASE STUDY 2.2 POVERTY AS A FORM OF CAPITAL

SUSAN L. SLOCUM

Poverty tourism is a type of tourism that involves financially privileged tourists visiting impoverished communities for the purpose of witnessing poverty firsthand. It is also known as ghetto, slum, or township tourism (Outterson, Selinger, & Whyte, 2011). It involves visiting some of the poorest and most vulnerable populations in the world, and there are very few regulatory policies to protect these people from exploitation. Steinbrink (2012) writes, "In spite of strong criticism coming from the international media, visits to poor urban areas in big cities in the South are unmistakably gaining in importance both in terms of tourism and in economic terms" (p. 214).

History

The concept of 'slumming' began in London and New York in the 1880s, when wealthy urbanites would visit immigrant communities to see how others lived. In the 1990s, black Africans in South Africa began to offer tours to white Africans to help explain and educate society on the apartheid restrictions and the impact it had on the lives on most South Africans. By the 1990s, international tour operators began offering poverty tour packages, and Rio de Janeiro, Brazil was the top poverty destination (Ma, 2010). Movies, such as *Cidade de Deus/City of God* (2002) or *Slumdog Millionaire* (2008) have been a major driver of the increase in urban slum tourism (Rolfes, 2010). While accurate statistics on the size and scope of poverty tourism are lacking, it is estimated that it has evolved into a multi-million-dollar industry with more than a million travelers each year.

Poverty as capital

The concept of capital is the ability to turn something into wealth. Cultural capital uses culture, in the form of art, theater, music, and dance, as a means to earn revenue, which is then used to increase social mobility. Cultural capital also consists of lived experiences, such as social norms, languages, and traditional lifestyles. Cultural tourism is a traveler's engagement with a country or region's culture, specifically the lifestyle of the people in those geographical areas, the history of those people, their art, architecture, religion(s), and other elements that helped shape their way of life. For many tourists, poverty is a way of life that is foreign and exotic, filled with notions of crime, drugs, prostitution, and other vices. Some researchers consider poverty tourism a vice in itself (Ma, 2010).

There are two primary types of poverty tourism: cultural or entertainment tours. Cultural tours focus on the lived experiences of slum dwellers and highlight how slum communities function. Cultural tours will incorporate a strong educational component (Ma, 2010). Entertainment tours focus on safari-like experiences where tourist view residents from the comfort of their vehicles. In a study conducted by Rolfes (2010), the primary reason tour operators offered poverty tours was for economic profit and as a way to diversify their tour options. Other reasons mentioned included "to show what life is like in the communities, to convey knowledge about culture and history, and to give an authentic insight into what they themselves called the real life" (p. 429). Monroe and Bishop (2016) show that tourism providers promote experiences they think tourists will pay to see and incorporate selling points that allow customers to visualize poverty.

Challenges to poverty tourism

No form of tourism is all good or all bad. The same applies to poverty tourism. While itineraries vary from tour to tour, many include a walking expedition through a neighborhood or a stop at a market, which allows tourists to interact directly with local people. There is an opportunity to sell locally-made products, and opportunities for visitor-host

Image 2.5 Viewing poverty in Laguna de Caratasca, Honduras

Source: Susan L. Slocum

interactions where community members can shape the narrative imparted to tourists. Tourists can visit orphanages or schools, where they can volunteer or donate money. Tours can demystify poverty and show firsthand that people who live in slums are not all miserable or criminal, despite their portrayal in the media. Lastly, it is hoped that tourists will leave with a new understanding of the causes of poverty, making them more inclined to support charitable organizations in the future.

However, when tourism is organized by tour companies that only seek economic profit, locals are marginalized from tourism and do not have an opportunity to turn their lifestyle into cultural capital. Poverty tourism can perpetuate images of misery and despair and ignore the complex social and organizational structures that comprise an impoverished community. This can perpetuate stereotypes and undercut the ingenuity and creativity that exists. Poverty tourism can also misrepresent the complex global phenomena that perpetuate poverty. The United Nations World Tourism Organization (2010), with help from the NGO SNV, provides the following guidelines when addressing poverty in tourism destinations. These are relevant to poverty tourism development as well.

Ten principles for pursuing poverty alleviation through tourism

1. All aspects and types of tourism can and should be concerned about poverty alleviation.
2. All governments should include poverty alleviation as a key aim of tourism development and consider tourism as a possible tool for reducing poverty.

3. The competitiveness and economic success of tourism businesses and destinations is critical to poverty alleviation – without this the poor cannot benefit.

4. All tourism businesses should be concerned about the impact of their activities on local communities and seek to benefit the poor through their actions.

5. Tourism destinations should be managed with poverty alleviation as a central aim that is built into strategies and action plans.

6. A sound understanding of how tourism functions in destinations is required, including how tourism income is distributed and who benefits from this.

7. Planning and development of tourism in destinations should involve a wide range of interests, including participation and representation from poor communities.

8. All potential impacts of tourism on the livelihood of local communities should be considered, including current and future local and global impacts on natural and cultural resources.

9. Attention must be paid to the viability of all projects involving the poor, ensuring access to markets and maximizing opportunities for beneficial links with established enterprises.

10. Impacts of tourism on poverty alleviation should be effectively monitored.

UNWTO and SNV (2010)

Sustainable tourism strives to provide access to cultural capital long into the future. However, is poverty something that should be sustained? When there is an economic incentive for the existence of poverty, there is little incentive to eradicate it and lose the opportunity to generate tourism revenue. There are a number of documented cases of orphanages or schools that seek donations from visitors, and yet if they use that money to improve the conditions of the facility, they will lose the donation opportunities. It is a catch-22 – poverty brings money (through donations, international aid, and tourism visits), and using this revenue to eliminate poverty stops the flow of financial support.

While poverty tourism remains controversial, it is a growing aspect of the tourism industry. As Monroe and Bishop (2016) write, "Perhaps slum tourism will ignite societal change in some places in the future, but for now, researchers agree, its most obvious positive effects occur on a more modest scale: improving lives and changing minds, one person at a time" (p. 4).

Reflective questions

1. Do you feel poverty tourism is an ethical option for tourism development? Why or why not?

2. If you were tasked with developing a township tour, how could you develop social and human capital to ensure that the benefits from tourism remained with the local community? What challenges would you face and how would you overcome them?

3. Research a tour operator that offers poverty tours. From the perspective of a consumer, how can you determine if they are using the UNWTO guidelines? How could they increase their transparency?

References

Ma, B. (2010). A trip into the controversy: a study of slum tourism travel motivations. 2009–2010 *Penn Humanities Forum on Connections*.

Monroe, E. & Bishop, P. (2016). Slum tourism: helping to fight poverty . . . or voyeuristic exploitation? Tourism Concern Research Brief, Retrieved from www.tourismconcern.org.uk/wp-content/uploads/2016/02/Slum-Tourism-Report-print-web.pdf.

Outterson, K., Selinger, E., & Whyte, K. (2011). Poverty tourism, justice, and policy. *Public Integrity*, 14(1), 39–50.

Rolfes, M. (2010). Poverty tourism: theoretical reflections and empirical findings regarding an extraordinary form of tourism. *GeoJournal*, 75(5), 421–442.

Steinbrink, M. (2012). We did the slum! – Urban poverty tourism in historical perspective. *Tourism Geographies*, 14(2), 213–234.

UNWTO and SNV (2010). Manual on tourism and poverty alleviation, practical steps for destinations. Retrieved from http://step.unwto.org/content/tourism-and-poverty-alleviation-1.

STUDY QUESTIONS

1. Determine which type of capital these are.
   - A national park that is open to the public
   - A 15th-century mosque that is closed to the public
   - A 15th-century mosque that is open to the public
   - A local craft market that happens every Saturday afternoon for tourists
   - Tourism donations that support a dance troupe of HIV widows
   - A hotel training program for local high school students
   - A tourism organization that lobbies the government on issues related to hotel worker benefits
   - A non-profit volunteer group that picks up litter in a public park

2. As a business owner, what could you do to increase social capital in your destination? What are some of the challenges you might face?

3. Develop a crowd sourcing campaign that supports a local small business idea. How can you get your customers to invest?

4. Research a local tourism policy in your region. Is it supportive of sustainable tourism development? How can you use this policy to support your business ideas?

5. What resources are in your local area to support tourism? How well are they managed? What advice could you offer to increase their ability to generate revenue without causing the negative impacts associated with tourism?

DEFINITIONS

Bonding social capital   social networks made up of homogeneous groups of people

Bridging social capital   social networks made up of socially heterogeneous groups that include people with different backgrounds

Built capital   any pre-existing or planned formation that is constructed or retrofitted to suit community needs

Capital   factors of production that generate wealth through investment

Capitalism   an economic and political system in which a country's trade and industry are controlled by private owners for profit, rather than by the state

Crowd sourcing   a financial model in which individuals or organizations solicit investment from a large, relatively open, and often rapidly-evolving, group of internet users

Cultural capital   the stock of values, arts, crafts, cultural knowledge, performance, social practices, and access to heritage resources

Environmental capital   includes natural capital, other natural assets, such as weather, and built capital

Factors of production   the inputs that are used in the production of goods or services in order to make an economic profit. The factors of production include land, labor, capital, and entrepreneurship

Financial capital   financial wealth that is used to start or maintain a business

Human capital   the stock of knowledge, habits, social and personality attributes, including creativity, embodied in the ability to perform labor so as to produce economic value

Human resources   the people who make up the workforce of an organization, business sector, or economy

Intangible culture   the practices and representations of artifacts, objects, and cultural spaces

Micro finance   the lending of small amounts of money at low interest to new businesses, generally but not exclusively, in the developing world. Also known as micro credit

Natural capital   the world's stock of natural resources, which includes geology, soils, air, water, and all living organisms

Non-renewable resources   resources that take millions of years to form and cannot be renewed in a human lifetime

Political capital   the ability to use power in support of political or economic positions

Private sector   the part of an economy that invests in profit-making businesses, such as hotel accommodations, restaurants, and entertainment (private industries)

Public sector   the part of an economy that is under government control, financed through tax revenue, and provides services for all members of society (public services)

Renewable resources   resources that are replenished naturally and can be used repeatedly

Social capital   the links, shared values, and understandings that enable individuals and groups in a society to trust one another and so work together

Tangible culture   physical cultural and historical artifacts, such as architecture or other built heritage

Chapter **3**

Globalization, localism, and sustainability

Overview

This chapter describes globalization and its implications for, and impact by, tourism, as well as its benefits, costs, and consequences in the context of the developed and developing global divide. In addition, the concept of localism, as a response to globalization, will be discussed. Finally, the relevance of globalization, localism, globalization from below, and glocalization (globalization and localism), in the context of sustainable tourism development, is explained. The chapter tool provides a strategy to engage both the local community and international tourism sector in collaborative sustainable tourism development.

CHAPTER OBJECTIVES

At the completion of the chapter, students will be able to:

- Define globalization and the role tourism plays in supporting globalization;
- Describe the benefits and costs of globalization;
- Explain localism and its relationship to globalization;
- Consider the practical benefits of globalization from below; and
- Analyze the importance of globalization and localism in the context of sustainable tourism development.

Introduction

The industrial revolution, one of the technological coups of world history, changed the economies of countries, primarily those of the developed regions and their interactions with other nations. Industrialization required access to valuable natural resources, often found in unde-veloped regions of the world, leading to a period of colonization of the world by European countries. **Colonization** is defined as the action of appropriating a place or domain for one's own use and establishing control over the indigenous people of an area. The exchanges among countries at an economic, social, cultural, and political level have taken various forms and, if the history of international alliances and wars is considered, fall into the categories of 'the good, the bad, and the ugly'. An example of 'the good' is the trade that occurred along the **Silk Road**, a network of routes in the ancient world linking regions of Asia and Europe that was established by the Han Dynasty of China (Mark, 2018). In reference to 'the bad', the colonization of African, Asian, and American native populations, which devolved from initial trade interactions, ultimately marginalized indigenous peoples. The horrific transatlantic slave trade and the establishment of the apartheid regime in South Africa signifies 'the ugly' of globalization.

Globalization

Increasingly, it has become apparent that there are links that bring the countries of the world together, particularly when it comes to their economic activities, but also culturally and envi-ronmentally. Globalization is one of the concepts that has been used to describe this phenom-enon. According to Friedman (2000), globalization may be described as,

> [T]he inexorable integration of markets, nation-states, and technologies to a degree never witnessed before – in a way that is enabling individuals, corporations and nation-states to reach around the world farther, faster, deeper, and cheaper than ever before . . . the spread of free-market capitalism to virtually every country in the world.
>
> (pp. 7–8)

In simpler terms, **globalization** is the process by which people and goods move easily across borders (Gray, 2017). While this definition points to the predominantly economic nature of these interactions between nations, it is has also resulted in cultural exchanges, resulting in a globalized (western) culture that is oftentimes referred to as the global village. According to Chang (1999), a **global village** is characterized by "instant communication, the proliferation of transnational corporations, and the pervasive influence of mass media and popular cultural trends from the West" (p. 91). It infers that the entire world has been condensed into one vil-lage through the use of electronic media.

Shangquan (2000) suggests that there are a number of influences that have contributed to the growth of globalization. These include: the increase in the size of national economies; the reduction in world trade tariffs; the tendency of economies to move in trade cycles together; the linkages among the monetary policies of different countries; and international influence over product markets (e.g. McDonald's, which originated in the USA is now a global brand, Image 3.1).

The World Trade Organization (WTO) has been influential in establishing a more integrated and interdependent global economy (Wallach, 2001). By establishing the rules of trade between nations, the WTO seeks to ensure that trade flows as smoothly and freely as possible by regu-lating commerce and negotiating exchange disputes. Other aspects influencing globalization include the movement of capital (described in Chapter 2), the movement of people perma-nently and temporarily across the globe, and the spread of information and knowledge (Inter-national Monetary Fund, 2002).

Image 3.1 McDonald's restaurant at the Bryggen World Heritage Site, Bergen, Norway

Source: Susan L. Slocum

Benefits of globalization

For the proponents of globalization, one key benefit is free trade. **Free trade**, or policies that seek to eliminate government-imposed barriers to trade (such as taxes and quotas), ensure that the flow of goods and services between, and among, countries is unhindered by tariffs and other forms of blockades. When companies enjoy monopolies in their local economies, complacency could arise. Free trade opens up markets to competition from abroad. An example of a free trade policy is the North American Free Trade Agreement (NAFTA), which was formulated between the United States, Mexico, and Canada on January 1, 1994 (United States Trade Representative, 2018). NAFTA focused on the elimination of restrictions, duties, and tariffs on products and services that are traded across borders, with a few exceptions on agricultural products traded with Canada. Another example is the elimination of trade barriers across member countries of the European Union. Free trade supports access to higher-quality, lower-priced goods, improves efficiency and innovation, and drives competitiveness in a global market.

Another benefit of globalization is increased economies of scale and comparative advantage. **Economies of scale** refers to a proportionate savings in costs gained by an increased level of production. For example, the unit cost of producing larger quantities is less than the unit cost of producing smaller quantities because fixed costs, such as the cost of rent on facilities, are divided up among a higher number of units, reducing the overall cost of each unit. **Comparative advantage** is when countries specialize in the production and export of the goods which they can produce relatively less expensively than other countries, because they possess specific resources, such as land, labor, and capital (Edgell & Swanson, 2013). Since globalization allows for the free flow of goods and services between countries, it allows countries to specialize in the production of goods and services with greater efficiency, leading to increased economies of scale. For example, tropical climates are more conducive to growing bananas and pineapples, which is why Central America is a leader in their production.

The final benefit is that globalization increases levels of investment. Because there is an ease in the flow of capital (financial and human capital, specifically), this can encourage companies to invest in economies which they would not have considered profitable pre-globalization. Using the example from above, one reason Central America has been so successful in the production of bananas and pineapples is because of international investment, specifically from the United States, for the modernization of agriculture in this region.

Globalization, through free trade, economies of scale, comparative advantage, and international investment has supported an increase in quality of life in many developing countries. It has opened new markets, increasing production and supporting international investment in traditionally poorer economies. It has also provided jobs to areas where high unemployment exists. It has lowered prices for basic necessities, such as food, building supplies, and energy, in both developed and developing regions.

Costs of globalization

Mowforth and Munt (2009) describe a number of costs attributed to globalization. Globalization has made the rich richer, while making the non-rich poorer, since it is the rich that have access to certain forms of capital (education and financing) and who invest in emerging industries and reap the profits from trade. While globalization decreases the costs of goods and services for consumers, this is done through decreased wages by hiring low-income workers in developing countries. China is generally named as one of the recipients of manufacturing jobs lost to American workers because wages are lower in China. This also increases employment insecurity since international corporations will easily relocate if wage rates change significantly. Globalization has been shown to decrease labor standards, including decreased safety standards and a reduction in bargaining power for workers (Mosley & Uno, 2007).

While import and export taxes have been reduced through free trade, there are about 161 countries who have value added taxes (VATs). **Value added tax** is tax collected in pieces along the production chain and can be as high as 21.6% in some European countries (Thompson, 2010). Moreover, globalization has allowed certain **multinational companies (MNCs)**, companies whose bases of operation are located in one country but then have subsidiaries in two or more other countries (Kogut, 2001), to avoid tax obligations in their home country, as well as the foreign countries in which they operate, by hiding profits in international financial institutions and through the practices of corruption or bribery (Tanzi, 2017).

Reductions in regulation on imports, financial transactions, and labor have had a number of negative social and environmental impacts. Globalization has contributed to the spread of deadly diseases and invasive species resulting from the movement of people and agriculture. There has also been a notable increase in child labor and human trafficking, both in developing and developed countries. Some MNCs have been found to operate in socially irresponsible ways towards their employees and the environment, as many developing countries lack social and environmental oversight, resulting in the exploitation of the countries in which MNCs operate. It is not surprising that there are increasing anti-globalization sentiments among many in the middle class, particularly in developed countries, who point the finger at globalization as the reason behind their economic, and in some cases, sociocultural, woes (Burgoon, Oliver, & Trubowitz, 2017).

Recent political occurrences in a number of countries appear to shed light on how deep the negative sentiments run against globalization. Coyle (2016) writes that the campaign slogan for those in support of the **Brexit vote** (the vote by the United Kingdom to leave the European Union), "Let's take back control", seems to highlight the feeling of having lost power over their agency by many Britons. Lester and dela Rama (2018) decry this apparent move towards **isolationism**, which refers to a national policy of avoiding political or economic entanglements with other countries, and **protectionism**, the policy of protecting domestic industries against foreign competition through the use of quotas, subsidies, and tariffs. Another example is the current United States administration's "America First" policy, which has caused some consternation globally. However, in early 2018, President Trump attended the World Economic Forum, in Davos, Switzerland, to point out to his fellow heads-of-state that putting "America First" did not, in fact, lead to sluggish economic growth and lackluster stock market gains (Pettypiece, 2018). Whether this apparent reversal from globalization is good or bad for the world economy is something that future economic, as well as sociocultural, trends will show.

Globalization and tourism

There is much debate about whether tourism is a byproduct of globalization or a cause of globalization. The reality is that tourism is both a cause and an effect of globalization (George, Mair, & Reid, 2009). Dwyer (2015) claims that the tourism sector has indeed profited from globalization (Figure 3.1). The advancements resulting from the generation of *technology* at an international scale, as well as technology collaborations globally (Archibugi & Pietrobelli, 2003), have contributed to the rapid mobility of people from place to place, increasing their discretionary time, and therefore their ability to engage in tourism-related activities. New technological innovations have also spurred the marketing reach of the sector, resulting in an increase in travel motivation to new destinations. *Social changes*, including increased consumerism and a growing global middle class, have opened up travel opportunities for many developing countries, increasing the accessibility of travel. *Political changes* include a reduction in travel restrictions, a world governance system that promotes sustainable travel, and an increase in the quality of tourism infrastructure. *Economic drivers* include the ease in conducting financial transactions at the international level, a decrease in travel costs, and more supply chain options for global companies (Dwyer, 2015).

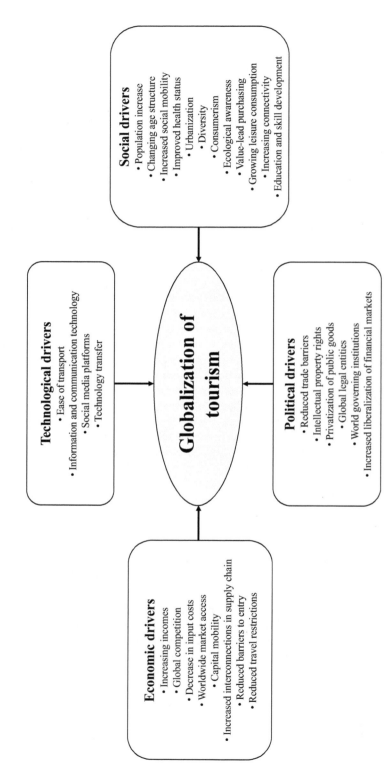

Figure 3.1 Drivers of globalization

Source: Adapted from Dwyer (2015)

Tourism also spurs globalization by bringing tourists together with local populations. The need to support tourism inherently changes the nature of local communities, impacts the way natural environments are used, and facilitates the flow of money on a global scale. Tourists can appear wealthier than the people in the destinations they visit, shifting power relations and bringing outside influences into a society. While Chapter 1 highlights many of the negative impacts of tourism, these impacts occur because tourism is a globalized industry, prone to all aspects of globalization. Now, however, it appears that a closer look at another important concept may be timely, the concept of localism.

Image 3.2 Handmade guitarra in Portugal

Source: Susan L. Slocum

Localism

Evans, Marsh, and Stoker (2013) write that the concept of localism is not a recent phenomenon, but that it predated the industrial revolution. It was the rise in **imperialism**, a policy of extending a country's power and influence through diplomacy or military force, which diverted attention away from the local in the nineteenth century. Ashworth and Tunbridge (2004) define **localism** as the belief in, and expression of, the unique character of localities. In other words, in contrast to the outward view inherent in globalization, localism turns the focus inwards to provide opportunities and empowerment to local communities by capitalizing on their unique attributes. Following Evans et al.'s (2013) assertion about the displacement of localism during the nineteenth century, it appears that the resurgence of the focus on localism (or locality) can be traced to the 1980s (Chang, 1999). Localism has resulted from dissatisfaction with globalization, feelings that communities are becoming homogenized by being steeped in western influences, and a loss of sense of place. Sense of place in the sociological context is "people's subjective perceptions of their environments and their more or less conscious feelings about those environments", and in the geographical context, it is described as "the affective bond between people and place or setting" (Cross, 2001, p. 2). In tourism, **sense of place** refers to what sets a place (destination) apart from others, and the strong feelings a place invokes in the people who live there or travel there as tourists. Weaver and Lawton (2014) indicates that sense of place is an important concept for tourism destinations because it enables them to brand themselves and helps to highlight their uniqueness as a way to be competitive and to engender loyalty. Another important aspect of localism is the focus on the agency of local institutions and local communities. Cooke (1989) states that "local communities are not mere recipients of fortune or fate from above, but are actively involved in their own transformation" (p. 296).

A related term, **neolocalism** (new localism), was coined by Flack (1997) and describes a renewed interest in preserving and promoting the identity of a community and restoring aspects that make it culturally unique. Whereas localism describes feelings of identity, neolocalism is the result of people cultivating local ties by choice, not by necessity (Schnell, 2013). In other words, neolocalism is the process of crafting localism through marketing and tourism product development. While destinations may have a unique sense of place that attracts visitors (localism), when they develop attractions or use unique cultural themes in special events, they are creating neolocalism.

One area where neolocalism is evident is in the growth of the microbrewery industry. The Brewers Association (n.d.) defines a **microbrewery** as one that produces a volume of less than 15,000 barrels of beer and sells at least 70% of it to locations off-site. Holtkamp, Shelton, Daly, Hiner, and Hagelman (2016), in assessing the role of neolocalism in the growth of microbreweries, suggest that microbreweries, through their targeted marketing strategies, help to emphasize the uniqueness of local identity. They quote the then president of Heineken USA, who stated that "people are looking for something very different as part of a behavioral statement . . . With a micro[brew], they're not drinking a brand at all, but an idea" (p. 66). They add that the use of local names and imagery by microbreweries enhances local marketing and is a form of neolocalism. Reid and Gatrell (2017) also add that locally-owned breweries tend to name their breweries and product after "local landmarks, historical figures, landscapes, or historical events" (p. 93) as a way to strengthen their local connections. From the discussions on globalization and localism above, a question that lingers is whether the way forward is to choose between the two, or to find a way to incorporate both frameworks, particularly in the context of sustainability, in the development of tourism.

Image 3.3 Two Silos Brewery, Manassas, Virginia

Source: Susan L. Slocum

Globalization and/or localism and sustainable tourism development

Chang (1999) indicates that the growth in tourism resulting from globalization poses a threat to local structures, cultures, and communities in destination regions. In developing countries in particular, there is concern that the expansion of tourism contributes to the subjugation of their local culture, and renders these countries unable to push back on the external forces, such as MNCs, that tend to be the source of much needed financial capital. George et al. (2009) add that tourism can contribute to cultural conflict, loss of diversity, cultural appropriation, staged authenticity, and leakages/loss of control. Thus, according to them, "[w]hen considering any tourism development, the host community and its local culture should be given precedence as the foundation on which all action is grounded" (p. 124). Simmons (1994) emphasizes that the positive and negative impacts of tourism are more evident at the local level. It would be easy, then, to point a finger at globalization as the problem and swing the pendulum totally towards localism or neolocalism. However, some believe that globalization and localism exist together; and that 'localizing global movements', and 'globalizing local attributes' do not constitute "two opposing views of what is happening in the world today, but two constitutive trends of global reality" (Friedman, 2000, p. 311).

Businesses, especially MNCs, such as Marriott International or Club Med, are often catalysts for globalization. MNCs generally have a corporate culture that aligns with the culture of their home country and bring this culture to their international locations. MNCs seeking to operate in developing regions or invest in rural regions are oftentimes viewed with suspicion or skepticism at the local level, based on the perception that they are there to take advantage of these regions (Ferdussy & Rahman, 2009). Some of these negative views are self-inflicted, as they have established a reputation of exploiting local resources and then leaving an area when these resources are gone (García-Cabrera, Suárez-Ortega, & Durán-Herrera, 2016). The reality, however, is that the capital these businesses bring is an important resource for economic development in many parts of the world. If these businesses are to be seen as honest brokers in the partnership towards sustainable tourism development, they must be dedicated to providing new opportunities and tools to the regions in which they do business. By providing technical training, promoting the active and powerful participation of local stakeholders, and being willing to collaborate with local representatives, they can allow the community to the take the lead in deciding the best plan for implementing tourism development that achieves the triple bottom line that is appropriate for the region. As García-Cabrera et al. (2016) suggest, "the successful implementation of sustainable tourism could benefit both local communities and foreign MNCs, as it would make it possible for these two parties to achieve their objectives in the long term" (p. 24). This is the practice of conducting business according to both local and global considerations.

Globalization from below

The coexistence of globalization and localism in the context of sustainable tourism development is known as **globalization from below** (Teo, 2002). Globalization from below is regulated by the local governance institutions as a way to guarantee the right to access capital and to regulate the global economy, both within and outside its jurisdiction (rather than being regulated by MNCs).

Community participation in the planning, decision-making, and implementation of sustainable tourism is integral to globalization from below. By involving community members in the development and execution of policies, global forces can be navigated, and neolocalism can be constructed throughout the tourism development process. Simmons (1994) suggests that the overall goal of a destination's tourism development strategy is to integrate the growth objectives of its community. Requirements necessary for this integration include: a clarification of the role that tourism will play in achieving the destination's economic, social, environmental, and political goals; democracy that allows for the full participation of its citizens; connections with other segments of the destination's structure; and policy that is systematic and steeped in research (Table 3.1).

Table 3.1 Globalization and localism in tourism development

	Globalization	Localism	Globalization from below (Policy) Glocalization (Management)
Infrastructure	Foreign direct investment for infrastructure	Seek local funding for infrastructure	Establish private–public partnerships to gain access to grant funding and international investment
	Employ international development professionals	Employ local development professionals	Ensure global companies hire local labor Provide training to develop local management skills
	Use international development standards	Use local development standards	Use international safety standards, but local design esthetics

	Globalization	Localism	Globalization from below (Policy) Glocalization (Management)
Environment	Establish resource protection policies that promote the use of natural resources for tourism growth	Establish resource protection policies that support local use of natural resources	Establish resource protection policies that mutually address the needs of the tourism industry and local resource use
	Develop a sense of place based on mass consumer demand	Develop a sense of place based on local community attributes	Develop a sense of place based on local community attributes that satisfy specific consumer markets
Product development	Serve global food with global safety standards	Serve local food with local safety standards	Serve both local and global food with the highest safety standards
	Develop cultural tourism products that are commodified for mass consumption	Develop tourism products that represent local culture	Develop tourism products that represent local culture and are appealing to global audiences
	Use the same tourism amenities in different destinations	Use the amenities available locally	Use some standardized features but maintain a distinct sense of character
	Provide global amenities using global technology	Provide local amenities using local technology	Provide local amenities using global technology
Destination development	Support ease of travel for tourists	Support lifestyle needs of the community	Support ease of travel for tourists that utilize local lifestyle options
	Promote global businesses that offer standardized experiences	Promote local businesses that offer localized experiences	Promote local businesses that offer a variety of experiences
Service quality	Maintain global customer service standards	Maintain local customer service standards	Maintain customer service standards that meet customer expectations
Marketing	Highlight globally recognizable experiences	Highlight local experiences	Educate the consumer to recognize uniquely local experiences
	Develop a brand that appeals to mass consumers	Develop a brand that reflects local attributes	Differentiate using a global brand that supports local attributes
Policy	Allow tourism power structure to determine appropriate policy	Allow local power structure to determine appropriate policy	Allow all stakeholders to determine appropriate policy
	Use international polices	Use local policies	Use international policies to inform local policy

Similarly, **glocalization** is the practice of conducting business according to both local and global considerations and is used by managers or businesses to develop global products customized locally to support diverse tourism products.

In the context of managing the triple bottom line of sustainability, therefore, there is a need to think globally and act locally. In other words, it is important for local businesses to be aware of global trends, take advantage of advancements and innovations resulting from globalization, but to translate them to fit the structure and culture of the local environment. For example, businesses could attempt to incorporate the mandates under the World Charter of Sustainable Tourism +20 (described in detail in Chapter 4), such as reducing poverty and hunger, providing quality education, and supporting the equitable use of valuable resources, for instance clean water, electricity, and ecosystems. By including elements of the World Charter of Sustainable Tourism +20 into their vision and mission statements (see tool in Chapter 1) and operating procedures, and taking into account local conditions and local needs, tourism businesses can be an asset to the overall development of tourism. Edgell and Swanson (2013) suggest that it is important that policymakers at the local level formulate tourism strategies that fit into the objectives of national tourism policies, but that also align with the aims of global organizations, such as the UNWTO.

Once again, it is not possible to discuss the enmeshing of globalization and localism in the context of sustainable tourism development without paying attention to the important role that politics plays in tourism development. It is easy to assume that politics is the domain of political scientists and politicians. However, Farmaki, Altinay, Botterill and Hilke (2015) state that, "[r]esearch has shown that, within western democracy, power is also exerted on government by strong industrial associations, lobbies, or private sector elites including external investors" (p. 181). This is true all across the world. Edgell and Swanson (2013) describe the key role that advocacy coalitions, groups with similar viewpoints, have on public policy issues. According to them, these groups can be made up of journalists, interest groups, policy analysts, researchers, legislators, and agency officials. Their ability to influence the formulation and implementation of policy cannot be ignored, and it is incumbent on all stakeholders, including the local community, to be proactive in the awareness of the actions and motivations of these groups. This is covered in more detail in Chapter 4.

SUSTAINABILITY TOOL: GLOBAL AND LOCAL STAKEHOLDER ANALYSIS

The German Federal Ministry for Economic Cooperation and Development (GFMECD) (2014) published a guide called *Tourism Planning in Development Cooperation: A Handbook* that offers a toolkit designed to promote the development of sustainable forms of tourism that are socially, culturally, ecologically, and ethically responsible, as well as economically successful. The handbook offers strategic, technical, and methodological recommendations to address major challenges and questions that arise in connection with tourism planning and the implementation of tourism projects in developing and emerging countries. The handbook "is aimed at international and local tourism consultants, those involved in development cooperation for tourism projects, national tourism organizations in the partner countries, and international and local tourism companies and associations" (p. 11).

Exploring stakeholder commitment

At a practical level, one of the key components to using tourism as a tool for sustainable development involves the establishment of strategic partnerships between communities and the tourism industry. Before a decision can be made as to whether tourism is an appropriate tool for development in a given region, a feasibility study should be conducted. The study should be designed to determine whether the community in the local area has a genuine interest in tourism development, and whether they can count on international investment that supports sustainability and community engagement goals. It is important to preserve the cultural identity of the local population if the area is to undergo tourism development, yet maintain a level of service that will serve the global tourists. There must be collaboration at the local, and at the global, level.

To ensure this, a preliminary stakeholder analysis, conducted through face-to-face interviews and information sharing with key actors from the area, must be performed. This analysis of the local population should focus specifically on whether the community has a genuine interest in tourism development, and whether the cultural identity and other important human rights of the local population would be appropriately protected if the area were to undergo changes related to tourism development. It is important to include members of poor and marginalized population groups, such as indigenous peoples, senior citizens, and youth. In evaluating the potential of tourism development for a given area, a number of questions should be considered. Table 3.2 lists some strategic criteria for review, as well as some key questions to assist in the assessment.

Once a community has expressed interest in tourism development, the next step is to engage the global tourism industry to determine their willingness to participate in community-based tourism initiatives, and for them to establish their needs and expectations related to their involvement. Working with MNCs can be challenging, as bottom-line profits will often be their first concern. However, they usually have a good idea of what tourists expect from their travel experience, such as service standards and transportation needs, as well as knowledge about marketing to attract visitation. Moreover, asking the global tourism industry about the role of

Table 3.2 Assessing the appropriateness of tourism development

Strategic assessment	Key questions
Tourism potential	Will the community and natural resources be attractive to tourism visitors?
Tourism products	Will the community have sufficient goods/services to provide a quality experience for tourists?
Tourism infrastructure	Does the community have sufficient infrastructure (roads, hotels) to support tourism?
Local community circumstances	Does the community have a genuine interest in tourism development?
	Will tourism development enhance people's livelihoods or provide other indirect benefits to the local community?
Competition	Will the community be able to provide tourism opportunities on its own or in collaboration with other destinations?
Factors that may impede tourism	Will the community be able to provide for the safety of tourists (crime, sanitation)? Will it be able to provide for the safety of local children and seniors?

the local community in developing the tourism product can support realistic expectations by community members in their level of involvement.

The last set of stakeholders that should be consulted include the governmental and nongovernment organizations (NGOs) that provide access to human, social, and financial capital. Research shows that what the global tourism industry expects and what local communities are capable of offering are not always well aligned (Salazar, 2012). Often local community members have never traveled or may lack knowledge specific to tourism development. Moreover, MNCs do not always have the time or resources to support knowledge exchange nor do they have access to grants that support local development. Therefore, channels of communication between the global and local stakeholders often occur through NGO and governmental channels. NGOs, in particular, are valuable stakeholders in tourism development through:

- Contributing to the development of policies and plans for the tourism industry;
- Assisting the government in developing a standard for responsible tourism;
- Assisting the government, private sector, and communities in implementing, monitoring, and evaluating responsible tourism;
- Attracting funding from donor agencies to develop specific community-based tourism projects;
- Assisting communities and community groups in organizing themselves, preparing themselves for tourism, and implementing tourism projects;
- Assisting the government in conducting tourism and environmental awareness programs among communities and the tourism industry at large;
- Liaising between the private sector and communities to generate more community involvement in the tourism sector and stronger private sector commitment to deliver education, training, and bridging courses to local communities.

Sustaining collaboration

Once stakeholder commitments are established, it is important to define the roles and responsibilities of each group in order to sustain these relationships over time. Specific tasks include creating an innovative tourism product, accessing investment capital, training a successful work force, marketing, and monitoring visitor feedback. The GFMECD (2014) recognizes a number of reasons why tourism development initiatives fail, including:

- Insufficient market research and market knowledge;
- Inadequate training;
- An overestimation of the market potential of a destination and its products;
- An overly narrow focus on local-scale issues without evidence of a market for these products;
- A lack of focus on target groups that lower the attractiveness and quality of many tourism products;
- Exclusion of the local population in decision-making on questions of protected area, wildlife, or cultural resource management;
- A failure to deliver direct or indirect economic benefits of tourism for the local population, or the fair distribution of these benefits;
- An imbalance between the interests of the tourism sector and those of the local population; and
- Clearly defined land use rights and ownership policies.

To avoid common pitfalls, all stakeholders should have some say in each task, although establishing areas of expertise can support best practice in decision-making. The challenge is to ensure that power dynamics do not hinder successful development and that inclusive decision-making is a priority.

In order to ensure involvement by all parties, the GFMECD (2014) advises that "it is important that the actors involved evaluate the achievement of their common objectives regularly and transparently by using appropriate indicators or a dedicated monitoring system in order to build stable and long-lasting business relationships" (p. 33). As new stakeholders enter the tourism industry, and others leave, maintaining these relationships and promoting the common goals of sustainable development must be an ongoing commitment for all involved. Forming these local partnerships empowers people residing in or around the tourism destination to have a voice in the decision-making, ensures a balance between local and global influences, and helps to ensure that the tourism development initiative is successful, from everyone's perspective.

Conclusion

Depending on the impact of globalization, people either feel strongly in support of it or may be opposed to it. While globalization can be credited with increased economies of scale and increased levels of investment, it can also be blamed for exacerbating the rich–poor divide, the loss of jobs, the ability of large MNCs to evade their tax obligations, and a loss of sense of place. These negative impacts have brought to the fore the move towards localism and neolocalism. In the context of sustainability or sustainable tourism development, it is clear that an interconnection between globalization and localism has become important. Businesses have to operate cognizant of these mixed feelings and strive to incorporate both perspectives into their vision, mission, and operational strategies.

CASE STUDY 3.1 CHILDREN AND TOURISM IN ZANZIBAR

SUSAN L. SLOCUM

The role of tourism in poverty reduction and child safety has been studied extensively by multinational organizations, such as United Nations International Children's Emergency Fund (UNICEF). In 2018, UNICEF published a Tourism Industry Impact Assessment called *Assessment of the Impact of Tourism on Communities and Children in Zanzibar*. The report asserts that over the 27-year period from 1990–2017, tourism grew from 42,000 international tourist arrivals in 1990, to more than 125,000 by 2005. By 2014 the number of tourists visiting Zanzibar had reached 311,000, and by 2017 it reached 433,000. The assessment on the impacts of tourism over these 27 years of growth concluded that benefits to the local community are largely unfelt. Most Zanzibari are still living on less than 300,000 TZS (US$130) per month, which is insufficient to provide basic necessities for a family, such as proper nutrition, schooling, and health services. Older adult Tanzanians see tourism as introducing inappropriate behaviors to the local community – particularly due to the way that tourists dress, and the locals also resent the introduction of alcohol as an element of everyday life. As such, many of the local adults choose not to engage in tourism services – and most of the workers in the tourism industry are from regions outside of the island of Zanzibar.

This is an example of the negative impacts of tourism on a local community that has not been an active participant in the planning of tourism development initiatives. If a formal assessment had been conducted in the 1980s involving the local community in Zanzibar – to invite them into the decision-making process around tourism initiatives – it likely would have been determined that the local community did not have a strong desire to participate in tourism development at that time. Further discussions aimed at articulating the potential economic benefits of tourism development, and the acceptable limits of tourism development for the community, could have changed the outcome, and minimized the perceived negative impacts by the locals.

In their investigation, UNICEF has uncovered extensive impacts to children and youth. While the report claims that these are "mainly indirect" (p. 8), in that it is the poor working conditions and salaries of their parents that affect their quality of life, there are a number of direct negative influences brought by tourism on the children of Zanzibar. Globalization has increased access to illegal drugs, primarily distributed through bars and nightclubs in the beach tourist areas. The rise in *beach boys*, those who "engage with individual tourists on and around the beach to provide any service or product the tourist might want" (p. 45), has provided a distribution network that moves drugs from tourism communities into resident villages. Alcohol consumption by youth is also on the rise. While begging on the beaches was not found to be common, tourist 'donations' are problematic in that children are more likely to engage with visitors rather than attending school, in hopes of receiving money. This has the potential to encourage aid dependence, an unsustainable reliance on donations over employment.

Image 3.4 Children in Zanzibar, Tanzania
Source: Seth Doyle on Unsplash

Other potential negative impacts are not as prevalent in Zanzibar as in other tourism destinations. The report found only sporadic instances of sexual abuse, although one could argue any sexual exploitation is too much. Moreover, while child labor was not found in the formal tourism sector, informal jobs (unregulated jobs with no fixed employer and no formal protections) were numerous. The Zanzibar Office of Chief Government Statistician (2016) reported that somewhere between 5 and 9% of Zanzibari children work in the informal economy, primarily in agriculture and fishing, two industries supported by the tourism sector.

UNICEF has offered a number of potential solutions to the problems incurred by tourism development. These include implementing education programs for children that focus on how they can protect themselves from everyday risks in relation to tourism. However, as long as tourism provides informal financial incentives, the probability that children in need of this training will attend is low. Another potential solution is to train tourism providers to recognize and act on illegal activities involving children. Evidence suggests that private industry has made poor progress in self-regulating activities. Moreover, tourists that engage in these types of activities (drug use and child sex) already know they are breaking the law and continue to do so.

The most efficient solution is to ensure that the citizens of Zanzibar earn adequate wages through tourism. In turn, this can ensure that families have enough money to pay school fees and support their children. Finding incentives to stay in school as a means to combat child exploitation and to allow children to gain the skills needed to be productive members of society is also an important resolution. By providing the tools these children need to grow up healthy and educated, the tourism sector is contributing to a quality workforce into the future.

Reflective questions

1. Considering the rapid increase in tourism on Zanzibar, and the perceived negative impact by locals, what might be done to change the situation for the better?
2. Considering that Islam is the predominant religion of residents of Zanzibar, what do you think the perception of locals might be of a large tourist presence, their behavior, and their activities?
3. In what ways might tourism on Zanzibar be used to positively impact childhood poverty reduction on the island?

References

United Nations International Children's Emergency Fund (2018). *Assessment of the Impact of Tourism on Communities and Children in Zanzibar*. Retrieved from www.unicef.org/tanzania/reports/assessment-impact-tourism-communities-and-children-zanzibar.

Zanzibar Office of Chief Government Statistician (2016). Zanzibar integrated labour force survey, 2014.

CASE STUDY 3.2 BUDAPEST HOUSE OF TERROR

MELANIE SMITH

The House of Terror was opened in 2002 under the direction of the first Orbán government in Budapest, Hungary. As a tourism product, it instantly became an extremely popular museum, but it has also been one of the most criticized because of its interpretation of history. The House of Terror is located in Andrássy Avenue, the former headquarters of the fascist Hungarian Arrow Cross party. Later, the building became the headquarters of the Communist secret police. The House of Terror, therefore, reflects both of Hungary's totalitarian regimes, but the focus is more on the Communist period, whose duration was much longer. On the cornice of the extended metal roof of the building, the word TERROR is carved, which casts a shadow onto the pavement below. Although this extension was controversial because the building is located within a World Heritage Site, the visual effect on passers-by, as well as visitors to the museum, is quite dramatic.

The House of Terror was established by Orbán's conservative government to warn of the dangers of socialism. Turai (2009) compares the House of Terror with Budapest's statue park that contains the unwanted and unwelcome statues of the Communist period, which were removed from public spaces. Whereas the statue park is located on the outskirts of the city in an empty, industrial area, the House of Terror is located in the heart of the city on the main avenue within a World Heritage Site. The reason for this, he argues, is because "this museum is used for direct political purposes: it does not encourage memory work but rather embodies memory politics, instrumentally controlling memory for political ends" (Turai, 2009, p. 102). Turai (2009) notes that a museum visit has a very different effect on locals compared to tourists who merely come to gaze upon Communism. Many locals, on the other hand, want to forget about their troubled past and get on with their lives (hence the removal of statues from public spaces in the city). However, the museum tries to provoke and retain outrage in locals and tourists alike. Right wing supporters of the House of Terror see it as a symbol of national identity (Sik, 2015), as well as standing as a warning to those who would foolishly vote for the socialists again.

On the other hand, the museum takes a 'victimization' approach to Hungary's role in the Holocaust and other acts of terror, denying the country's responsibility (unlike Budapest's Holocaust Museum which was established in 2004 and tries to counterbalance the denial) (Sik, 2015). One review by Dougherty (2017) questions the use of the words "twin occupations" for the Nazi and Communist regimes within which Hungarians were also perpetrators and "enthusiastic collaborators" (n.p.). However, this responsibility-denying narrative continued in 2014 when a monument was established in Liberty Square (Szabadság Tér) in Budapest, which depicted Hungary's victimhood at the hands of the Nazis. This monument was as controversial as the House of Terror when it first opened, with protests continuing even today.

The House of Terror was also originally criticized for taking a 'theme-park approach' to history, but it could hardly be described as a fun day out! Rátz (2006) notes the extreme bias in the interpretation of everyday life within the socialist system, where residents received free education, healthcare, and affordable social housing. Instead, sinister

Image 3.5 House of Terror, Budapest, Hungary

Source: Melanie Smith

music (composed by a well-known musician) provides the soundtrack for the numerous exhibits that refer to the hardships of everyday life with their tales of informants and secret police, as well as interrogations, torture, and executions. Emphasis is placed on the deportations of Jews and Gypsies from Hungary by the Nazis, as well as a Gulag room depicting the banishment of thousands of Hungarians to Siberian labor camps. In the atrium, there is a wall of victims. Visitors are transported to a prison in the basement via an excruciatingly slow lift where they are forced to listen to the description of an execution.

The museum is rather stylized and dramatic, as it was designed by a film and theatre stage designer, and it makes use of spectacular media audio-visual technology to create its narratives. Visual intensity was the main aim of the designer. Indeed, it even received a commendation from the European Museum Forum in 2004 for its innovative approach to interpretation and visitor experience creation. On the other hand, random objects and artefacts are strewn around the museum and it is not always clear whether they are authentic, what they represent, or how they are connected. Often, the objects are not labelled. Rátz (2006) argued that the House of Terror should not even be called a museum because of the lack of collections management. Apor (2014, p. 331) suggests that "the purpose of the display is to produce general experiences and impressions and to discourage systematic interpretation of the events evoked". Apor (2014) argues that the museum does not help the visitor to understand the historical context in which events took place, and the interpretation does not reveal its complexity. Nor does the museum allow the visitors to understand the fates of the victims and develop compassion for them. Visitors emerge visually and sensorially stimulated but also disorientated and puzzled by what they have just seen. The souvenir shop offers a lighter touch, where Communist-themed souvenirs like refrigerator magnets and mugs can be purchased or visitors can sip a cappuccino in a Soviet style factory canteen. However, as stated by Dougherty (2017), "You look, and you cannot turn away. You cannot leave this House unchanged."

Reflective questions

1. While there were many atrocities during Nazi and Soviet control, do you feel this museum provides an accurate narrative in relation to Hungary's history? Why or why not? What changes could you make to improve on the narrative?

2. How do you think the local community feels about the sense of place communicated through the House of Terror? Do you feel tourist attractions should be used as political tools? Why or why not?

3. How is this museum's anti-socialist message different from other educational materials, such as conservation messages, that only present one side of a story? Should all educational material be balanced? Why or why not?

References

Apor, P. (2014). An epistemology of the spectacle? Arcane knowledge, memory and evidence in the Budapest House of Terror, *Rethinking History*, 18(3), 328–344.

Dougherty, M.B. (2017) Through the House of Terror, *National Review*, December 18, www.nationalreview.com/magazine/2017/12/18/through-house-terror/.

Rátz, T. (2006). Interpretation in the House of Terror, Budapest, in M. K. Smith and M. Robinson (Eds) *Cultural Tourism in a Changing World: Politics, Participation and (Re)presentation*, Channel View Publications, p. 244.

Sik. D. (2015). Memory transmission and political socialization in post-socialist Hungary, *The Sociological Review*, 63(S2), 53–71.

Turai, H. (2009). Past unmastered: hot and cold memory in Hungary, *Third Text*, 23(1), 97–106.

STUDY QUESTIONS

1. Look at the selection of restaurants in your hometown. How is globalization represented in the food choices available? How is localism represented in the food choices available?

2. Write a paragraph that describes the sense of place for your hometown. How could you use that to develop tourism? How could you use it to market your town as a destination?

3. List the positive attributes of multinational corporations that operate in the tourism industry. List the positive attributes of locally-owned businesses. Which provides more positive impacts to a community?

4. Find the minutes of a local policy meeting online. What elements of politics are inherent in the meeting minutes? What political groups were recognized as contributing to the meeting?

5. What strategies could you use as a manager to ensure all stakeholders are involved in the decision-making process? What challenges do you think you would face? How best can you overcome these challenges?

DEFINITIONS

Brexit vote   the vote by the United Kingdom to leave the European Union

Colonization   action of appropriating a place or domain for one's own use and establishing control over the indigenous people of an area

Comparative advantage   when countries specialize in the production and export of the goods which they can produce relatively less expensively than other countries because they possess specific resources, such as labor, capital, and land

Economies of scale   a proportionate saving in costs gained by an increased level of production

Free trade   policies that seeks to eliminate government-imposed barriers to trade

Global village   the world characterized by instant communication, the proliferation of transnational corporations, and the pervasive influence of mass media and popular cultural trends from the West

Globalization   the process by which people and goods move easily across borders

Globalization from below   globalization that is regulated by the local governance institutions

Glocalization   the practice of conducting business according to both local and global considerations

Imperialism   a policy of extending a country's power and influence through diplomacy or military force

Isolationism   a national policy of avoiding political or economic entanglements with other countries

Localism   the belief in and expression of the unique character of localities

Microbrewery   a brewery that produces a volume of less than 15,000 barrels of beer, and sells at least 70% of it to locations off-site

Multinational company   a company whose base of operation is found in a specific country, but who has subsidiaries in two or more other countries

Neolocalism (new localism)   a renewed interest in preserving and promoting the identity of a community and restoring aspects that make it culturally unique

Protectionism   the policy of protecting domestic industries against foreign competition through the use of quotas, subsidies, and tariffs

Sense of place   what sets a place (destination) apart from others, and invokes strong feelings in people who live there or travel there as tourists

Silk Road   a network of routes linking regions of Asia and Europe in the ancient world that was established by the Han Dynasty of China

Value added tax   sales tax collected in pieces along the production chain

Chapter **4**

Governance of sustainable tourism

Overview

This chapter provides a deeper look into key components of the governance and policy for sustainable tourism. It identifies some important documents and organizations that guide tourism development and addresses the key role of politics in the decision-making process. This chapter also considers the obstacles facing tourism stakeholder groups, including public sector agencies, private businesses, and local communities, when it comes to participation in the act of governance. The cost–benefit analysis tool is introduced, along with calculating net present value.

CHAPTER OBJECTIVES

At the completion of the chapter, students will be able to:

- Define governance;
- Describe the important tourism governance agreement documents;
- Explain the characteristics of important governance organizations and their role in sustainable tourism;
- Articulate the role of politics and lobbying in tourism development;
- Understand the challenges facing different stakeholder groups in governance participation; and
- Develop a cost–benefit analysis including the calculation of net present value.

Introduction

The overarching goal of sustainable tourism is ensuring that development is done in such a way that the benefits of tourism, such as income opportunities, revenue generation, and job creation, outweigh the costs of tourism, such as commodification of the destination's culture, revenue leakage, and the degradation of the destination's natural environment (Weaver & Lawton, 2014). In other words, sustainable tourism must maximize benefits and minimize costs. A key avenue towards achieving this goal is through good governance.

According to Hall (2011), governance may be described as simply the act of governing. This modest definition does not highlight the complexities inherent in the concept of governance, especially when it comes to sustainable tourism development. A more nuanced description of governance in the tourism context is that **governance** is about the ways in which society allocates, controls, and coordinates resources (Bramwell & Lane, 2011). "Governance can be equated with strategic leadership, in that governance is the process of determining future development paths, and establishing policies that determine appropriate behaviors" (Slocum & Curtis, 2017, p. 178). **Policies** are definitive courses of action that determine present and future decisions. For governments, these rules are either laws or regulations that all businesses and members of the community must obey. **Laws** are the system of rules designed to regulate behavior, whereas **regulations** determine how the laws are enforced and the penalties for violation. In business, governance is setting the policies that employees must follow and the penalties for noncompliance.

The goal of effective governance, and the resulting policy documents, related to tourism is to ensure certain standards are maintained in order to establish the optimal level of development, control growth, maintain communities and environments, and ensure a quality tourism product or experience (Slocum & Curtis, 2017). Governance occurs at many different levels and through many different organizations. At the destination level, local governments generally take the lead in governance by developing policy instruments, such as providing information and education, granting financial incentives for businesses, putting in place regulations that encourage sustainable tourism business practices, or dissuading practices that would be detrimental to the triple bottom line of tourist destinations (Bramwell & Alletorp, 2001). These local policies generally align with national policy objectives, but not always.

Good governance requires involving members of a community in decision-making. It also requires that individuals who hold positions of power are held to the same legal and ethical standards as the general public. Governing officials must follow and abide by the same rules and laws as the general public, and be similarly held accountable for their actions. Good governing agencies maintain a practice of transparency, operating openly so that the general public remains aware of policies under consideration, even if they are not directly involved in creating policy.

Governance also occurs within organizations. Tourism businesses have documents, policies, and guidelines that govern their operations and culture, including policies on the adoption of sustainability. Sustainability policy may be drafted as a response to the growing call for corporate social responsibility. It can support access to the green traveler market, achieve higher levels of profitability, and encourage economies of scale (Weaver & Lawton, 2014). **Benchmarking** is the process of comparing a business's process and performance metrics to industry best practices from other companies or destinations and can be used to track performance over time and inform effective policy directives at the business level. While business policies related to sustainability are on the rise, the percentage of businesses that actually employ sustainable practices is small, thus the need for government leadership, even though a mix of government intervention and business self-regulation is more typical (Bramwell & Alletorp, 2001). Therefore, local governmental policies often influence business policies related to sustainable tourism.

From an industry perspective, the instruments of governance for sustainable tourism exist at international levels, regional levels, national levels, and local levels, and vary by destination or country. This chapter will focus on governmental regulatory policies, whereas business governance is covered throughout the rest of the book.

Image 4.1 Butchart Gardens, Brentwood Bay, British Columbia, Canada

Source: Susan L. Slocum

Instruments for the governance of sustainable tourism

International governing organizations for sustainable tourism

When it comes to sustainable tourism development at the international level, one preeminent organization is the United Nations World Tourism Organization (UNWTO). The UNWTO is an agency tasked with the responsibility of promoting tourism that is responsible, sustainable, and universally accessible (UNWTO, 2019a). The UNWTO began in 1947 as the International Union of Official Travel Organisations (IUOTO) (UNWTO, 2019b) and following its creation, successive meetings of the United Nations General Assembly saw to the expansion of its activities. The IUOTO established modern definitions of the terms 'visitor' and 'tourist' and supported the simplification of international travel formalities, a general resolution on tourism development, including technical cooperation, freedom of movement, and the absence of discrimination. In 1970, at the IUOTO General Assembly in Mexico City, the statutes for the UNWTO were adopted, and in 1975, after the 1st General Secretariat was established in Madrid, the agreement was signed to make the newly-formed UNWTO an executing agency of the United Nations (UNWTO, 2019b).

Another important organization of relevance to the tourism industry is the World Travel and Tourism Council (WTTC). The WTTC is an organization that was formed in 1990 and is made up of 170 executives from companies that represent all aspects of the tourism industry around the globe (WTTC, 2019). The goal of the WTTC is to make governments and decision-makers aware of travel and tourism's contributions to individual economies, as well as the global economy more broadly. The main areas of focus of the WTTC are security and travel facilitation, crisis preparedness, management and recovery, and sustainable growth. The WTTC has conducted research in about 185 countries over the past 25 years and has released a number of publications. One such document, the *Governing National Tourism Policy* (WTTC, 2015), asserts that for tourism to thrive, governments need to:

- Provide adequate infrastructure;
- Provide incentives for private sector investment;
- Create easy access, including good transport connectivity and visa facilitation;
- Enact intelligent taxation policies; and
- Implement policies to encourage growth in demand.

International governing documents for sustainable tourism

An important component of governance has to do with the international documents and the underlying multilateral agreements reached by stakeholders of tourism development at various gatherings, such as summits and general assemblies. A **multilateral agreement** is a treaty between three or more sovereign states that stipulates established guidelines that are mutually agreed upon by participating nations. While many of these agreements occur at the international level, they have implications for the governance of sustainable tourism at the national, regional, and/or local level, as they often inform local policies and regulations. What follows is a series of international governing documents related to sustainable tourism, presented in chronological order.

One of the earlier documents governing sustainable tourism is the "Tourism bill of rights and tourist code" (UNWTO, 1985). This agreement was adopted by the 6th General Assembly of the United Nations in Sofia, Bulgaria in 1985. Areas covered in the agreement include: steps towards the harmonious growth of tourism; integration of tourism within overarching development goals; the rights and responsibilities of local residents; and the rights and responsibilities of tourists.

Another international governing document is the "Global code of ethics for tourism", adopted by the General Assembly of the UNWTO in 1999 and acknowledged by the United Nations General Assembly in 2001. It is not a legally binding document, but it provides an avenue through the World Committee on Tourism Ethics (WCTE) by which to raise issues of ethical practices related to tourism development (UNWTO, 1999). The "Global code of ethics for tourism" comprises ten stipulations that cover the breadth of sustainable tourism development:

Article 1: Tourism's contribution to mutual understanding and respect between peoples and societies;

Article 2: Tourism as a vehicle for individual and collective fulfilment;

Article 3: Tourism as a factor of sustainable development;

Article 4: Tourism as a user of the cultural heritage of mankind and contributor to its enhancement;

Article 5: Tourism as a beneficial activity for host countries and communities;

Article 6: Obligations of stakeholders in tourism development;

Article 7: Rights to tourism;

Article 8: Liberty of tourist movements;

Article 9: Rights of the workers and entrepreneurs in the tourism industry; and

Article 10: Implementation of the principles of the "Global code of ethics for tourism"

Image 4.2 Berlin Wall, Germany

Source: Susan L. Slocum

As the international community continues to adopt sustainable practices, the United Nations has published an agenda to support increased sustainability in many industries. Starting with the Millennium Development Goals in 2000, and the recently revised Sustainable Development Goals in 2015, pressure for governments and international funding agencies (such as the World Bank and International Monetary Fund) to put the needs of communities and the environment first in future development initiatives is on the rise. The important (yet lofty) aims of these goals are listed in Table 4.1 (United Nations, 2015).

Table 4.1 Millennium and Sustainable Development Goals

Millennium Development Goals (2000) To be achieved by 2015	Sustainable Development Goals (2016) To be achieved by 2030
Eradicate extreme poverty and hunger	End poverty in all its forms everywhere
Achieve universal primary education	End hunger, achieve food security and improved nutrition and promote sustainable agriculture
Promote gender equality and empower women	Ensure healthy lives and promote well-being for all at all ages
Reduce child mortality	Ensure inclusive and equitable quality education and promote lifelong learning opportunities for all
Improve maternal health	Achieve gender equality and empower all women and girls
Combat HIV/AIDS, malaria, and other diseases	Ensure availability and sustainable management of water and sanitation for all
Ensure environmental sustainability	Ensure access to affordable, reliable, sustainable, and modern energy for all
Develop a global partnership for development	Promote sustained, inclusive, and sustainable economic growth, full and productive employment, and decent work for all
	Build resilient infrastructure, promote inclusive and sustainable industrialization and foster innovation
	Reduce income inequality within and among countries
	Make cities and human settlements inclusive, safe, resilient and sustainable
	Ensure sustainable consumption and production patterns
	Take urgent action to combat climate change and its impacts by regulating emissions and promoting developments in renewable energy
	Conserve and sustainably use the oceans, seas, and marine resources for sustainable development

Table 4.1 continued

Millennium Development Goals (2000) To be achieved by 2015	Sustainable Development Goals (2016) To be achieved by 2030
	Protect, restore, and promote sustainable use of terrestrial ecosystems, sustainably manage forests, combat desertification, halt and reverse land degradation, and halt biodiversity loss
	Promote peaceful and inclusive societies for sustainable development, provide access to justice for all and build effective, accountable, and inclusive institutions at all levels
	Strengthen the means of implementation and revitalize the global partnership for sustainable development

Source: United Nations (2015)

The first multilateral agreement established on sustainable tourism was the "World charter of sustainable tourism +20" (World Charter +20), which was adopted at the 2015 World Summit on Sustainable Tourism in Vitoria-Gasteiz, Basque Country, Spain (World Summit on Sustainable Tourism, 2015). The original charter introduced the concept of sustainable tourism, and twenty years later, the "World charter of sustainable tourism +20" seeks to continue the success of sustainable tourism development by:

- Bringing benefits to local communities;
- Supporting green growth and economies;
- Fostering innovation;
- Safeguarding cultural and natural heritage; and
- Protecting the environment.

A key component of the "World charter of sustainable tourism +20" are the mandates it places on different stakeholders, as described in Table 4.2.

Other tourism organizations important to the governance of sustainable tourism through their publications include those listed in Table 4.3. These organizations, and the documents they publish, are important resources for businesses in the tourism industry. While it appears that in many instances the agreements upon which the documents are based are not legally binding, they are still useful because they provide benchmarks that set the standards for sustainable practices. Businesses should familiarize themselves with these documents, and with the operations of these organizations, to ensure that internal business governance strategies are compatible with international tourism policies. As businesses engage in the global tourism industry, it is helpful to understand the best practices inherent in these agreements. This will help managers meet the ever-increasing requirements for sustainable practices sought by the emerging and sophisticated sustainable traveler market (discussed in Chapter 5).

Table 4.2 World charter of sustainable tourism +20

Stakeholders	Mandates
Tourism industry	• Contribute to the creation, development, and implementation of sustainable tourist products and services that encourage respectful use of natural, cultural, and intangible heritage and that transmit the destination values and identity through the tourism experience; • Integrate sustainability into policies, management practices, and operations; • Encourage investors and increase investments designed to achieve a greener sector; • Engage in local destination management and support the economic, social, and cultural well-being of local communities; • Build capacity for sustainable tourism and apply this capacity to internal operations as well as for influencing the decisions of other stakeholders; • Enhance the capacity of tourism businesses and organizations to improve environmental performance and sustainability through innovation; • Reduce waste generation in tourist activities through prevention, reduction, recycling, and reuse; • Improve water quality by reducing consumption, avoiding pollution, eliminating dumping, and minimizing the release of hazardous chemicals and materials; • Implement eco-efficient technologies and processes in all areas of the tourism industry, including buildings and infrastructure, resource management, and transport; • Promote maximum penetration of renewable energy in the destinations with the aim of reducing the carbon footprint in the tourism sector; • Use and promote appropriate instruments for measuring, enlarging and marketing the sustainable tourism offer, such as certification programs; and • Inform consumers about their options to travel responsibly.
Governments and international organizations	• Integrate sustainability in national and international tourism policies, strategic plans, and operations for meeting national sustainable development objectives, and the UN Sustainable Development Goals (SDGs); • Encourage national, regional, and international financial and development institutions to provide adequate support to programs and projects related to sustainable tourism; • Strengthen legislative and policy frameworks for sustainable tourism, including those for environmental protection and the conservation of natural and cultural heritage, and human and labor rights;

Table 4.2 continued

Stakeholders	Mandates
	• Plan through a participatory process, including partnerships at local, national, regional, and international levels to ensure that all stakeholders, especially local communities, indigenous peoples, women, and disadvantageous groups, can influence how tourism is developed and managed;
	• Facilitate cooperation and collaboration between government agencies responsible for tourism, finance, trade, and those responsible for culture, conservation, and the environment;
	• Improve the contribution of sustainable tourism to poverty eradication, including through securing wider benefits to communities as a viable and sustainable economic development option;
	• Enhance international support for implementing effective and targeted capacity-building to support national plans to implement all sustainable tourism development goals including monitoring and reporting of tourism impacts;
	• Provide finance and incentives for tourism-related public infrastructures that mitigate social and environmental impacts;
	• Integrate cultural and natural heritage conservation into tourism planning, giving special attention to intangible heritage, due to its extreme vulnerability to disruption and deterioration;
	• Ensure that tourism stakeholders are encouraged and supported to develop peace and conflict resolution through the promotion of intercultural dialogue that promotes equality and freedom of expression; and
	• Use the UNESCO designated sites as learning places to foster the harmonious integration of tourism with cultural and natural heritage.
Consumers	• Encourage use of local sustainable products and services that generate local employment and benefits;
	• Evaluate the environmental, sociocultural footprint and economic implications of their decisions; and
	• Choose more sustainable products and services over less sustainable options.
Local communities and destinations	• Ensure that destination tourism governance includes all stakeholders, especially at the local level and that the responsibilities of each stakeholder are clearly defined;
	• Empower local communities and indigenous peoples and facilitate their involvement in planning and developing tourism;
	• Adopt necessary measures to maximize the economic benefits for the host community and create stronger linkages with the local economy and other economic activities in the destinations;
	• Preserve destination values by outlining processes to monitor change, evaluate threats, risks, and opportunities, and permit public and private leaders to sustain the destination's sense of place;

Stakeholders	Mandates
	• Promote low carbon development strategies in tourism-related infrastructure, operations and services, including buildings and infrastructures, resource management, and transport;
	• Promote a tourism that is inclusive and accessible for all, and enhance accessibility to all parts of the tourism value chain, including the physical environment, transport systems, information and communications channels, and a complete range of hospitality sector facilities, services, and tourist activities;
	• Consider the carrying capacity of destinations, not only in the case of natural sites but also urban areas, especially when the quality of life of the residents is compromised;
	• Ensure that seniors' knowledge of traditions and cultural and natural heritage is retained and effectively transmitted to young people as a means of inter-generational integration of sustainability; and
	• Support education in tourism and sustainable development at all levels in each destination.
Researchers, developers, and trainers	• Build new alliances between science and tourism since scientific research and its contribution to knowledge is critical for the sector's ability to address the new challenges of sustainable tourism;
	• Create new set-ups for closer relations between research hubs and the tourism industry;
	• Facilitate green technological innovation in tourism by establishing bridges between developers and tourism stakeholders;
	• Identify effective ways to accelerate the diffusion of eco-innovation in the sector, including via effective communications, recognition, training, and incentives where appropriate;
	• Develop and offer learning and training about sustainable tourism management and integrate this into existing learning and training; and
	• Encourage professionals and policy makers to use indicators when making decisions to evaluate the sustainability performance of tourism activities.
Nongovernmental organizations and networks	• Revitalize the global and regional partnerships for sustainable tourism and strengthen their implementation;
	• Promote and facilitate sharing and exchange of know-how and best practices to inspire the replication of success stories on sustainable tourism;
	• Promote guidelines for the behavior of tourists at destinations using social networks, media and other communication channels, such as information from service providers and operators along the whole tourism value chain; and
	• Make information available to all destinations about green products available to their businesses.

Source: World Summit on Sustainable Tourism (2015)

Table 4.3 Tourism governance organizations and publications

Name of organization	Example(s) of sustainability-focused publications	Scale of governance
Asia-Pacific Economic Cooperation (APEC)	Voluntourism best practices: promoting inclusive community-based sustainable tourism initiatives (Final Report)	Regional
Caribbean Tourism Organization (CTO)	Caribbean sustainable tourism policy framework Guide to internet resources on sustainable tourism	Regional
European Network for Sustainable Tourism Development (ECOTRANS)	Sustainability in tourism: a guide through the label jungle The VISIT initiative: tourism eco-labelling in Europe – moving the market towards sustainability	Regional
International Council on Monuments and Sites (ICOMOS)	Conservation of intangible heritage	International
Organization for Economic Cooperation and Development	Database to measure the economic impacts of tourism to inform policy-making	International
United Nations Conference on Trade and Development (UNCTAD)	Is the concept of sustainable tourism sustainable? Developing the sustainable tourism benchmarking tool	International
United Nations Environment Program (UNEP)	Advancing sustainable tourism: a regional sustainable tourism situation analysis	International

Politics and the governance of sustainable tourism

Yasarata, Altinay, Burns, and Okumus (2010) describe the politics of tourism development as "a struggle for power and underpinned by the question *cui bono* (who benefits)" (p. 345). **Politics** are the processes of making decisions that apply to members of a group and can include negotiation with other political subjects, making laws, and exercising force, including warfare against adversaries. In other words, politics is about how things get done rather than what needs to be done. There is no question that in order to work towards the development of sustainable tourism, solid comprehensive policies must play a key role. However, it is important to note that these policies must incorporate three key elements if they are to do so effectively: they must be based on rigorous research; they must involve the powerful and active participation of all stakeholders; and they must acknowledge and harness the reality of politics. While it might be easy to overlook the key role that politics plays in the formulation and implementation of these policies, there are enough examples to indicate politics' important role.

For example, Edgell and Swanson (2013) outline the history of the formulation of the National Tourism Policy in the early 1980s in the USA. They describe the three phases of research that were conducted, the deliberations that occurred in congress, and how with a stroke of a pen, President Jimmy Carter vetoed the bill that would have set the policy into law in 1980. It was not until President Ronald Reagan was elected in 1981 that the veto was reversed and the USA had its first tourism policy. It was a change in politics that eventually allowed the policy to take effect.

A number of tourism businesses understand the importance of playing an active role in communicating with politicians at all levels of government to ensure that the needs and interests of the industry are taken into consideration when policies are being developed. This is called **lobbying** and is defined as the process of trying to persuade elected officials to take particular actions or change certain laws. The WTTC is actively engaged in lobbying, both at the international level and with national and regional governments. Other organizations involved in lobbying include the Cruise Lines International Association, the International Association of Tour Managers (United Kingdom), and the Tourism and Transport Forum Australia. Figure 4.1 shows the top travel lobbying expenditures in the US, as an example of the breadth of lobbying, including both industry associations and multinational corporations (Center for Responsible Politics, 2018).

As an example, the Virginia Restaurant, Lodging, and Travel Association (VRLTA) is an advocacy organization that lobbies on behalf of the tourism industry in the Commonwealth of Virginia, in the USA. It is made up of members of a variety of statewide industry associations including restaurant, hotel, travel, and hospitality, as well as industry suppliers. The VRLTA understands the importance of monitoring and influencing political mechanisms at both the state and federal levels. They are interested in local issues, such as the policies surrounding the disbursement of the hotel room tax, Alcoholic Beverage Control (ABC) laws, the public school-year calendar (to support an extended summer travel season), proposed food tax increases, and competition from informal sector operators. As a lobbying organization, the VRLTA was instrumental in influencing the Commonwealth to pass laws allowing local communities to regulate **Airbnb** (a website that allows travelers to find low-budget informal accommodation in the prospective destination). Local jurisdictions can now impose taxes on rental income and can use zoning laws to determine where rentals are located (VRLTA, 2019). This policy

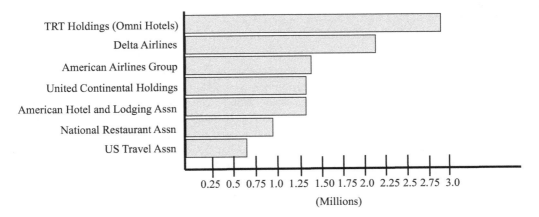

Figure 4.1 USA tourism lobbying efforts (2017–2018)

Source: Center for Responsible Politics (2018)

supports the local tourism sector by creating an even playing field for Airbnb properties and traditional hotel properties.

Industry organizations are dependent on membership support. Membership of these organizations is a smart business decision, because businesses can reap many benefits, such as a louder advocacy voice, the goodwill of other members, increased influence through collaborative lobbying partnerships, and economies of scale when resources are pooled together to further the political interests of members. Without involvement from tourism business managers, policymakers may overlook the needs of this sector and establish policies that directly counter sustainability efforts.

Edgell and Swanson (2013) suggest there are two ways in which policy decision-makers (and implementers or politicians) can be motivated to support policies that promote sustainable tourism development, namely "money and information" (p. 191). Money, in this case, plays a role in the political donations given to candidates deemed to be supportive of the industry's interests, as well as procuring the human and other resources needed to lobby the decision-makers. While politicians are elected to represent their voters, the divergent views of the voter base results in favoring the more vocal or influential groups, in many cases the lobbyists. Information includes using the knowledge-based resources inherent in scientific inquiry. However, due to the influence of the more vocal voices, such as lobbyists, the decisions made are not always logical or in the best interest of the majority. In certain instances, when comparing multiple projects, Edgell and Swanson (2013) suggest that the technique of logrolling or vote trading may come into play. **Logrolling** is the practice whereby two or more legislators agree to trade votes for bills that they each would like to see passed.

Even though local communities form an important group of stakeholders, there are barriers to their participation in the political process, particularly in developing countries. Tosun (2000) recognizes apathy in the local community, a lack of expertise, and a lack of financial resources as primary reasons that local communities do not engage in the political process. Businesses, if they seek to be true partners in development, should look for opportunities to provide the support and resources needed to facilitate active and powerful participation of the local community in order to ensure the sustainability of tourism development in these regions. It is imperative that any destination or country that is serious about the development of sustainable tourism take the necessary steps to encourage and facilitate the participation of all stakeholders in its governance. The tool in Chapter 6 covers this in more detail.

It is important to note the difference that exists between the role of politics in developed countries and those in developing countries. Yasarata et al. (2010) explain that in developed countries, policy-making and implementation of sustainable tourism development is more or less decentralized, but the case is different for developing countries where in many cases, "the ruling elites of developing countries [rationalize] their decisions under cover of bureaucratic traditions" (pp. 345–346). As a result, policy-making and its implementation are hindered by the struggles between government entities, political parties, the private sector, and the local communities. Understanding these different contexts becomes key, particularly for multinational corporations (MNCs), since that knowledge can guide their engagement in different destinations in which they operate and contribute to the development of tourism that achieves the triple bottom line of sustainability. Local businesses also need to understand how policy decisions are made, and the local politics that can impact the success of sustainability activities of the tourism industry.

Image 4.3 Markets in Marrakech, Morocco

Source: Susan L. Slocum

Think globally, act locally

Some of the best ways to hold your governing authorities to account, and to ensure that sustainable tourism policies are implemented at the local level, are to get involved and participate in these types of conversations. Not everyone is interested in running for elected office, however most local government agencies and elected officials hold town hall meetings that are open to the public. If you are unable to attend, often you can find the minutes of the meetings are available to read later. If you have a particular area of interest or expertise, say – clean water or affordable housing – you can look to join a specific board or commission. These groups are often comprised of people who care deeply about the issues at hand and are willing to use their voice for positive change. Boards and commissions are often tasked with reviewing and providing input into policies prior to their enactment. So, the best ways to ensure that good governance exists in your local community, and that the policies being formulated support the values of sustainable tourism development, are to stay informed, and get involved.

SUSTAINABILITY TOOL: COST–BENEFIT ANALYSIS

A tool relevant to information sharing and the influencing of decision-makers is the cost–benefit analysis. According to Prest and Turvey (1965), the **cost–benefit analysis** is a technique used to determine the desirability of proposed projects by quantifying and calculating their relevant costs and benefits. This tool allows planners to enumerate different policy options in order for policymakers to choose the best alternatives when making development decisions. Businesses can also use this tool to support fiscally responsible investments and to determine the best sustainability initiatives, or corporate policies, that reap the highest rewards for all stakeholders. If the calculated benefits turn out to be greater than the calculated costs, the project would typically be

Table 4.4 Applicable benefits and costs to tourism

Example	Description	Benefit	Cost
Support infrastructure	Hotels Visitor center Transportation needs	Salaries and wages of employees Use by local residents	Construction costs Parking costs Traffic congestion
Support services	Fire, emergency medical, police, water, sewer, solid waste	Tax relief to local residents	Tax expenditures on social services Expansion of infrastructure
Tourist expenditures	Payments for services	Sales tax payments Increases in property taxes from new construction	Calculate leakages
Cultural impacts	Cultural conflict or cultural cohesion	Development of arts, crafts, and other cultural product markets Increases in social capital	Increased crime Marginalized minority groups
Marketing	Destination and business marketing	Increases in visitor numbers	Marketing expenditures
Environmental impacts	Preservation or destruction to natural ecosystems	Construction/preservation of parks or natural areas	Increases in traffic, pollution, and waste

Source: Adapted from Goldman, Nakazawa, and Taylor (1994)

deemed an efficient project. When faced with choosing between options, a logical decision would be to choose the project that quantifiably indicates more benefits than costs.

A cost–benefit analysis is evaluating two or more proposed policy initiatives, tourism development projects, or business strategies in monetary terms. As an example, adopting a policy that encourages tourism visitation would require a cost–benefit analysis between what is occurring without tourism and what would happen with tourism. Table 4.4 shows some examples of benefits and costs related to tourism development (Goldman, Nakazawa, & Taylor, 1994). It is important to note that cost–benefit analysis:

- Involves a specific geographic study area;
- Cannot double count benefits or costs;
- Involves a specific time period; and
- Must discount future benefits and costs using the net present value.

Net present value is a measure of discounted future cash inflows and outflow in present day monetary terms. Money in the present is worth more than the same amount in the future due to inflation and to earnings from investments that could be made with the money during the intervening time. The **discount rate** represents the rate of return that could be earned if the money was collected today and invested. The formula to calculate net present value is:

$$NPV = C^0 + \underline{C^1} + \underline{C^2} + \ldots + \underline{C^n}$$
$$(1+r) \quad (1+r)^2 \quad (1=r)^n$$

Where C^0 = the initial investment, $\underline{C^1}$ = cash flow, r = the discount rate, n = the number of years.

As an example, if an investment earns €1,000 each year, starting in year one, and the discount rate is 5%, then the net present value is:

$$NPV = 1,000 + \underline{1,000} + \underline{1,000} = 1,000 + 952.38 + 907.03 = €2,859.41$$

$$(1 + 0.05) \ (1 + 0.05)^2$$

Conducting a well-executed cost–benefit analysis requires the analyst to follow a logical sequence of steps:

1. **Ask relevant questions** – What policy or project is being evaluated? What alternatives are there? How is social well-being measured? What is the appropriate scale of development?
2. **Determine standing** – Whose costs and benefits are to count? What is the relevant time horizon over which costs and benefits are considered? How will peoples' preferences change over time? What is the level of uncertainty over time?
3. **Ascertain access to capital** – What are the budget constraints? Is there additional capital available? What aspects of a policy should take financial priority?
4. **Measure impacts** – What are the costs and benefits to the environment and society? How can benefits and costs be distributed equally across the community? What are the long-term consequences of environmental degradation?

Measuring the benefits of a policy can include anything from additional income to an increased quality of life, or a cleaner environment. Costs may consist of forgone opportunities, cash outlays, and externalities. All costs and benefits must be given a common unit of measurement, such as a dollar value, in order to be comparable. In sustainable tourism, quantifying social and environmental benefits and costs can be a complicated and difficult process. The cost of pollution can be measured in relation to the cleanup costs or the benefit of protected areas can be measured by the amount of revenue earned in admission fees. Job creation can be a good basis for measuring social benefits or an increase in petrol usage can be the basis to measure increased traffic congestion. A reduction in health care costs could be a benefit to increases in recreational opportunities developed through tourism.

Lastly, cost–benefit analysis can be used to determine the appropriate scale of development. For example, if a policy states that development must add zero pollution, then the only solution would be zero tourism. More people visiting a destination will always result in some additional pollution. However, zero tourism would also have zero social benefit, meaning there would be no new tourism jobs, for example. Therefore, finding the appropriate level of tourism requires an understanding of the appropriate increases in pollution (cost) and the appropriate level of new jobs (benefit).

Unfortunately, politics can play a negative role in cost–benefit analysis, especially if powerful or influential people gain from certain policies or have better access to the benefits. Often it is the marginalized members of society that incur many of the costs. Ensuring that the cost–benefit analysis is done by neutral parties and that politics do not influence the results are important considerations if the analysis is to be reliable and accurate. Moreover, providing transparency throughout the process and using appropriate measurement tools can increase support for policies and ensure that the predictions are as accurate as possible.

Table 4.5 has an example of a cost–benefit analysis of tourism development over two years. The town of Happy Valley is considering a policy to increase tourism. There are two options, to build a conference center or to build a theme park. All Year 2 benefits and costs are discounted at 5%. The interest rate on a loan or bond is also 5% over 20 years. One key difference between a conference

Table 4.5 Cost–benefit analysis for Happy Valley

	Conference center				Theme park			
	Year 1		Year 2		Year 1		Year 2	
	Benefit	Cost	Benefit	Cost	Benefit	Cost	Benefit	Cost
Facility								
Purchase of land		$50,000				$50,000		
Construction costs		$1,000,000				$1,500,000		
Maintenance				$10,000				$15,000
Supplies and equipment		$50,000		$47,619		$30,000		$28,571
Investment costs								
Interest payed on a loan or bond		$2,500		$2,381		$3,750		$3,571
Income								
Sales tax revenue	$50,000		$47,619		$73,000		$69,524	
Property tax revenue	$16,000		$15,238		$16,000		$15,238	
Hotel tax revenue	$25,000		$23,810		$6,000		$5,714	
Social costs and benefits								
New employment income	$500,000		$476,190		$300,000		$285,714	
Small business income	$250,000		$238,095		$300,000		$285,714	
Traffic congestion		$75,000		$71,429		$120,000		$114,286
Emergency services		$25,000		$23,810		$45,000		$42,857
Environmental costs and benefits								
Additional landfill		$15,000		$14,286		$20,000		$19,048
Additional energy		$17,000		$16,190		$27,000		$25,714
Additional water and sewage		$12,000		$11,429		$15,000		$14,286
Pollution costs (air and water)		$8,000		$7,619		$12,000		$11,429
Total benefit/cost	$841,000	$1,254,500	$800,952	$204,762	$695,000	$1,822,750	$661,905	$274,762
Yearly profit/loss	−$413,500		$596,190		−$1,127,750		$387,143	
Total profit/loss over 2 years	$182,690				−$740,607			

center and a theme park is that conference attendees usually stay for multiple days, whereas many theme park visitors may come only for the day. While this is a simplistic example, the results show that building the conference center is a better decision than building a theme park.

Conclusion

Governance plays an important role in the development of sustainable tourism. It contributes to the achievement of the overarching goal of maximizing benefits and minimizing costs. Governance is at its best when it fosters the participation of key stakeholders, such as public agencies, private businesses, and local communities. Even though the agreements described in the chapter are typically non-binding legally, they provide information and guidance on best practices that are important when it comes to the practice of governance at international, regional, national, and local levels. Similarly, membership of the organizations is key because it provides opportunities for businesses and other stakeholders to benefit from the knowledge and expertise of fellow members. Moreover, these organizations can offer strength in numbers that become advantageous when businesses have to advocate for their interests as they contribute to sustainable tourism development. Businesses must understand the dynamics of politics, which play a significant role in the formulation, adoption, and implementation of policies.

CASE STUDY 4.1 THE POLITICS OF AIRBNB

SUSAN L. SLOCUM

Introduction

In 2007, Brian Chesky and Joe Gebbia, the founders of Airbnb, had just moved to San Francisco and were struggling to find jobs. They noticed that most hotels were fully booked, so they bought a few air mattresses and set them up in their living room as a way to earn extra money. They charged $80 per night. The following year, Nathan Blecharczyk, Chesky's former roommate, joined the team and three entrepreneurs started a website, Airbedandbreakfast.com, which officially launched on August 11, 2008. To help pay for the site, they created special breakfast cereals 'Obama O's' and 'Cap'n McCains', named after the 2008 US presidential candidates. Their success drew attention and they received moderate funding to grow the company. By March 2009, the site had 10,000 users and 2,500 listings (Rao, 2009).

Airbnb is an online platform through which ordinary people rent out spaces as accommodation for tourists that can range from a living room futon to an entire island, but generally comprise a private room or an entire apartment or house. While a majority of the properties listed on Airbnb are primary residences, corporate owned housing is on the rise (O'Neill & Ouyang, 2016). As part of the sharing economy, Airbnb has eliminated the need for small accommodation businesses to maintain complicated website technology and has allowed small businesses an opportunity to compete with major hotel chains (Guttentag, 2015). Moreover, Airbnb handles much of the marketing for small businesses.

Airbnb also offers a number of advantages for visitors. Compared to major hotel chains, Airbnb presents relatively less expensive lodgings and offers opportunities for guests to have a more authentic experience by living among local residents. Visitors may get access to local information by property owners and interact with neighbors or see non-touristy areas of a destination. Some destinations market Airbnb as a place for "living like the locals do" (Guttentag, 2015, p. 1197).

Image 4.4 Airbnb property, Amsterdam, the Netherlands

Source: Emily O'Connor

Increasing regulations

Technology corporations specialize in innovation and can often outpace legislation or policy-making, and frequently encounter legal issues. In most municipalities, short-term housing rentals are illegal (where properties are zoned as residential only), and a lack of regulation has allowed rental properties to avoid paying certain taxes, including income tax on earnings and accommodation taxes that hotels must pay (Coté, 2012). Many communities, as well as the hospitality industry, have filed law suits against Airbnb. For example, the city of New York filed a law suit in 2016 claiming violations of local housing laws and a court recently dismissed a law suit in Paris claiming Airbnb authorized illegal listings. Moreover, the US senate has investigated Airbnb's influence in rising housing prices in some cities, and a law suit filed in 2019 alleges that real estate brokers are using Airbnb to sublet newly built, unsold apartments.

Airbnb has recently purchased a number of other companies, including luxury vacation rentals (such as Luxury Retreats International in Canada, and HotelTonight, a website for booking last minute hotel rooms), which highlights a changing direction towards commercial, mainstream, hotel-like services. In response, cities around the world have begun regulating the short-term rental markets, including Los Angeles, Amsterdam, Mallorca, Barcelona, Paris, and Tokyo.

Social consciousness and sustainability

Airbnb has used their global influence by entering the political arena, using its market power and reach to address numerous social issues. These include fighting for marginalized communities and supporting sustainability issues. As many of these programs are in their infancy, time will tell if Airbnb will become a leader in corporate social consciousness. Some of their initiatives include:

- In 2017, the company acquired Accomable, a start-up focused on travel accessibility, which allows travelers with disabilities to better find lodging that can accommodate their needs.

- In 2018, Airbnb refused to list properties in the West Bank of Jerusalem in protest over the Israeli occupation of Palestinian lands. However, in 2019, after settling numerous lawsuits, the company rescinded the ban, quoting:

  > We will continue to allow listings throughout all of the West Bank, but Airbnb will take no profits from this activity in the region. Any profits generated for Airbnb by any Airbnb host activity in the entire West Bank will be donated to non-profit organizations dedicated to humanitarian aid that serve people in different parts of the world.
  >
  > (Airbnb, 2019)

- Airbnb has established a sustainability council with the goal to support greener accommodation choices and to reduce mass tourism by driving travel to lesser-known places, which spreads tourism benefits and reduces overcrowding. The Board includes well-known sustainable tourism advocates, including Taleb Rifai, the former Secretary General of the United Nations World Tourism Organization (UNWTO), Rosette Rugama, MD of Songa Africa and Amakoro Lodge, and former Director General of Rwanda Tourism.

- Airbnb has set up a disasters response page to help displaced families of natural disasters find a place to stay. They have waived their standard fees, allowing hosts to use the online platform for free.

Reflective questions

1. Do you feel individuals operating in the sharing economy should be subject to the same laws and taxes as corporations? What impacts do you foresee in regulating these economies?

2. How would you suggest hotels compete with Airbnb? Do they sell the same product? Why or why not?

3. Should multinational corporations use their power to influence international politics? Why or why not?

References

Airbnb (April 9, 2019). Update on listings in disputed regions. Retrieved from https://press.airbnb.com/update-listings-disputed-regions/.

Coté, J. (April 4, 2012). Airbnb, other sites owe city hotel tax, SF says. *San Francisco Chronicle*. Retrieved from www.sfgate.com/bayarea/article/Airbnb-other-sites-owe-city-hotel-tax-SF-says-3457290.php.

Guttentag, D. (2015). Airbnb: disruptive innovation and the rise of an informal tourism accommodation sector. *Current issues in Tourism*, 18(12), 1192–1217.

O'Neill, J.W. & Ouyang, Y. (2016). From air mattresses to unregulated business: an analysis of the other side of Airbnb. Pennsylvania, PA: Penn State School of Hospitality Management.

Rao, L. (March 4, 2009). Combinator's Airbed and Breakfast casts a wider net for housing rentals as AirBnB. *TechCrunch*.

CASE STUDY 4.2 WILDLIFE TOURISM AUSTRALIA AND THE GOVERNMENT

RONDA J. GREEN

In primary school, I thought there would always be vast tracts of jungle in Africa and the Amazon to explore, and polar bears safely roaming the Arctic. I also imagined that anyone in the government would have a wide understanding of the topics they spoke about. By the end of high school, I was somewhat disillusioned, so I took a job managing a holiday farm where I could not only teach horse-riding and care for domestic animals, but also learn about the wildlife. I soon found I needed a degree for my conservation efforts to be taken more seriously by a wider audience, so I entered university and emerged with a PhD in zoology.

Realizing politicians and other government representatives do not always understand, accept, or care about the results of academic research, I became interested in the use of tourism to advance an understanding and appreciation of wildlife and their needs. I wanted to demonstrate to governments and developers an economic reason for preserving wilderness and protecting species. I started my own wildlife tourism company in 1996, and a couple of years later was invited to join the Wildlife Sector of the Cooperative Research Centre (CRC) for Sustainable Tourism, where I authored and co-authored several reports. In 2001, The CRC held Australia's first-ever national wildlife tourism conference, resulting in the formation of a new national body, Wildlife Tourism Australia (WTA), of which I became vice-chair. Our motto is "promoting the sustainable development of a diverse wildlife tourism industry that supports conservation". Currently, I am the chair, with a team of nine other committee members, including academics and tour guides.

So, what has WTA done since then, and how have we involved government? We developed a website with a great deal of information to be used by the tourism industry, conservation managers, academic researchers, and by government at all levels. We also host many events and represent WTA at many events run by others. We have sent numerous reports to governments in support of wildlife conservation.

We opposed the development of a marina in a stretch of woodland-fringed coastline, offered suggestions for protecting the dwindling populations of koalas in Brisbane, contributed to Western Australia's Department of Conservation and Land Management's

Image 4.5 Tassie Devils at the Devils at Cradle Sanctuary, Tasmania, Australia

Source: Ronda Green

review of human–wildlife interactions, commented on the federal government's Green Paper (a medium- to long-term strategy for tourism), contributed suggestions to the federal government's "Whale and dolphin watching guideline review", and sent numerous other submissions and letters to federal, state, and local governments. We have lobbied governments against the culling of fruit bats without permits, the potential impacts of proposed major tourism development in Far Northern Queensland, and various other topics. We have been asked, more than once, by Ecotourism Australia to offer our perspectives on the wildlife aspects of their eco-certification program, and accordingly suggested criteria for minimal-impact marine and terrestrial (including nocturnal) wildlife viewing.

We started a wildlife research network designed to put tour operators involved in research or conservation monitoring in touch with each other, and also with academic researchers and traveling citizen scientists. We were given space in the Australian Citizen Science Association pavilion at the World Science Festival in Brisbane in 2019, where we presented information and activities.

We have had our frustrations with some politicians. A former state premier promoted his state as the 'ecotourism capital' but also talked extensively about opening up national parks to horse-riding, motor bikes, off-road vehicles, accommodations, and even hunting. Unexpectedly sitting next to him at a conference, I said such activities could be appropriate in some situations, but we first needed research into where the vulnerable species and vulnerable habitats are, and we needed to plan appropriately. His response was that no research was needed, they just needed to start doing it and then see if it was sustainable. Well, if kangaroos or emus later disappeared we might notice, but a rare frog or other small creature could easily disappear before anyone knew it was there. I approached his tourism minister to ask if myself and our secretary, representing WTA, could speak with her about sustainability in tourism, but – although I stressed we supported tourism, including appropriate tourism in national parks – she insisted she was only allowed to discuss tourism policy and we would have to see the environment minister about sustainability. We were not sorry they lost the next election.

On the other hand, we have had considerable support. One local government gave us two separate grants to run a series of workshops and a two-day wildlife exposition, and various politicians are happy to speak at or open our events and talk to us about important issues. Our workshops and conferences are often attended by politicians or government employees, including local councilors, national parks personnel, the national threatened species commissioner, and others.

Our reach to governments has expanded somewhat to other countries. As chair of WTA, I have been invited to lecture to a number of tourism groups from Indonesia and one from Sri Lanka, all including representatives from government as well as the tourism industry. The United Nations World Tourism Organization (UNWTO) commissioned me to present a talk and chair a panel discussion in Fiji on the impacts of climate change on wildlife tourism at the UNWTO Regional Seminar on Climate Change, Biodiversity, and Sustainable Tourism Development in 2018. Government representatives of many countries were amongst the participants.

Professor Noel Scott (University of Sunshine Coast) and I are currently working with the UNWTO on a survey of responsible wildlife tourism throughout Asia and the Pacific, focusing on positive examples (regarding animal welfare, conservation, visitor education, and supporting local communities), including some government partnerships, that can be emulated by others starting businesses or seeking to improve existing ones.

We hope that our efforts over the years have had at least a few positive impacts, modified some negative moves, and sparked ideas for the kinds of habitat management and wildlife tourism that will support excellent visitor education and biodiversity conservation. We certainly intend to keep trying.

Reflective questions

1. Go to www.wildlifetourism.org.au and find a specific project that interests you. How has Wildlife Tourism Australia included government in this project? How has government involvement enhanced the success of this program?

2. Do you think being a non-profit organization (and an NGO) has helped or hindered WTA? Why?

3. As an owner of a tourism business, why might you join WTA? How would it benefit your business and your customers?

STUDY QUESTIONS

1. Find a local business policy or government policy online. Determine which aspects constitute laws and which aspects constitute regulations.

2. Find a tourism policy online. How well does it address the Sustainable Development Goals? Explain what elements are missing and why you feel they are missing.

3. Write a policy that governs the appropriate behaviors of tourists. Explain how you would enforce this policy.

4. You are tasked with meeting your local politician to encourage her support for sustainable tourism. Write a one-page draft argument in favor of sustainable tourism. Be sure to provide quantifiable support for your arguments.

5. Are projects that are shown to be more quantifiably beneficial than costly always supported by policymakers? Provide support for your answer.

DEFINITIONS

Airbnb   a website that allows travelers to find low-budget informal accommodation in the prospective destination

Benchmarking   the process of comparing a business's process and performance metrics to industry best practices from other companies; it can be used to track performance over time

Cost–benefit analysis   a technique used to determine the desirability of proposed projects by quantifying and calculating their relevant costs and benefits

Discount rate   the rate of return used to discount future cash flows

Governance   the ways in which society allocates, controls, and coordinates resources

Laws   the system of rules designed to regulate behavior

Lobbying   the process of trying to persuade elected officials to take particular actions or change certain laws

Logrolling   the practice whereby two or more legislators agree to trade votes for bills that they each would like to see passed

Multilateral agreement   a treaty between three or more sovereign states that stipulates established guidelines that participating nations mutually agreed upon

Net present value   a measure of discounted future cash inflows and outflow in present day monetary terms

Policy   a definitive course of action that determines present and future decisions

Politics   the process of making decisions that apply to members of a group

Regulation   a policy tool that governs how laws are enforced and the penalties for violation

Chapter 5

The sustainable traveler

Overview

This chapter explains customer segmentations and the importance of finding the appropriate consumer for sustainable tourism products and services. A number of consumer movements related to sustainability are explained, and the demographic, geographic, psychographic, and behavioral characteristics of tourists within these consumer groups are described. While people may not be limited to a single, specific group, there are common traits that signify potential customers within these segments. Additionally, this chapter highlights common themes that sustainable travelers look for in their vacation experiences, and a tool to measure customer satisfaction is provided.

CHAPTER OBJECTIVES

At the completion of the chapter, students will be able to:

- Define market segmentation and the four ways to group similar tourists;
- Differentiate current consumer movements related to sustainability;
- Describe sustainable consumption;
- List the similarities and differences between tourists that fall into current consumer movements;
- Recognize common themes that sustainable travelers look for in their vacation experiences; and
- Conduct customer service feedback research.

Introduction

Although sustainable development and sustainable business practices are essential in making tourism a more ethical industry, businesses must satisfy their customers' needs in order to be successful. Therefore, businesses and destinations must understand consumer demand for sustainability and find appropriate target markets that are motivated by low-impact tourism options. This is done through **market segmentation**, or the activity of dividing a broad consumer base, normally consisting of existing and potential customers, into sub-groups of consumers (known as segments) grounded in some type of shared characteristics. Segmentation assumes that consumers with similar profiles will exhibit similar purchasing patterns, motivations, interests, and lifestyles, and that these characteristics will translate into similar travel preferences (Reid & Bojanic, 2009). There are four ways in which segments are determined: demographic, geographic, psychographic and behavioral traits of tourists. **Demographic segmentation** divides consumers into categories such as age, income, race, family size, and socioeconomic status. **Geographic segmentation** divides markets according to physical location criteria. In practice, markets can be segmented as broadly as continents and as narrowly as neighborhoods, but in tourism it is generally done by country of origin or destination. For example, British tourists may seek a distinctly different type of holiday than Chinese tourists, while visitors to Peru may seek a dissimilar type of vacation than tourists to the Maldives. **Psychographic segmentation** separates consumers by lifestyle choices, including their activities, interests, and opinions. In tourism, people interested in outdoor activities will generally be interested in different services than those interested in cultural activities. For example, there is evidence that people who enjoy biking trips are also interested in local craft beers (Slocum & Curtis, 2016). **Behavioral segmentation** splits consumers into groups according to their observed behaviors, such as how often they travel, if they use a loyalty program, or whether they are price conscious. Finding avenues to determine the right customers for a tourism product can be a tricky business.

Understanding the attitudes of tourists towards sustainability, and dividing them into groups, falls within the behavioral segmentation process. The result is **tourism typologies**, or the classification of tourists based on psychological characteristics. The goal is to provide insight into the minds of consumers and determine how they prioritize sustainability in relation to their overall travel experience. The United Kingdom's Department for Environment, Food and Rural Affairs (DEFRA) (2008) conducted a study to better understand the attitudes that drive sustainable behavior in British consumers. They found the following six consumer segments:

- **Greens:** Driven by the belief that protecting the environment is critical; try to conserve whenever they can;
- **Conscious with a conscience:** Aspire to be green; primarily concerned with waste; lack awareness of other behaviors associated with broader environmental issues such as climate change;
- **Currently constrained:** Seek to be green but feel they cannot afford to purchase organic products; pragmatic realists;
- **Basic contributors:** Skeptical about the need for behavioral change; desire to conform to social norms; lack awareness of social and environmental issues;
- **Long-term resistance:** Have serious life priorities that take precedence before a behavioral change is a consideration; their everyday behaviors often have a low impact on the environment, but for other reasons than conservation; and
- **Disinterested:** View greenies as an eccentric minority; exhibit no interest in changing their behavior; may be aware of climate change but have not internalized it to the extent that it enters their decision-making process.

As consumers become more aware of environmental and social challenges, there are increasing opportunities for businesses and destinations to target and keep long-term customers committed to sustainability. The goal is to move consumers up within the tourism typologies, towards greater awareness of the importance of making sustainable choices.

Image 5.1 Shopping in Mostar, Bosnia

Source: Susan L. Slocum

Sustainable consumption

Sustainable consumption is included in the Sustainable Development Goals (#12) (United Nations, 2015), which highlights the importance of consumption patterns in the journey towards sustainable development (see Table 4.1, Chapter 4). **Sustainable consumption** is defined as the use of goods and related products which bring a better quality of life to those who produce them, while minimizing the use of natural resources, toxic materials, waste, and pollutants over the product life cycle, so as to not jeopardize the needs of future generations (Seyfang, 2008). It involves engaging consumers through awareness-raising and education on sustainable consumption and lifestyles, providing consumers with adequate information through standards and labels, and engaging in sustainable public procurement, among other informational practices. Figure 5.1 shows the attributes of sustainable consumption.

Figure 5.1 Attributes of sustainable consumption

Gössling and Hall (2013) divide sustainable consumption into four typologies:

- Business as usual;
- Green growth;
- Traditional sustainable; and
- Steady state.

The *business as usual* approach defines sustainability in purely economic terms and consumption is based on a wide variety of mass commodities. This approach is encouraged by mass tourism, resulting in significant standardization of the tourism product. A *green growth* approach seeks to balance the economic, environmental, and social aspects of sustainability and encourages greater efficiency through the promotion of green economic growth via technological and market solutions (i.e. waste reduction). The *traditional sustainable* approach is based on traditional methods of production that promote opportunities for the poor. The emphasis is placed on small-scale business development that is culturally and ecologically sensitive to local needs. The *steady state* approach is characterized by the balancing of natural capital/natural systems within consumption practices. It incorporates appropriate production levels with environmental conservation, where sufficiency is more important than efficiency. The traditional sustainable approach and the steady state approach provide opportunities for tourists to sample local products, learn about environmentally friendly behaviors, and support local people. Both approaches also draw tourists interested in activities related to ecotourism or cultural tourism.

Sustainable consumption has been used to determine a variety of attributes that segment sustainable tourists by psychographics. For example, positive attitudes toward sustainable tourism and higher levels of kinship with other groups are common attributes in sustainable tourists (Passafaro et al., 2015), and sustainable tourists are more inclined to accept diversity in society and the environment. They also possess high levels of agreeableness in their personality, making them more open to new experiences. López-Sánchez and Pulido-Fernández (2016) use sustainable intelligence (sustainable knowledge, behaviors, attitudes, values, and willingness to pay for a more sustainable products or services) as a means to segment tourists. They recognize that some visitors, labeled 'pro-sustainable tourists', are willing to pay more for sustainable options, whereas the group labeled 'reflective tourists' hold sustainability values but will not pay more for sustainable options. The reasons for a lack of willingness to pay by reflective tourists include: "government should be the entity that assumes these investments; companies generate the greatest impacts, so they must assume these costs; and a sustainable destination does not have to be more expensive but should be more efficient at using its resources" (p. 66).

Demographic variables are less conclusive when predicting sustainability behaviors. Ample evidence suggests that sustainable tourists may have higher education and income levels (Boley & Nickerson, 2013), although there is no evidence that these traits predict sustainable consumption patterns. Mair and Laing (2013) found that younger age groups (ages 18–39) have stronger environmentally friendly behaviors, whereas López-Sánchez and Pulido-Fernández (2016) found the youngest segment to have the least sustainable behaviors. Scholars recognize that younger generations (specifically millennials and Generation Z) have been raised within the sustainable development paradigm and possess more knowledge about sustainability than older generations. However, the perception that sustainability is more expensive, and recognizing that younger generations are not yet in high income brackets, may mean they are less inclined to pay more for sustainable consumption options. There is also evidence that national culture plays a role in pro-sustainability attitudes, with collective societies (such as Japan and Korea) more inclined to adopt sustainability than individualistic societies (such as the United States and Australia) (Kang & Moscardo, 2006).

There are numerous studies that support the idea that women have a stronger commitment to sustainable consumption and behave more sustainably. Women have traditionally been viewed as consumers and men as producers, and women are estimated to make upwards of 80% of consumption decisions in the household (Khan & Trivedi, 2015). Although gender studies specifically related to tourism are rare, women generally report deeper environmental attitudes and behaviors than men (Skanavis & Sakellari, 2008). Han and Hyun (2018) found that elements of eco-concern and anticipated travel impacts were less prominent in the sustainable behaviors of female college students, but sense of obligation was more influential in females. Therefore, providing specific rules related to behaviors may have more influence for female travelers, whereas listing specific negative impacts destinations face may encourage more sustainable behaviors in males.

There have been a few attempts to determine the relationship between at-home sustainable consumption and travel-related behaviors. Barr, Shaw, Coles, and Prillwitz (2010) acknowledge that, "whilst individuals are relatively comfortable with participating in a range of environmental behaviours in and around the home, the transference of these practices to tourism contexts can be problematic" (p. 474). Mehmetoglu (2010) shows that education, environmental concern, and personal norms positively predicted in-home sustainable consumption practices. When traveling, environmental concern and personal norms were associated with

Image 5.2 Giant's Causeway, Northern Ireland

Source: Susan L. Slocum

higher levels of sustainable consumption, but also household income and gender played a role in sustainability values. Older people were more likely to possess a conservative political orientation, which led to more hedonistic values that resulted in less sustainable consumption values. With tourists who ranked as high- or medium-sustainable consumption at home, Slocum and Curtis (2016) show a decline in sustainable behaviors when they travel. Those with low sustainability practices at home showed no change while traveling. Moreover, they conclude that people traveling to experience culture were less likely than nature-based tourists to engage in sustainable behaviors when traveling. McDonald, Oates, Thyne, Alevizou, and McMorland (2009) determine that while sustainability criteria are often considered during the initial travel-planning phase, they are commonly compromised in favor of price, convenience, and journey time.

Within sustainable consumption, there are many different social movements gaining recognition. Three of these movements, LOHAS, localism, and slow travel, are discussed in more detail.

The LOHAS movement

The LOHAS movement began in late 1999 in response to mass consumerism. It gained international recognition after the *New York Times* published a full-page article in 2003. **LOHAS** stands for Lifestyles of Health and Sustainability and is a social and economic movement that reflects a marketplace of goods and services that are immersed in meaningful personal values related to oneself, as well as the social and natural world. Emerich (2011) equates LOHAS with a spiritual movement because it includes references to personal transcendence (moving beyond mainstream consumption), eschatology (death of the planet), and salvation of the earth and its populations related to karma (cause and effect).

While accurate statistics that represent the size of the LOHAS market are not readily available, Szakály, Popp, Kontor, Kovács, Pető, and Jasák (2017) estimate that the market for LOHAS labeled brands, products, and services is approximately $355 billion dollars in the United States and $546 billion worldwide. They also approximate that 29% of the Japanese population, 33% of New Zealanders, and 25% of Australians participate in LOHAS purchases, and that the trend is growing in China. LOHAS consumers regularly purchase organic food, support corporate social responsibility, including fair trade, ethical behavior, and social justice, as well as search for individualistic values (e.g., wellness, enjoyment, comfort, and personal improvement). Ray and Anderson (2000) recognize five distinct values inherent in LOHAS consumers as shown in Table 5.1.

Segmenting consumers as LOHAS is problematic for a number of reasons. LOHAS consumers appear in all demographic levels, including age and income brackets. They mainly live in urban areas and are equally distributed between genders (Urh, 2015). They tend to favor technological developments, but still enjoy nature, living a self-centered life, while thinking about others

Table 5.1 LOHAS values and purchasing behaviors

Values	Purchases
Authenticity	Sustainable tourism, ecotourism, or alternative tourism
	Locally grown food
Health consciousness	Organic food
	Organic and natural personal care products
	Complementary, alternative, and preventive medicine (naturopathy, Chinese medicine, etc.)
	Exercise
Ethical values	Fair treatment of animals
	Socially responsible investments
	Fair trade products
Individualism	Literature in the mind/body/soul
	Spirituality
Environmental consciousness	Hybrid and electric cars, biking, and walking
	Green and sustainable building
	Energy efficient electronics/appliances
	Natural household products (paper goods and cleaning products)

Source: Adapted from Ray and Anderson (2000)

and being realistically open to spiritual ideas. Moreover, "most LOHAS consumers have no idea they've been labeled as such and don't have much sense of belonging to any particular group outside of the mainstream" (Heim, 2011, p. 172). Therefore, since LOHAS consumers do not know they are LOHAS consumers, they are proving to be a difficult market to target.

It is not surprising that the LOHAS market is attracted to voluntourism (volunteer tourism), food tourism, and ecotourism. **Voluntourism** is tourism that provides opportunities for people to do volunteer work while also participating in tourism, as a way to 'do good' or 'give back' to a community, and provides avenues for civic-minded travelers to give back to the areas they visit (Hudson & Hudson, 2017). On top of volunteering, LOHAS consumers are more inclined to donate to environmental or community causes while traveling. **Food tourism**, defined as the desire to experience a particular type of food or the produce of a specific region while traveling, is a natural fit for the LOHAS segment as eating healthy food is an important value. Food tourism is considered a form of cultural tourism where the visitor is exposed to traditional recipes and locally grown food items. Not only does it fulfill the need for individualism, it can provide an authentic experience that supports local businesses. Ecotourism is also a form of tourism with potential to reach LOHAS consumers. **Ecotourism** is described as a low impact nature-based tourism which contributes to the maintenance of species and habitats either directly through a contribution to conservation and/or indirectly by providing revenue to the local community sufficient for local people to value, and therefore protect, their wildlife heritage area as a source of income (Goodwin, 1995). Although ecotourism is discussed in more detail in Chapter 7, since LOHAS consumers are interested in physical and emotional well-being, they are a good target market for ecotourism experiences (Urh, 2015).

Localism

The rise of **localism**, as a response to globalization, was discussed in Chapter 3 and is defined as the belief in and expression of the unique character of localities (Ashworth & Tunbridge, 2004). Flack (1997) recognized this phenomenon as an attempt to reassert the "distinctively local" (p. 38) in response to a landscape increasingly devoid of the unique. While the primary line of research in localism involves food and agricultural tourism, including wine/craft beer tourism and farm stays, other local tourism products are comprised of homestays, bed and breakfasts, heritage sites, local crafts, and local artisan products, such as dancing, literature, and music. Tourist activities may include cooking schools, pick-your-own farm products, watching craft beer being produced, learning about medicinal herbs, and connecting production processes (or artisan works) with the history and landscape of the area. Neolocalism has been shown to encourage local sourcing, influence environmentally friendly production methods and consumption patterns, and encourage support for local causes and charities (Graefe, Mowen, & Graefe, 2018). Moreover, local production boosts the use of local products within the production process, increasing the indirect and induced impacts of tourism. It is not surprising that local products and experiences have become a cornerstone of tourism marketing (Holtkamp, Shelton, Daly, Hiner, & Hagelman, 2016).

Localism is embedded in a search for the nostalgic past, rooted in agriculture, rurality, and family and social ties long lost through urbanization (Schnell, 2011). It involves not just exploring a locality, but becoming immersed in it. However, it has also become a social movement where consumers seek out local experiences as a means to connect with local residents. It involves a sense of place and exploring local, unique, quality, and personal aspects of a community. A **locavore** is defined as a person whose diet consists only or principally of locally grown or produced food (Slocum & Curtis, 2017) and **locavists** are people that travel closer to home and invest locally in their communities with money, time, and personal energy (Hollenhorst, Houge-Mackenzie, & Ostergren, 2014).

There is very little data on the demographics or psychographics of locavists, however there are some behavioral statistics and trends that have been uncovered for locavores. For example, locavores commonly use direct markets to purchase fresh produce, such as farmers' markets, consumer supported agriculture (CSA) programs, farm stands, farm shops, or will shop at grocery stores or specialty shops that source locally. Locavores are also willing to pay price premiums for locally grown food. Slocum and Curtis (2017) claim that "locavores seek fresh, high-quality, safe food and are motivated by a desire to support local farmers, preserve agricultural open space, and develop personal relationships with local farmers or at least know where their food was produced" (p. 106).

While most studies have emphasized locavores, there is evidence that these traits can be applied to localists on a broader scale. Therefore, we can presume that they are interested in having close relationships with the people they visit and the artisans or communities that provide unique experiences. Locavists are generally tourists that remain closer to home when they travel. They may be **excursionists** (also known as day-trippers), who are travelers that live in close proximity to a destination and only stay for a short visit. Excursionists have been shown to provide a larger economic impact through local purchases of groceries and gasoline, but will not usually book hotel accommodations. They are also more inclined to be repeat visitors (Oh & Schuett, 2010). Schnell (2011) shows that local travelers possess five core values:

- A desire for educational vacations;
- A need for relaxation;
- An appreciation for nature;
- Connections with the exotic; and
- A feeling of environmental virtue.

Slow tourism

The rise of slow tourism is a result of the increased pace of life many people feel at home. Fullagar, Markwell, and Wilson (2012) write, "being slow was once an entirely derogatory term that signified one's inability to keep up . . . slowness today is invoked as a credible metaphor for stepping off the treadmill, seeking work–life balance, or refusing the dominant logic of speed" (p. 1). Originating from the slow food movement, as a direct response to increased fast food, **slow tourism** is a philosophy of travelling that allows visitors to experience the authentic side of a destination by spending an extended

Image 5.3 Local artisan, Tokyo, Japan

Source: Susan L. Slocum

amount of time in one area. Rather than traveling with a proverbial bucket-list of activities or sites, slow tourists will stay in one location, usually removed from mainstream attractions, and immerse themselves with locals. They may engage in canoe-trips, walking pilgrimages, leisure cycling trips, or place-based experiences (Fullagar et al., 2012).

The rise of **slow cities**, a development strategy that promotes the slow philosophy to urban living by providing a political agenda of local distinctiveness within urban development, has brought about a changed mindset for many urban residents. Robinson, Heitmann, and Dieke (2011, p. 117) write,

> *The preservation of local and cultural heritage, as well as the integration of local production and support of independent businesses, are some of the key issues for a slow city. Impacts of commercialization and the development of mass tourism are discouraged and avoided, and there is extensive concern for the local environment by promoting sustainable travel modes.*

In turn, these residents seek slow experiences when traveling, such as the enjoyment of discovery, learning, and sharing, which results in more memorable experiences.

Heitmann, Robinson, and Povey (2011) claim that slow tourists generally avoid long-haul travel and prefer to stay close to home, as they prefer to use local transportation and avoid negative environmental impacts, such as greenhouse gas emissions. However, they also recognize that backpack tourists, on long-haul tours, may also qualify as slow tourists. For example, slow tourists may travel to the African continent and live in a small beach town for a month. Slow tourists look for long-term accommodations, and may be frequent users of Airbnb or homestays/farmstays. They are less likely to plan out the details of their trip in advance and prefer to seek local input into excursions and attractions. They avoid stress, noise, and urban pollution, so are generally found in rural or remote areas. Moreover, since slow tourists are interested in cultural immersion, they may be inclined to learn the local language and seek out new learning experiences, such as local cooking. They may also be voluntourists who want to give back to the community they are visiting. Since slow tourists stay for an extended period of time in destinations, they will have a lifestyle that allows for lengthy vacations, such as retirees, gap year students, or self-employed individuals. Moreover, because they value spontaneity, they will often use local websites or tourist information centers to look for last minutes activities or even destinations.

SUSTAINABILITY TOOL: MEASURING CUSTOMER SATISFACTION

At all levels within an organization, it is important to measure decisions in relation to customer satisfaction in order to ensure the sustainability of the company. Several marketing studies show that sustainability and corporate social responsibility can significantly influence the customer's experience through customer–company identification, consumer–product attitudes, customer engagement in responsible behavior, and customer donation practices (Luo & Bhattacharya, 2006). **Customer satisfaction** in tourism is generated by providing an experience (tourism product) that meets or exceeds the customer's expectations and is a key driver in the long-term success and profitability of a business (Gruca & Rego, 2005). It is important to remember that a company's image appeals to a multifaceted group of customers, as well as a variety of different stakeholders, and that this image can enhance the perceived value received through the consumption of the tourism product. One must also recognize that each visitor may possess very different motivations for traveling to a destination, for example, travel could be for pleasure, business, to visit friends and relatives, or to attend a conference. Each of these customers will have different needs and expect different outcomes related to their travel experience. It is also important to realize that a tourist's satisfaction involves the entire travel experience, much of which may be beyond any one company's control. A bad meal or a delayed flight could have a profound impact on a tourist's view of their entire trip. Therefore, working with industry partners within a destination can support a more unified, and hopefully satisfactory, tourist experience.

Quality assurance

The first step in measuring customer satisfaction is an assessment of the service and product quality. In sustainable tourism, there are two important aspects to quality assurance: the service being provide to the customer; and the quality of the resources that the tourists are visiting. Tourists expect certain service standards, such as the amenities associated with a 3-star hotel versus a 5-star hotel. They expect good food, although food preferences vary based on specific attributes of the customer (Slocum & Curtis, 2017). However, their satisfaction is also derived from the sites they are visiting, and overcrowding or litter can distract from their experience. Therefore, quality assurance should also include aspects of the major tourist attractions in the area, as well as the service provided by any particular business.

Data collection

When conducting research, there are two types of data to consider – primary data and secondary data. **Primary data** are collected to address specific problems, or to investigate specific tourism trends. **Secondary data** are collected, analyzed, and presented to answer different questions or to solve different problems than those that the data was originally collected to investigate. Examples include federal documents that report tourism statistics as a means to measure tourism (primary data), which in turn are used by a local agency to benchmark their progress in relation to other destinations (secondary data). Secondary data are generally less time intensive and can be less expensive than conducting primary data research. However, secondary data are not always appropriate to the situation or challenges you may be facing (Slocum & Curtis, 2017). This tools section will focus on primary data collection for the purpose of evaluating customer satisfaction.

There are four types of tools used to gather information about customer satisfaction: surveys, interviews, audits, and inspections. Surveys and interviews involve all stakeholders, including tourists, other businesses, local community members, and government agencies. Surveys and interviews can be conducted to evaluate the level of quality and the socially acceptable limits of change within a destination.

Surveys

Surveys are the most common method of primary data collection because they are cost effective and do not require an extensive amount of time to complete. Many businesses have ongoing surveys that allow them to monitor changes in real time. Surveys can be collected in person, over the phone, via the internet, or through the mail. Surveys generally collect **stated data**, which is data that reflect what respondents say they will do, which may or may not be what they actually do. However, in relation to customer satisfaction, surveys allow respondents to rate their satisfaction, usually on a scale of 1 (dissatisfied) to 5 (highly satisfied).

One of the key disadvantages of survey data collection is that the surveys are usually designed by a person inside the business structure and the questions may be biased towards specific activities deemed important by the management team (rather than what is important to the customer). They can also lack detailed descriptions that help explain what is happening within the visitor experience. For example, a business may ask customers to evaluate the check-in process at a hotel. A customer may rate the check-in process as a '3', but the lack of detail may not explain what occurred during the registration process that left the customer less satisfied. To accommodate the lack of detail in survey questions, adding an open comment area, where customers can elaborate on their experiences, may help, however the response rates to open-ended questions are generally low as answering them requires more time to complete the survey. The longer the survey, the less likely a customer will fill it out completely.

Interviews

Interviews provide rich detail to help explain the 'why' and 'how' of a situation, thus helping the interviewee understand the questions more fully. There are two types of interviews: individual interviews and focus groups. **Focus groups** are groups of two or more people who are answering the interview questions simultaneously. Rather than rating a business on its customer service (on a scale of 1 to 5), interviews allow participants to provide detailed feedback through storytelling, and offer other vital information to help explain a situation. For example, rather than asking if a person is satisfied with their tour guide, an interview provides a detailed narrative as to what specific behaviors increased or reduced their satisfaction, how a tourist would have preferred a situation to be handled, and what repercussions ensued. In interviews, customers may share aspects of their personal life that you would not think to ask in a survey. Interviews provide extensive details that help frame their reaction to issues encountered during their stay.

Interviews can be very time consuming and not all tourists can commit to being involved in an interview or focus group. Instead, interviews can be more useful when gauging the involvement (or lack of involvement) of locals working in tourism, or managers of local attractions who often see the negative repercussions of increased tourism. One aspect of interviews is determining when you have enough information. A general rule is to conduct interviews until you reach saturation. **Saturation** is when your interviewees are repeating information uncovered in previous interviews, and when no new knowledge is being acquired. In order to be effective, interviews can be conducted over a short period of time, but should be repeated to ensure that changes made to your service or to the attractions in response to survey/interview/focus group data are being received positively by your customers. Your interviewees should also be diverse so that you make sure to get a wide variety of perspectives.

Sustainability and customer satisfaction

Monitoring sustainability is discussed in more detail in Chapter 8, but gathering customer feedback about your sustainable practices is an important part of being a sustainable business. The connection between visitor management (discussed in Chapter 12) and customer service is the way in which you inform the visitor of your commitment to sustainability, and the role that they play in ensuring you can meet your goals. Educational programs should enhance the tourist experience, rather than distract from it. Policies necessary to preserve tourism resources should be evaluated based on both the effectiveness of resource protection and the level of satisfaction/dissatisfaction they impart on the visitor. If a policy does little to protect the resource and distracts from visitor satisfaction, then it is probably the wrong policy.

The old adage that 'the customer is always right' must be approached lightly when operating under the strong form of sustainability. It is your job to balance the needs of your customer with the needs of the environment, economy, and society in which you do business. By the sheer definition of sustainability, the customer includes future generations that have the right to experience your destination in the same condition as the customers that are currently visiting.

Using surveys and interviews provides valuable feedback on how successful you are in communicating your sustainability message. It is important to measure your success by conveying why certain visitor management policies are in effect, as this will change customers' expectations, and in turn increase their satisfaction. If customer satisfaction is declining after changes to the tourism product, this is a clear sign that you are not being effective in your educational message. Often, visitors may have ideas in support of sustainability practices that you may not realize, and they generally know what other customers expect and how to keep them happy. So, keep asking!

Lastly, remember that all your stakeholders are valued in a sustainable business. This means gathering feedback from the local community, suppliers, and governmental and nongovernmental partners who also have needs that must be met through tourism. As a facilitator of change, your research can provide valuable insights that can extend your sustainability commitments to other businesses and stakeholders in your destination.

Conclusion

In order for a sustainable business to be successful, it must understand its customers and target its products to fit the needs of the market segments. This chapter has highlighted a number of consumer markets that are interested in sustainable travel. It is recognized that many similarities exist between these consumer groups. The purpose is not to provide a definitive typology of the sustainable traveler, but to showcase the values, motivations, and interests resulting from these social movements. Most people will not limit themselves to a single consumer group, and businesses may recognize common traits that appeal to potential customers within and between these segments. Obviously, the types of customers that will patronize your establishment will be based on the amenities you choose to offer as part of your tourism product. However, this chapter has attempted to highlight common themes that sustainable travelers look for in their vacation experiences and has offered ways to gauge feedback to ensure customer expectations are met. Sustainability commitments must be appropriately communicated so that tourists can play an active role in safeguarding a destination.

CASE STUDY 5.1 TRAVEL BUMS AND BUMMERS

KELLY MCMAHON

Suzie and Kella, best friends since high school, had been travelling together for decades. Both women had studied sustainability in college and considered themselves sustainable travelers. This is a story about their recent trip to Sri Lanka. You decide whether (and how) sustainable their choices and actions were.

Sri Lanka is an island in Southeast Asia, in the Indian Ocean located off the southern tip of India. Kella lived in Seattle, which is approximately 8,000 miles from the capital city of Sri Lanka, Colombo. Suzie lived in Washington, DC, approximately 9,000 miles away. After flights half way around the world, the two women booked a hotel for their first two nights in Colombo but made no further plans beyond researching the areas of the country that they wanted to visit and local transportation options.

After recovering from their jetlag, the women decided to travel by train to the town of Kandy, located in the central mountain region. Before departing Colombo, they booked a two-night homestay with a local family via the website www.homestay.com using their smartphone. The train ride was comfortable enough (though sometimes crowded) but the scenery was outstanding and the cooler temperatures that arrived with the train's ascent made it worthwhile. More than a dozen foreign backpackers disembarked the train a few stations before Kandy.

Upon their arrival, the property owner came to pick them up at the train station. The property ended up being gorgeous, with lushly planted and lovingly maintained

Image 5.4 Train to Kandy, Sri Lanka

Source: Susan L. Slocum

grounds, and their room was in a separate building with its own bathroom, a private balcony, and beautiful furnishings. Breakfast was served each morning in the garden, and the proprietors provided them with a multitude of ideas for attractions in the surrounding area. The two women learned that the grandfather of the property owner had been the King of Kandy (a system of local governance put in place by the English when they decolonized the island in 1948). Fascinating!

Among the religions of Sri Lanka, about 70% of residents are Buddhist, 13% Hindu, and 12% Muslim. Desiring to visit some of the many temples in the region, Suzie and Kella hired a taxi and proceeded into what turned out to be the most congested and packed traffic jam. Previously unknown to them, it was a religious holiday, and thousands of locals were similarly proceeding to the temples for religious pilgrimages. They ended up disembarking the taxi and walking to the temples on foot, among the throngs of locals walking in the same direction. Access to the temples required tourists to pay a small entry fee, which was waived for local worshipers.

After Kandy, they booked another homestay at a place in Badula, and boarded the train. Upon arriving at the station, an incredibly shocking sight awaited them. There was a dead man laying uncovered on the platform. A few men and a child stood by with somber looks on their faces. It seemed that the man had been hit by a train several hours earlier. Kella and Suzie quickly hailed a tuktuk (rickshaw) to take them to their accommodation. Death was not a sight they were accustomed to seeing up close and in public. They talked about this for hours, noting how American culture tends to hide death, especially from children, and that it would be a very different childhood growing up where death (even violent death) was not shielded from view.

Once dropped at their homestay, the travelers walked up a dirt driveway towards the home. There was a cow grazing lazily in the front lawn. At first glance, the residence appeared to be uninhabited and their suspicion was confirmed when they knocked on the front door and nobody answered. There was obvious construction underway, but no human activity that day. The women sat down to ponder what to do and played with a very friendly dog. They greatly enjoyed his company. Ultimately, they were able to get in touch with the owner, and several hours later he arrived to let them in. He explained that the property was presently closed for remodeling (though, since the website had allowed the women to book a reservation, he agreed to let them stay). It was an awkward night, a small breakfast was provided in the morning. They stayed two nights and explored local waterfalls during the day.

Their next stop was the southern beaches. The women took a series of buses and booked their homestays a day in advance. Accommodations were smaller, with multiple family members and generations living in the same house. It seemed quite a bit more expensive to live in this region, which appeared to be heavily dependent on tourism as a part of the economy. Car traffic was heavy and exhaust fumes were prevalent. Vehicles driving on the dirt roads kicked up dust, and with the increased heat and humidity, it stuck to the bodies of the women as they walked around town. The beaches were nice, with relatively little garbage (though enough to be disturbing to these travelers), and the soft sand led from the ocean to a series of small restaurants with outdoor decks for dining al fresco. Breakfast was typically included at their accommodations, and often served on balconies or decks overlooking the ocean.

Their final stop was back in Colombo the day of their late-night flights back home. They spent the day visiting with the cousin of Kella's friend, who was a local who offered them delicious mangos, giant-sized cashews, and wine. They learned that her husband was a prominent figure in local sports recruiting, somewhat of a star in Sri Lanka, and that he was frequently travelling for business.

Reflective questions

1. Describe these travelers in terms of their behaviors and choices. What type of traveler are they?

2. Did these two women make sustainable choices while travelling? What else could they have done to be more sustainable?

3. What types of things could Sri Lanka do to market the country to sustainable travelers? Are there actions you would take to enhance travelers' experiences while visiting?

CASE STUDY 5.2 A TRIP TO PORTUGAL

JOHN READ

Over their summer break, two academics, Jack and Lynn, decided to spend a few days in Portugal before a conference that they were both attending. Wanting to spend time in the mountains, they booked an Airbnb in Peneda-Gerês National Park near the Portuguese–Spanish border. Jack enjoys hiking, especially to see historic sites like ruins, while Lynn was more interested to see the waterfalls that were within the park. As we trace some of the adventures that they took within the national park, reflect on the challenges Jack and Lynn experienced and their overall satisfaction with their trip.

On their first day of exploring, Jack and Lynn decided to walk around the village that they were staying in and explore some of the trails. After walking to the end of the village they came to the Moinhos de Parada (the Mills of Parada) and decided that this would be a good trail to begin their adventure. As they were walking along the trail, Jack commented on the trail markers that were used to designate the proper path to take. He had seen trail markers within the village, as well as a descriptive image for what the trail markers meant (see Image 5.5). To know that you were headed in the correct direction, the path was marked by painted lines that looked like an equals '=' sign on rocks located along the side of the path. When you reached a fork in the path, the trail marker that indicated the incorrect path was a set of crossed painted lines that looked like an 'x'.

As they were hiking down the trail they began to notice that the path was poorly maintained and looked like it had seen little use in the recent past. The trail markers were still visible though, so they continued their hike that led them down into the bottom of a forested valley beneath the village. Knowing that they were on a trail that was named for the disused mills in the area, the pair were intrigued when they came across their first mill which was located just on the other side of a closed metal gate that was painted green. It appeared that there was a very old path on the other side of the gate that continued to lead deeper into the valley. This being their first hike in the village, the pair decided that they did not want to accidentally trespass by passing through the gate. They instead decided to continue along the path that they were already on which began to take a winding route up the opposite side of the valley. After a period

Image 5.5 Park map, Peneda-Gerês National Park, Portugal

Source: John Read

of walking, the trail opened up into a field that was located behind the local café. Realizing that they must have missed the route they were supposed to take, the pair decided to stop and have a beer before venturing off to find a trail that was more clearly marked.

Their next day in the national park was dedicated to waterfall viewing. Waking at sunrise, they started their day with an hour and a half drive before reaching the town with the waterfall. After arriving in the town, the pair wandered around until they eventually found a path that was marked with the '=' sign, indicating that they were on an officially marked trail. Walking down this path, they came to a three-way fork with paths that led down a hill, straight ahead, and up a hill. The path that led downhill and straight ahead were marked with an 'x', the path that led up the hill was marked with the '=' sign. Observing two groups, one heading downhill and the other heading up the hill, they decided to follow the marked path and the group that was headed up the hill. Proceeding to hike for 20 minutes uphill, they reached the plateau and found a fork in the road. Jack consulted the map function on his cellular phone and realized that this path had led them to the top of the waterfall with no way to access the pools at the bottom. After taking a brief break by the stream that fed the waterfall, the pair hiked down the mountain and again reached the area where the path forked in three directions. After a little exploring, they took the path that led straight ahead, past the 'x' trail marker and finally reached the base of the waterfall. Jack took a swim and enjoyed the cold waters while Lynn sat and ate her lunch.

On the drive back to their Airbnb, an interesting event occurred. While passing through an area of the National Park with poorly maintained roads, they were stopped and charged a fee of €2. The explanation for the fee was that automobiles were the greatest source of impact on the environment within the park. Receiving no other explanation, they paid the fee and continued their drive. That evening, they looked up the fee information on their computers and realized that automobiles are prohibited from driving through the 'Mata de Albergaria', which is the oldest forest in Portugal, on the weekends unless the vehicle is headed to Spain (as Jack and Lynn were) or the occupants live within that region of the park. Having not been stopped on their initial entry that morning, they realized that they must have travelled early enough for the fee collection officials to have not yet arrived. Of course, they had visited the forest and its waterfalls earlier in the day before their hike, so felt that the fee applied to them even if it was not collected when they arrived.

Reflective questions

1. Jack and Lynn appear to be interested in nature-based independent travel. What demographic, psychographic, and behavioral traits do you think they possess? Explain your answer.
2. The park used a number of strategies to reduce the impact of tourists. How do you think these affected Jack and Lynn's satisfaction with their experience? How best can the park manage environmental impacts with visitor satisfaction?
3. Based on this case study, which typology best applied to Jack and Lynn? Do you think they were appropriate for the resources at the park? Why or why not?

STUDY QUESTIONS

1. In the following scenarios, determine which type of market segmentation each company uses. There may be more than one segment.
   - Disney cruises markets to middle- and high-income families.
   - Marriott Hotel's guests are primarily business travelers.
   - Coach tours in Europe appeal to first-time travelers who value comfort and safety.
   - Intrepid Travel promotes customized travel to out-of-the-way places for small groups or independent travelers.
   - Las Vegas promotes itself under the slogan *What Happens in Vegas, Stays in Vegas*.
   - Costa Rica has become known as the ecotourism capital of the world.
2. Research a new consumer trend not discussed in this chapter. Describe how it could be used by a tourism business. Would it also be appropriate for a sustainable business? Why or why not?
3. Create a new tourist experience for visitors to your hometown. How could you adapt it to appeal to a sustainable consumer? More specifically, how could you adapt it to appeal to a LOHAS consumer? How about to a locavist? How about a slow tourist?

4. You are interested in marketing to sustainable consumers. What avenues might you use to communicate your sustainability initiatives to ensure that your target markets receive the message?

5. You have just implemented a number of sustainability initiatives at your hotel. How would you go about measuring your customers' response to the changes? What is the best way to determine if these changes are adding to the consumer experience?

DEFINITIONS

Behavioral segmentation   splits consumers into groups according to their observed behaviors

Customer satisfaction   generated by providing an experience (tourism product) that meets or exceeds the customer's expectations

Demographic segmentation   divides consumers into categories such as age, income, race, family size, and socioeconomic status

Ecotourism   low impact nature-based tourism which contributes to the maintenance of species and habitats either directly through a contribution to conservation and/or indirectly by providing revenue to the local community sufficient for local people to value, and therefore protect their wildlife heritage area as a source of income

Excursionist (also known as a day-tripper)   a traveler that lives in close proximity to a destination and only stays for a short visit

Focus group   a group of two or more people who are answering interview questions simultaneously

Food tourism   the desire to experience a particular type of food, or the produce of a specific region while traveling

Geographic segmentation   separates markets according to physical location criteria

Localism   the belief in and expression of the unique character of localities

Locavist   a person that travels closer to home and invests locally in their communities with money, time, and personal energy

Locavore   a person whose diet consists only or principally of locally grown or produced food

LOHAS (Lifestyles of Health and Sustainability)   a social and economic movement that reflects a marketplace of goods and services that is immersed in meaningful person values of self as well as the social and natural world

Market segmentation   the activity of dividing a broad consumer base, normally consisting of existing and potential customers, into sub-groups of consumers (known as segments) based on some type of shared characteristics

Primary data   data collected to address specific problems, or to investigate specific tourism trends

Psychographic segmentation   separates consumers by lifestyle choices, including their activities, interests, and opinions

Saturation   when interviewees are repeating information uncovered in previous interviews and when no new knowledge is being acquired

Secondary data   data collected, analyzed, and presented to answer different questions or to solve different problems than those that the data was originally collected to investigate

Slow cities   a development strategy that promotes the slow philosophy to urban living by providing a political agenda of local distinctiveness within urban development

Slow tourism   a philosophy of travelling that allows visitors to experience the authentic side of a destination by spending an extended amount of time in one area

Stated data   data that reflect what respondents say they will do, which may or may not be what they actually do

Sustainable consumption   the use of goods and related products which bring a better quality of life to those who produce them, while minimizing the use of natural resources, toxic materials, waste, and pollutants over the product life cycle, so as not to jeopardize the needs of future generations

Tourism typology   a classification of tourists based on psychological characteristics

Voluntourism   tourism that provides opportunities for people to do volunteer work while also participating in tourism as a way to 'do good' or 'give back' to a community

Chapter **6**

Mass tourism

Overview

This chapter provides a general introduction to mass tourism and explains the impacts of a number of different mass tourism types. It describes the evolution of tourism destinations that has led to the rise of mass tourism, which can result in economic dependency and negative social and environmental impacts. It highlights the green economy and the process of greening mass tourism, as well as the concept of sustainable mass tourism. Anyone working in tourism operations should be aware of the interrelationship between all elements in the tourism system and how small changes can impact overall sustainability. An overview of the Global Reporting Standards is provided as a tool to support increased transparency in sustainable operations.

CHAPTER OBJECTIVES

At the completion of the chapter, students will be able to:

- Define mass tourism, sustainable mass tourism, and the differences between them;
- Identify different types of mass tourism;
- Describe the tourism life cycle;
- Evaluate the impacts of dependency;
- Differentiate green tourism from sustainable tourism;
- Explain the interrelationships between the elements of tourism; and
- Describe the Global Reporting Standards and categorize the four principles for defining the contents of a sustainability report.

Introduction

Prior to the mid-nineteenth century, travel was reserved exclusively for the rich – such as the grand tour – a cultural exploration undertaken mainly by young men of the upper class as part of their education. Generally, only small groups within a family traveled for pleasure, often to experience the refined cultures of Europe. In 1849, Thomas Cook organized the first international tourist group excursion, taking tourists to Belgium, Germany, and France, followed by the first round-the-world group tour where visitors traveled to the United States, Japan, China, India, Palestine, and Egypt. It is not just that Cook developed affordable tours for ordinary people, but it was how he packaged these tours that gave him the reputation as the "father of mass tourism". By negotiating group rates for train seats, boat passage, and hotel rooms, Cook was able to collect commissions to support his business venture. His business model is still used by tour operators today.

Mass tourism is the aggressive development of standardized travel packages that result in tens of thousands of visitors going to the same destination (Bramwell, 2004). Not all types of mass tourism are exactly the same, although most visitors within a mass tourism destination enjoy the same amenities and activities as other visitors in that destination. Often in mass tourism destinations, the number of tourists can be substantially larger than the number of residents on any given day, and over time, these communities have become dependent on tourism revenue to support their economy.

Image 6.1 American football game

Source: Susan L. Slocum

Mass tourism results in increased pollution, environmental degradation, deforestation, inefficient energy use, and cultural exploitation (UNEP, 2011). In particular, the amount of water 100 guests would use in a luxury hotel for 55 days could support 100 families in poor countries for three years (Tourism Concern, n.d.). Not all of this water is used by tourists for drinking or washing, but it is used to support tourism operations in the form of landscape maintenance, swimming pools, golf courses, and food preparation. Moreover, the travel and tourism industry is responsible for about 5% of yearly greenhouse gas emissions (GHG) (UNWTO, n.d.). Many developing countries are unable to process waste, specifically because they do not have the capacity to store trash within landfills, accommodate recycling, nor can they adequately process human waste in the quantities associated with mass tourism.

Many of the most visited sites in the world are facing degradation because of mass tourism. Examples of destinations under threat from mass tourism visitation are listed in Table 6.1.

Table 6.1 Destinations under threat from overdevelopment

Attraction	Location	Threat
Great Wall	China	Sections of the wall have been sprayed with graffiti and 30% of the fortification has disappeared due to natural erosion and human damage
Great Barrier Reef	Australia	Climate change and increasing ocean temperatures are killing coral and marine life. Some scientists predict that the reef could become extinct by 2050
Sistine Chapel	Vatican City	Flash photography and the carbon dioxide exhaled by millions of tourists are destroying Michelangelo's artwork
Atlantic City	New Jersey, USA	Increased competition for casino gambling worldwide, and increased poverty and crime in the area has resulted in a drastic reduction in tourist numbers
Acapulco	Mexico	Over development and increased drug-related crime have made some beach destinations dangerous for foreigners. Acapulco has been listed as Mexico's most violent city since 2012
Costa del Sol	Spain	The proliferation of tourism infrastructure and the presence of thousands of visitors each year have led to much of Spain's Mediterranean coast being paved over, degrading the natural environment and decreasing the quality of the tourist experience
Angkor Wat	Cambodia	Some claim that corruption has resulted in the embezzlement of tourism revenue by government agents, resulting in tourism sites falling into disrepair, and the destruction of ancient temples

Understanding mass tourism

Types of mass tourism

The most familiar type of mass tourism is the sun, sea, and sand destinations (**3S destinations**), such as Cancun Mexico or Majorca Spain. One of the key challenges of 3S destinations is that most of the hotels, resorts, and many restaurants are owned by foreign corporations, so very little of the economic impact stays in the local economy (Scheyvens, 2002). Moreover, these destinations usually offer all-inclusive resorts, where the guest pays for lodging, food (sometimes alcohol), and recreational activities in advance. This reduces the incentive for visitors to leave the resort and interact with local people or the local economy. The vacation makers use vast quantities of energy and water and create large amounts of waste, which is a high price to pay for little commercial return. Many resorts own the beachfront, which is reserved only for tourists, isolating the local population from their traditional recreational and fishing opportunities. Insufficient housing for the vast number of employees can also reduce quality of life for residents. Moreover, construction of hotels, roads, and parking lots affects rain run-off, increasing erosion to the beach and washing pollutants into the oceans. Some beaches, such as Waikiki Beach in Honolulu, Hawaii, must replenish the sand on a regular basis. In 2012, the sand reconstruction project at Waikiki cost $2.4 million and was funded jointly by businesses and the government (Riker, 2016).

Urban destinations also fall within the definition of mass tourism. While urban infrastructure areas are generally better equipped for accommodating large numbers of tourists (by having established public transportation and advanced waste treatment options), there are still local environmental and social impacts related to urban tourism. For example, Hong Kong is the most visited tourist city in the world, receiving 58.5 million visitors in 2017 (China Tourism Commission, 2018), yet had only 7.4 million residents the same year. The economic benefits of tourism have resulted in increases in property values, forcing many local shops to close, which have been replaced by international retail chains. Local residents are finding it harder to live in Hong Kong, with property inflation rates estimated at more than 14% annually (Delmendo, 2017). Modern development has changed the character of the city, resulting in a decline of tourism visits over the past five years. New initiatives to decrease GHG emissions, as a means to improve air quality, and the plan to develop new green spaces, such as urban parks, are designed to offer new tourism services that also positively increase the quality of life for residents.

Cruise ship tourism is the fastest growing segment of the travel industry. It is estimated that in 2018, there were 511,000 beds available on over 50 cruise lines, resulting in 27 million cruise passengers, with an additional 27 new ships being debuted that year. The Caribbean receives the highest number of cruise ship visits, almost 35% of the total market share, and Americans are the largest travel group, making up 11.5% of all passengers (Cruise Lines International Association, Inc., 2017). Much like all-inclusive resorts, cruise passengers buy their excursions from the cruise line so that 50% to 75% of the revenue is kept by the cruise company rather than going to local excursion agencies (Brida & Zapata, 2009). Cruise companies are also powerful entities that can demand larger ports or dense development at embarkation locations because there are always other destinations trying to recruit cruise ship visitation. From an environmental perspective, cruise ships generate a number of waste streams into the marine environment, including sewage, greywater, hazardous wastes, oily bilge water, ballast water, and solid waste. Since the cruise industry remains largely unregulated, it is impossible to accurately measure the environmental costs of the sector (Brida & Zapata, 2009).

Image 6.2 Cruise ship, Cabo San Lucas, Mexico

Source: Susan L. Slocum

Cultural heritage sites also risk drawing tourists on a mass scale. The United Nations Educational, Scientific and Cultural Organization (UNESCO) (2003) defines **cultural heritage** as the legacy of physical artefacts and intangible attributes of a group or society that are inherited from past generations, maintained in the present, and bestowed for the benefit of future generations. According to Timothy (2011), cultural heritage tourism is significant as an economic activity because "the past and its resources lie at the core of much of global tourism today, and people by the hundreds of millions travel worldwide each year to seek out and experience places of historical significance" (p. 15). In other words, cultural heritage tourism forms a large part of mass tourism. While heritage tourism can bring well-needed economic benefits, many sites are managed by government agencies who receive much of the revenue through concession contracts and entrance fees. Since the inception of UNESCO's World Heritage list, many of the 1,073 places in 167 countries have seen a rapid increase in mass tourism. Heritage destinations, such as the Taj Mahal in Agra, India or the Great Pyramid in Giza, Egypt, are facing challenges related to sustainability. Moreover, increased visitation often isolates local people who have the strongest connection with heritage resources and the history behind them. Too many tourists can disrupt the experiences at sacred sites and lead to overuse, pollution, and inadequate maintenance of ancient sites. Even though it is difficult to isolate the international tourist arrivals and receipts for cultural heritage tourism specifically, cultural heritage is often a primary reason for visitation to certain destinations (McKercher & du Cros, 2002).

Finally, natural areas suffer from mass tourism development. Whether it is alpine ski areas, such as Matterhorn Ski Paradise in Switzerland or Whistler Blackcomb in British Columbia, Canada, or national parks, such as the Grand Canyon in Arizona and the Serengeti in Tanzania, visitation has drastically changed the landscape of high use natural areas. In relation to national parks, many parks were designed to specifically exclude traditional peoples, who were forcibly removed from the park boundaries when the area was designated (Hamin, 2001). Therefore, the socio-cultural impacts generally occur outside the park in neighboring communities that function as **gateway communities** and who continue to face restricted use of their natural resources. For example, while many tourists are allowed to hunt in nature reserves, local people are forbidden from hunting and often cannot afford the expensive hunting permits sold to tourists. Often, these communities once used the natural resources as sources of food, medicine, and building materials, which must now be bought on the open market. While tourism does generate revenue to support conservation efforts in these areas, the impact of millions of tourists on the natural landscape can be disastrous. In relation to ski areas, increased development affects the migratory process of animals, the clearing of large piste areas can invite invasive species, and artificial snowmaking and grooming increases erosion and sediment loads that leach into riparian areas (Rixen & Rolando, 2013).

The Tourism Area Life Cycle

Tourism destinations generally evolve over time rather than being created with mass tourism in mind. Butler (1980) recognized an evolutionary pattern to tourism development as shown in Figure 6.1. In the *Exploration stage*, wanderers begin to venture into areas not traditionally known as tourism destinations. These may be small villages located in remote areas or areas neighboring already established tourism hotspots. When tourists are impressed with an area, they may return home and tell their friends about the new and unique region and

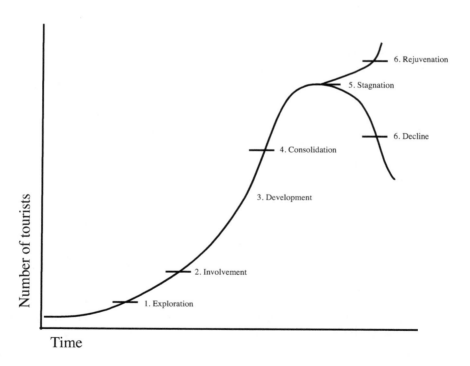

Figure 6.1 Butler's Tourism Area Life Cycle

Source: Adapted from Butler (1980)

encourage others to visit there. In these spaces, there are no specific tourism businesses and most enterprises are locally owned and serve the residents in the community. As more visitors are attracted by the unspoiled landscape, local entrepreneurs begin to realize the economic significance of tourism and provide facilities and services specifically aimed at tourists.

Destinations now enter the *involvement stage*, where hotels or hostels are built to higher comfort standards than those that service locals, and restaurants begin to cater to the desires of tourists. In the *development stage*, tourist numbers increase and begin to outnumber the local population. Many locals tolerate the unwanted impacts of tourism because they see substantial economic benefits. As more tourists access these locations, transportation, roads, and tour companies increase accessibility for tourists. Also, during the development stage, foreign entrepreneurs see the potential for profit and begin to open tourism-related businesses that better serve the tourists' needs than the local businesses.

The increasing number of tourists begins to change the nature of the area, impacting the local ambience and causing destruction to the natural resources through increased construction of accommodations and new business facilities, resulting in the *consolidation stage*. By this phase, indigenous populations and local businesses are isolated from the local resources and may be forced to move further away because of inflation and increased development. The *stagnation stage* results when the tourism landscape becomes dominant with little room for further expansion. Resorts become urbanized and capacity levels are reached or exceeded. By this phase, the destination loses the local quality that made it attractive to tourism in the first place.

It is important to note that once mass tourism has been established in a destination, it is not possible to return to an unspoiled natural and cultural environment. For example, Disney World Orlando will not return to the native swamp lands that once occupied that area of Florida. Nor would we necessarily want to return Orlando to its natural state now that over 250,000 people call that area home. Once mass tourism is established, communities become dependent on tourism. **Economic dependency** is an unending situation in which economies and their economic agents (those who produce, buy or sell goods within an economy) rely on one aspect or thing in order to be successful. When an economy becomes dependent on tourism as the one thing that makes it successful, all economic sectors in that area can fail without the help of tourism. For example, restaurants and hotels need tourists to visit in order to succeed, but also service stations, grocery stores, and other businesses may rely on tourists as part of their customer base. This is how communities become dependent not only on the direct effects of tourism, but also on the indirect effects. If the majority of local jobs are in the tourism industry, that locality can also become reliant on the induced effects of tourism. If the local residents are unable to earn adequate income through tourism jobs, local grocery stores and service stations may also suffer. Once a destination reaches the consolidation phase, the area has become dependent on tourism and has lost the ability to generate economic returns from other industries. As tourism declines, these destinations and businesses must find new avenues to differentiate themselves by creating new attractions or finding new travel markets that can support the changing nature of the experience. If they cannot, they risk losing tourism as an economic driver, and the local economy may suffer.

Butler's model predicts that all destinations will follow the same path unless they actively pursue other development options. In the *rejuvenation stage*, destinations may develop artificial attractions, such as theme parks or boardwalks, to draw additional tourists to the area. At the time Butler developed the Tourism Area Life Cycle model, the concept of sustainability did not yet exist. However, recent scholars have recognized the power of sustainability as a diversification process that can lead to the rejuvenation stage. By means of the weak form of sustainability (see Chapter 1), mass tourism enterprises can use thresholds of acceptable change to develop indicators that are appropriate for urban and high-use destinations. This can be done by **greening** tourism or attempting to mitigate the environmental consequences of economic activities.

Sustainable mass tourism

Weaver (2012) highlights a new emerging destination type called **sustainable mass tourism**, which promotes economic, environmental, and socio-cultural enhancements to areas already witnessing mass tourism. Within sustainable mass tourism, destinations and businesses actively engage with sustainable mechanisms that reduce the negative impacts of tourism, specifically resource use (water, energy, waste), and provide for a more inclusive form of tourism for local residents. Peeters (2012) agrees that "the only sustainable future for tourism lies in sustainable mass tourism" (p. 1040). Within Weaver's model, he describes three distinct development paths that still result in fully regulated, high-volume tourism or sustainable mass tourism:

- Incremental path;
- Organic path; and
- Induced path.

The *incremental path* is characterized by a high level of regulation that occurs before mass tourism levels are reached. He claims this path is more common near vulnerable areas, such as

Image 6.3 Viewing the *Mona Lisa*, Paris, France
Source: Susan L. Slocum

nature parks and coral reefs. The *organic path* is the opposite, where regulation to support sustainability happens after a destination has reached a state of unsustainable mass tourism. Regulation is often a response to increasing negative impacts to an area. This organic path is very similar to what Butler describes as the rejuvenation stage of development and is the most common form of sustainable mass tourism today. The *induced path* lies between the incremental and organic paths in relation to both the scale of tourism and the level of regulation, and occurs when scale and regulation are jointly developed.

Greening mass tourism

In order to understand greening, it is important to understand the green economy. The concept of the green economy advanced in response to the 2008 economic crises and was widely praised as providing new opportunities for business (Makower, 2009). The United Nations Environment Programme (UNEP) (2011) defines the **green economy** as an economy that results in improved human well-being and social equity, while significantly reducing environmental risks and ecological scarcities. Newton (2015) challenges whether the green economy is consistent with economic growth, resulting in numerous "shades" of green that focus "from narrow concerns about climate change on one end of the spectrum to more extensive critiques of the environmental sustainability of modern capitalism on the other end" (p. 36). Allen and Clouth (2012) see the green economy as a means of supporting sustainable development by focusing on specific changes that must be made in order for economic systems to operate more sustainably. Greening strategies are most commonly used in mass tourism businesses because they can decrease operating costs, are relatively easy to incorporate, and do not require total buy-in from all businesses in a mass tourism destination.

There are two primary ways businesses can support the greening of mass tourism. One is to find avenues to reduce resource use, specifically resource waste, and the second is through the use of sustainable supply chain management. Supply chain management is discussed in more detail in Chapter 9, however many of the same principles apply to both methods of the green business model. Businesses or destinations can choose green options that reduce the carbon footprint of their operation, resulting in a decrease in the negative impacts of tourism. These strategies apply not only to hotels, cruise ships, tour operators, and airlines, but can be used by small businesses, such as hostels, museums, local tourism guiding agencies, wineries/breweries and attractions. Table 6.2 provides a general overview of sustainable mass tourism strategies.

Table 6.2 Overview of sustainable mass tourism strategies

Goal	Strategy
Reduce greenhouse gas emissions	Use clean energy (solar, water, wind power)
	Support public transportation
	Encourage walking, hiking, or biking
	Support carbon off-set programs
	Use hybrid or electric vehicles for shuttle services
	Buy locally in order to reduce transportation emissions

Table 6.2 continued

Goal	Strategy
Reduce water consumption	Low flow technologies for toilets and showers
	Use native plant species in landscaping that do not need additional water
	Collect grey water to use on golf courses or in landscaping
	Allow pool water to recirculate
	Reduce the amount of laundry by supplying towels and changing linens less frequently
Reduce energy consumption	Insulate windows and doors
	Use energy-efficient fixtures and electronic appliances
	Lock and unlock the electricity supply to a room so that it can only be used when the room is occupied
	Minimize the use of air conditioning by using ceiling fans or natural air flows
	Use energy-efficient appliances
	Erect LEED-certified buildings
Reduce pollutants	Use organic materials whenever possible
	Use natural fertilizers for landscaping and natural cleaning agents
Reduce waste	Reuse materials whenever possible
	Recycle or set up a community recycling program
	Use plated food service rather than buffets to reduce food waste
	Compost all food waste
Improve quality of life	Hire locally
	Provide job skills training for the community to ensure they have the skills to succeed in tourism
	Buy local food to support indirect revenue sources for locals
	Buy local artisan products for gift shops
	Support local charities
	Donate used items to locals in need (linens, dishes, etc.)
	Educate tourists on local customs and traditions
	Celebrate the local culture through décor and business themes

Tourism as a system

It is important to remain cautious as tourism businesses try to implement sustainability or green practices because tourism is a complex system where decisions in one area can have negative impacts in other areas. A **system** is described as an interdependent series of elements that interact in order to achieve some end result (Beni, 2001). Leslie (2000) emphasizes that it is necessary to use a holistic view when analyzing tourism because the holistic approach includes all of tourism's key characteristics, such as the movement of people, transport, accommodation, and activities at the destination regardless of whether tourism is considered a business sector or an academic field of research. Figure 6.2 shows the systems approach to implementing sustainability. According to Lohmann and Netto (2016), to effectively evaluate a system, consideration must be given to:

- The environment (the system's location);
- Units (the system's parts);
- Relationships (the relationships among the system's units);
- Attributes (the quality of the units and the system itself);
- Inputs (what enters the system);
- Output (what leaves the system);
- Feedback (control of the system to keep it working properly); and
- A model (a system design to facilitate its understanding).

For example, when promoting public transportation, there is a risk that local taxi drivers will encounter fewer tourists, lowering wages or eliminating jobs. One common practice by

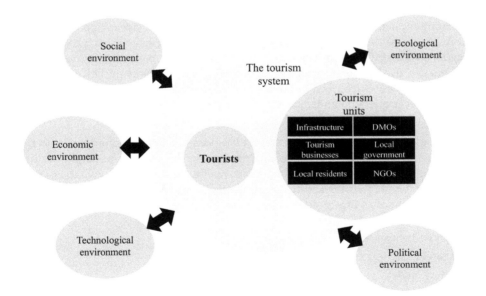

Figure 6.2 A systems approach to implementing sustainability

hotel establishments is to open organic gardens on premises. This supports reducing GHG emissions from long-haul food transport, the use of chemical fertilizers in food production, and lowers the cost of purchasing organic food. However, it also reduces the indirect effects of tourism through a reduction in purchases from local farmers. Supporting local charities can provide valuable aid to impoverished regions, but can also encourage aid dependence. Promoting local culture can celebrate regional differences and instill pride in a community, yet can also lead to the **commodification** of culture, where the transformation of goods, services, ideas, and people into commodities or objects of trade is changed in order to meet tourists' expectations and to earn revenue. In other words, within the system, changes to mass tourism in one area must be carefully considered to ensure they are the appropriate strategies for a given environment and that the interrelationship between all aspects of tourism is considered.

Fyall and Garrod (1997) assert that achieving sustainability is a four-stage process. The first step is to define and establish the concept of sustainable tourism. The second step is to determine the conditions required to achieve sustainable tourism. The third step is to develop a framework for measuring the progress of sustainable tourism. The final step is to develop a set of techniques to evaluate sustainable tourism, which is the topic discussed in the following tools section.

SUSTAINABILITY TOOL: SUSTAINABILITY REPORTING

Reporting on sustainability accomplishments is an important part of showcasing a business and destination, both to stakeholders and to the general public. The Global Sustainability Standards Board (GSSB) provides a set of globally recognized standards that identify an organization's significant impacts on the economy, the environment, and/or society. According to the GSSB (2016), "The Global Reporting Initiative (GRI) creates a common language for organizations and stakeholders with which the economic, environmental, and social impacts of organizations can be communicated and understood" (p. 3). The Standards provide a global framework for comparability across the industry, thereby enabling greater transparency and comparability of organizations around the world. The GRI is designed to report both the positive and negative impacts, but can also be used to evaluate the success of sustainability initiatives. The GRIs are divided into four series, described in Table 6.3. Discussing all of the GSIs is too extensive for this book, however a general understanding of the reporting content is important for tourism practitioners.

If an organization wants to claim that its report has been prepared in accordance with the GRI standards, it must apply the two Reporting Principles in the analysis: principles for defining report content; and principles for defining report quality. Report content guarantees the accuracy of information in a sustainability report, which is important for stakeholders to make a truthful assessment of an organization. The report content includes:

- Stakeholder inclusiveness;
- Sustainability context;
- Materiality; and
- Completeness.

Report quality provides information on how to ensure the report content is accurate and that measurements are unbiased. The report quality must include tests, which are tools to help an

Table 6.3 The Global Reporting Initiative's universal standards

Series description	Universal standards
100 series	The 100 series includes three universal standards:
	GRI 101: Foundation is the starting point for using the set of GRI Standards. GRI 101 sets out the Reporting Principles for defining report content and quality. It includes requirements for preparing a sustainability report in accordance with the GRI Standards, and describes how the GRI Standards can be used and referenced. GRI 101 also includes the specific claims that are required for organizations preparing a sustainability report in accordance with the Standards, and for those using selected GRI Standards to report specific information.
	GRI 102: General Disclosures is used to report contextual information about an organization and its sustainability reporting practices. This includes information about an organization's profile, strategy, ethics and integrity, governance, stakeholder engagement practices, and reporting process.
	GRI 103: Management Approach is used to report information about how an organization manages a material topic. It is designed to be used for each material topic in a sustainability report, including those covered by the topic specific GRI Standards (series 200, 300, and 400) and other material topics.
	Applying GRI 103 with each material topic allows the organization to provide a narrative explanation of why the topic is material, where the impacts occur (the topic boundary), and how the organization manages the impacts.
Topic-specific Standards 200 series – Economic topics 300 series – Environmental topics 400 series – Social topics	The 200, 300, and 400 series include numerous topic-specific Standards. These are used to report information on an organization's impacts related to economic, environmental, and social topics (e.g., Indirect economic impacts, Water, or Employment).
	To prepare a sustainability report in accordance with the GRI Standards, an organization applies the Reporting Principles for defining report content from GRI 101: Foundation to identify its material economic, environmental, and/or social topics. These material topics determine which topic-specific Standards the organization uses to prepare its sustainability report.
	Selected topic-specific Standards, or parts of their content, can also be used to report specific information, without preparing a sustainability report.

Source: Global Sustainability Standards Board (2016)

organization determine whether it has accurately applied the principles. Report quality is covered in the completeness description and includes:

- Accuracy;
- Balance;
- Clarity;
- Comparability;
- Reliability; and
- Timeliness.

Stakeholder inclusiveness

The GSSB defines **stakeholders** as entities or individuals that "can reasonably be expected to be significantly affected by the reporting organization's activities, products, or services" (p. 8). Stakeholders can include employees, contract workers, shareholders or business owners, suppliers, local community members or residents, NGOs or other civil society organizations, and vulnerable groups (e.g. the homeless, minority populations, children, the elderly, and migrant workers). Reports must include "reasonable expectations and interests of stakeholders" (p. 8), even if they are unable to articulate their concerns. The report should differentiate between categories of stakeholders and should use common methodologies to assess their perspectives, such as surveys, monitoring the media, collaborative activities, or scientific research. The goal is to make sure their needs are properly understood. It is important to note that an organization may encounter conflicting views or expectations and must be able to explain how it balanced them when making decisions about its reporting. Tests for stakeholder involvement include:

- The reporting organization can describe the stakeholders to whom it considers itself accountable;
- The report content draws upon the outcomes of stakeholder engagement processes used by the organization in its ongoing activities, and as required by the legal and institutional framework in which it operates;
- The report content draws upon the outcomes of any stakeholder engagement processes undertaken specifically for the report; and
- The outcomes of the stakeholder engagement processes that inform decisions about the report are consistent.

Sustainability context

Contextualizing the information in the report includes describing how an organization contributes, or plans to contribute in the future, to the improvement or deterioration of economic, environmental, and social conditions at the local, regional, or global level. The goal is to report the organization's performance within the broader concepts of sustainability. Examples include addressing limits on resources, optimal pollution levels, and socioeconomic objectives. Some of these may be global challenges, such as greenhouse gas emissions, or they may be local challenges, such as community development, clean water, or educational standards. When reporting on topics that have positive or negative local impacts, it is important to provide insight regarding different influences in different locations, or within different communities around a single location. The report should also address impacts across specific operational divisions (e.g., transportation, accommodations, food and beverage, attractions, philanthropic activities). The relationship between sustainability and organizational strategy should be explicit in the report. Tests for sustainability contexts include:

- The reporting organization presents its understanding of sustainable development, drawing on objective and available information, and authoritative measures of sustainable development, for the topics covered;
- The organization presents its performance with reference to broader sustainable development conditions and goals, as reflected in recognized sectoral, local, regional, or global instruments;
- The organization presents its performance in a manner that communicates its impacts and contributions in appropriate geographic contexts; and
- The organization describes how economic, environmental, and/or social topics relate to its long-term strategy, risks, opportunities, and goals, including in its value chain.

Materiality

Materiality determines which topics, or significant impacts, are relevant and important and, therefore, essential to the report. Not all material topics are of equal importance, and the report should prioritize each item. Figure 6.3 shows an example how materiality can be represented, where items in the top right corner would receive the highest priority, next are those in the bottom right corner, and those in the bottom left corners would be the lowest priority.

An organization should use a combination of internal and external factors when determining whether a topic is material. Internal factors include the organization's overall mission, vision, and competitive strategy. Materiality can also be evaluated by the priorities recognized in the stakeholder assessment, or the organization's influence on upstream entities, such as

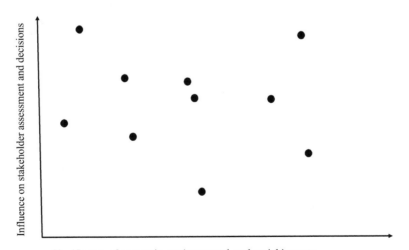

Figure 6.3 Materiality of impacts

suppliers, or downstream entities, such as customers. External factors may include international standards, certification requirements, and laws or regulation that an organization must follow. The tests for materials include:

- Reasonably estimable economic, environmental, and/or social impacts (such as climate change, HIV/AIDS, or poverty) identified through sound investigation by people with recognized expertise, or by expert bodies with recognized credentials;
- The interests and expectations of stakeholders specifically invested in the organization, such as employees and shareholders;
- Broader economic, social, and/or environmental interests and topics raised by stakeholders such as workers who are not employees, suppliers, local communities, vulnerable groups, and civil society;
- The main topics and future challenges for a sector, as identified by peers and competitors;
- Laws, regulations, international agreements, or voluntary agreements of strategic significance to the organization and its stakeholders;
- Key organizational values, policies, strategies, operational management systems, goals, and targets;
- The core competencies of the organization and the manner in which they can contribute to sustainable development;
- Consequences for the organization which are related to its impacts on the economy, the environment, and/or society (for example, risks to its business model or reputation); and
- Material topics are appropriately prioritized in the report.

Completeness

Completeness encompasses the list of material topics covered in the report, as well as topic boundaries and timelines. This section will include information collection (for example, compiling data that shows the impacts on all entities and where these impacts occur) and appropriateness of the information provided. Together, the topics covered in the report must be accurately communicated to enable stakeholders to assess an organization. GSSP suggests that "in determining whether the information in the report is sufficient, the organization considers both the results of stakeholder engagement processes and broad-based societal expectations that are not identified directly through stakeholder engagement processes" (p. 12).

The **topic boundary** is a description of where impacts occur for each material topic, and in which ways the organization is involved with those impacts. Organizations can be involved with impacts through their own activities or as a result of their business relationships with other enterprises. You are expected to report not only on impacts you cause, but also on your contributions to impacts that are directly linked to your activities, products, or services through your business relationships.

Time refers to the evaluation period presented in the report. Businesses are expected to present impacts in the reporting period in which they occur. However, some impacts may produce minimal short-term impacts, which may have a long-term cumulative effect (sometimes irreversible effects) on the economy, environment, and/or society. In making estimates of future impacts (both positive and negative), the reported information is expected to be based on well-reasoned estimates that reflect the likely size and nature of impacts in order to provide a reasonable representation of the organization's sustainability practices. Tests for completeness include:

- The report takes into account impacts the reporting organization causes, contributes to, or is directly linked to through a business relationship, and covers and prioritizes all material information on the basis of the principles of materiality, sustainability context, and stakeholder;
- The information in the report includes all significant impacts in the reporting period, and reasonable estimates of significant future impacts when those impacts are reasonably foreseeable and can become unavoidable or irreversible; and
- The report does not omit relevant information that substantively influences stakeholder assessments and decisions, or that reflects significant economic, environmental, and social impacts.

For more information on global reporting, visit www.globalreporting.org.

Conclusion

This chapter has provided an overview of mass tourism and has introduced many of the sustainability challenges specific to mass tourism. Explicit issues are addressed in more detail relating to 3S tourism, urban tourism, the cruise industry, World Heritage cultural sites, and nature-based tourism. Using Butler's (1980) Tourism Area Life Cycle model, this chapter has explained the process of how tourism development can change small undiscovered places into mass tourism destinations, and the problems associated with economic dependency on tourism in these areas. Although mass tourism is generally considered irreversible, sustainability can play an important role in revitalizing areas in decline. Sustainable mass tourism relies heavily on regulation to control the growth and restrict operational practices in a destination, whereas green tourism relies on voluntary individual operations through reducing resource use that often results in financial saving by a company. It is important to note that as a system, changes in one area of tourism may have unintended side effects, so monitoring and reporting sustainability practices is important. One common reporting mechanism is the Global Sustainability Standards Board's Global Reporting Standards, which increases transparency and offers a globally recognized report standard.

CASE STUDY 6.1 SUSTAINABILITY OF BEIJING OLYMPIC GAMES VENUES

QIJING WANG AND XIAOTAO BAI

Introduction

The 29th summer Olympic Games were held from August 8 to 24, 2008 in Beijing, China. This was the first time that China hosted the summer Olympic Games. As the largest comprehensive sporting event, the 2008 Beijing Olympic Games needed many large venues to accommodate the athletes and spectators, and 37 venues were used in total. There were 11 newly constructed main venues, such as the National Stadium and the National Aquatics Center, 11 renovated venues, and nine temporary venues. Some events (football, sailing and equestrian events) were held outside Beijing.

The slogan of the 2008 Beijing Olympic Games was *One World, One Dream* which embodied the essence of the Olympic spirit and the universal values of unity, friendship, progress, harmony, participation, and dreams. The core values of 2008 Olympic Games included Green Olympics, High-tech Olympics, and the People's Olympics. Within the Green Olympics theme, there were three connotations. The first was that the Olympic Games should be planned and executed within the guidelines of sustainable development to protect environmental resources and ensure ecological balance. The second was to promote the construction of environmentally friendly infrastructure and improve the ecological environment in host cities. The third was to carry out extensive educational activities on environmental awareness (Gu, 2006).

From the perspective of large-scale sporting venues, sustainable development includes two aspects. The first is sustainable development during the construction of green buildings, focusing on energy usage, material conservation, and environmental protection. The second is sustainable development in the functional sense, both during and after the Olympics. During the events, the space must meet the needs of the competitions, exhibitions, social events, etc. However, development must also consider long-term use, with the potential to adapt the facilities to population growth, shifting recreational demand, and varying functions of the venues after the event is complete (Yuan, 2006).

Energy conservation and environment protection

Making the most of renewable energy is the highlight of Beijing's Olympic venues. The 31 newly built or renovated venues, without exception, use solar and geothermal energy, as well as other renewable energy sources, saving about 10 million kilowatt hours of electricity and more than 2,000 tons of coal every year. The energy savings from the 168 building efficiency projects are equivalent to reducing CO_2 emissions by 200,000 tons per year (Sun, 2009).

Besides solar energy technology, the application of new materials in water conservation, energy reduction, and environmental protection has been given full consideration. All venues were designed with natural lighting and ventilation in mind. At the same time, through wall and window insulation, heat recovery, and other measures, the venues' energy saving indicators have exceeded the relevant national standards (Yu, 2007).

Sustainable development in the functional sense

As the largest comprehensive sporting event, the Olympic Games are characterized by large-scale construction requirements, long preparation time, and short holding time (Wang, 2002). Therefore, the utilization of large venues after the event is very important.

Sustainable venues

As the main stadium for the 2008 Olympic Games, the National Stadium (Bird's Nest) hosted the opening and closing ceremonies of the Olympic and Paralympic Games, the track and field competitions, and the football finals. Today, the National Stadium actively holds football, track and field, equestrian, skiing, and other large-scale international sports events through a market-oriented business model, which vigorously promotes concerts, performances, and other cultural events.

Other venues have been successfully transformed after the game. The National Aquatics Center, National Indoor Stadium, Beijing Workers' Stadium, and Cadillac Arena have found alternative uses. Now they can hold cultural and sporting activities and provide venues for corporate meetings, team training events, and physical exercise opportunities for local residents. Wukesong stadium undertook a huge transformation and now it can host all kinds of large- and medium-sized concerts, basketball events, motorcycle races, and conferences.

There are six venues at a local university that were built or extended for the Games. After the Games, except when being used for campus activities, these venues are also open to residents in a market-oriented way. Sometimes these venues host various commercial performances and sports events. The utilization rate of these venues is very high (Zhou, 2011).

Abandoned venues

Although most of the venues achieved the goal of sustainable use, there are still some venues that are not being utilized after the Games. Shunyi Olympic Rowing-Canoeing Park, which held the canoeing, has dried up and turned into a muddy ruin. Chaoyang Park Beach Volleyball Ground is now unused and abandoned. After the Games, Laoshan Bicycle Moto Cross (BMX) Venue was abandoned until January 2019, when it was transformed into the National Team Dry Ski Training Center. The two main reasons for the low utilization rate of some venues is because some venues are far away from the city and have poor public transport, and some sports, like canoeing and beach volleyball, are not popular in Chinese culture.

Reflective questions

1. Do you think it is necessary to design large-scale venues as local landmarks? Is it more sustainable to use them for tourism (market-oriented events) or for local recreational opportunities? Why?

2. How can you manage the contradiction between geographical location and sustainability?

3. Are there other ways to improve the utilization of Olympic venues? What infrastructure do you think should be included in the venues to help achieve sustainable development?

References

Gu, S. (2006). Discussion about the development of the Olympics and green Olympic Games in Beijing. 2006 Annual Conference Review of China Environmental Resource Law Research Institute. April, 2006.

Sun, D. (2009). Research on environmental heritage of Beijing Olympic Games based on sustainable development. Beijing International Studies University.

Wang, Y. (2002). The stadium construction and later usage for hosting country in Olympic Games. *China Sport Science and Technology*, 2002(03), 14–16.

Yu, J. (2007). The green Olympics will leave a rich environmental legacy. *Science and Culture*, 8, 30–31.

Yuan, G. (2006). A research on the sustained development of the functions for the stadiums and gymnasiums for Beijing Olympic Games – reflections on the status quo of the management of large-size public stadiums and gymnasiums in China. *Journal of Capital Institute of Physical Education*, 2006(1), 23–25.

Zhou, C. (2011). The comparative study for the post-games uses of Beijing Olympics venues in college. South China University of Technology.

CASE STUDY 6.2 SUSTAINABLE GREENSPACE MANAGEMENT: THE NATIONAL CHERRY BLOSSOM FESTIVAL

MARGARET J. DANIELS

The National Cherry Blossom Festival (NCBF) is an annual cultural celebration held in Washington, DC, on the National Mall and Memorial Parks (National Mall), an urban parkland that encompasses 146 acres and is home to iconic structures such as the Washington Monument and Lincoln Memorial. The NCBF commemorates the gift of over 3,000 cherry trees from the government of Japan to the United States government, spans four weeks, includes a wide array of traditional and modern artistic programs, and is enjoyed by over 1.5 million visitors (NCBF, 2019). The event coordination is managed by NCBF, Inc., a not-for-profit organization, in conjunction with the National Park Service (NPS), Downtown DC Business Improvement District, Destination DC, DC Events, and a host of member organizations (NCBF, 2019).

Annually, NPS receives over 3,000 applications for public gatherings on the National Mall, resulting in more than 14,000 event-days (NPS, 2019). Of these, the NCBF, first launched in 1935, is the largest and longest event (NCBF, 2019). What makes this festival particularly unique is its natural resource dependency. While the festivities include diverse cultural activities and performances, the primary draw is the blossoming cherry trees themselves, with the five-stage blooming period carefully tracked through the NPS Bloomwatch and widely publicized (NCBF, 2019). Visitors experience the extraordinary cherry trees by walking around the Tidal Basin Loop Trail, a 2.1-mile trek that is home to the majority of the trees, with the Thomas Jefferson Memorial adjacent to the southeast of the loop and Martin Luther King, Jr. Memorial readily accessible from the northwest.

While it is illegal to climb the cherry trees, remove branches or pick blossoms, quantitative data collection coupled with photographic documentation illustrate consistent infractions (see Park et al., 2010). Complicating the issue is that the density of visitors makes enforcement uneven at best and nearly impossible during peak visitation periods. During the post-peak phase, when the blossoms begin to fall, visitors delight in deliberately shaking the trees to create a rainfall of blossoms, with overzealous adults seeking picture-perfect moments more likely to violate greenspace policies than children. Further greenspace degradation occurs on the narrow pathways, where bottleneck areas force pedestrians to walk on the grass and step on the sensitive tree roots, resulting in long-term erosion and necessitating periodic replacement of the famous trees in high impact areas.

Image 6.4 Jefferson Memorial during the National Cherry Blossom Festival, Washington, DC

Source: Margret J. Daniels

The symbolic and cultural importance of the cherry trees situate them within the NPS visitor use management framework known as the *Visitor Experience and Resource Protection* (VERP), as falling within the Limits of Acceptable Change (LAC) processes, first established in 1985 (Cole & Stankey, 1997). LAC processes include the development of standards, assessment of current conditions, and the formulation/implementation of policies that uphold visitor use and carrying capacity standards while striving to reconcile the incompatible goals of usage and protection.

Short-term steps that are being taken by NPS and NCBF to minimize and mitigate the greenspace impacts of the festival include the following:

- Education via *Paddles the Beaver,* the cartoon mascot of the festival. Large cutouts of Paddles carrying a stop sign that states, "STOP: Please don't pick the blossoms or climb the trees" are strategically situated around the tidal basin, while brochures featuring Paddles and more detailed natural resource policies are widely available online and at the festival;

- NPS park rangers and uniformed NCBF staff are courteous, well-informed, and available to educate visitors about policies specific to the cherry trees;

- US park police are highly visible on horseback and have enforcement capabilities; and

- Endow a Cherry Tree campaign, which is an ongoing fundraiser managed by the Trust for the National Mall (2019), is resulting in an endowment for the ongoing preservation and protection of the trees.

Long-term strategies for tidal basin greenspace management before, during, and after the festival are aligned with the umbrella initiatives *National Mall Plan* and *Save the Tidal Basin Campaign* (National Trust for Historic Preservation, 2019; NPS, 2010), which suggest that a minimum of $500 million will be required to address pedestrian and deferred maintenance projects such as:

- Widening of the tidal basin loop trail to minimize soil, grass, and root damage and improve difficult walking terrain;
- Rebuilding the sea wall, which is slowly sinking and subjecting the southern portion of the walking path to daily flooding during high tide, making the path areas impassable and compromising the root systems;
- Design of designated trail shoulder areas for photo opportunities that will not impede the flow of pedestrian traffic;
- Improved interpretation such as permanent plaques placed at the base of each cherry tree that collectively act as consistent reminders of natural resource policies; and
- The addition of a tidal basin visitor center to centralize educational endeavors.

When considering tourism resource vulnerability, urban destination managers tend to focus attention on macro level issues, such as the potential loss of economic impact, diminished air quality, and traffic optimization (e.g., Daniels et al., 2018). While these areas of concentration are critical, they can overpower the resource impacts of individual events. Collectively, however, the thousands of events hosted in most urban areas lead to resource degradation that can be irreversible. In the case of the tidal basin's fragile cherry trees, dilapidated sea wall, and crumbling pathways, the restoration plan has been documented and publicized for well over a decade, yet no meaningful progress has been made. The viability of the NCBF is at risk unless and until a financial commitment to sustainable greenspace management is made.

Reflective questions

1. How would you suggest the National Park Service fund the capital improvement projects needed to protect the urban environment? What are some of the challenges that would result from your funding ideas?
2. Urban park space is an important resource for local communities. Do you feel large-scale events, such as the National Cherry Blossom Festival, are valuable to the community? Why or why not?
3. You have a budget of $1 million to address sustainability issues at the National Mall. How would you prioritize the spending of this money? Which projects would you fund first and why?

References

Cole, D.N. & Stankey, G.H. (1997). Historical development of limits of acceptable change: conceptual clarifications and possible extensions. Proceedings – limits of acceptable change and related planning processes: progress and future directions. Retrieved from www.fs.fed.us/rm/pubs_int/int_gtr371.pdf.

Daniels, M.J., Harmon, L.K., Vese Jr., R., Park, M., & Brayley, R. (2018). Spatial optimization of tour bus transport within urban destinations. *Tourism Management*, 64, 129–141.

National Cherry Blossom Festival (2019). About the festival. Retrieved from https://nationalcherryblossomfestival.org/about-us/.

National Park Service (NPS) (2010). Final National Mall Plan/Environmental impact statement. Retrieved from www.nps.gov/nationalmallplan/FEISdocs.html.

National Park Service (2019). Permits and reservations. Retrieved from www.nps.gov/nama/planyourvisit/permitsandreservations.htm.

National Trust for Historic Preservation (2019). Save the tidal basin. Retrieved from https://savingplaces.org/savethetidalbasin#.XQQ0uxZKheN.

Park, M., Daniels, M.J., Brayley, R.E., & Harmon, L.K. (2010). An analysis of service provision and visitor impacts using participant observation and photographic documentation: The National Cherry Blossom Festival. *Event Management*, 14, 167–182.

Trust for the National Mall (2019). Endow a Cherry Tree Campaign. Retrieved from www.nationalmall.org/cherrytrees.

STUDY QUESTIONS

1. Describe a mass tourism destination that you have visited. How did you know it was mass tourism? What negative impacts from tourism did you observe?
2. Find a tourism destination for each stage of Butler's Tourism Area Life Cycle. What challenges do you imagine they are facing?
3. How is sustainable mass tourism different from green tourism? Can you find an example of each and explain why they are classified as sustainable mass tourism or green tourism?
4. Since tourism is a system, what unintentional impacts could occur when implementing the following sustainability initiatives? Are they positive or negative impacts?
   - Pay people money to bring their recycling directly to a recycling center.
   - Ban food or alcohol at the beach.
   - Host a local craft fair at your hotel.
   - Buy used linens from a charity shop.
   - Encourage tourists to use public transportation.
   - Source food from a local farm.
   - Hire local workers.
5. Find one negative impact caused by tourism in your community. Using the Global Reporting Standards' report content, provide a report that assesses one solution that you think could be effective. Remember to report both the positive and negative results of your decision as all elements in the tourism system are interrelated.

DEFINITIONS

3S destinations   sun, sea, and sand destinations

Commodification   the transformation of goods, services, ideas, and people into commodities, or objects of trade

Cultural heritage   the legacy of physical artefacts and intangible attributes of a group or society that are inherited from past generations, maintained in the present, and bestowed for the benefit of future generations

Economic dependency   an unending situation in which economies and economic agents rely on one aspect or thing in order to be successful

Gateway community   a community neighbouring a national park or nature area

Green economy   an economy that results in improved human well-being and social equity, while significantly reducing environmental risks and ecological scarcities

Greening   the act of becoming more aware and attempting to mitigate the environmental consequences of economic activities

Mass tourism   the aggressive development of standardized travel packages that result in tens of thousands of visitors going to the same destination

Materiality   determines which topics, or significant impacts, are relevant and important

Sustainable mass tourism   a type of mass tourism which promotes economic, environmental, and socio-cultural enhancements within a destination

System   an interdependent series of elements that interact in order to achieve some end result

Topic boundary   a description of where impacts occur for each material topic, and in which ways the organization is involved with those impacts

Chapter **7**

Alternative tourism

Overview

This chapter describes alternative tourism as a form of community-based tourism. It provides a list of issues that should be considered when developing alternative, also known as niche, tourism. Using ecotourism, cultural tourism, food tourism, and rural tourism as examples, this chapter highlights some concerns and challenges facing alternative tourism development. Specific management considerations are discussed, and tools to engage communities in alternative tourism development decision-making are provided.

CHAPTER OBJECTIVES

At the completion of the chapter, students will be able to:

- Differentiate alternative tourism from mass tourism;
- Explain the development considerations for alternative tourism;
- Discuss community-based participation in the context of alternative tourism;
- Define environmentalism, preservation, and conservation in relation to tourism;
- Describe ecotourism and cultural tourism; and
- Explain the steps of community engagement.

Introduction

Mass tourism is firmly grounded in the economic growth paradigm, where quantity is privileged over quality. In other words, an economy must be growing by selling more units or acquiring more visitors in order to be considered successful. This philosophy promotes the western value of **capitalism**, an economic and political system in which a country's trade and industry are controlled by private owners for profit, rather than by the state (Rosser, Rosser, & Barkley,

2003). While capitalism is discussed in more detail in Chapter 2, suffice it to say that capitalism has many negative consequences, since it promotes mass production and consumption as a means of maximizing profit. Because all resources can be used for profit, access to capital is generally concentrated within the wealthy class (known as the capital class) which isolates the poor and less privileged. Within the sustainable development paradigm, community-based development, rather than profit, is emphasized, and equitable distribution of resources is prioritized.

Alternative development grew in response to mainstream economic growth policies to rebalance traditional top-down, western-centric, profit-oriented development (Sharpley, 2009). **Alternative development** is defined as development that emanates from, and is guided by, the needs of individual societies (Brohman, 1996). Alternative development recognizes that each community has varying

Image 7.1 African-American Monument, Savannah, Georgia

Source: Susan L. Slocum

desires in relation to development, and that economic decisions should be grounded in the unique attributes of each area. It implies that local populations better understand the problems they face and the potential solutions that can mitigate negative impacts. It also works on the premise that local residents should be able to access tourism amenities because "whenever the amenities for tourists are much more advanced than those of the local residents, this can lead to resentment towards tourists" (Boxill, 2004, p. 270).

Alternative tourism is a direct response to unsustainable mass tourism. **Alternative tourism** is tourism that is appropriate for the local environment, social and cultural values, and that optimizes local decision-making, enhances the local economy, and promotes meaningful encounters between tourists and the local community (Sharpley, 2009). It uses the strong form of sustainability discussed in Chapter 1 and attempts to reduce the negative consequences of tourism by developing appropriate types and levels of tourism based on the resources, needs, and cultures of a region. Activities that fall within this relatively new type of tourism include walking tours, bird safaris, guided nature walks, horse riding, barge and canal tours, bicycle tours, home and farm stays, and independent travel (Eadington & Smith, 1992).

Understanding alternative tourism

Alternative tourism is generally described as small-scale and locally owned. It requires a shift for regional tourism development agencies to focus on developing a community enhancement strategy. While profit for local businesses is important, it should not occur at the expense of

Figure 7.1 Alternative tourism development considerations

culture, the environment, or community cohesion. Guyette (2013) suggests that small-scale development involves less risk because it involves lower investment (in the form of financial capital) and relies on cultural or environmental capital, such as local knowledge of ecosystems and using traditional forms of production and consumption. She writes, "The difference (is) viewing culture as an attraction versus maintaining a way of life. Culture is a way of life in the viewpoint of traditional communities, not something to be used for profit" (p. 52). Therefore, creating a common vision and targeting specific types of visitors, as well as determining the appropriate number of tourists, can support a quality experience, preserve the way of life for hosts, and capture adequate profits at the local level. To be successful, alternative tourism should address the many issues shown in Figure 7.1.

Alternative tourism should include a variety of stakeholders and provide avenues for the development of human capital (education and jobs), access to financial capital (loans), information and access to new technologies, improvements in establishing a competitive product (tourism experience), and a strategy for interaction between travelers and hosts (Lane, 2009). Because alternative tourism promotes the local ownership of tourism businesses, it is important to recognize that some local residents are uneducated about the needs of tourists or may lack general business skills. Therefore, alternative tourism must promote capacity building and capacity development for the communities that engage in new forms of tourism. **Capacity building** is defined as a process that supports only the initial stages of building or creating capacities and assumes that there are no existing capacities at the start. In turn, alternative tourism must encourage **capacity development**, or the process through which individuals, organizations, and societies obtain, strengthen, and maintain their capabilities to set and achieve their own development objectives over time (United Nations Development Programme, 2009). Alternative tourism should enhance the identity, self-esteem, and self-confidence of local residents while simultaneously providing adequate incomes (Boxill, 2004).

Alternative tourism should also increase quality of life for local residents. Providing a safe and secure community and using the rule of law to ensure that local residents (as well as tourists) are treated fairly is vital to the support of alternative tourism strategies. Moreover, ensuring adequate wages and making sure tourists pay a fair price for locally produced goods, services, and experiences should be included in the planning. **Fair pricing** means that the revenue earned from a product or service is equitably shared between the producer, the supply chain, and the end seller. Alternative tourism supports positive host-visitor interactions, so ensuring that residents maintain access to the tourism resources, whether they be natural areas, historical sites, or religious experiences, must be safeguarded.

Alternative tourism also focuses on providing a quality experience for the visitor. Alternative tourists are covered in more detail in Chapter 5, but research suggests that these travelers are specifically looking for immersive experiences that are significantly different from their lifestyles at home and from those usually available through mass tourism. Often called explorers, **alternative tourists** generally enjoy meeting new people, expect to learn something new when they travel, appreciate a wide range of activities, seek out challenges, are concerned with social issues, and embrace change (Sohn & Yuan, 2013). Therefore, alternative tourism providers must craft the tourist experience to ensure an original, educational, and authentic experience.

Community-based tourism

Community-based tourism (CBT) is an effective approach used to develop alternative tourism. The Caribbean Tourism Organization (CTO, n.d.) lists a number of definitions of community-based tourism as shown in Table 7.1. In short, **community-based tourism** is a collaborative approach to tourism in which community members exercise control through active participation in the appraisal, development, management, and/or ownership of enterprises. They ensure that activities deliver net socioeconomic benefits to community members, conserve natural and cultural resources, and add value to the experiences of local and foreign visitors. Community members adopt this approach towards both alternative tourism activities in a community, and the supply of goods and services to the tourism industry.

Salazar (2012) highlights the importance of CBT in the context of sustainability, "CBT presents a way to provide an equitable flow of benefits to all stakeholders affected by tourism through consensus-based decision-making and local control of development" (p. 10). He also states that "[as] a particular alternative form of tourism, CBT suggests a symbolic or mutual relationship where the tourist is not given central priority, but becomes an equal part of the [tourism] system" (p. 10). He proposes fours dimensions of CBT that are significant when it comes to sustainability. These are:

- CBT needs to be economically viable where the revenue exceeds costs;
- CBT must be ecologically sustainable such that the value of the environment does not decrease;
- The distribution of costs and benefits must be equitable among all participating stakeholders; and
- There needs to be a transparent leadership organization established that is recognized by all stakeholders, whose role is to represent the interests of the community.

Table 7.1 Definitions of community-based tourism

Source	Document/ agency	Definition
SNV (n.d.)	Background paper on sustainable tourism	Community-based tourism consists of tourism initiatives which are owned by (one or more) communities, or as joint venture partnerships between communities and the private sector. Furthermore, it is based on four principles, being: • Economically viable; • Ecologically sustainable; • Institutionally consolidated; and • With equitable distribution of costs and benefits over participants
Dilys Roe (n.d.)	International Institute for Environment and Development (IIED)	Community-based tourism initiatives aim to increase local people's involvement in tourism. They are mainly small-scale (campsites, guesthouses, craft markets, local excursions) although can include partnerships with the private sector
World Wildlife Fund (2001)	n/a	Community-based ecotourism is where the local community has substantial control over, and involvement in, its development and management, and a major proportion of the benefits remain within the community
Mountain Institute (2000)	n/a	Community-based tourism is a visitor–host interaction that has meaningful participation by both, and generates economic and conservation benefits for local communities and environments
Mann (2001)		Community-based tourism is tourism that consults, involves, and benefits a local community, especially in the context of rural villages in developing countries and indigenous peoples
REST (2006)	n/a	Community-based tourism is tourism that takes environmental, social, and cultural sustainability into account. It is managed and owned by the community, for the community, with the purpose of enabling visitors to increase their awareness and learn about the community and local ways of life
APEIS-RISPO (2006)	n/a	Community-based tourism is defined by its objectives as to gain local economic development, reach some forms of participation, provide socially and environmentally responsible experiences for visitors, and bring a positive effect on the conservation of natural and/or cultural resources in national parks

Table 7.1 continued

Source	Document/ agency	Definition
Jamaica Community Tourism Manual (2004)	Quoted in Pantin, D. and Francis, J. (2005)	Community tourism is both an integrated approach and collaborative tool for the socioeconomic empowerment of communities through the assessment, development, and marketing of natural and cultural community resources, which seek to add value to the experiences of local and foreign visitors and simultaneously improve the quality of life of communities
CTO (n.d.)	Manual of the Caribbean Regional Sustainable Tourism Development Programme	A collaborative approach to tourism in which community members exercise control through active participation in appraisal, development, management and/or ownership (whole or in part) of enterprises that delivers net socioeconomic benefits to community members, conserves natural and cultural resources and adds value to the experiences of local and foreign visitors. This encompasses both tourism activities in a community and goods and services supplied to the tourism industry by one or more community members

Source: Adapted from Caribbean Tourism Organization (n.d., p. 7)

Types of alternative tourism

Alternative tourism is often called **niche tourism**, where specific tourism products are tailored to meet the needs of a particular audience or market segment, and locations with specific niche products are able to establish and position themselves as niche tourism destinations (Ali-Knight, 2011). Other words that are used to describe alternative tourism include responsible, green, eco, soft, or slow tourism. Different types of alternative tourism are provided in Table 7.2.

While there are many commonalities within alternative tourism, the types of alternative tourism established will depend on the specific resources available, and the cultural and environmental amenities that a destination offers. Using community-based tourism strategies, a synergy between nature, culture, and the needs of the visitor can be addressed in a holistic way to assess and/or establish tourism development. While all alternative tourism destinations possess the risk of developing into mass tourism (per Butler's Tourism Area Life Cycle predictions outlined in Table 6.1), allowing for community decision-making can ensure that growth levels stay within a community's acceptable levels of change. The most common types of alternative tourism include ecotourism and cultural tourism.

Ecotourism

Before explaining ecotourism, it is important to distinguish between the concepts of environmentalism, preservation, and conservation as they relate to human uses of the environment. **Environmentalism** is a social movement that is based on political and ethical views of the

Table 7.2 Types of alternative tourism

Niche tourism	Definition
Adventure tourism	Exploration or travel with a certain degree of risk, and which may require special skills and physical exertion
Agritourism	Any agriculturally based operation or activity that brings visitors to a working farm or ranch
Culinary tourism or food tourism	The exploration of food as the purpose of tourism
Cultural tourism	A traveler's engagement with a country or region's culture, specifically the lifestyle of the people in those geographical areas, the history of those people, their art, architecture, religion(s), and other elements that helped shape their way of life
Dark tourism	Travel to places historically associated with death and tragedy
Disaster tourism	Travel to a disaster area for pleasure, usually out of curiosity
Ecotourism	Low impact nature-based tourism which contributes to the maintenance of species and habitats either directly through a contribution to conservation and/or indirectly by providing revenue to the local community sufficient for local people to value, and therefore protect, their wildlife heritage area as a source of income
Educational tourism	Visiting another country to learn about the culture, study tours, or to work and apply skills learned inside the classroom in a different environment
Film tourism	The growing interest in and demand for locations which have become popular due to their appearance in films and television series
Food tourism	The desire to experience a particular type of food or the produce of a specific region while traveling
Medical tourism	Traveling to a foreign country to obtain medical treatment
Rural tourism	A country experience, which encompasses a wide range of attractions and activities that take place in agricultural or non-urban areas
Scientific tourism	Travel by researchers, academics and higher degree students, in order to conduct research
Slum tourism or poverty tourism	Cases in which financially privileged tourists visit impoverished communities for the purpose of witnessing poverty firsthand
Soft tourism	A type of adventure tourism that requires little or no experience and is low risk
Voluntourism or volunteer tourism	Doing volunteer work while also participating in tourism as a way of 'doing good' or 'giving back' to a community

environment. Most environmentalists are people who are dedicated to protecting the environment and the resources it provides to ensure life for all species. Although environmental scientists and environmentalists may have a similar passion for the world we live in, they differ in the way they approach and address their passion. In particular, environmentalists generally support the preservation perspective and often believe that humans should be barred from some sections of the environment in order to ensure it remains as pristine as possible. Environmental scientists generally try to find ways that allow for human use, while still protecting the natural resource as habitat for other species to thrive.

The question that lies at the heart of the debate is whether humans are considered a part of the natural environment (are people animals?). Many religions believe that people were given dominion over nature's plants and animals to serve their needs, such as Adam and Eve in the Garden of Eden. **Anthropocentrism** explicitly states that humans are the sole bearers of intrinsic environmental value and that all other living things are here to sustain humanity's existence (Burchett, 2014). **Ecocentrism** extends the concept of inherent worth to all living things, regardless of their usefulness to humans.

These paradigms lead to two differing management philosophies (Lowe, 1989). **Preservation**, rooted in ecocentrism, is the principle that lands and their natural resources should not be consumed by humans and should instead be maintained in their pristine form. **Conservation**, more aligned with anthropocentrism, is the principle that the environment and its resources should be used by humans and managed in a responsible manner. While natural areas may have been initially set aside under the premise of preservation, using natural areas for tourism is a conservation practice. In other words, allowing humans to use the environment for recreational and educational purposes, and generating money to fund protective measures within these natural areas, is saying that humans have the right to access and use the environment even if negative impacts result. One of the primary goals of conservation is to minimize these impacts through monitoring and best practice. There may be instances where both paradigms collide, or where one set of values is more appropriate for a given area, at a given time.

Nature-based tourism includes any tourism activities that involve the use of natural areas, such as 3S tourism (sea, sand, and sun), visits to national parks, or cruise ship tourism.

Image 7.2 Canoeing the River Spey, Scotland
Source: Susan L. Slocum

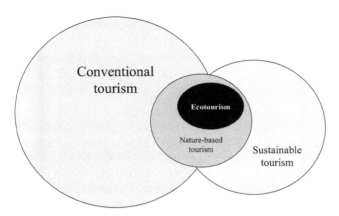

Figure 7.2 Ecotourism as a form of nature-based tourism

Ecotourism is a more sustainable subset of nature-based tourism (see Figure 7.2). While the term 'ecotourism' is relatively new, the concept of environmentally responsible travel to natural areas has been practiced and studied since the mid-1960s (Fennel, 2015). **Ecotourism** is defined as low impact nature-based tourism which contributes to the maintenance of species and habitats either directly through a contribution to conservation and/or indirectly by providing enough revenue to the local community for local people to value, and therefore protect, their wildlife heritage area as a source of income (Goodwin, 1995, p. 288).

By encouraging development that is appropriate to the ecosystem, ecotourism is grounded in the concept of sustainable use, often measured by carrying capacity. **Carrying capacity** considers the amount of use any given land or environment can endure over time without degrading its suitability for that use (Fennel, 2015, p. 175). Carrying capacity is extremely hard to measure because it involves an understanding of the ecosystem itself, as well as the types of uses being considered and the impacts of these uses. For example, the number of canoers on a river may have a different impact than horseback riders on a trail next to a river. Building zip lines or chair lifts require the removal of trees in the short term, but reduces the potential for hikers to tread on, and destroy, native grasses over the long term. Environmental degradation can occur when there are constant levels of visitation over a long period or when there is a high volume of visitors for a short period in a concentrated area. Moreover, carrying capacity takes into consideration the long-term use of a resource for tourism and recreation, therefore involves visitor satisfaction with regard to crowding (Hammitt & Cole, 1987). **Crowding** can occur when visitors perceive that too many people are in a given area, spoiling the atmosphere, ambiance, or user experience. Each visitor may have a different perception of what constitutes crowding.

In tourism, it is important to find a balance between human use and the protection of the resource. From the conservation perspective, managers must determine if environmental degradation threatens future supplies of the natural resources to ensure that the landscape can sufficiently support the economic needs of future generations. If natural resources are overused, resource shortages could become so severe as to threaten future standards of living. Wallace and Pierce (1996) identified six criteria that must be followed if tourism is to be considered a form of ecotourism aimed at mitigating natural resource degradation:

- Minimal impacts to the environment and to local people;
- Awareness and understanding of an area's natural and cultural systems and the involvement of visitors in issues affecting those systems;
- The conservation and management of legally protected and other natural areas;
- Early and long-term participation of local people in the decision-making process that determines the kind and amount of tourism that should occur;

- Directing economic and other benefits to local people that complement rather than overwhelm or replace traditional practices (farming, fishing, social systems etc.); and
- The provision of special opportunities for local people and nature tourism employees to utilize and visit natural areas.

Cultural tourism

Cultural tourism is a traveler's engagement with a country or region's culture, specifically the lifestyle of the people in those geographical areas, the history of those people, their art, architecture, religion(s), and other elements that help shape their way of life. In addition, it may be characterized by how a place uses its cultural resources (cultural capital) to attract visitors (Aidoo, 2010). Chapter 6 explained cultural heritage tourism as a form of mass tourism, however, cultural tourism can also fit within alternative tourism if it meets the criteria of small-scale and local. Cultural tourism as a form of alternative tourism should also highlight elements of intangible heritage, such as the practices and representations of artifacts, objects, and cultural spaces.

Cultural tourism provides valuable opportunities to promote and showcase local traditions or historical narratives. McKercher, Ho, and Cros (2004) suggest ways to transform a country's or region's cultural heritage resources into its tourism product. One way is mythologizing a cultural resource by transforming the assets from the mundane to the extraordinary and in the

Image 7.3 Avaldsnes Viking Farm, Norway
Source: Susan L. Slocum

process, converting a physical place or a cultural practice into a place of spiritual or secular significance. For example, the city of New Orleans has a unique culture emanating from the African slaves forced to appropriate the practice of Catholicism by the French colonial authorities. Voodoo is now a major draw for tourists to that area. Another transformative process is story telling based on either historical facts or a piece of fiction. A third way is to make the culture triumphant or extraordinary by setting it apart from common places (such as is common with battlefield sites). Making cultural heritage into a spectacle, special event, or transforming fantasy into reality, even if the latter is experienced in a fleeting and vicarious manner, is another way to enhance the tourism product. Lastly, making the experience fun, lighthearted, and entertaining is important for engaging the visitor.

One form of cultural tourism is food tourism. **Food tourism** is defined as "the desire to experience a particular type of food or the produce of a specific region while traveling" (Hall & Sharples, 2008, p. 10) and includes agritourism, gastronomy tourism, or culinary tourism. The growth in food tourism can be attributed to the globalization of food distribution and the pressure to standardize food production, which has eroded the culinary traditions of regions through the invasion of western food values (Slocum & Everett, 2010). Ilbery and Kneafsey (1998) suggest that food and drink tourism can reassert cultural distinctiveness by providing ways for tourists to 'taste' local culture. Locals can showcase their traditional food, which is derived from historic landscapes, traditional farming heritage, and cultural celebrations (Slocum & Curtis, 2017). Moreover, sourcing local food can increase the economic impact of tourism, reducing economic leakages, and supporting farmers or women in small businesses. There is ample evidence that tourists will travel specifically to try local food, and vacations around food production and culinary specialties are on the rise (Slocum & Curtis, 2017).

Another cultural tourism opportunity is rural tourism, which is closely related to food tourism. **Rural tourism** can be defined as a country experience, which encompasses a wide range of attractions and activities that take place in agricultural or non-urban areas (Irshad, 2010). It includes farm-based holidays, nature holidays, ecotourism, adventure holidays (walking, biking, horse riding), sport and health tourism, hunting and angling, educational travel, arts and heritage tourism, cattle rides, and ethnic tourism. Rural areas in particular face many hardships related to a lack of economic development options outside of agriculture, resulting in rural-to-urban migration, aging populations, and a declining tax base (Albrecht, 2014). Finding employment opportunities that pay a good wage and are interesting to younger generations can help retain young talent and provide new avenues of tax revenue to support basic necessities, such as decent schools, roads, and health care options. Rural areas can offer a much-needed break to travelers from urban areas who seek a slower pace of life, rejuvenation, and idyllic landscapes. Irshad (2010) reminds us that "as a general rule, rural communities are challenged to take full advantage of the tourism industry due to lack of sufficient infrastructure to support year-round visitors" (p. 2).

One potential side effect of cultural tourism is the commodification of culture. **Commodification** is the transformation of goods, services, ideas, and peoples into commodities, or objects of trade. Commodification can lead to changing cultural representations in order to meet consumer expectations and can result in an inauthentic experience for visitors. In turn, traditional culture is blended with the tourist representation, which can be passed down to future generations. In sustainability, the goal is to allow communities to interpret and represent their culture in ways that ring true to them while still finding avenues to transform the culture into cultural capital that can generate wealth for individuals and communities (Shepherd, 2002). Again, ensuring that the community is involved in the development of cultural products has shown to curb commodification.

Empowering community

Empowerment is the process of becoming stronger and more confident, especially in controlling one's life and claiming one's rights. Timothy (2011), in describing the planning model for community-based tourism, asserts that in order for tourism to be sustainable, it is vital to remember the importance of the residents (community) as "part of the cultural product," as well as respecting "their concerns, desires, and interests" (p. 264). He suggests that there are two main areas where community-based participation and empowerment in cultural tourism is important: having agency in decision-making; and participating in the socioeconomic benefits of tourism. With regard to having agency in the decision-making, Timothy (2011) describes four degrees of empowerment, as shown in Table 7.3.

Managing alternative tourism involves overcoming many challenges since stakeholders are more actively engaged in the details of the tourism product development than would occur in mass tourism. One key aspect to the success of alternative tourism from a business perspective is the level of social capital at a destination and the willingness of the local community to engage in the development process. Communities are not homogeneous, meaning that every person in a community may have a different idea on how to develop tourism (Prince & Ioannides, 2017). Therefore, community and business leaders may be tasked with finding consensus between everyone involved in the decision-making process.

Sustainable tourism requires a future-oriented perspective and many stakeholders may have pressing needs, or may want to maximize their earning potential rather than thinking along the lines of future generations. Businesses, in general, possess a short-term perspective, especially when there are outside investors seeking a quick return on their investment (Lane, 2009). Moreover, existing businesses may use unsustainable practices because they lack knowledge about sustainability or feel that their customers' expectations require a certain level of pampering and consumerism. Old habits die hard, and often people are reluctant to change the way they operate (Weaver, 2009).

A key component of ensuring the socioeconomic benefits of CBT, particularly when it comes to the representation of cultural tourism and ecotourism, is the education of and

Table 7.3 Degrees of empowerment in community-based cultural tourism

Degree of empowerment	Description
Imposed development	Ideas and plans from outside the community imposed without public input
Token involvement	Local community feedback sought on externally determined initiatives mainly to check off that requirement
Meaningful participation	Significant input is sought from the local community, as well as other stakeholders, but the ownership still remains external to the community
True empowerment	The local community initiates the goals, programs, and projects, even though external assistance may still be sought

Source: Adapted from Timothy (2011)

awareness-building within the local community. Done right, this will enable the community to understand the significance of the development process, and the roles they must play in maintaining the natural and cultural resources and their interpretation. Encouraging innovation and providing the tools for running a successful business are important aspects of the curriculum. Support for grant writing can also be incorporated as a means for ensuring that development funds are made available to community members, and that they are used wisely. Lastly, sharing the tools to prevent commodification of culture and establishing open communication channels to monitor changes in the social structures will empower those starting out in alternative tourism.

Marketing a destination increases visitation, which can change the nature of the tourism product over time and impact the destination's life cycle (Butler, 1980). As Prince and Ioannides (2017) write, "The goals of households, businesses, and organizations that strive to subsist from alternative tourism often become contradictory since, on the one hand, they seek to pursue their idealistic mission while, on the other hand, they have to recognize the daily realities that are shaped by the global capitalist system" (p. 349). Therefore, it is important to develop a tourism brand based on sustainability and social responsibility as an avenue for encouraging responsible visitor behaviors in a way that generates revenue (discussed in more detail in Chapter 12).

SUSTAINABILITY TOOL: COMMUNITY ENGAGEMENT

Tourism development has a varied history of resulting in both positive and negative impacts to destinations and host communities. In order to realize the tourism industry's potential for sustainable development, governments, the private sector, and local community members alike must work together as equal partners to envision and maintain the economic benefits to the local destination, while ensuring negative impacts to the environment and cultural heritage are avoided (or minimized). Developing a tourism product requires a strategic balance between the global tourism entities, such as tour operators and corporate hoteliers, and the local community and its assets.

Building a community that supports alternative tourism and educating potential businesses about the advantages of maintaining small, locally-run businesses, and appropriate levels of tourism, is important in creating consensus about tourism development options. One way to ensure that alternative tourism remains sustainable is to encourage honest debate about the costs and benefits of growing the tourism industry (Prince & Ioannides, 2017). Alternative tourism development should include knowledge transmission regarding conflict resolution (mediating different perspectives), how the tourism product is represented and marketed (ecotourism, cultural tourism), and ways to find value in tourism–host interactions outside of the economic incentives. Conversation surrounding acceptable levels of social and environmental change should also be included.

As a practitioner of alternative tourism development, you may find yourself playing a role in these conversations, or you may find yourself in a leadership position uniting the community around the notion of alternative tourism. Either way, developing social capital and ensuring a community-based approach to tourism provides you with an opportunity to interact with stakeholders, suppliers, and partners who embrace similar sustainability values. Collectively, you can help ensure that the voices of everyone involved are heard in an inclusive and respected way. Table 7.4 provides a series of inclusive strategies for alternative tourism.

Table 7.4 Alternative tourism development strategies

Goal	Strategy
Keep the size of development appropriate to the area	Mitigate growth through effectively targeting sustainably-minded tourists and ensure that tourism revenue remains in the economy to reduce excessive growth strategies
Locals should have the opportunity to take part in decision-making, be employed, trained, and empowered, and become owners of tourism products	Build social capital and create avenues for constructive dialog that is inclusive. Reduce conflict by establishing a safe and effective conflict resolution process
Local goods and services should be procured	Ensure local businesses understand the needs of tourists and that they produce quality, yet culturally appropriate supply options
Local entrepreneurship and small business development should be promoted	Avoid duplication or copycat businesses and find opportunities where tourists' needs are not being met. Encourage entrepreneurship in these areas and provide basic training for new businesses
Local cultures should be respected and protected	Using community-based development strategies, find a consensus on how culture should be represented and establish a guideline for acceptable levels of change. Remember that there may be numerous cultures represented in any single community
Natural, cultural, and heritage resources should be preserved	Invest in the maintenance and preservation of cultural and heritage resources to ensure that tourism visitation does not degrade the resource. Ensure local access to heritage resources and, if appropriate, set aside times for local visitation that are not interrupted by tourism visitation (specifically with religious sites)
Developments should be sensitive to the environment	It is important to balance the needs of the community with the needs of tourists and not to privilege tourism use of natural resources. Establish a system to monitor environmental changes
Interactions between tourists and locals should be encouraged	Ensure that tourist–host interactions are not only beneficial for the tourists, but that local residents gain insight and reap tangible rewards above and beyond just profitable encounters

The 'to dos' of community engagement

The United Nations Educational, Scientific, and Cultural Organisation (UNESCO) (2015) provides some basic guidelines when engaging destination stakeholders. They write (p. 4),

> *Remember that dialogue educates all parties. People start to learn each other's languages and terminologies, and over time, understanding grows. Stakeholders will have a greater sense of the limits of growth, the responsibilities that fall upon everyone in the destination to protect its natural or cultural heritage, and also how to deliver benefits sustainably to local people. Successful, sustainable initiatives have been developed with active, local buy-in and support – local people are the heart of sustainable tourism.*

Step 1: *Talk and listen to the host community and businesses*. Community engagement requires building relationships between businesses, governments, non-governmental organizations, and the local community. Everyone must feel that their concerns are relevant and a priority, and that they will be taken seriously. Make sure everyone understands both the positive and negative impacts of tourism so they can learn throughout the process of relationship-building. They must approach tourism with their eyes wide open.

Step 2: *Identify and communicate sustainable, economic local opportunities*. Think strategically about how local people and businesses can benefit from tourism and the use of their natural and cultural resources. Appropriate action does not happen automatically; it requires conscious efforts and investment to identify new opportunities, including transportation, accommodation, food and drink, retail, leisure, or guiding and interpretation opportunities. Remember that the community is the key attraction to your destination and build the visitor experience around experiencing and respecting the knowledge, values, stories, culture, and activities of the host community. UNESCO also reminds us to encourage, celebrate, and reward individuals and businesses that act responsibly, giving them a competitive advantage and ensuring businesses buy into sustainable practices.

Step 3: *Empower the host community by telling their story in the site*. Incorporating local stories into the tourism narrative helps establish respect for local people and communicates it to tourists in a way that locals will value. UNESCO states, "research has shown that tourists spend less than 10% of their time in museums or galleries – the rest of the time is spent in airports, railway stations, taxis, hotels, restaurants, bars, shops, on the street, by the pool, or on the beach" (p. 5). Storytelling provides context to what the visitor is seeing and takes an artifact out of history to show its modern relevance. Help people become ambassadors by crafting their own story. Moreover, tour guiding should be considered a "professional activity of the highest standard" and should be managed just like any other resource.

Step 4: *Show long-term commitment*. The last hurdle to overcome is securing community development funds and establishing guidelines for businesses. Development funds, usually from local or international nongovernmental organizations, signal long-term commitment to the community and can reduce skepticism. These funds should be invested in community assets that support both tourism and local needs and should be designed to empower the local community. It is important to balance long-term strategic planning with things that can be accomplished immediately as a means to establish integrity in the development process. UNESCO (2015) claims that "these quick wins are a statement of intent and credibility that will sustain the initial enthusiasm of stakeholders" (p. 5). Lastly, develop clear rules and regulations for what is expected of the host community and businesses. Often your business partners simply want to know what they can and cannot do.

Conclusion

This chapter has explained alterative tourism, a form of small-scale tourism that is appropriate to specific locations and the resources available. Distinctly different from mass tourism, one of the primary goals of alternative tourism is to ensure community involvement as a means to avoid the negative impacts of large-scale tourism development. Alternative tourism supports capacity building and capacity development, ensures that the region provides quality tourism products that preserve the way of life for hosts, and captures adequate profits at the local level. A variety of alternative, or niche, experiences are covered, including ecotourism and cultural tourism. Community-based tourism provides avenues to support active participation in the appraisal, development, management, and/or ownership of tourism resources. Managing alternative tourism can be challenging, but the development of social capital, finding avenues to mitigate conflict, and reaching a consensus on development priorities can help to ensure alternative tourism avoids the pitfalls of Butler's Tourism Area Life Cycle patterns.

CASE STUDY 7.1 FARMSTEAD VERES: FAMILY VACATIONS IN THE BELARUSIAN VILLAGE

ALESIA SMIAKHOVICH

In the 1990s, the country of Belarus became independent from the former Soviet Union. As a new country, many people struggled to adapt to a difficult economic situation where market-based knowledge replaced the government decision-making of the communist regime. However, a welcoming environment encouraged and supported the start-up of new entrepreneurial businesses in rural areas. Small business development received support from the State, including a number of tax incentives and small business loans.

The area where Farmstead Veres spreads out today was just abandoned land at the fall of the Soviet Union. In 1991, Mikhail Makey – a local agriculturist – and his wife purchased the land to become farmers and start a new life. From the very beginning, the family could discern the opportunity of abundant nature, traditional culture, and a welcoming society in the area, and so they settled into the Zelva region to create an opportunity for authentic leisure experiences. Owning only a field-engine and a car, they began to scatter the fields with seeds to establish a garden. Step by step, what started as a family farm turned into one of the most successful country estates in modern Belarus.

Veres is the first country estate in Belarus that is also a farmstead. As a form of agricultural tourism, it is an example of how agricultural entrepreneurship and rural tourism, modern standards of comfortableness, and old local traditions are seamlessly united within the principles of sustainability.

By the time I had a chance to stay at Veres, I had already been to several Belarusian and European rural houses and knew that the heart and soul of every house is, in many respects, the host. They are the people who construct the stone buildings, forage for decorations, clear the fields, plant the gardens, and welcome the guests. Mikhail and Irina Makey put out the welcome mat and invited us to a dinner of traditional Belarusian Draniki (potato pancakes filled with meat). All the recipes served at Veres belong to either the locals or to the Makey's family culinary traditions. Baked meat (the winner of the local culinary contest), meat gravy with home-made sausage, fluffy pancakes (Machanka), homebrew, and infusions are the signature dishes. In the kitchen, there are several hired helpers who cook and serve the guests. The family manages a large farm with geese, turkeys, chickens, pearl hens, pigs, and a greenhouse. Most of the homegrown products are used in the kitchen, the rest is sold to local cafés, restaurants, and to several Russian export purchasers.

The country estate offers a variety of options for tourists. The estate includes a three-story farmer's house that can accommodate 14 people and includes a traditional banya (Russian sauna), a Russian stove, and three types of family korchma, which provide seating for 30–40 people to share daily meals or celebrate festive occasions. Hunter's Hall seats 120 people for seminars and feasts and includes an exhibition of an ancient flour-mill. Besides the main apartments, the family also runs its own café by the side of the road leading to the estate and a grocery store in the neighboring village.

Surrounding the country estate, there are numerous small and big art features that appeal to the eye: a huge wooden ship in the backyard, a tiny elf in a flower bush, beaten gates, and a straw hat. These are the work of a local metalsmith, carpenter, and welder who are permanently employed at the estate.

Veres is not just an ordinary country estate: it has much more to offer. Every summer, Belarusian children come here to take part in a farmer's school, where they live as country people do. In the morning, they collect chicken eggs and milk the cows to prepare

Image 7.4 Farmstead Veres, Belarus

Source: Alesia Smiakhovich

the breakfast using fresh farm products. During the day, they learn to harvest hay, as well as weeding and watering the garden. After fruitful work, they relax in a beautiful arboretum park around the farm with more than 250 species of trees and shrubs. They can take a walk by the stream or catch fish in the lake. In the near future, the family plans to launch an international farmer's school for English-, Polish-, and Czech-speaking guests.

During the year, the Makeys organize workshops for children in decoupage, basket weaving, and flower arranging. An artisan comes from the local village to teach visitors how to work with black earth. Both the carpenter and the welder also hold workshops that emphasize local traditions.

One part of the formula for success is active engagement in the community. It has become a tradition to organize organic parties in Veres to promote the principle of respect for the national culture, the appreciation of nature, and sustainable consumption. This is evidenced in the Easter Island Festival, where young Belarusian designers work with organic materials to create a traditional straw mythological creature that sits on a hill over the small river that runs through the country estate. A visit to Veres also provides an opportunity for younger and elder generations to gather at festivals, share stories, and learn from each other.

Reflective questions

1. What are some of the strengths and weaknesses with the Makeys' business model? How can they overcome some of their weaknesses?

2. What about Veres would appeal to international tourists? What aspects may deter international visitors?

3. How can Veres enhance what they already have to offer? What additional partnerships would be needed to offer new products and services?

CASE STUDY 7.2 ANTARCTIC CRUISE TOURISM: ALTERNATIVE OR MASS TOURISM?

JOHN READ

Antarctica is one of those places that spurs the imagination and holds great allure for individuals that want to see an isolated environment with beautiful landscapes and animals that can be seen nowhere else in the world. As tourism goes, Antarctica is a relatively new destination with mainstream cruise expeditions beginning in 1991. This corresponded with the formation of the International Association of Antarctic Tour Operators (IAATO) in the same year. In the last 20 years, Antarctic tourism has increased exponentially as this remote destination becomes more accessible, with the addition of ice-breaking vessels, reductions in annual sea ice, and lower prices.

Ecotourism, as previously defined in this chapter, involves low impact nature-based tourism, which contributes to the maintenance of species and habitats either directly through a contribution to conservation and/or indirectly by providing revenue to the local community. Antarctic tourism seems to fit well into this category, especially for the purposes of observing wildlife. As it pertains to conservation efforts, however, Antarctica is not the best fit as a location for ecotourism, especially from Goodwin's (1995) definition of conservation. With no indigenous peoples in the Antarctic, funding for conservation that is generated from tourism goes to "ensure that private sector travel to the Antarctic makes a worthy contribution to the protection of the continent" (IAATO, 2018, n.p.).

Ice-free areas make up less than 1% of the Antarctic continent, and native flora and fauna compete for this limited space. This small area is condensed even farther when viewed through the lens of tourism hotspots. The findings of Bender, Crosbie, and Lynch (2016) show that during the 2012–13 season, over 76% of all tourist landings took place in a combined area of less than 200 hectares, which is the same size as the second smallest country in the world, Monaco. These tiny areas are the epicenter of native flora, fauna, and tourist convergence. This results in competition for space and a high likelihood of human–wildlife conflict in these hotspots. The area with the highest concentration of tourist visits during the 2017–18 season was Neko Harbor, which is located along the Antarctic peninsula. It saw, on average, over 100 visitors at the site per day during the November to April season.

Travelling to tourism hotspots in the Antarctic has a high carbon dioxide (CO_2) impact. Over 86% of tourists travel to the port of departure from a foreign continent, requiring the use of an aircraft in addition to the cruise vessel. The most recent numbers from Farreny et al. (2011) found that the average emission cost for one passenger to go on an

Image 7.5 Tourist observing Adélie penguins in an ice-free area of Antarctica

Source: John Read

Antarctic cruise was 5.44 tons of CO_2. When this is extrapolated to the number of tourists that visited the Antarctic during the 2017–18 season, it would be the equivalent CO_2 emissions to driving approximately 554 million miles in an average passenger vehicle and would require 266,599 acres of forests to sequester (United States Environmental Protection Agency, 2015). These emissions not only have an effect on the local Antarctic environment but also the global environment as they are a major driver of climate change.

With a high carbon output and potential for conflict, Antarctic tourism would appear to be moving from a form of alternative tourism to unsustainable mass tourism. For some scientists though, this is not the case. Researchers around the world are seeing many advantages of increased tourism to one of the most remote regions in the world. Tourism has provided opportunities for supporting partnerships, with many member vessels of IAATO supporting science-based research. These vessels provide logistical support for scientists, their equipment, and the research stations during their regularly scheduled voyages by providing transportation, supplies, and other support services. This partnership has also engaged tourists to participate in Antarctic science. Citizen science projects have become a pivotal source of data for many scientists whose research would be impossible or cost prohibitive to obtain on the scale that Antarctic tourists are able to generate. Some of these citizen science projects involve cloud observations, seabird surveys, phytoplankton sampling, whale and seal observation, sea ice observation, and others (The Polar Citizen Science Collective, 2018).

What is human–wildlife conflict?

Human–wildlife conflict can be viewed in two contexts: 1) wildlife behavior conflicting with human goals (e.g., safety, satisfaction, property), or 2) human behavior conflicting with wildlife safety and well-being (e.g., harassment, noise, direct mortality due to hunting, destruction of habitat) (Cline, Sexton, & Stewart, 2014).

What is citizen science?

Citizen science involves "the collection and analysis of data relating to the natural world by members of the general public, typically as part of a collaborative project with professional scientists" (The Polar Citizen Science Collective, 2018).

Reflective questions

1. Should Antarctica be labelled as an ecotourism destination? Why or why not? Should it be labelled as a mass tourism destination? Why or why not?

2. In what ways can tourism benefit a destination without indigenous people or systems to directly support conservation? What is needed to monitor tourism when there is no local community nearby?

3. The concept of carrying capacity was discussed earlier in the chapter. Based on this case study, what are the implications of carrying capacity in Antarctica? Do you think it has been reached? Why or why not?

References

Bender, N.A., Crosbie, K., & Lynch, H.J. (2016). Patterns of tourism in the Antarctic Peninsula region: a 20-year analysis. *Antarctic Science*, 28(03), 194–203.

Cline, R., Sexton, N., & Stewart, S.C. (2014). *A Human-Dimensions Review of Human-Wildlife Disturbance: A Literature Review of Impacts, Frameworks, and Management Solutions*. Open-File Report 2007–1111, 1–88. Retrieved from https://web.archive.org/web/20140316165127/www.fort.usgs.gov/Products/Publications/21567/21567.pdf.

Farreny, R., Oliver-Solà, J., Lamers, M., Amelung, B., Gabarrell, X., Rieradevall, J., Boada, M., & Benayas, J. (2011). Carbon dioxide emissions of Antarctic tourism. *Antarctic Science*, 23(06), 556–566.

Goodwin, H. (1995). Tourism and the environment. *Biologist*, 42(3), 129–133.

International Association of Antarctic Tour Operators (2018). Financial Support – IAATO. Retrieved November 23, 2018, from https://iaato.org/financial-support.

The Polar Citizen Science Collective (2018). The Polar Citizen Science Collective. Retrieved November 23, 2018, from www.polarcollective.org/projects/.

United States Environmental Protection Agency (2015). Greenhouse Gas Equivalencies Calculator [Data and Tools]. Retrieved November 23, 2018, from www.epa.gov/energy/greenhouse-gas-equivalencies-calculator.

STUDY QUESTIONS

1. List the primary differences between mass tourism and alternative tourism.
2. Research an alternative tourism product. How have they incorporated the elements of alternative tourism (Figure 7.1)? What aspects are missing? How can they improve to become more inclusive?
3. Develop a plan to enhance capacity building or capacity development in your region. Which would you use and why? What, specifically, should be done that is not currently being done?
4. This chapter has separated ecotourism and cultural tourism as a way to explain their difference. What are their similarities? Can something be both ecotourism and cultural tourism? If so how?
5. You have been tasked with starting a community-based tourism program to support unique opportunities for your hotel guests. Write your introductory speech to be presented at your first community meeting.

DEFINITIONS

Alternative development   development that emanates from, and is guided by, the needs of individual societies

Alternative tourism   tourism that is appropriate to the local environment, social and cultural values, and that optimizes local decision-making, enhances the local economy, and promotes meaningful encounters between tourists and the local community

Alternative tourist   a visitor who generally enjoys meeting new people, expects to learn something new when they travel, appreciates a wide range of activities, seeks out challenges, is concerned with social issues, and embraces change

Anthropocentrism   the philosophy that humans are the sole bearers of intrinsic environmental value, and all other living things are there to sustain humanity's existence

Capacity building   a process that supports only the initial stages of building or creating capacities and assumes that there are no existing capacities at the start

Capacity development   the process through which individuals, organizations, and societies obtain, strengthen, and maintain the capabilities to set and achieve their own development objectives over time

Capitalism   an economic and political system in which a country's trade and industry are controlled by private owners for profit, rather than by the state

Carrying capacity   the amount of use any given land or environment can endure over time without degrading its suitability for that use

Commodification   the transformation of goods, services, ideas, and people into commodities, or objects of trade

Community-based tourism   a collaborative approach to tourism in which community members exercise control through active participation in the appraisal, development, management, and/or ownership of enterprises that delivers net socioeconomic benefits to community members, conserves natural and cultural resources, and adds value to the experiences of local and foreign visitors

Conservation   the principle that the environment and its resources should be used by humans and managed in a responsible manner

Crowding   when visitors perceive too many people in an area, spoiling the atmosphere, ambiance, or user experience

Cultural tourism   a traveler's engagement with a country or region's culture, specifically the lifestyle of the people in those geographical areas, the history of those people, their art, architecture, religion(s), and other elements that helped shape their way of life

Ecocentrism   the philosophy that there is inherent worth to all living things regardless of their usefulness to humans

Ecotourism   low impact nature tourism which contributes to the maintenance of species and habitats either directly through a contribution to conservation and/or indirectly by providing enough revenue to the local community for local people to value, and therefore protect, their wildlife heritage area as a source of income

Empowerment   the process of the process of becoming stronger and more confident, especially in controlling one's life and claiming one's rights

Environmentalism   a social movement that is based on political and ethical views of the environment

Fair pricing   ensuring that the revenue earned from the product or service is equitably shared between the producer, the supply chain, and the end seller

Food tourism   the desire to experience a particular type of food or the produce of a specific region while traveling

Nature-based tourism   any tourism activities that involve the use of natural areas

Niche tourism   specific tourism products that are tailored to meet the needs of a particular audience or market segment

Preservation   the principle that lands and their natural resources should not be consumed by humans and should instead be maintained in their pristine form

Rural tourism   a country experience which encompasses a wide range of attractions and activities that take place in agricultural or non-urban areas

Chapter **8**

Marketing for sustainability

Overview

This chapter explains basic marketing for sustainable organizations including factoring in visitor expectations and motivations when evaluating customer satisfaction. The unique attributes of destination marketing and management are clarified, and an explanation of the marketing mix and a SWOT analysis are provided. Product, distribution, pricing, and promotion in relation to sustainability are explored. The tools section lays out the requirements for a business plan and a marketing plan.

CHAPTER OBJECTIVES

At the completion of the chapter, students will be able to:

- Define marketing and apply it to sustainable tourism;
- Explain the relationship between expectations, motivations, and satisfaction;
- Describe how to apply the marketing mix to sustainable tourism;
- Apply product, distribution, pricing, and promotional strategies to the development of tourism products;
- Conduct a SWOT analysis to assess competitive advantage; and
- Develop a business and marketing plan to inform strategies for a successful organization.

Introduction

Consumerism is a direct result of increased marketing as businesses attempt to influence consumer decision-making to attract more sales. **Marketing** refers to the activities of a company associated with buying and selling a product or service, which includes advertising, selling, and delivering products to people. Marketing has become a very powerful force that affects all people in most aspects of their lives (Swarbrooke, 1999). The primary goal of marketing in tourism is to increase visitation, which appears to be in conflict with the goals of sustainable tourism (Buhalis, 2000). However, marketing can also be used to attract sustainability-minded travelers, to form visitors' expectations, and to promote responsible tourist behaviors. Therefore, marketing within sustainable tourism should include the following activities (Swarbrooke, 1999, p. 217):

- **Assessment** – Practitioners should be outward looking, interpreting current and future trends and determining their competitive advantage;
- **Consumer-responsiveness** – Practitioners should collect detailed knowledge on current and prospective customers in order to understand the needs and expectations of different consumer segments;
- **Innovation** – Practitioners should develop culturally and environmentally sensitive products and services and find ways to add value; and
- **Balance** – Practitioners should balance long-term requirements of sustaining capital with short-run needs to satisfy customers and investors, while generating adequate profits to continue operations.

Marketing involves shaping a company or destination's identity in such a way that it leads to positive images through "the creation and communication of the meaning, relevance, and value

Image 8.1 Tourist resort, Fiji

Source: Susan L. Slocum

of the organization and its product for identified consumers and other stakeholders" (Pomering, Noble, & Johnson, 2011, p. 958). One primary marketing activity involves understanding potential customers, specifically their expectations for sustainable travel, and their motivation for choosing a specific trip. **Expectations** are strong beliefs that something will happen which are derived from the need to fulfill a goal that has some intrinsic value or attractiveness (Heckhausen, 1989). These expectations lead to **motivations**, the desire or willingness to do something or go somewhere to fulfill these needs. When tourists have high expectations, they are more willing to search for tour information and learn about a destination's culture and environment and to invest time and other resources to research a journey (Lee, Jeon, & Kim, 2011). When a business or destination meets a customer's expectations, the likelihood of customer satisfaction increases. Customer **satisfaction** in tourism is achieved by providing an experience (tourism product) that meets or exceeds the customer's expectations and is a key driver in the long-term success and profitability of a business (Gruca & Rego, 2005). Chapter 5 provides tools to measure satisfaction.

Marketing in tourism

In tourism, there are two primary types of marketing: business marketing and destination marketing. **Business marketing** is marketing the actual products, services, or experiences that a single business entity offers. This could include the amenities offered at a particular location, the activities in which the tourist can engage, or specific services that create added value to the tourist product. Examples include luxury accommodations, specific excursions available, or unique opportunities for visitors, such as sourcing local food in a restaurant, offering a spa service, or highlighting a particular natural environment (private beach or amazing vistas). Business marketing generally includes those products and services that an individual business can control. **Destination marketing** is marketing for a specific location that generally includes all activities, sights, and tourism businesses in a destination. Destination marketing is vital in the overall success of any tourism business because if a visitor does not choose a specific destination, then there is no point in engaging in business marketing. For example, a tourist may want a unique cultural experience learning about indigenous peoples. The first choice they must make is which indigenous group they want to visit. Let's say the tourist wants to visit the Quechua peoples of South America. The tourist must choose between a number of countries where the Quechua live, including Peru, Bolivia, Chile, Colombia, and Ecuador. Once a country (or multiple countries) are chosen, visitors must decide which locations within that country they will visit. Destination marketing helps a location differentiate themselves from other regions that may offer similar tourism products. Once a tourist chooses a specific location, only then can the individual businesses begin to compete for that visitor.

Destination marketing and management

Destination marketing is usually done by a **destination marketing and management organization** (DMO), which is an organization that represents destinations and helps to develop long-term travel and tourism strategies. The role of a DMO is two-fold: within marketing, the DMO must establish and manage a destination's brand and promote travel opportunities within their region; and within management, the DMO must support business development to ensure the amenities offered meet the needs of the tourists (Figure 8.1). In other words, they must facilitate the overall development of tourism products for a destination.

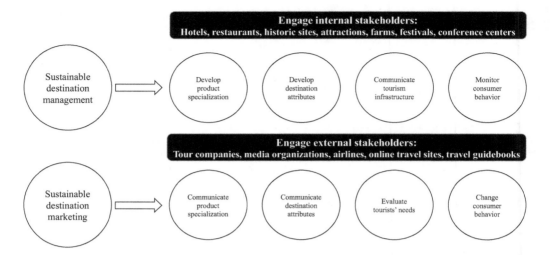

Figure 8.1 Destination marketing and management roles

DMOs come in various forms and have labels such as Tourism Board, Convention and Visitors Bureau, or Tourism Authority. They may be funded through membership fees paid by individual tourism businesses, or they may receive tax support from a national, regional, or local government, such as taxes on tourists (e.g., an accommodation tax), which is used to support destination marketing. Slocum and Curtis (2017, p. 160) explain,

> *DMOs are as diverse as the destinations that support them, but they all have a common goal: to ensure that tourists are aware of the destination by communicating the businesses, events, attractions, and opportunities available in their area; to encourage tourists to choose their destination over others; and to ensure that the destination has the amenities to satisfy its customers.*

Part of the destination product development process includes recruiting and maintaining the appropriate mix of businesses that support tourism, such as a wide range of accommodations, attractions, and other support businesses, like grocery stores, transportation options, and eating establishments. More specifically, the tourism product of a destination is the variety of experiences that entices a diverse set of tourist typologies.

While the tools used in business marketing and destination marketing are similar, destination marketing requires the development of social capital and collaboration between all tourism businesses in a destination. Collaboration strategies are discussed in more detail in Chapter 9 in relation to value chain management, but the same strategies work in developing networks between community stakeholders in a destination. Networks allow information exchange and are a vital element when diversifying into new industries or markets because different economic sectors possess varied information related to product development, distribution, and integrated marketing strategies (Montanari & Staniscia, 2009). DMOs are responsible for establishing and nurturing these networks to ensure that all members of a community have a voice in the way tourism is developed and marketed. Networks should include internal stakeholders, such as tourism businesses and local residents, as well as external stakeholders, such as tour companies, airlines, and travel promotion media. However, collaboration can be difficult, especially when these stakeholders have differing ideas on how to develop and promote tourism. Having a DMO can help support consensus building and ensure that a more bottom-up form of tourism planning is pursued.

The marketing mix

The **marketing mix** is a combination of factors that can be controlled by an organization to influence consumers to purchase its products. The purpose of developing the marketing mix is to evaluate the four primary elements that influence a company's ability to achieve its marketing objectives. Those four elements are: product; distribution; price; and promotion. Within each element, it is important to assess what expectations the consumer may have, how an organization can meet these expectations, and how this compares to what the competition is doing.

In terms of sustainable tourism, value should be created for tourists, the physical environment, the socio-cultural environment, and the organization or firm in order to meet the triple bottom line of sustainability. Therefore, in sustainable tourism, each element of the marketing mix must take into account impacts on the environment and society, as well as the consumer, and each of the marketing mix elements should support the organization's vision and mission statements of increased sustainability (Pomering, Noble, & Johnson, 2011). Table 8.1 provides a list of important questions that should be addressed in the marketing mix.

Table 8.1 Elements of the marketing mix

Marketing mix		
Product or service	What does the customer want from your product/service?	What needs does the product/service satisfy? What features does it have to meet these needs?
	How and where will the customer use your product/service?	Are there any features missing? Will the customer use all the features?
	What is the product/service to be called?	How is it branded?
	How does the product affect the environment and society?	Does tourism use add additional stresses to the environment? Do tourist/host interactions have a positive influence on both parties? How can you change how tourism uses resources to ensure more sustainable results?
	How is your product differentiated from the competitors?	Why would the consumer choose your product/service over the others?

Table 8.1 continued

Marketing mix		
Place (distribution)	Where do buyers look for your product or service?	Do they shop online, through a tour operator, or purchase once on vacation (in-country)?
	How can you access the right distribution channels?	Do you need to use a sales force? Should you attend trade fairs? Do you have partnerships with tour operators?
	How do tourists access your location?	Do you work with transportation companies or do tourists drive themselves to your location? Once they arrive at a destination, how do they get around to the various sights?
	How do your distribution choices affect the environment and society?	Are there transportation options that reduce greenhouse gas emissions? Are there transportation options that support traditional industries?
	How is your distribution strategy differentiated from the competitors?	How does your distribution strategy reduce barriers to travel and ease visitation compared to your competition?
Price	What is the value of the product or service to the buyer?	Are there established price points for products or services in this area? Is the customer price sensitive?
	What discounts should be offered to trade customers, or to other specific segments of your market?	Will a small decrease in price gain you extra market share? Or will a small increase be indiscernible, and so gain you extra profit margin?
	How do your pricing choices affect the environment and society?	Does your pricing take into account external costs? Does your pricing strategy provide opportunity to increase the indirect and induced economic impacts? Does your pricing strategy allow for opportunities to give back to your community?
	How will your price compare with your competitors?	What type of pricing strategy should you use? Does the price match the value received compared to the value of your competitors?

Marketing mix		
Promotion	Where and when can you get your marketing messages across to your target market? When is the best time to promote?	Will you reach your audience by advertising online, in the press, on TV, on radio, or on billboards? By using direct marketing mailshots? Through PR? On the internet?
	Is there seasonality in the market?	Are there any wider issues that suggest or dictate the timing of your market launch or subsequent promotions?
	What is the role of your website in purchasing decisions?	Can tourists book travel through your website or is it for information only?
		How much time do tourists spend on your website?
		What additional information should be provided (about the destination or other activities in the region)?
	How do your promotional choices affect the environment and society?	Are you representing your community in a way that instills pride?
		Does your community identify with the promotional representation you present?
		Does your promotion accurately address environmental issues that encourage responsible travel?
	How do your competitors do their promotions?	Should you compete in the same market as your competitors?
		How can you stand out from the competition?

The sustainable product or service

Organizations may have multiple products, services, or experiences which are available to their customers, and organizations should break down each one in relation to each market segment they serve. As a reminder from Chapter 5, **market segmentation** is the activity of dividing a broad consumer base, normally consisting of existing and potential customers, into sub-groups of consumers (known as segments) based on some type of shared characteristics. Tourism products may vary based on resources available, seasonality, and market conditions and not all products may appeal to all market segments. For example, winter activities may be different from summer activities at a mountain resort. Knowing the specific expectations of winter visitors and how they differ from summer visitors is an important part of developing the tourism product. Moreover, understanding specific experiences that may cross over to different market segments is also important. At a mountain resort, skiing may be a winter product, hiking a summer product, but other amenities, such as spa treatments or skating opportunities, may appeal to both markets.

All products or services offered should align with the overall brand that an organization presents to potential customers. A **brand** is a unique name, term, sign, symbol, design or combination of these that identifies the goods or services of one seller or group of sellers and differentiates them from the competition (Keller, 1993). A brand provides information that influences the expectations of tourists, and may motivate them to choose a particular business or destination over other options. **Attributes** are the descriptive qualities that a

Image 8.2 Angkor Wat, Cambodia

Source: Susan L. Slocum

visitor believes a destination or business has, such as physical characteristics like beaches, nightclubs, or outstanding food choices. **Benefits** are the personal values each visitor attaches to these attributes (such as adventure, relaxation, or learning). A brand should invoke an image of the attributes and the benefits that visitation could fulfill. It should be unique to a specific business or destination and be readily identifiable to current or future customers. The products that are offered should enhance the brand, and if a new product idea conflicts with the brand, that may be a signal that the product idea is a bad fit for the organization, business, or destination. Managing a brand is synonymous with managing the overall reputation of an organization.

Product development can become more complex when assessing the role of sustainability within different product options and different target markets. In a weak form of sustainability, the goal may be to ensure that a product (or the use of a product) does not damage the environment or society in which an organization does business. This could include making sure that hikers stay on designated paths or providing opportunities for local artisans to access tourist markets. From a strong sustainability perspective, a product should find avenues to enhance or improve the environment or society in which it operates. An example is providing voluntourism opportunities or other avenues for tourists to support or donate to local charities or social causes, such as local conservation efforts. If the local culture is part of the product, practitioners need to ensure positive host–guest interactions so that hostilities or conflicts of interest do not arise. As a tourism provider, each product or service should be evaluated in relation to the level of sustainability it can achieve, and then this product or service needs to be evaluated in relation to the target market that is interested in the determined level of sustainability.

Distributing sustainable tourism

Distribution strategies are discussed in detail in Chapter 9 in relation to value chain management, though they are also applicable to marketing decisions. A **distribution channel** is a chain of businesses or intermediaries through which a good or service passes until it reaches the end consumer. In tourism, visitors must come to the destination to consume tourist products and services, so the distribution channel includes the process of booking travel and transporting visitors, as well as the goods and services they consume in-country. Since booking partnerships and supply chains are covered in Chapter 9, this section focuses on transportation issues related to sustainability.

Greenhouse gas (GHG) emissions are a serious concern that relates to the tourism distribution channel. **Greenhouse gases** are gases that enter the earth's atmosphere and trap heat, causing a warming of the atmosphere (United States Environmental Protection Agency, 2018). These gases include carbon dioxide, methane, nitrous oxide, and fluorinated gases. Carbon dioxide enters the atmosphere through multiple channels: the burning of fossil fuels (coal, natural gas, and oil) or wood products; solid waste; the destruction of trees, wetlands, and everglades (which trap and store GHGs); and the result of certain chemical reactions (e.g., manufacture of cement). Any form of transportation that uses petroleum products emits carbon into the atmosphere. Carbon dioxide is removed from the atmosphere (or sequestered) when it is absorbed by the ecosystem as part of the biological carbon cycle, so preserving or planting natural ecosystems can help offset carbon emissions. Transportation is a leading cause of carbon dioxide emissions, and tourism is responsible for about 5% of global carbon emissions (United Nations Environment Programme & United Nations World Tourism Organization, 2007). The United Nations World Tourism

Organization (n.d.) provides the following suggestions to mitigate carbon emissions in the tourism industry:

- Reducing carbon emission – Considering alternative means of transportation;
- Measuring the carbon footprint associated with the travels – Using a carbon emission calculator through one of the carbon-offset organizations (available online);
- Offsetting the carbon emission – Purchasing certified carbon credits or supporting offset projects, such as: tree planting; renewable energy; energy conservation; and environmental education;
- Changing operating patterns – Given that winter sports, beach, or health-wellness tourism (to name but a few) require very specific climate conditions, the diversification of products and services decreases the dependency on climate shifts;
- Adapting tourist destinations – A difficult and long-term measure, which involves the modification of economic circuits, new technologies, intensive training efforts, and changing the minds of all the people involved, including the tourists; and
- Mitigating global warming – Implementing action plans to reduce carbon emissions or modernizing through carbon friendly technologies.

Addressing sustainable transportation issues can be a challenge for sustainable tourism businesses. Long-haul travel is usually outside of a destination's or business's control, but local transportation can include public transportation, biking, walking, ride-sharing, or the use of hybrid, electric, or natural gas-powered vehicles. These forms of transportation can also enhance the visitor's experience and become activities in their own right. As with any part of the marketing mix, it is important to understand the tourists' expectations to ensure that transportation options meet the expectations of customers.

Pricing sustainable tourism

Pricing strategies are an effective way to differentiate a product or service from the competition because consumers are often price sensitive. Table 8.2 explains a number of determinants for price sensitivity. There are three general pricing strategies: cost-based pricing; demand-oriented pricing; and competition-oriented pricing. **Cost-based pricing** is determined by calculating the cost of production plus a per-unit profit margin on each item sold. Cost-based pricing is the easiest strategy as input costs are generally known to the organization. However, this strategy lacks incentives for businesses to reduce their operating costs, is not based on consumer demand, and makes it difficult to adjust prices when input costs rise (Slocum & Curtis, 2017). **Demand-oriented pricing** is based on consumers' **willingness to pay**, or the maximum price at, or below, which a consumer will definitely buy one unit of a product. Chapter 5 highlights a number of consumer trends that support an increase in willingness to pay for sustainable products, services, and experiences. **Competition-oriented pricing** is the practice of setting prices based on the prices of other comparable businesses or products. The three forms of competition-oriented pricing are **parity pricing**, setting the price equal to the competition, **premium pricing**, setting the price higher than the competition, or **penetration pricing**, setting the price lower than the competition. A combination of all three strategies is recommended, as it is important to know the costs of doing business, to have a general idea of what the market will allow, and to know how a pricing strategy relates to other travel options available to the consumer. In other words, a pricing strategy must ensure adequate profits to reinvest in an organization and keep the doors open.

Table 8.2 Determinants of consumer price sensitivity

Effect	Description
Substitution effect	When there are many similar products available, a price increase in one product will cause consumer to switch to one of the less expensive options
Unique value effect	Consumers will be less price sensitive if the product or service is unique, has no substitutes
Switching cost effect	When consumers face large costs to switch products, such as the time required to seek information or to make an additional stop at a retail outlet, they are less price sensitive
Difficult comparison effect	Consumers are less price sensitive when it is hard to compare products or services
Price-quality effect	Consumer perception that a higher price indicates a higher quality product, reducing the impulse to switch to a less expensive option
Expenditure effect	Consumers are more sensitive to price changes on large, expensive products rather than small, inexpensive ones
Fairness effect	Consumers may be willing to pay more for a product if they feel the value provided is higher than competing products
Inventory effect	Consumers are willing to pay more for a product when it's in season just in advance of a holiday, rather than after the holiday
End-benefit effect	Consumers may be willing to pay more for products that have an end-benefit such as protecting the environment, preserving agricultural open space, or supporting family farms

Source: Adapted from Slocum and Curtis (2017)

The challenge with standard pricing strategies is that they only consider **private costs**, which are the costs the firm pays to purchase capital equipment, hire labor, and buy materials or other inputs. In sustainable tourism, it is important to consider **external costs**, which are costs to society, regardless of who pays for them (Becken, 2007). For example, large-scale hotels often use pesticides, herbicides, or other chemicals to maintain attractive landscapes. The private cost of these chemicals is the price a hotel pays to purchase them. However, these chemicals often leach into the soil or may be included in the run-off after a hard rain, and may be washed into the ocean or other waterways. These chemicals may kill fish and make people or livestock sick when they drink or play in the water. The cost of treating these illnesses or the loss of fishing revenue would be considered the external cost of the hotel's operations. When you combine the private costs and the external costs, you have the **social cost** of doing business.

Sustainable tourism takes into account the social cost of production when determining the price of their goods or services. External costs are hard to calculate and even harder to distribute in the form of compensation to those that incur the external cost (the person that gets sick in the previous example). One solution is to collect money through a pricing strategy and use this money to support the entire community, such as investing in a school or a health care center. Finding avenues to decrease indirect and induced impacts can also help support those negatively impacted by external costs, for example choosing not to use toxic herbicides and

Image 8.3 Dunhinda Falls, Sri Lanka

Source: Susan L. Slocum

pesticides. Another solution might be helping tourists or tourism businesses become aware of the external costs they may bring to a community or ecosystem and encouraging them to alter their behavior.

Promoting sustainable tourism

The final aspect of the marketing mix is the promotion of the tourism product. There are a variety of media through which an organization can promote its business or services, including radio or television advertising, fliers, brochures, trade shows, billboards, or the internet. A common promotional strategy involves partnerships with travel agencies, online booking sites, or working with tour operators. The key to a successful promotional strategy is knowing how visitors book their vacations and understanding their motivation for travel. All promotional material should reflect both the experience that is being sold and the role sustainability plays in overall operations. A promotional strategy can help formulate the expectations guests have prior to their trip.

In promotion, be sure to highlight sustainability accomplishments and explain how and why an organization is dedicated to sustainable tourism. This can include the vision and mission statements on websites, and highlight how sustainability will enhance the visitor experience. One helpful promotional strategy is to apply for a well-known and recognizable sustainability certification (covered in Chapter 10). Many tourists interested in sustainable tourism will look for certifications (Black & Crabtree, 2007). Certifications provide transparency in operational practices, which may appeal to particular market segments. The promotional strategy is the business's or destination's way of communicating competitive advantage, and promotional materials should accurately showcase what is being done in relation to sustainable tourism. Beware, if the marketing material does not accurately reflect the actual experiences offered, word-of-mouth could destroy an organization's brand and its reputation. Online rating sites, such as TripAdvisor, help ensure that any discrepancies can easily be discovered by potential customers.

Assessing competitive advantage

One task that all organizations should perform periodically is a comparison between their marketing mix and that of their competitors. This is usually done through a **SWOT analysis** (Figure 8.2). SWOT stands for strengths, weakness, opportunities, and threats in relation to business competition. Strengths and weaknesses are internal to an organization, whereas opportunities and threats are external.

Strengths and weaknesses may include an organization's access to resources and capital (such as human capital, natural capital, or cultural capital), technology, financing, and partnerships (social capital). An organization's strengths and weakness can change over time as technology or market forces alter the competitive environment. What is currently a strength may become a weakness or may become obsolete over time. It is important to be honest when evaluating the internal situation, as acknowledging weaknesses is an important first step in overcoming them.

Opportunities and threats relate to things outside the control of any single organization. They include overall economic conditions, technology changes, changes in government policy, and legal regulations. **Environmental scanning** is the process of monitoring the external environment and should be an ongoing process within business planning. Being involved with a local chamber of commerce, DMO, visitor center, or industry association can enhance an organization's ability to conduct environmental scanning.

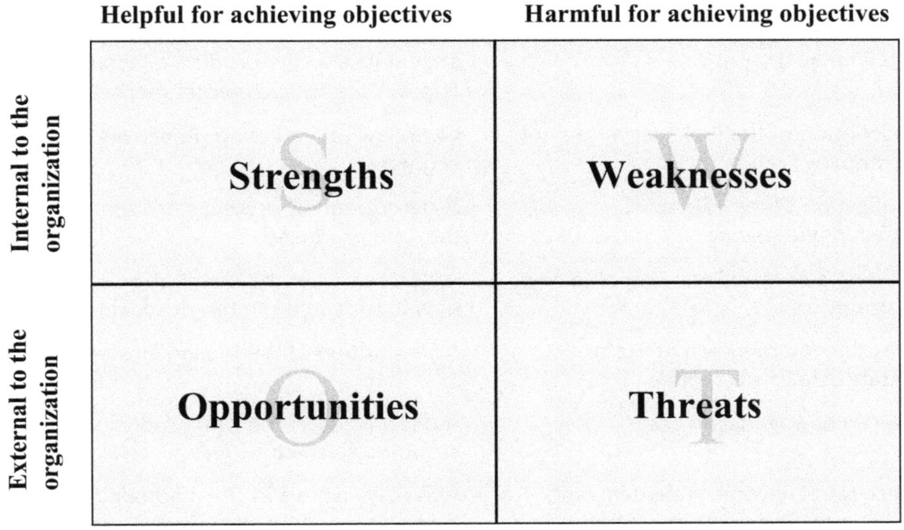

Figure 8.2 Elements of a SWOT analysis

In an ideal world, a company or destination will try to match their strengths with the opportunities available. For example, offering a sustainable travel experience (internal strength) is well aligned with the rise of the LOHAS movement (external opportunity). However, when a weakness aligns with a particular threat, the long-term viability of the business or destination may be at stake. For example, the environmental degradation of a local beach (internal weakness) in partnership with rising airfares (external threat) can result in tourists finding a better vacation experience elsewhere. Therefore, the SWOT analysis should be an ongoing evaluation tool and part of the business and marketing plan process.

SUSTAINABILITY TOOL: DEVELOPING BUSINESS PLANS AND MARKETING PLANS

Business and marking plans are written documents that aid an organization in planning and executing the marketing mix successfully. Business plans focus on strategic implications, such as internal investment, organizational structures, and long-range planning. The business plan is generally shared only with key executives within the company and external members of the financial community and is written to target potential investors, stockholders, and accountants. Marketing plans focus on defining and accessing a distinct target market and developing the products or services that distinguish an organization from its competitors (Slocum & Curtis, 2017). Specific components of each are described in Table 8.3. Generally, how the document is used determines which type of document an organization will utilize. It is important to note that both a business plan and a marketing plan should

Table 8.3 Comparing business plans and marketing plans

Business plan	Marketing plan
Executive summary	Executive summary
Mission and vision statement	Mission and vision statement
Overview of the business	Overview of the business environment or industry including a company's competitive advantage
A description of products or services and how they are produced	A detailed description of the target market segments and the product or service appropriate to each target market
A description of the business model for the company	Overview of marketing objectives by market segment
Identification of the executive leadership and management team	A description of products or services and how they are produced
Marketing summary including objectives and strategies	A description of the distribution channel and how it adds value to the products or services
Tactics the company will utilize to generate sales and revenue	A description of the pricing strategy
Overview of advertising plans	A description of the promotional strategies, including sales objectives
Balance sheet, income statement, and cash flow statement or projected financial statements for the next five years	A SWOT analysis of the marketing mix in relation to strengths, weaknesses, opportunities, and threats

be updated regularly, as the documents should be used to guide the strategic decisions of a company and must be kept current.

Goals and objectives

Both business plans and marketing plans need to explicitly state the organization's goals and objectives. A **goal** is an envisioned future state that people commit to achieving, and an **objective** is a measurable step taken to achieve a goal. The business plan will include overall business aims, such as hiring goals, market share, long-term financing need, and company structure. The marketing plan will specify goals related to the marketing mix and strategies related to achieving competitive advantage. Here are some examples of goals and objectives.

Goal – Establish long-term supply partners that enhance the sustainability of our product.

- Objective – Research and select the most appropriate certification label to inform our supply chain partners;
- Objective – Establish four contractual agreements with sustainable vendors;
- Objective – Work with each vendor to expand their selection of sustainable product lines.

Goal – Educate our visitor on the value of sustainable behavior.

- Objective – Research best practice in sustainable tourist behavior;
- Objective – Establish one educational activity to highlight appropriate sustainable behavior for tourists;
- Objective – Monitor consumer response to educational activities and make adjustments as needed.

Goal – Hire committed and well-trained employees that support our vision.

- Objective – Offer in-house training related to customer service and sustainability practices;
- Objective – Establish a program that encourages employees to improve overall operations;
- Objective – Offer employee incentives (health insurance, training, community involvement opportunities) to retain committed and qualified employees.

It is important to establish a timeline when each objective should be completed and to understand which objectives must be completed in which order. For example, there is no point in working with a specific vendor to offer a sustainable product line until a contractual relationship has been established. The timeline also ensures that certain objectives are not overlooked, and that the organization as a whole is successful in achieving the overall goal, and not just a few objectives.

Competitive analysis

A SWOT allows an organization to assess its overall competitive advantage; understanding the competitive environment, both globally and locally, helps an organization differentiate itself from the competition. When writing a business or marketing plan, it is important to ask the following questions:

- Who is the competition? Which destinations offer similar experiences on a global scale and which businesses offer similar experiences on a local scale?

- How many competitors operate in the market? Are they large or small?
- What types of tourism products do they offer? Are they similar or different from our tourism products? How are they different?
- What pricing strategy do they use? How does our pricing strategy compare? Do we offer added value for the price we charge?
- Who is their target market? Are we competing for the same customers?

When determining a business or marketing strategy in relation to the competition, an organization may choose to compete directly by offering similar products to similar market segments, or it may choose to offer a very different visitor experience. When competing directly, an organization must ensure that they are exceeding the value being offered by the competition. When developing different products, it is important to understand exactly what those differences are. For example, from a destination perspective, beach resorts may be similar across a number of Caribbean Islands, so a destination may focus on luxury, accessibility, or a variety of recreational activities as a source of competitive advantage and value enhancement. However, adding components that are unique to a specific destination, say cultural components that highlight unique traditions or historical perspectives, may help distinguish a destination as offering a different type of tourism experience. The same applies to businesses within a destination. When tourist products are similar, it may be appropriate to compete by price, or a business may choose to offer specific products that are different from the competition. Either way, a business practitioner must know what the competition is offering in order to ensure that a brand is distinctive.

Financial statements

When developing a business plan, financial statements are required. When writing a marketing plan, they are not required but an organization should be aware of the cost of marketing goals and the projected return on investment. There are generally three types of financial statements. A balance sheet is a snapshot of the financial condition of a business at a point in time and changes on a day-to-day basis. They are generally completed monthly or annually. A **balance sheet** contains an organization's assets (what they own), their liabilities (what they owe), and owners' equity (owners investments including the sum of profits and losses over time). Assets minus liabilities minus equity should equal zero (it should balance). An **income statement** shows the net return of a business, its revenue minus its expenses, or its profit (or loss). The revenue is determined by the number of customers multiplied by the price charged to each customer, as well as any incidental revenue streams, such as gift shop sales, excursions, or food and beverage sales. The expenses come from money that is used to pay the operating costs of an organization. The income statement reflects year-to-date totals. The **cash flow statement** shows how changes in balance sheet and income affect cash and cash equivalents and breaks the analysis down to operating, investing, and financing activities.

When starting a new business, projected financial statements show how a company will ensure profitability over time and are necessary when a company does not have a solid record of accomplishment. The challenge with projected financial statements is getting accurate information about tourist numbers, market conditions, regulatory requirements, and estimating expenses. Information about tourist numbers, market conditions, and regulatory requirements may be available through DMOs or industry associations. In many developed countries, there are census data that can also be used to estimate demographic and geographic information. In relation to expenses, these data can be collected by seeking bids from reputable vendors or searching the internet for prices relating to inputs an organization may use. With projected financial statements, it is important to be thorough and as accurate as possible to ensure that an investment is profitable in the long run.

Conclusion

This chapter has provided an overview of strategic marketing in relation to sustainable tourism. By explaining the relationship between expectations, motivation, and satisfaction, this chapter has highlighted the need for branding and reputation management in order to achieve success. Many of the same tools are used in business marketing and destination marketing. However, destination marketing requires additional attention to destination management, wherein all stakeholders work together to ensure the appropriate mix of tourism products in a destination, as well as the overall marketing strategies to ensure tourists choose a particular destination. Through the development of strategies relating to product development, distribution, pricing, and promotion, the marketing mix establishes competitive advantage over other, similar tourism products. The SWOT analysis can be used to determine the strengths, weaknesses, opportunities, or threats of an organization or destination in relation to the competition. Developing business plans or marketing plans can assist in the accomplishment of strategic goals and objectives.

CASE STUDY 8.1 THE MARKETING MIX OF AIRLINE SUSTAINABILITY

SUSAN L. SLOCUM

Introduction

Sustainability in the airlines industry is a controversial topic. Over 4.1 billion passengers used airlines for travel in 2017, releasing over 859 million tons of carbon dioxide (CO_2) into the atmosphere (Air Transport Action Group, 2019). That's 2% of all the CO_2 caused by humans (International Air Transport Association, 2019). Airlines make up a significant part of the tourism distribution channel, and their impact is important to the overall sustainability of the tourism industry. While the airline industry is heavily regulated globally, there is very little, if any, regulation regarding sustainability. Therefore, airlines generally self-regulate and are finding ways to become more sustainable using a number of their marketing mix elements.

Sustainable product development

Aircraft manufacturers have put extensive focus on improving fuel consumption. For example, the Boeing 787–9 Dreamliner and the Airbus A350–900 use 40% less fuel than comparably sized jets. Airlines are also moving towards using biofuel, a mixture of jet fuel and ethanol (made from corn) or other vegetable oils (including flaxseed, algae, or camelina) in an effort to reduce carbon emissions (ethanol is controversial as agriculture is also a large producer of GHG emissions). Better maintenance and the process of 'cold-spraying' jet engines with water during the flight (reducing engine temperature and fuel consumption) have also helped make aircraft more fuel efficient.

There are also a number of practices that, while annoying to passengers, have greatly improved the sustainability of airlines. Planes that are heavier burn more fuel, so the elimination of free checked baggage has been effective at getting people to pack lighter and reduce the weight of the aircraft. Moreover, airlines continually add more seats to the plane in order to transport more passengers, resulting in fewer flights overall. Lastly, using GPS technology, pilots are better able to select fuel-efficient routes based on current weather data.

Sustainable distribution

Dichter, Sørensen, and Saxon (2017) claim that more than 60% of an airline's expenses go to suppliers. Moreover, most airports only have one or two suppliers, and airlines are in long-term contracts with these companies. Therefore, using sustainable suppliers has become an important strategy to improve airline sustainability. For example, United Airlines uses eco-friendly cleaners and supports women-owned businesses in their supply chain. Today, most airlines recycle and compost waste, as shown by KLM Airlines who claim that everything on the meal tray is recyclable, most food (including cooking oil) is certified fair trade, and chicken is sourced locally. Asian Airlines and Alaska Airlines serves Rainforest Alliance certified coffee, and Alaska Airlines uses compostable utensils and coffee mugs made from recycled plastic. British Airways assert that the fish, tea, and coffee are sourced sustainably and their cookies, made at a bakery in Scotland, are organic. Vegetarian and vegan food is also on the rise aboard planes.

Another sustainable practice is the use of e-tickets that do not require printing paper tickets. Many low-cost airlines do not even require a boarding pass, as passengers only need a valid identification to board and seating is open. Moreover, many airlines and airports are reducing paper consumption in their offices.

Sustainable pricing

Price is still a major determinant of how consumers choose airlines. The price of air transportation rarely takes into account the full cost of the negative externalities

Image 8.4 Tourists flying into the back country of Alaska

Source: Susan L. Slocum

incurred in air traffic (social costs). Pollution is the most obvious externality, but waste, water use, and noise are also important externalities. Mayer (2013) stresses that air travelers will pay up to 10% more in airfares as a response to the environmental impacts of flying, and as many as 45% would pay an additional 20% of the price. One practice is carbon offsets, where passengers pay a third party who, in turn, offers services that reduce carbon in the atmosphere, such as planting trees. Most airlines provide links to carbon offset programs, but require customers to pay separately for this service. Harbour Air Seaplanes (the largest sea plane carrier in British Columbia, Canada) includes carbon offsetting in the price of its tickets to cover the externalities associated with emissions.

One current trend in airline pricing has been to unbundle services and allow passengers to pay only for what they use. This strategy has reduced overall consumption of food items, drinks, and such things as disposable napkins, cups, and silverware, as well as overall packaging materials. Pay-as-you-go services, such as luggage fees, encourage people to travel lighter and reduce baggage handling waste. Low-cost carriers, such as easyJet, Southwest, or IndiGo have been very successful, but generally rank low in overall sustainability, primarily because they do not have sustainability plans nor do they monitor sustainability (Chen, Jiang, & Larson, 2016).

Sustainable promotion

Promotion includes the communication of environmental policies and sustainability accomplishments to the general public. As there is no specific certification for the airline industry, most sustainability is communicated through websites, and reporting measures are determined by the airline company itself, increasing the opportunity for greenwashing. Almost all airline companies have a sustainability page on their website and external reporting of the world's "most sustainable airlines" is on the rise.

Reflective questions

1. Although only 10%–20% of customers report a willingness to pay extra for sustainability, would promoting sustainability efforts improve public relations for airlines? Why or why not? Why don't airlines promote more of their sustainability accomplishments?

2. Using the distribution channel to lower operating costs and achieve sustainability objectives is a smart business move. What challenges, other than those mentioned in the case study, do airlines face with regard to sustainable sourcing?

3. Do you think using a marketing mix approach to sustainability is helpful for companies? Why or why not? What other methods might be better suited to help managers realize sustainability opportunities?

References

Air Transport Action Group (2019). Facts and figures. Retrieved from www.atag.org/facts-figures.html.

Chen, X., Jiang, C., & Larson, P. (2016). Sustainability reporting of airlines: performances and driving factors. Retrieved from http://ctrf.ca/wp-content/uploads/2017/05/CTRF2017ChenJiangLarsonAirTransportation.pdf.

Dichter, A., Sørensen, A.J., & Saxon, S. (2017). Buying and flying: next-generation airline procurement. McKinsey and Company. Retrieved from www.mckinsey.com/industries/travel-transport-and-logistics/our-insights/buying-and-flying-next-generation-airline-procurement.

International Air Transport Association (2018). Fact sheet climate change and CORSIA. Retrieved from www.iata.org/pressroom/facts_figures/fact_sheets/Documents/fact-sheet-climate-change.pdf.

Mayer, R. (2013). Environmental marketing in the airline sector: an evaluation of market segments, green image and eco-positioning (Doctoral dissertation Loughborough University).

CASE STUDY 8.2 TRIPADVISOR: REVIEWS YOU CAN TRUST?

SUSAN L. SLOCUM

Introduction

The internet has become the primary source for travelers in their search for destination information. Specifically, Web 2.0 has helped destination websites evolve from static sources of marketing information to dynamic user-generated content. Roque and Raposo (2016) explain that, "The Web 2.0 phenomena embodied in the form of applications, services, and communities is gradually changing how society communicates, consumes, and contributes to the creation and distribution of information" (p. 59). Social media, in particular, provides a multidirectional flow of information where a person initially receives information about a destination, and then provides future tourists the material they learned after their travels by sharing stories, photos, and videos. Kaplan and Haenlein (2010) list six primary types of social media:

- Social networking sites (i.e. Facebook, LinkedIn);
- Content communities (i.e. YouTube, Flickr, SlideShare);
- Blogs, social virtual worlds (i.e. Second Life);
- Virtual game worlds (i.e. World of Warcraft);
- Collaborative projects (i.e. Wikipedia, Wikitravel); and
- Consumer review websites and rating (i.e. TripAdvisor).

Destination marketing and management organizations (DMOs) are responsible for building a destination's image. They are responsible for maximizing the visitor experiences while ensuring the sustainability of a destination. Their primary function is to establish a recognizable brand that ensures the destination remains competitive. Balancing the needs of tourists with the needs of a community requires extensive collaboration and partnerships to ensure that the destination brand provides a collective and unique message.

Social media is a cost-effective means to increase word-of-mouth (WOM) advertising for DMOs. WOM advertising is perceived as more trustworthy than other forms of advertising because consumers feel it is authentic, tied to emotion, and is voluntary. In other words, tourists believe that WOM is not paid for by corporations, and therefore results from honest experiences. However, this is not always the case. If travel experiences do not match WOM, the impact can be devastating to a destination.

TripAdvisor

TripAdvisor is the largest social media sharing site for travel-related information. It was founded in 2000, four years before the existence of Facebook, and has been owned by the online booking agent Expedia since 2004. Its strength lies in the user's ability to compare multiple destinations on one site, unlike other sites that only provide information on a single destination (such as a particular destination's webpage). It is estimated that 456 million people visit TripAdvisor every month – that's about one in every 16 people on earth (Kinstler, 2018). While TripAdvisor can provide opportunities for lesser-known destinations, Kinstler (2018) reminds us that "TripAdvisor reviews are also a ruthless audit of the earth's many flaws" (n.p.).

Like many social media giants, TripAdvisor has been bombarded with fake news. The company has found themselves in a position to determine what is real and what is not, as well as what constitutes freedom of speech. Evidence suggests that there are companies that will flood the website with positive reviews, for a price, or use fake reviews to sabotage the competition. Using algorithms, the company must determine the difference between a post about sex trafficking or sex tourism from a post about sexual

Image 8.5 Kasbah du Pacha el Glaoui in the High Atlas of Morocco receives a 4.5 rating on TripAdvisor

Source: Susan L. Slocum

abuse. A quick review of the TripAdvisor site lists the best place to find prostitutes, yet in 2019, a woman who was sexually assaulted by her tour guide was restricted from posting her story on the site (Mzezewa, 2019). In 2011, the UK's Advertising Standards Authority ordered TripAdvisor "not to claim or imply that all the reviews that appeared on the website were from real travelers, or were honest, real or trusted", forcing TripAdvisor to change its motto from "Reviews You Can Trust" to "Know better. Book better. Go better".

TripAdvisor has established 'destination experts', the people who have posted over 500 entries in a six-month timeframe. Furthermore, the more a person posts, the more 'badges' they receive, implying that the information provider has certain qualifications, without verification. TripAdvisor will send email reminders to encourage posts, elevating a person's status as they engage more with the website. In fact, a Tunisian hotel received TripAdvisor's coveted '2016 Traveler's Choice Award' even though it had been closed for a year after 30 guests were killed in a terrorist attack (Stimmler-Hall, 2016). One must question where these 'votes' originated.

When the US Federal Trade Commission began an investigation into the business practices at TripAdvisor, change was inevitable. Today, about one-third of TripAdvisor's staff work on fraud detection. At the World Cup in 2018, TripAdvisor "found 1,300 suspicious accounts, removed 1,500 reviews from the site, and put 250 restaurants on a 'special watch list' of establishments that might attempt to buy fake reviews in the Russian host cities" (Kinstler, 2018, n.p.). Also, in 2018, the owner of PromoSalento was sentenced to nine months in prison and an 8,000 euro fine for posting fake reviews about hospitality businesses in Italy.

Marketing through TripAdvisor

As a business or destination, engaging with TripAdvisor is a necessary evil in business and destination marketing. In fact, there is no way to opt out of TripAdvisor reviews. Therefore, managers must manage the reviews they receive. Zhang and Vásquez (2014) provides some tools to enhance the co-creation of travel experiences online:

- Express gratitude and thank reviewers;
- Apologize for sources of trouble;
- Invite reviewers for a second visit;
- Show proof of action in correcting issues;
- Acknowledge complaints and provide feedback;
- Respond to specific complaints rather than using generic responses;
- Refer to previous customer reviews;
- Avoid reoccurring problems;
- Solicit responses or comments via email;
- Add a personal voice by using pronouns and signatures.

Reflective questions

1. How can a company counter fake news about their establishment or destination? How will this support brand management?

2. Is TripAdvisor responsible for managing fake stories? Why or why not?

3. Should government regulate social media? Why or why not?

References

Kaplan, A.M. & Haenlein, M. (2010). Users of the world, unite! The challenges and opportunities of social media. *Business Horizons*, 53, 59–68.

Kinstler, L. (2018). The world's biggest travel site has turned the industry upside down – but now it is struggling to deal with the same kinds of problems that are vexing other tech giants like Facebook, Google and Twitter. *Guardian*, August 17. Retrieved from www.theguardian.com/news/2018/aug/17/how-tripadvisor-changed-travel.

Mzezewa, T. (2019). TripAdvisor modified its approach to reviews and sexual assault. Did it go far enough? *The New York Times*, May 16. Retrieved from www.nytimes.com/2019/05/16/travel/tripadvisor-safety-sexual-assault-reviews.html.

Roque, V. & Raposo, R. (2016). Social media as a communication and marketing tool in tourism: an analysis of online activities from international key player DMO, *Anatolia*, 27(1), 58–70.

Stimmler-Hall, H. (2016). What you don't know about TripAdvisor: how the world's largest travel monopoly ultimately hurts travelers and small businesses. *Medium*. Retrieved from https://medium.com/choking-on-a-macaron/what-you-don-t-know-about-tripadvisor-15d31d745bdc.

Zhang, Y. & Vásquez, C. (2014). Hotels' responses to online reviews: Managing consumer dissatisfaction. *Discourse, Context & Media*, 6, 54–64.

STUDY QUESTIONS

1. Determine if the following actions represent expectations, motivations, or satisfaction.

- At a dinner party, a person tells the story of an amazing tour guide they had on a recent trip;
- A husband and wife search for a travel package that includes both shopping and hiking;
- A person reads reviews of different travel operators that organize trips to Morocco;
- A foodie books a week-long cooking school in southern Italy;
- Someone posts travel pictures on Facebook;
- A school group travels to a local museum as part of a history project.

2. Your hometown offers walking tours through the historic district. How would the tour company's marketing differ from the DMO's marketing? Why?

3. As you start a new company, how would you gather information about your competition? How would you differentiate your business from the competition? Why?

4. In sustainable tourism, how are the elements of the marketing mix different from traditional tourism?

5. Develop a SWOT analysis for your hometown.

DEFINITIONS

Attribute   a descriptive quality that a visitor believes a destination or business has, such as physical characteristics, like beaches, nightclubs, or outstanding food choices

Balance sheet   contains an organization's assets, liabilities, and owners' equity

Benefit   the personal values each visitor attaches to each attribute

Brand   a unique name, term, sign, symbol, design, or combination of these that identifies the good or services of one seller or group of sellers and differentiates them from the competition

Business marketing   marketing the actual products, services, or experiences that a single business entity offers

Cash flow statement   shows how changes in balance sheet and income affect cash and cash equivalents, and breaks the analysis down to operating, investing, and financing activities

Competition-oriented pricing   the practice of setting prices based on the prices of other comparable businesses

Cost-based pricing   price is determined by calculating the cost of production plus a per-unit profit margin on each item sold

Demand-oriented pricing   price is based on consumers' willingness to pay

Destination marketing   marketing for a specific location that generally includes all activities, sights, and tourism businesses in a destination

Destination marketing and management organization (DMO)   an organization that represents destinations and helps to develop long-term travel and tourism strategies

Distribution channel   the chain of businesses or intermediaries through which a good or service passes until it reaches the end consumer

Environmental scanning   the process of monitoring the external environment

Expectations   strong beliefs that something will happen which are derived from the need to fulfill a goal that has some intrinsic value or attractiveness

External cost   a cost to society, regardless of who pays for it

Goal   an envisioned future state that people commit to achieving

Greenhouse gas   a gas that enters the earth's atmosphere and traps heat, causing a warming of the atmosphere

Income statement   shows the net return of a business, its revenue minus its expenses, or its profit

Marketing   the activities of a company associated with buying and selling a product or service, which includes advertising, selling, and delivering products to people

Marketing mix   a combination of factors that can be controlled by a company to influence consumers to purchase its products and consists of four primary elements: product, distribution, price, and promotion

Market segmentation   the activity of dividing a broad consumer base, normally consisting of existing and potential customers, into sub-groups of consumers (known as segments) based on some type of shared characteristics

Motivation   the desire or willingness to do something or go somewhere to fulfill specific needs

Objective   a measurable step taken to achieve a goal

Parity pricing   setting the price equal to the competition

Penetration pricing   setting the price lower than the competition

Premium pricing   setting the price higher than the competition

Private cost   the cost the firm pays to purchase capital equipment, hire labor, and buy materials or other inputs

Satisfaction   providing an experience (tourism product) that meets or exceeds the customer's expectations

Social cost   The combination of private costs and external costs of production

SWOT analysis   the strengths, weaknesses, opportunities, and threats related to business competition

Willingness to pay   the maximum price at or below which a consumer will definitely buy one unit of a product

Chapter **9**

Supply and value chain management

Overview

This chapter explains the similarities and differences between supply chain management and value chain management in relation to upstream and downstream activities. In addition, ensuring customer expectations are met requires both horizontal and vertical collaboration between service providers within the tourism value chain. This chapter specifically highlights input suppliers and tour operators as important components of sustainability and introduces reverse logistics in relation to tourism. Building collaboration and sharing knowledge is a prerequisite for successful value chain partnerships. A tool to help managers choose suppliers is also explained.

CHAPTER OBJECTIVES

At the completion of the chapter, students will be able to:

- Explain supply chain management and value chain management;
- Differentiate between upstream and downstream suppliers;
- Describe horizontal and vertical collaboration;
- Categorize the sustainable attributes of input supply chains and tour packages;
- Explain reverse logistics;
- Evaluate the importance of knowledge sharing along the value chain; and
- List important criteria, and the relationship between criteria, for the selection of supply chain partners.

Introduction

Sustainability is a growing focus among tourism businesses as companies recognize the opportunity to gain competitive advantage within an increasingly saturated industry environment. Jones, Hillier, and Comfort (2016) write, "boardroom agendas and growing numbers of companies acknowledge sustainability as one of the emerging drivers of competition, and as a significant source of both opportunity for, and risk to, long-term competitive advantage" (p. 41). However, it is recognized that many managers are not fully aware of what constitutes sustainable tourism nor what actions are needed to ensure that sustainability principles are accurately and effectively being implemented (Salzmann, Ionescu-Somers, & Steger, 2005). Because tourism is a complex system with wide-ranging stakeholders, sustainability requires cooperation among many different industries and a variety of tourism products, services, and experiences. Therefore, Sigala (2008) argues that supply chain management is a critical tool that provides information and access for tourism suppliers to enhance tourism sustainability.

Tourism organizations must design innovative products that not only satisfy the needs of their customers, but also differentiate themselves from the numerous other tourism businesses and destinations. The **tourism supply chain** (TSC) is a network of tourism organizations involved in a series of diverse activities, including the provision of an entire spectrum of components of tourism products and services, beginning with flights and accommodation and ending with the sale of tourism products in the destination (Zhang, Song, & Huang, 2009). Supply chain management covers all aspects of a product's production cycle, such as raw materials, processing, manufacturing, distribution, retailing, customer use, and final product disposal. Many of the

Image 9.1 Local products at SeaTac Airport, Washington

Source: Susan L. Slocum

negative impacts resulting from tourism originate along the tourism supply chain. Therefore, finding an appropriate distribution channel is a vital step in achieving a company's sustainability objectives. Szpilko (2017) recognizes that "cooperation between multiple business partners in a tourism supply chain constitutes an important determinant of the success of a product on the tourist market, and assuming that it is successful, contributes to the optimization of the business activities" (p. 688).

The supply stream

Tourism businesses provide end services to visitors, or may be somewhere along the supply chain providing goods and services to other tourism businesses. The terms upstream and downstream help explain where in the supply chain a business may be located. **Upstream activities** refer to the inputs that a company buys to make or sell its product and includes suppliers, purchases, and production lines. **Downstream activities** include all selling activities, such as tour operators and concessionaires (e.g. on-site restaurant contractors, transportation companies, or travel booking websites). Figure 9.1 shows a simple example of a tourism supply chain; although there are many variations to this model and all businesses buy and sell along the supply chain.

Within the supply chain, businesses will collaborate in order to increase their bargaining power with certain suppliers or to ensure a certain level of quality along the supply chain. There are two types of collaboration. **Horizontal collaboration** is collaboration between firms at the same level of the tourism supply chain, such as tour operators that work together to buy airline seats in bulk at a discounted rate. With travel agents and tour operators, horizontal collaborative groups are commonly called consortiums. A **consortium** is an association of two or more companies with the objective of pooling their resources to achieve a common goal. For example, if someone books an all-inclusive package with a well-known travel company, they may be able to find lower airline prices than others could find independently. This is because travel companies buy a large number of airline tickets at a discount for all of their customers. **Vertical collaboration** is collaboration between firms at different levels within the supply chain, such as supply inputs (upstream collaboration) or the businesses to which they sell their final products (downstream collaboration). Table 9.1 show some common reasons why hotels, as an example, may consider collaboration.

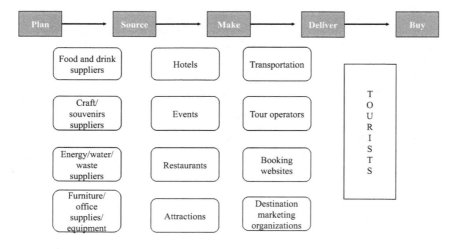

Figure 9.1 Supply chains in tourism

Table 9.1 Hotel collaborations

Objective	Horizontal collaboration	Vertical collaboration	
		Downstream	Upstream
Destination marketing	Combine services and sell as a package (e.g. rooms and cultural shows and dinner with a discounted price)	• Supplier selection • Order fulfilment and replenishment • Sales and promotion	Meeting, information sharing about room booking and reservations, demand forecasting
Infrastructure development	Ensure a variety of quality and price selections in a destination (e.g. 3-star and 5-star accommodation choices)	Hotels and transportation companies to ensure adequate airport shuttle service	Hotel and conference center partnerships to ensure meeting attendees have adequate accommodations
Customer satisfaction	Provide a list of hotel restaurants to ensure variety in food service	Ensure production inputs meet customer expectations (e.g. linens, food quality, complementary room amenities)	Provide a variety of activities to do while visiting (e.g. museums, theme parks, entertainment)
Sustainability	Ensure tourism minimizes negative impacts to the community	Provide sustainable products and packaging	Ensure customers have sustainability options throughout their stay (e.g. local sourcing restaurants, public transportation options)

The value chain

One way to look at a supply chain is to see how it provides extra value to the customers. A **value chain** is a system that describes how private businesses in collaboration with governments and civil society receive or access resources as inputs, add value through various processes (planning, development, financing, marketing, distribution, pricing, positioning, among others) and sell the resulting products to visitors. The value chain describes the full range of activities that are required to serve a visitor, including the supply chain. The difference between a value chain and a supply chain is that a supply chain is the process of all parties involved in fulfilling a customer request, while a value chain is a set of interrelated activities a company uses to create competitive advantage. In other words, the supply chain is about the inputs and outputs of a firm, whereas the value chain is about the customer experience. The value chain should be driven by the passion, pride, and confidence of key stakeholders so that visitors experience the best that a destination has to offer. Therefore, hotels, meeting planners, restaurants, airlines, destination marketing organizations, and attractions will collaborate to ensure that the destination fulfills a customer's expectations, that the travel experience is rewarding, and that visitors recommend the destination to family and friends. If sustainability is truly rooted within the mission of a company, it is linked to every business decision and collaborative partnership along the value chain (Jonker & de Witte, 2006).

As an example, many tourism businesses, such as hotels, restaurants, and special event companies, purchase linens such as bed sheets, towel, tablecloths, or napkins. From a supply chain perspective, a manager may look at thread count (quality), color selection, ease of distribution (how quickly a replacement can be shipped), and cost. From a sustainability value chain perspective, a sustainable business may consider how the linen is made (mass produced versus handmade), construction material (synthetic fiber versus organic cotton), or where the product is made (imported versus supporting local producers). A business will make hundreds of supply chain decisions, and managers must consider how each of these decisions support the overall mission of sustainability and, ultimately, customer satisfaction. Choosing a sustainable supply chain is the most impactful way a company can support the triple bottom line of sustainability.

Types of value chains

Each business is just one step in the overall value chain that serves a tourist. Therefore, finding the appropriate supply network and developing collaborative partnerships is a vital management activity since each business may have limited control over the entire customer experience. However, tourism businesses are often integrated into several value chains simultaneously. Determining how these collaborations add to the sustainability agenda of a business should influence the decisions being made. Therefore, a look at the different types of value chains in tourism is necessary.

Input supplies

Every business needs products to serve a tourist; from the food a tourist eats, to the office supplies necessary to run the operation. These are called **backward linkages** in the supply chain, or channels through which information, material, and money flow between a company and its suppliers. Many of these types of inputs have complicated supply chains, involving a number of distributors between the input's production and delivery to the company that utilizes them. Most of these inputs are purchased in bulk, and a manager may look for a distributor that claims similar sustainability values. However, in practice, distributors will carry a variety of product lines to maintain a larger market share and may carry traditional products as well as sustainable options. Moreover, because of the global nature of supply chains, the distributor may not know the production processes of every item they carry. For example, many cleaning supplies use harsh chemicals that not only pollute the environment where they are used (such as leeching into water supplies), but generate extensive pollution in the production process. All-natural cleaning supplies are on the rise, but not every country has regulations requiring a list of the chemical used in cleaning products. A distributor may carry products labeled as 'all natural', but may not know how 'all natural' is defined in the countries that produced the cleaning supplies, assuming they even know which countries manufactured their inventory. Other issues that may concern sustainable businesses include water and energy consumption throughout the production and distribution process, as well as the amount of waste generated. Therefore, transparency in the production process is important for making solid sustainability purchasing decisions.

Another issue in the purchase of inputs is considering the employment practices of suppliers during the production process. Globalization has eased the transfer of inputs, so that managers rarely know who produced them. A sustainable business may be concerned with the wages paid throughout the production process, health and safety issues for employees, or whether a supplier maintains a relationship with the local community where inputs are processed. Again, not all distributors will have information related to these issues, so sourcing through distributors who can provide details related to their sustainable practices is ideal.

One way to ensure products meet sustainability objectives is through certification. While certification is discussed in more detail in Chapter 10, **certification** is defined as a type of label indicating that compliance with standards has been verified by an outside agency. Buying products that have a sustainability certification rating can help sustainable businesses make educated purchasing decisions. Labels, such as 'organic' or 'Fair Trade', can ensure that the inputs used in a business have minimal negative impacts on the triple bottom line. It is important to note that not all sustainability certifications are the same, so careful research into the criteria used in a certification is important.

Another sustainability strategy is locally sourcing as many inputs as possible. The goal of sourcing locally is to ensure that the profits from inputs remain in the local economy and support small business development (Lane, 2009) as a way to avoid economic **leakages** (see Chapter 1). It also increases transparency when a business can visit the production site of its inputs. Another advantage is the reduction in greenhouse gas emissions associated with long-haul distribution (Gössling & Hall, 2013). Sourcing locally can offer the visitor unique cultural experiences, where local food or other traditional items add value by enhancing their exposure to the destination's traditional production practices. Many sustainable businesses pride themselves on sourcing locally.

Package tours

Tourism services, in the form of transportation, lodging, attractions, tours, and food and beverages, can be purchased by tourists as a package in advance of travel at a lower cost, rather than independently at a higher cost (Yamamoto & Gill, 1999). This is because of economies of scale. **Economies of scale** refer to a proportionate saving in costs gained by an increased level of production. Pongsathornwiwat, Huynh, and Jeenanunta (2017) recognize five reasons why tourists may purchase package deals when traveling:

- Package deals are a convenience for tourists;
- They guarantee security and safety while traveling;
- Tourists can view online ratings of entire packages rather than searching each aspect of a destination individually;
- Package deals are generally more affordable; and
- Tourists can save time during the planning stages.

As a sustainable business, it is important to use appropriate distribution channels for the products and services produced or provided. Many tourism businesses find that being included in a package deal is beneficial to their bottom line and an effective distribution strategy. Sigala (2008) highlights three benefits of being part of a package for tour operators:

- They greatly influence the volume and direction of tourism flows;
- They integrate and affect attitudes and practices of numerous tourism suppliers and stakeholders; and
- They lead to widespread benefits due to their large size.

Image 9.2 Tourist boats in Halong Bay, Vietnam

Source: Susan L. Slocum

By bundling services within a destination, tour operators provide a value distribution option for many tourism businesses.

However, choosing a tour operator that has sustainability options throughout the entire package can be difficult. One feature to look for are tour operators who use local tour companies and local tour guides in-country to ensure that jobs go to local residents. Another aspect to consider is whether the educational material that tour companies give to travelers encourages responsible behavior, specifically information about appropriate behavior in natural areas and cultural norms in the country visited. Educating the tourist can be a valuable way to reduce the negative impacts of tourism (see Chapter 12).

Reverse logistics

Reverse logistics is the process of transporting goods and services backward along the supply chain, such as returning defective products or disposing of waste. Reverse logistics can be expensive, but good management can save a company money as well as reduce unintended impacts on communities (Sarkis, 2012). The first step in analyzing reverse logistics is to assess the complex questions of why, when, how, and where reverse flows occur along the supply chain, and then identify where inefficiencies may occur. Since reverse logistics are not primary activities for tourism businesses, they are often overlooked. Škapa (2014) acknowledges that services, such as tourism products, are intangible, meaning they cannot be stored as inventory, and are hard to recognize as reverse logistics. However, tourism is made up of a number of tangible products that enhance the experience. Table 9.2 shows some examples of tangible flows from tourism that may have reverse flows along the supply chain.

Table 9.2 Tangible reverse flows from tourism

Broad category	Sample items
Product return/complaint	Return of meals and drinks
	Return of semi-finished products/ingredients
	Accommodation complaints
Waste	Food and drink waste
	Packaging
	Water and sewage
	Equipment destroyed by customers
Re-usable service components	Linens
	Food service items
	Machinery/equipment
Returnable packaging	Returnable bottles
Financial flows	Revenue, profit
Customer "returns"	Loyalty programs
	Repeat customers
Documents	Customer questionnaires
	Customer orders
	Proof of payment

Source: Adapted from Škapa (2014)

In sustainability, reverse logistics should include a process for the reduction of waste, the reuse of items, and a recycling plan as a means of reducing pressure on landfills. An **integrated waste management plan** is a working document that outlines the process of managing waste that is created through tourism consumption, implementing disposal methods that reduce harm to the environment, and waste reduction methods, such as reusing, recycling, and composting. Likely avenues to dispose of toxic substances, human waste, and chemicals should also be included in the waste management plan. Figure 9.2 shows the process of developing the plan. It involves the practice of reduce, reuse, and recycle (the 3Rs), which can help to cut down on the amount of waste thrown away. The 6Rs conserve natural resources, landfill space, and energy, as well as save land and money that communities must use to maintain waste in landfills. The 6Rs include:

- Step 1: Rethink/reinvent by considering and questioning consumption habits. As people begin to question what they think they 'really' need, they will become increasingly self-aware of their effect on the environment. This self-awareness may influence their behavior, values, and consumption habits.
- Step 2: Refuse by making the choice to not generate waste. By avoiding certain products that appear to be more wasteful than others (such as excessive packing materials or short shelf-lives), and by purchasing sustainable products, consumers can cast their financial 'vote' in support of sustainably-minded products.

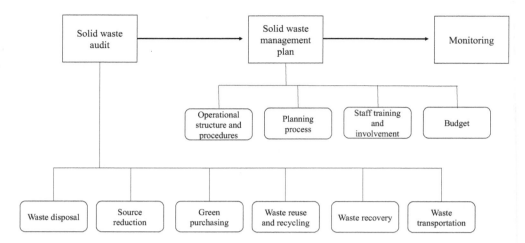

Figure 9.2 Integrated waste management

- Step 3: Reduce the amount of waste generated. This is usually done by reducing the amount of inputs a business or a tourist uses throughout the tourism product experience. Most waste is generated through packaging, so purchasing in bulk can help to reduce waste. Also, eliminate one-time use products and disposables (paper plates, plastic water bottles, straws, and utensils).

- Step 4: Reuse or repair the waste that is generated. Reusing boxes and other packaging material, as well as buying used items, can reduce the amount of waste sent to landfills. Moreover, buying products made from recycled materials supports recycling activities.

- Step 5: Recycle waste. Many recycling centers will take plastic, glass, paper, cans, and wood products, but other items, such as electronic equipment, batteries, and heavy metals, may need to be taken to special recycling facilities. Food waste can be composted and used as fertilizers for landscaping.

- Step 6: Replace or rebuy by purchasing products made from recycled material. Consumers can promote recycled products by purchasing items that incorporate items in whole or in part from material recovered from the waste stream. Consumers can look for labels on packages that include a percentage of recovered materials.

Building supply chain partnerships

As tourism moves away from focusing on mass tourism and towards a more customized travel experience, establishing effective partnerships is vital to the success of any business. Since the tourist views the entire holiday as a seamless series of experiences and activities, it is important for one entity to control the overall development of the tourism product. This is usually the tour operator, but could also be an event management company, hotel, or cruise line. **Focal companies** in the supply chain, with direct contact to end customers, and having bargaining power over other actors in the supply chain. From a sustainability perspective, focal companies should organize communication channels between stakeholders comprising a variety of viewpoints and interests, including other businesses along the supply chain, local authorities within the destination,

Image 9.3 *Game of Thrones* and *Star Wars* filming location, Dubrovnik, Croatia

Source: Susan L. Slocum

and civil society, such as nongovernment organizations. Pongsathornwiwat, Huynh, and Jeena-nunta (2017) write, "Successful service (provision) depends on involving various supply chain members and different operational functions to design, form, and bundle tourism products that can satisfy customers' preferences successfully" (p. 40). The goal is to build relationships and collaboratively determine sustainability targets appropriate to the destination (Seuring, Müller, Westhaus, & Morana 2005).

Effective collaboration along the value chain builds social capital within the industry or the destination, which can facilitate information exchange, support collective access to resources, and allow for new business prospects and innovation. Therefore, the focal company must establish trust, commitment, coordination, communication, information exchange, participation, and effective resolution techniques, in order to ensure the long-term success of the value chain. Moreover, if value chain members offer inadequate service, the focal business has the authority to censure or drop them. When selecting a value chain member, it is vital that the products and company's values align with other members of the collaborative partnership.

Sharing knowledge

One of the key barriers to sustainability is a lack of knowledge about suitable sustainability practices by managers or businesses (Lee & Slocum, 2015). An effective value chain focuses on sustainability options for travelers and should include information and training on sustainability practices appropriate for different aspects of the travel package. While much of this information can be learned through the certification process, it is the responsibility of the focal company to provide ongoing opportunities to improve the tourism product. This requires the focal company to have a breadth of knowledge about the implementation of sustainability at all levels of the value chain. For example, hotels may be interested in reducing their consumption of water (especially in arid landscapes), energy, and waste, whereas a transportation company may need technology that helps reduce travel time (and greenhouse gas emissions) between deliveries. Restaurants may need information about where to buy local produce and learn about sustainable agricultural production. While the focal company may not be an expert in sustainability for all industries, they need to have access to information and should include a variety of experts to support information exchange for all value chain members.

There are many effective ways of sharing knowledge along the value chain. The most common way is through certification and many focal companies will require a certification label (discussed in more detail in Chapter 10). However, certifications vary from country to country and from industry to industry, so finding appropriate certifications can be time consuming, and some certification may have substandard requirements. Certifications provide an avenue to benchmark performance. **Benchmarking** is the process of comparing a business's process and performance metrics to industry best practices from other companies and can be used to track performance over time. Benchmarking allows the focal company to see where their partners' strengths and weaknesses lie, and where a company may need help to improve its sustainability performance.

Other focal companies may provide ongoing training to their suppliers or partners, which is expensive but ensures that all value chain members are striving towards the same levels of sustainability and customer satisfaction. A value chain may have a partnership website that provides resources or contact information for approved suppliers. Lastly, newsletters and case studies help showcase best practice tools or can stimulate innovation along the value chain. These communication tools can also provide information to assist in the benchmarking process by highlighting the practices of similar businesses along horizontal collaboration channels (Font, Walmsley, Cogotti, McCombes, & Hausler, 2012).

Lastly, it is important for knowledge sharing to be a two-way channel of communication. All members along the value chain should be aware of the practices of other collaborative partners. Some focal companies require extensive reporting on an annual basis to ensure that member businesses are maintaining or improving performance. Many hotel management companies will require their franchise owners to report energy, water, and waste consumption numbers to ensure constant improvements over time. Tour operators may require information on community development projects or conservation initiatives that businesses support. The goal is to avoid finding discrepancies through customer complaints or decreased sales; although this is all too often the way information is transferred.

SUSTAINABILITY TOOL: CHOOSING SUPPLY PARTNERS

Tourism businesses often have a number of suppliers from which to choose. For example, a hotel chain or international tour operator may want to offer guided tours of a local cultural heritage site. There may be dozens of local tour companies that offer the excursion, so choosing the best company may be a challenge. Most businesses make hundreds of supply chain decisions since tourism experiences require an extensive list of inputs. As Pongsathornwiwat, Huynh, and Jeenanunta (2017) write, "Successful service process depends on involving various supply chain members and different operational functions to design, form, and bundle tourism products that can satisfy customers' preferences successfully" (p. 40). Determining which suppliers offer the best service, the best product, and do so in a sustainable manner can be a very challenging task.

Tourism businesses face two specific challenges when choosing supply chain partners: determining suitable evaluation criteria for supply-partner selection in the context of the tourism supply chain; and understanding the relationships between criteria that influence successful performance for suppliers. Product and service quality are obvious issues of consideration, as is cost and customer service reputation; however, from a sustainability perspective, there are other considerations as well. Businesses and destinations must address demand uncertainty as tourism visitation is influenced by global economic and political changes. Therefore, finding suppliers that help reduce risk should be a core selection criterion. This can be done by determining the past performance of suppliers and their ability to adapt to market forces. Moreover, a reputation as a sustainable business, above and beyond just certification, should also be included. Table 9.3 provides some selection criteria to consider.

Table 9.3 Suitable evaluation criteria for tourism partner selection

Main criteria	Sub-criteria	Brief description
Supplier's performance	Flexibility	Ability to change a requirement rapidly
	Capacity	Ability to support the buyers' requirement
	Service-oriented	Perceived ability to deliver a good service
	Sustainability	Goods and services conform to the established sustainability criteria
Supplier's profile	Reputation	Has a good view of customers
	Performance history and relationship closeness	Ability to sustain the best performances
	Sustainability	Is well known as a sustainably-minded company
Product's characteristics	Product cost	Suppliers can provide the lowest cost for us
	Product quality	The supplier can provide the best product/service for us
	Novelty	Suppliers can support and design innovative product
	Sustainability	Has a track record of sustainable production

Table 9.3 continued

Main criteria	Sub-criteria	Brief description
Partner's compatibility	Organizational culture	Understands different cultures
	Communication and coordination	Communicates and coordinates effectively
	Symmetry in organizational size	Is large enough to offer a variety of products or services, yet small enough to provide customized service
	Trust and commitment	Has a high level of mutual trust and commitment to work together
	Strategic goals fit	Adopts a win–win strategy together
	Conflict resolution	Ability to negotiate and compromise when conflicting
	Sustainability	Maintains long-term supply partners
Risk factors	Political stability	The political status at the destination
	Economy	The economic status, such as currency exchange rates at the destination
	Sustainability	Evidence of staying power through past instability

Source: Adapted from Pongsathornwiwat, Huynh, & Jeenanunta (2017)

Choosing a value chain partner

It is important to note that the main criteria in Table 9.3 are not easily visible when evaluating potential suppliers, even if they are the primary considerations for selection. Therefore, an organization must determine appropriate ways to learn about potential suppliers and the relationships between what can be known about a potential supply partner and what that information may infer about a company. Figure 9.3 shows the interrelationship between the criteria mentioned in Table 9.3.

Customer service

Evidence suggests that companies that are customer service oriented generally transfer that commitment to the supply chain (Liburd, 2012). This usually translates into a superior reputation for a firm. Since it is hard to judge a company's level of commitment before establishing a partnership, reputation is a good measure of the level of service that can be expected. Reputations can be evaluated by looking at customer reviews online or talking with other businesses that may already have a relationship with a specific firm. Competitors may want to help their suppliers be successful as well as establish a good reputation for the overall destination, so may be willing to provide a reference. Beware of testimonials that a potential supplier offers as part of the sales narrative. Always contact these references to make sure they are valid. Another

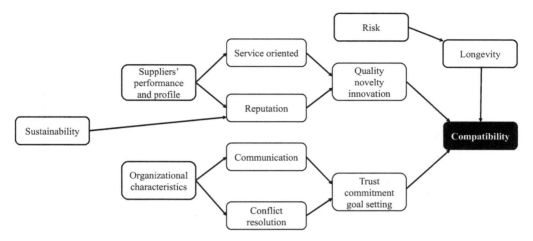

Figure 9.3 Relationships between criteria and successful performance
Source: Adapted from Škapa (2014)

avenue is to evaluate respectable horizontal organizations and track their value chain. If a highly reputable sustainable business is using a specific food distributor, there is a good chance that distributor meets general sustainability criteria.

Innovation

There is also a strong connection between service quality and innovation, as companies that are known for exceptional tourism products are more inclined to generate new products and services (Lee, Chang, & Chen, 2013). Often innovation comes from collaborative partnerships, so finding a supply chain partner that can enhance the tourism product is a major advantage, specifically if this partner is a focal company that can control the overall value chain. The right partner can actually help improve business performance and find specific areas where tourism services are limited in a destination or support new sustainable product options. Again, online reviews and recommendations can provide information on service quality, and websites highlight the diversity in the products or services offered.

Collaboration

Lastly, firms that communicate efficiently and are willing to take the lead in collaboration are also more likely to align strategic goals along the supply chain and engage in conflict resolution (Pongsathornwiwat, Huynh, & Jeenanunta, 2017). Ensuring that the organizational values align with others in the supply chain not only reduces conflict, but it is more likely that you will be able to find a compromise that improves both organizations' operations. Part of the communication strategy includes the level of commitment to sustainability. Asking to see certain strategic planning documents can help provide information on how a supplier plans to increase its sustainability or how a supplier monitors its impacts. Keep in mind that many companies will not share strategic plans in their entirety, but may be open to conversation about long-term sustainability strategies or a specific sustainability project under development if it supports the overall success of the value chain.

Conclusion

One key way to minimize negative tourism impacts is through supply chain management. Establishing partnerships between upstream and downstream members of the supply chain, and building both horizontal and vertical collaboration, are important steps in ensuring sustainability in all the products and services sourced by a company. Focal companies are leaders in the value chain and need to ensure that businesses collaborate and share knowledge in relation to best practice and effective sustainability measures. Benchmarking allows companies to measure improvements in sustainability that can be communicated throughout the value chain. While tourism businesses have many suppliers from which to choose, establishing effective selection criteria and understanding the relationship between elements within the criteria is important. The tool in this chapter guides managers on the selection of value chain members that will serve and support the sustainability agenda.

CASE STUDY 9.1 FOCAL INFLUENCE: THE CASE OF TUI

SUSAN L. SLOCUM

Introduction

TUI Group (Tourism Union International) is the world's largest tour operator. Headquartered in Hanover, Germany, TUI owns 1600 travel agencies, 380 hotels, 17 cruise ships, retail stores, and six European airlines with a fleet of over 150 airplanes. TUI covers the entire tourism value chain, serving 27 million customers in 180 regions and employing over 9,000 people (TUI Group, 2019a). TUI's commitment to sustainability is evident in their mission: "A key feature of our corporate culture is our global responsibility for economic, environmental, and social sustainability. This is reflected in more than 20 years of commitment to sustainable tourism" (TUI Group, 2019a, n.p.).

In 2015, TUI launched its *Better Holidays, Better World* Strategy. The goal was to cut the carbon intensity of its airline, cruise, and ground operations by 10%, deliver 10 million greener and fairer holidays per year, and invest €10 million per year to support good causes and enhance the positive impacts of tourism by the year 2020 (TUI Group, 2018a). Its four primary goals include:

- Reducing the environmental impacts of holidays;
- Creating positive change for people and communities;
- Pioneering sustainable tourism across the world; and
- Building the best place to work where people are passionate about what they do.

TUI used a materiality assessment (see Chapter 6) to assess their impacts on nature and society across the value chain. They used both quantitative and qualitative tools with 2,800 stakeholders to determine the business relevancy of sustainability and to prioritize sustainability criteria. Results indicated that precedence should be given to the following issues (TUI Group, 2018a):

- Resource efficiency and waste;
- Child protection;

- Local value creation and communities; and
- Emissions.

Value chain practice at TUI

TUI is undoubtedly one of the most powerful influencers for sustainable tourism primarily because of their size and market reach, making them the obvious focal company in the tourism value chain. This position allows TUI to demand sustainability practices both upstream and downstream in their supply chain.

Upstream initiatives

TUI has been actively engaged in lowering carbon emissions by working with Bio-Port Holland to develop more sustainable forms of jet fuel. They are encouraging research into new plant-based fuel (biofuel) options, working with organizations such as AlgaePARC (a partnership with Wageningen University & Research) to improve algae-based jet fuel and to build full-scale algae production facilities. Their new fleet of planes use a blend of traditional jet fuel with 30% sustainable fuel, from a certified supplier.

TUI encourages all member hotels and hotel partners to obtain certification that meets the Global Sustainable Tourism Council (GSTC) standards. Moreover, minimum expectations for accommodation suppliers are set out in a mandatory clause in their contracts. In 2018, 9.2 million TUI customers stayed in a certified hotel, 1,520 contracts

Image 9.4 TUI plane ready for take-off

Source: Tim Dennert on Unsplash

were signed with certified hotels, and 78 TUI hotels (81%) received sustainability certification (TUI Group, 2019c).

In 2019, the TUI Group published its third *Modern Slavery Statement* which lays out the steps to be taken to prevent acts of modern slavery and human trafficking from occurring in its supply chain. Their approach involves (TUI Group, 2019b):

- Expanding policies by creating the Global Employment Statement and re-launching their Employee Code of Conduct, which explicitly contain modern slavery provisions that apply to their employees, business partners, and suppliers;
- Increasing the number of hotels with independent sustainability certifications and establishing approaches to assessing modern slavery risk in non-accommodation supply chains; and
- Engaging stakeholders in modern slavery prevention by initiating new projects that focus on addressing child protection and youth empowerment in at-risk destinations.

Downstream initiatives

TUI works with hotel suppliers to drive environmental and social sustainability by highlighting sustainability certification accomplishments to their customers. They publish the *Guidelines for Environmental Sustainability for Hotels* and *Supplier Code of Conduct* for use by all their partner hotels.

In partnership with the Association of British Travel Agents, TUI supported the launch of the first *Global Welfare Guidance for Animals in Tourism* which requires all animal excursions to publicize their guidelines and support animal welfare audits of all animal-related excursion partners. In 2016, they discontinued all excursions involving elephant rides or shows and replaced them with elephant-friendly excursions where customers can visit and learn about elephants in their natural habitat.

In Andalusia, Spain, TUI is connecting local farmers with destination supply chains through direct training and technical support to130 farmers and 60 chefs. In Malaga, Spain, they are supporting women in food-based business initiatives. Approximately 70 underprivileged women are supported through promotional activities related to cooking schools, shopping at local markets, and guided tours.

Lastly, they strive to engage 5 million travelers in sustainable tourism. This is being accomplished through kids' club activities, local schools, and donation programs. They are also working to be recognized as a sustainability leader, which is monitored through customer surveys and feedback questionnaires.

Discussion

The information provided above came from TUI publications and information sources, so its credibility should, naturally, be questioned. Further research shows that in 2017, TUI Cruises received recognition at the World Responsible Tourism Awards, and in 2018, TUI UK & Ireland received the *Best for Communicating Responsible Tourism* award by the same organization. The Pacific Asian Travel Association (2015) writes "As a group, (TUI) has shown exemplary sustainable tourism practices, and its latest development, the

Sustainable Holidays Plan, is no exception" (n.p.). They appear to be taking their focal role in sustainability seriously.

One of TUI's goals includes building the best place to work where people are passionate about what they do. In April 2018, TUI was admonished by the *Guardian* newspaper for "their lack of women in leadership roles" (Kollewe & Butler, 2018). Moreover, when the UK government required all major corporations to report gender pay scales, it was shown that TUI paid female employees, on average, 45% less than male employees (Barr & Topping, 2018). TUI responded by saying "We know that our gender pay gap is not an equal pay issue, rather a lack of representation in specific roles such as pilots, engineering, technology and senior management" (TUI, 2018b, p. 1).

Reflective questions

1. List three areas of the supply chain not covered by TUI's sustainability initiative. How would you go about addressing sustainability issues with these suppliers?

2. Do you feel the equal treatment of employees (based on gender, race, religion, or sexual orientation) should be covered in a sustainability initiative? Why or why not?

3. How does TUI benefit from being a focal company that influences sustainability? What are some of the disadvantages of being a focal company?

References

Barr, C. & Topping, A. (2018). Firms touted as 'top employers' for women pay them less than men. *Guardian*, February 28. Retrieved from www.theguardian.com/news/2018/apr/08/firms-touted-as-top-employers-for-women-pay-them-less-than-men.

Kollewe, J. & Butler, S. (2018). Top UK companies under fire over lack of women in boardroom. *Guardian*, April 17. Retrieved from www.theguardian.com/business/2018/apr/17/top-uk-companies-women-boardroom-persimmon-bp-tui.

Pacific Asian Travel Association (2015). TUI Travel. Retrieved from https://sustain.pata.org/wttc-tui-travel/.

TUI Group (2018a). 2018 Sustainability report. Retrieved from www.tuigroup.com/en-en/responsibility/reporting-downloads.

TUI Group (2018b). TUI UK & Ireland gender pay gap report 2017/18. Retrieved from www.tuigroup.com/damfiles/default/tuigroup-15/en/about-us/our-business/TUI-UK-Ireland-Gender-Pay-Gap-Report.pdf.48123346d52936dd73ffe2d67ab31724.pdf.

TUI Group (2019a). About TUI Group. Retrieved from www.tuigroup.com/en-en/about-us/about-tui-group.

TUI Group (2019b). Modern slavery statement 2018. Retrieved from www.tuigroup.com/en-en/responsibility/msa.

TUI Group (2019c). Certification. Retrieved from www.tuigroup.com/en-en/responsibility/sus_business/hotel/certification.

CASE STUDY 9.2 LOCAL SOURCING IN BRAZIL: SUSTAINABLE OR EXPLOITIVE?

SUSAN L. SLOCUM

Introduction

Fishing is often the main source of income for people who live near coastal areas, specifically on islands. It is not surprising that coastal areas also act as huge attractions for tourists. Sourcing local fish would seem like a sustainable way to engage local communities in the tourism supply chain. However, not all fisheries are equally sustainable, and tourists' fish preferences have the potential to impact the sustainability of the industry. Some fish species have longer life spans and lower fertility rates, other fish play a key role in controlling the abundance of other species and can maintain a balance in the ecosystem, and some fishing techniques may destroy the seabed or require unsustainable baitfish (Rahel, 2016).

Consumers dictate demand for certain fish species, which changes over time. These preferences are shaped by a variety of factors, including sustainability values, the ability to make sustainable choices, peer pressure, or media influence (Vermeir & Verbeke, 2006). Moreover, consumers are often misinformed that eating local has few consequences on the ecosystem (Edwards-Jones, 2010).

Fernando de Noronha Marine Protected Area (MPA)

Fernando de Noronha is a series of volcanic islands 350 kilometers (217 miles) off the northeast coast of Brazil. The largest island is a protected national marine park and ecological sanctuary that has been designated as a UNESCO World Heritage Site. There are just over 5,000 residents and visitor numbers are restricted to 400 tourists a day, although as flights to the island escalate, there is pressure to increase this number (Lopes, Mendes, Fonseca, & Villasante, 2017). The rise in tourism has put growing pressure on water use, sewage, and garbage, and the Marine Protected Area (MPA) administration has warned that carrying capacities for the reserve have been ignored. There are 70 inns or *pousadas*, mostly personal homes, open to tourists. The government charges tourists a fee to support roads, hospitals, and schools.

The MPA is divided into 2 regions: 70% is a no-take fishing zone that allows controlled tourism (scuba diving and snorkeling) but no fishing access, and 30% is a sustainable use zone that allows fishing, accommodations, and developed tourism uses. Because seasonal swells reduce fish populations in the areas open to fishing, local fishermen want access to the closed areas, specifically to catch sardines which are used as baitfish for other species. In the past, park officials have granted access to this area, but recent management changes have resulted in the enforcement of rules, and local fishers caught in the no-take zone have been fined and arrested (Lopes et al., 2017).

Tourism fish consumption

Lopes et al. (2017) surveyed a number of hotels, restaurants, fishers, and tourists to better understand the local fish supply chain in Fernando de Noronha. They learned that 81% of the fish sold to tourists comes from local fishers, and the remainder comes

Image 9.5 Fernando de Noronha, Pernambuco, Brazil

Source: Pantai on Flickr

from mainland Brazil. About half of the fishers (56%) do not use a middleman, allowing them to keep a higher percentage of the profit margin. About 17% of all fish went to locals, the remainder to tourists or tourist establishments. Twenty-one of the 41 restaurants prefer to buy fish from the island, but also import fish when they cannot find enough local supply. The most commonly imported species are the same species usually caught locally (dolphin fish, yellowfin tuna, and wahoo).

The research showed that restaurants serve the same fish that is demanded by tourists rather than what is readily available in the surrounding ocean, requiring fishers to seek specific types of fish. Pelagic species (those that live neither close to the bottom nor near the shore) offer more boneless meat and are preferred to reef fish or deep-water species. According to the IUCN *Red List of Threatened Species*, yellowfin tuna is a near threatened species and wahoo is under threat, but not yet endangered. Dolphin fish (also known as Mahi Mahi) is more resilient because it reaches maturity at a faster rate, therefore producing more offspring. Lopes et al. (2017) recognize that the more threatened species, such as barracuda and black jacks, are luckily not in high demand. Lastly, many pelagic fish species are the top predators in the aquatic food chain and provide a natural balance in the ecosystem.

It was determined that tourists prefer their fish to be served as filets, which requires the removal of bones from the meat. Lopes et al. write, "Some estimates suggest that only

10% of the world's fish that is killed by fisheries ends up being used as food. The remaining is discarded (thrown overboard for having no economic interest), spoiled, turned into fishmeal, or wasted in inedible portions" (p. 131). This can be especially problematic in areas that suffer from inadequate waste facilities and infrastructure, such as Fernando de Noronha. Locals, on the other hand, tend to prefer reef fish, which are generally cooked and eaten whole, generating less waste.

Local fisheries are dependent on access to sardines, which are used as bait for pelagic species. Sardines are found in the reef area that constitutes the no-take zone of the MPA. While these no-take zones are exploited for commercial tourism use, access to these fish is vital to the long-term sustainability of the local fishing industry. Additionally, sardines are a major food source for the near-endangered lemon shark, which thrive within the protected areas.

Reflective questions

1. Develop a marketing campaign to encourage visitors to consumer more sustainable fish varieties, such as reef fish. What aspects would you highlight? Why?

2. How do you balance the needs of a fishing community with the needs of tourism markets? How do you balance tourism markets with global threats to certain fish populations? How do you determine whose needs take precedence?

3. Overall, is the tourism supply chain in Fernando de Noronha sustainable? Why or why not? What could be done differently?

References

Edwards-Jones, G. (2010). Does eating local food reduce the environmental impact of food production and enhance consumer health? *Proc. Nutr. Soc*, 69, 582–591.

Lopes, P.F.M., Mendes, L., Fonseca, V., & Villasante, S. (2017). Tourism as a driver of conflicts and changes in fisheries value chains in Marine Protected Areas. *Journal of Environmental Management*, 200, 123–134.

Rahel, F.J. (2016). Changing philosophies of fisheries management as illustrated by the history of fishing regulations in Wyoming. *Fisheries*, 41, 38–48.

Vermeir, I. & Verbeke, W. (2006). Sustainable food consumption: exploring the consumer attitude – behavioral intention gap. *J. Agric. Environ. Ethics*, 19, 169–194.

STUDY QUESTIONS

1. Describe how a supply chain in tourism is similar or different from a supply chain in a manufacturing industry. What specific challenges do tourism businesses face? Does being sustainable increase or simplify supply chain management for tourism? Why?

2. Explain a simple supply chain that gets the tourist from her place of residency to a destination. Explain how this would be different from a value chain perspective.

3. You are a manager of a historic site. How would you build collaboration between other tourism businesses in your destination to ensure the protection of your site? What conflict might arise?

4. The first step in benchmarking is understanding industry best practice. Where would you look for tourism best practice if you were running a casino in an indigenous community? What if you were running a youth hostel in the center of an urban destination? What differences would you expect in the best practices for each scenario?

5. Research suppliers of table linens and choose one for your value chain. What aspects of the selection criteria do they meet? Where could they improve?

DEFINITIONS

Backward linkage   a channel through which information, material, and money flows between a company and its suppliers

Benchmarking   the process of comparing a business process and performance metrics to industry best practices from other companies; it can be used to track performance over time

Certification   a type of label indicating that compliance with standards has been verified by an outside agency

Consortium   an association of two or more companies with the objective of pooling their resources to achieve a common goal

Downstream activities   all selling activities such as tour operators and concessionaires

Economies of scale   a proportionate saving in costs gained by an increased level of production

Focal companies   companies in the supply chain, with direct contact to end customers, and having bargain power over other actors in the supply chain

Horizontal collaboration   collaboration between firms in the same level of the tourism supply chain

Integrated waste management plan   a working document that outlines the process of managing waste that is created, implementing disposal methods that reduce harm to the environment, and waste reduction methods, such as reusing, recycling, and composting

Leakage   when consumer goods and services are imported from abroad or when tourism revenue leaves an economy

Reverse logistics   the process of transporting goods and services backward along the supply chain, such as returned or defective products, or the disposal of waste

Tourism supply chain (TSC)   a network of tourism organizations involved in a series of diverse activities, including the provision of an entire spectrum of components of tourism products/services, such as flights and accommodation, ending with the sale of tourism products in the tourism region

Upstream activities   the inputs that a company buys to make or sell its product and includes suppliers, purchases, and production lines

Value chain   a system which describes how private businesses in collaboration with governments and civil society receive or access resources as inputs, add value through various processes (planning, development, financing, marketing, distribution, pricing, positioning, among others), and sell the resulting products to visitors

Vertical collaboration   collaborations between a firm at different levels within the supply chain, such as inputs, or the partners to which they sell their final products

Chapter **10**

Certification

Overview

This chapter describes the importance of certification by explaining the benefits of certification, in terms of both attracting sustainable-minded customers and developing a sustainable supply chain. It highlights the certification process and the stakeholders needed to establish a reputable ecolabel. The chapter also discusses greenwashing and how to recognize the difference between green marketing and green management. It concludes with an explanation of the EU Ecolabel Tourist Accommodation Criteria in the tools section.

CHAPTER OBJECTIVES

At the completion of the chapter, students will be able to:

- Explain the difference between standards and criteria as they relate to certification;
- Recognize the top-rated tourism certifications globally;
- List the five stakeholders in the certification process and their responsibilities;
- Describe the difference between green marketing and green management;
- Explain greenwashing and how to recognize it; and
- Apply the principles of the EU Ecolabel Tourist Accommodation Criteria.

Introduction

As discussed in Chapter 4, transparency is required for good governance, which applies equally to a destination or a sustainable business. Communicating a commitment to sustainability not only allows sustainably-minded consumers to find a reputable organization with whom to do business, but it also helps to differentiate sustainable businesses along the supply chain. Promoting sustainability is very different from proving sustainability, therefore finding ways to communicate accomplishments in a way that is trustworthy and verifiable is an important part of business planning. Moreover, a business is only as sustainable as its supply chain, so choosing vendors that support a commitment to sustainability is very important for establishing a sustainable business or destination.

Ecolabels and certifications are proliferating in the tourism market and there are now so many different sustainability labels and certifications that it can be difficult to determine which ones are legitimate and representative of high-quality standards. Even though this may be the case, choosing to seek out and work with companies that have voluntarily sought and achieved sustainable certification is critical. From a supply chain perspective, some certifications are considered more valuable than others, based on their overall adoption and the resulting public and consumer recognition. For example, certifications such as Leadership in Energy and Environmental Design (LEED), Energy Star, Fair Trade, Marine Stewardship Council, and Forest Stewardship Council are very well-known and universally accepted as high-quality certifications. However, other quality labels may not be as commonly recognizable. When making supply chain purchasing decisions, it is strongly encouraged that decision-makers perform research into the widely accepted certifications and labels for a particular product, service, and region.

Understanding certification

The first step for any certification body is to determine the appropriate behaviors expected of a business by setting **standards**, or the technical specifications or criteria to be used consistently as rules, guidelines, or definitions, to ensure that materials, products, processes, and services are complying with best practice. Standards provide a common set of business practices that are recognized by an industry as appropriate or "good enough". Some businesses may require higher principles if they want to be seen as better than their competition, whereas other businesses may feel that the standards are acceptable. Standards should be the minimum requirements for any organization claiming sustainable business practices.

A **certification** is a type of label indicating that compliance with standards has been verified by an outside agency. In other words, it is a written guarantee that is used to communicate quality and conformity along the supply chain. The purpose of certification is to achieve voluntary standards, which meet or exceed baseline standards or legislation (Dodds & Joppe, 2005). Certifications may have multiple tiers, such as bronze, silver, and gold that imply increasing levels of compliance. It is important to note that most certification programs work regionally, rather than globally, making it difficult for travelers to distinguish among the standards used in any individual program. Table 10.1 shows the sustainability labels that are internationally

Table 10.1 International sustainability labels

Certification	Certifying institution	Description
Biosphere Responsible Tourism	Instituto de Turismo	Certifies accommodations, restaurants, amusement parks, golf courses, attractions, and entire destinations, (e.g. biosphere regions and cities in Europe and Latin America)
Blaue Schwalbe	Fairkehr GmbH	The Blaue Schwalbe was the first ecolabel for tourist accommodations and properties located in travel areas that can be reached easily without flying or private cars

Table 10.1 continued

Certification	Certifying institution	Description
Certification for Sustainable Tourism	Instituto Costaricense de Turismo	Certifies hotels, local tour operators, and car rentals in Costa Rica
EarthCheck	EarthCheck Pty Limited	Certifies hotels, activities, attractions, restaurants, transport, and mobility services and destinations
ECO Certification Program	Eco Tourism Australia	Awarded to accommodations, tours, and attractions offered by nature-based tourism operators in Australia
Ecotourism Kenya	Ecotourism Kenya	The Kenyan certificate is awarded to hotels, lodges, and camps
EU Ecolabel	European Commission	The official European Union label is awarded to accommodation establishments and campsites
Fair Trade Tourism	Fair Trade Tourism	Certifies tour operators in South Africa, Madagascar, and Mozambique
Green Globe	Green Globe	Certifies businesses, conference centers, hotels, resorts, and attractions
Green Key	Foundation of Environmental Education	A worldwide ecolabel awarded to leisure infrastructures such as hotels, hostels, campsites, holiday parks, small accommodations, conference centers, restaurants, and attractions
Green Leaf Foundation	Green Leaf Foundation	Certifies hotels, spas, and holiday resorts in Thailand
Green Tourism Business Scheme	Green Tourism	Awarded to hotel chains, management groups and hospitality brands; green suppliers, destination partners, local authorities, and agencies in the UK and Ireland
Ibex Fairstay	Ibex Fairstay, independent authority	A Swiss label for sustainability management awarded to accommodation establishments, hostels, and clinics
Legambiente Turismo	Legambiente Turismo	Works closely with Italian tourist destinations, hotels, campsites, guesthouses, restaurants, tour operators, and agro-tourism farms
Nordic Swan	Ecolabelling Sweden	Certifies a broad range of businesses, including hotels, restaurants, and conference facilities
Österreichisches Umweltzeichen für Tourismus	Austrian Federal Ministry for Agriculture, Forestry Environment and Water Management	Austrian Ecolabel was the first national ecolabel for tourism worldwide. It is awarded to accommodations, restaurants, travel packages, green meetings, events, conference centers, and event locations

Certification	Certifying institution	Description
Rainforest Alliance Certificate	Rainforest Alliance	Certifies hotels, restaurants, and inbound tour operators in Central and South America
TourCert	TourCert gGmbH	Awarded to tour operators, travel agencies, and accommodations
Travelife	ABTA Ltd (for accommodations), ECEAT (for tour operators)	The Travelife label uses different standards and verification procedures for accommodations and tour operators
Viabono	Viabono GmbH	Awards all types of accommodation providers, conference centers, restaurants, holiday packages, and vendors as well as canoe rentals, nature parks, and local tourism destinations in Germany

Source: Adapted from Plüss, Zotz, Monshausen, & Kühhas (2016)

recognized by the Global Sustainable Tourism Council (Plüss, Zotz, Monshausen, & Kühhas, 2016). To be acknowledged, the label has to take into account not only the environment and economy, but also the social dimension of sustainability and must carry out a transparent third-party verification procedure.

The certification process

The certification process should be designed to be transparent and easily understood in order to effectively communicate the standards being met. There are two primary uses for certifications, one to communicate to suppliers that a business has established a commitment to sustainability; and the other to consumers who are looking to travel more responsibly. The process is very similar regardless. Business owners may be looking to work with sustainable suppliers and should know which certifications are reputable, or they may be trying to find a certification that communicates with customers, and they may want a label that is easily recognizable. Therefore, it is important to understand the certification process in order to choose a certification scheme that mirrors an organization's commitment and dedication to the sustainability process and reaches the appropriate audience. Figure 10.1 shows the steps involved in establishing a certification (Font & Buckley, 2001). It is important to note that each of the five steps should be conducted by different agencies in order to ensure that there is no conflict of interest or to prevent any organization from easily manipulating the system to receive a certification they did not earn (Font, 2002). In the end, it will erode the reputation of the certification and create distrust between parties.

Funding bodies

The **funding body** is the organization that pays to develop and oversee a certification program. Since certifications generally do not generate a profit, in fact they can be very costly to run, the

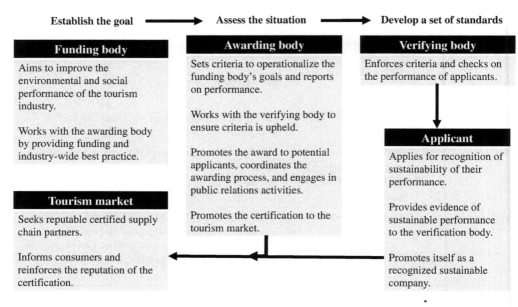

Figure 10.1 The certification process

Source: Adapted from Font & Buckley (2001)

funding body is usually a government, NGO, or industry association. The funding body must be committed to sustainability and be willing to incur a financial loss in order to encourage more ethical behaviors by businesses. Therefore, ecolabels need to be assessed against the objectives or core mission of the funding body. For example, in Table 10.1, the Rainforest Alliance is a nonprofit NGO dedicated to the preservation of the rainforest and certifies companies that support agricultural practices that ensure the long-term survival of the rainforest (such as shade grown coffee that does not encourage burning down the rain forest in order to grow coffee beans). Fair Trade Tourism supports adequate pay and working conditions for poor communities and certifies businesses that purchase fair trade supplies. Generally, funding bodies are focused on the environment, although recognition of social sustainability is on the rise.

Having a *funding body* that is separate from the *awarding body* and *verifying body* increases credibility in the mind of the consumer, provides more transparency, and ensures the long-term survival of the certification program (Font, 2002). The funding body's job is to ensure the reputation of the certification by setting the standards and regulating the verification measures. Funding bodies may provide direct financial support or may provide in-kind support (offices, salaries, marketing), whereas the application fees (fees paid by businesses applying for certification) pay for the verification process and are collected by the awarding body.

Funding bodies generally want to be associated with good causes. As an NGO, funding a certification project may encourage more people to donate to the organization, or as a trade association, may encourage more members to join an association. As a government, they may want to show local residents that their tax money is being used to promote a more sustainable destination. Funding bodies may want to generate money through price premiums for certified goods and service, which can be used to increase wages, increase economic impacts, or support conservation efforts. The Fair Trade certification has allowed poor farmers in developing countries to charge a price premium for their certified agricultural goods, which has increased their

Image 10.1 Hermitage, St Petersburg, Russia

Source: Susan L. Slocum

wages (Lyon, 2006). The more a funding body is aligned with the outcomes of a certification program, the more successful the program is, generally. In other words, association with a good cause can provide worthy public relations for the funding body.

Awarding bodies

Funding bodies do not necessarily possess the management skills essential to run a certification program. Therefore, once a funding body is committed to developing a certification, they hire an agency to set up and manage the specifics of the program. This agency is the **awarding body**, and they set the standards for the award and promote it to the public. Awarding a conservation certification requires different knowledge than certifying special events, and business practices in Chile may be different than those in Tanzania, so ecolabels tend to be regional (or national), or may be industry specific. Awarding agencies may target a region (Europe) or a sector (hotels) depending on their area of expertise. The process of developing and implementing a certification is outlined in Table 10.2.

The awarding body must balance the needs of the funding body with that of the end consumer. They need to ensure that the standards are rigorous enough to meet the needs of the funding body, but also practical enough that businesses can comply with the regulations. This is usually done with input from all stakeholders, including potential applicants and end-users. The goal is to effect change within the tourism industry, so the standards should require applicants to become more aware of their operational practices and encourage them to continually improve over time. By establishing a tiered system (bronze, silver, gold), a business may start at the

Table 10.2 The certification development process

Phase	Tasks
Phase 1 Positioning and planning	• Who else is doing similar work • Overlaps and collaborations • Stakeholders and participants • Intended effect on tourism consumption
Phase 2 Development and consultation	• Evaluation of environmental impacts • Evaluation of social impacts • Evaluation of economic impacts • Outlining the criteria • Developing a support system for applicants
Phase 3 Management and marketing	• Budgeting of ecolabel management costs • Negotiating terms between funding and awarding bodies • Disseminate information to the general public

bronze level as they begin the process of becoming more sustainable, but still have an incentive to strive for better operations over time as they learn more about sustainability. The awarding body should also know who else is offering a sustainability certification and determine ways to improve upon what is already being offered. Since certifications generally lose money, if the needs of industry and the tourists are being met, there may not be a need for a new certification program.

Once the awarding agency has determined the level of behavior that is deemed sustainable, they must establish a set of criteria that must be met by the applicants. **Criteria** are the standards established for a certification to be awarded to a business, and should meet both regulatory requirements and consumer expectations. Because businesses are of different sizes and require a different combination of inputs, awarding agencies usually allow a business to establish a base line and then make improvements over time, or may set criteria that are based on the implementation of specific practices or technologies.

As an example, let us consider a theme park, which is a water-intensive business. A city may have water use standards, which are enforced by allowing a business to use a certain amount of water at a discounted price, and then the city may raise rates as the business uses more water. Tourism certification criteria may want to encourage theme parks to save even more water than the regulatory standards. One way this can be done is to measure how much water a theme park used in one year, and then set a requirement of a 20% reduction the next year in order to maintain a certification. Another way involving technology improvements is to require theme parks to treat the water they use and then use this treated water in their rides or water displays. Therefore, the criterion may be to build a water treatment plant that pumps used water through the plant and back into the theme park to be reused. Generally, an awarding body will use some combination, such as building a small water treatment plant that allows 20% of the water used by the park to be recycled.

A common criterion is to require businesses to use certified suppliers. For example, buying certified organic produce is a common requirement for restaurants seeking certification. Fair Trade is another way for a business to ensure that people are making a fair wage along the supply chain. Again, certification agencies may require some combination of using certified suppliers and changing the business practices.

One key responsibility of the awarding body is to supply tools to help businesses learn about sustainability and information about how to implement the criteria. In the hotel business, a

Image 10.2 Local sourcing at Big Bend National Park, Texas

Source: Susan L. Slocum

common way to encourage water reduction practices is to reduce the amount of laundry a hotel washes each day. This is done by encouraging guests to reuse their towels rather than getting clean towels each day. One could argue that this is a very elementary form of sustainability and is generally designed to save the hotel money rather than to develop a more sustainable operation. A reputable certification program would help hoteliers save water in other ways. This could be done through technologies, like low-flow toilet flushes or aerators in showerheads (this mixes air with water so less water flows out of the shower). However, most of the water a hotel uses is for swimming pools, watering the landscaping, and in the kitchen. Informing hotels about native plant species that are adaptable to the natural rain patterns or using waste cooking water to irrigate the landscape is part of a successful certification program. In short, if you want to know if a certification is reputable, look first at the criteria and then at the tools provided to support sustainable behaviors by the applicants.

Verifying body

A **verifying body** enforces certification criteria and checks on the performance of applicants. In other words, they make sure that the applicant is actually doing what they say they are doing. Verifying the practices of a business is a time consuming and tedious process that is generally done through invoices and purchase orders. The verifying body will have auditors who will look at a company's purchases over the past year to ensure that suppliers are certified and that the products being used in the production process comply with the criteria set forth by the awarding body. For example, a criterion may support decreases in pollution by requiring the use of chemical-free cleaning products in a hotel. The verifying body can see what cleaning products are being purchased through a company's invoices. Table 10.3 highlights many of the evaluation criteria that a verification agency will require.

It is very important that the verifying body is a separate entity from the funding body and the awarding body. Most applicants pay a small fee each year to the awarding body, so there is an

Table 10.3 Evaluation criteria

Core competency	Example evaluation criteria
Business management	Has a formal business plan to guide operations
Policies for purchasing and suppliers	Reduce, reuse, recycle/uses certified suppliers
Customer service and relations	Group size
Training and human resources development	Percent of staff accredited
Resource protection and sustainability	Has minimal impact policies
Water, waste, and energy conservation	Works with communities to establish thresholds
Social and community contribution	Employs/consults with local people
Packaging	Works with local agencies
Marketing and promotion and delivery	Uses customer/market research in product development
Interpretation and education	Promoting sustainable behaviors to visitors

incentive for the awarding body to approve certification in order to continue to collect fees. In turn, the awarding body pays the verification agency to conduct the audit. Since the verifying body is paid a flat rate for an audit and does not receive money directly from the applicant, they are indifferent as to whether the applicant meets the sustainability criteria or not. In other words, there is no conflict of interest, and the verifying body can be unbiased when conducting the audit. There are many certifications that have the same organization acting as the awarding body and the verification body, which is generally a red flag that they are not truly transparent and unbiased.

Applicants and industry

There is no point in offering a certification program if there are no businesses interested in being sustainable. Luckily, pressure from consumers and local communities, who often feel the impact of exploitive business practices, is helping industry understand the need to be sustainable, or at least to be perceived as sustainable. We will discuss **green marketing**, or the communication of sustainable practices to consumers, whether real or not, in more detail in the next section, but **green management**, or the actual practice of employing sustainability production techniques, is the prime motivation for certification (Rivera, 2002).

There are four primary reasons that businesses seek sustainability certifications: altruism, marketing and competitive advantage, cost saving, and price premiums (Rivera, 2002). **Altruism** is the belief in, or practice of, disinterested and selfless concern for the well-being of others and can be a strong motivation to engage in sustainability behaviors. Many firms want to be the ethical leader because they believe strongly in the values of sustainability. Specifically, they want to preserve environmental resources and ensure a quality of life for all members of society, and they want to influence others to do the same. Other businesses may want to be seen as environmentally friendly to gain competitive advantage over similar businesses and recognize that consumers will ultimately learn whether the sustainability claims of a particular business exist in practice. However, the most common reason to choose sustainability is to incur cost savings or increase revenue from smart business practices. Often reducing the amount of water, waste, and energy consumed reduces expenses and improves the bottom line of a company's financial statements. This is generally considered a form of weak sustainability. Lastly, as shown with the Fair Trade example earlier in the chapter, being sustainable generally means a company can charge more for their products and services, even if there is a reduction in costs by becoming sustainable. It is important to note that many of these benefits come from green marketing rather than green management, so finding a transparent and reputable certification program can help supply chain members and the general public determine the difference.

Tourism market

Ultimately, a certification must be recognizable, and believable, by the end user. In relation to tourists, it is important to remember that stated values often differ from actual behaviors. Tourists may want to be more sustainable, but may get caught up in the excitement of the travel experience and do not always follow through with sustainable actions. However, certification allows tourists to make informed decisions during the planning process when they are likely to be more rational (Luo & Deng, 2008). Because ecolabels cannot be applied to specific tourist segments (income, age, lifestyle, education), they must be designed to appeal to the consumption or cultural needs of tourists covering their overall travel experience. Moreover, ecolabels

Image 10.3 Silver Diner, Fairfax, Virginia
Source: Susan L. Slocum

often preach to the converted, as those who believe in sustainability will seek out sustainability certifications.

The same can be said for business supply chains. Companies seeking certification, or those who demonstrate altruism related to people and the environment, will be more inclined to look for eco-certifications with their business partners. Often awarding bodies will list the businesses they certify on their website, which allows industry to build social capital around sustainability and provides valuable resources for managers just entering the sustainability arena. As a sustainable company, seeking out certification can provide a number of valuable resources and education on how to implement more ethical practices in a company's operations.

Greenwashing

Greenwashing is the act of misleading consumers regarding the environmental practices of a company or the environmental benefits of a product or service. Greenwashing occurs when companies promote themselves as sustainable (green marketing), but fail to be transparent. Moreover, some businesses may actually lie to the public. Evidence that an organization is greenwashing occurs when significantly more money or time has been spent on advertising green practices than is actually spent on environmentally sound procedures. Greenwashing efforts can range from changing the name or label to evoke the natural environment on a product that contains harmful chemicals, to multi-million dollar advertising campaigns portraying highly polluting companies as eco-friendly.

Alves (2009) highlights the seven greenwashing sins:

- Hidden trade-offs – not telling the whole story, such as buying local from a mass distributor that pollutes the local environment;
- No proof – making claims that cannot be substantiated;
- Vagueness – making general sustainability statements, such as "we value our community" without actually saying what they are doing to support their community;
- Irrelevance – making claims about things unrelated to the industry in which a business practices;
- Fibbing – essentially lying;
- Lesser of two evils – claiming one aspect of a product is sustainable when other aspects are highly questionable; and
- Worshiping false labels – using substandard or unreputable certifications or labels.

It is important to note that using certifications can be a common form of greenwashing. There are many certifications that allow a company to self-report their activities or that have an awarding body that is paid only when a certification is approved. In order to ensure that a company is truly working towards sustainability, make sure that the ecolabel has a separate verifying body, and that there is transparency in the standards, criteria, and certification processes.

Certification training in tourism

In 2009, the Global Sustainable Tourism Council (GSTC) was formed to establish global sustainability criteria for both tourism destinations and the tourism industry. As a non-profit, neutral certification body, the GSTC evaluates tourism businesses against minimum sustainability standards and issues certifications. GSTC is also a global **accreditation** body that can officially recognize another organization as being qualified to perform a particular activity. Through an intensive and extensive evaluation process, the GSTC accredits other certification bodies' practices and designates a mark of quality.

GSTC offers a *Sustainable Tourism Training Program* that includes an exam leading to a Certification in Sustainable Tourism. This certification is designed for individuals working in the tourism industry, and the certification is intended to demonstrate one's knowledge of sustainable tourism practices. Attaining this certificate can be a boost to one's resume, demonstrating to potential employers that s/he has knowledge of sustainable tourism practices, which can influence decision-makers on sustainability-enhancing choices.

Individual countries also are adopting sustainable tourism practices and certification bodies. For example, Costa Rica's Tourism Board and the Costa Rica National Accreditation Commission have created a *Certification for Sustainable Tourism* (CST). This body certifies tourism businesses on a scale of one to five related to the sustainability of the activities and services offered by their local tourism businesses. The United Nations has recognized Costa Rica's success with their CST, stating that "in its four years of operation in Costa Rica, CST has been able to objectively measure sustainability of operating businesses, improve business environmental and social practices, and motivate businesses to improve practices and clients to choose sustainable tourist businesses" (United Nations, 2001, n.p).

In January 2017, the European Union Ecolabel Tourist Accommodation Criteria introduced stricter environmental and social requirements for hotels, campsites, hostels, and bed and breakfasts that wish to be awarded with the prestigious EU Ecolabel. These criteria provide efficient guidelines for hotels and camping sites looking to lower their environmental impact while providing flexibility to support guest satisfaction. The criteria focus on environmental hotspots, such as the over-consumption of water and energy, waste management, and the use of toxic substances (EU Ecolabel, 2018).

Hotspot 1: lack of environmental engagement

It is difficult for companies to monitor and measure their environmental performance and progress without a defined environmental action plan. Using an environmental management system helps companies define the right targets appropriate for their environment by using a precise environmental policy, action program, and internal evaluation process that measures the impact of their actions. For example, the EU Ecolabel requires training of staff and provision of information to raise awareness on environmental practices employed by the company. Data on the energy, water, food, and product consumption per guest/night, as well as the number of toxic substances used must be monitored and reported. Becoming certified by an environmental management system, such as *ISO 14001* or the *Environmental Management and Audit Scheme* (EMAS), can aid companies in the development of an environmental action plan.

Hotspot 2: unnecessary carbon emission and use of energy

Tourist accommodations can consume large amounts of energy, which contributes to unsustainable levels of carbon emission that cause climate change. This is often caused by poorly managed energy consumption. The EU Ecolabel provides information for preventive maintenance on all appliances and devices in an effort to reduce the overuse of energy due to leakage and the malfunctioning of installations. They require a 98% threshold on energy efficiency in seasonal space heating, water heating appliances, household air conditioning, and air-based heat pumps. Similarly, up to 50% (and 100% after two years of certification) of the lighting must be of Class A type (the most efficient form of LED lighting). Temperature in common areas and rooms must be regulated with automatic switch-off options, and hotels and camping sites cannot use any heating or air conditioning in outside areas. A hundred percent of energy must be purchased from renewable energy sources (depending on the number of suppliers in the region), while coal and heating oils with more than 0.1% sulphur content are prohibited.

Hotspot 3: inefficient use of water

Water is be often wasted in tourist accommodations due to inefficient systems and equipment. The EU Ecolabel provides options to minimize the amount of water wasted in tourist accommodations through requirements on the average water flow rate of taps (which should not exceed 8.5 liters/minute) and toilet flushing (which should be equal or below 4.5L). The EU

Ecolabel provides information on suppliers of EU Ecolabel toilets and urinals or equivalent ISO 14001 Type I label products. Criteria state that hotels and camping sites cannot change sheets and towels every day unless explicitly requested by guests and encourage tourist accommodations to have an optimized pool management policy, which includes the recycling of rainwater and grey water (sink water). Lastly, efficient irrigation systems and the use of native plants (which require less water) are stipulated.

Hotspot 4: reducing pesticides and chemical substances

Tourist accommodations can have a detrimental impact on the environment through the use of pesticides and chemical substances used for cleaning, landscaping, and restoration services. The EU Ecolabel limits the polluting effects of cleaning services by providing options to outsource laundry and cleaning services to providers awarded with an ISO 14001 Type I label. Tourist accommodations are encouraged to purchase detergents and rinse-off cosmetics, which have less impact on the environment, through suppliers with an ISO 14001 Type I label. Accommodations are urged to procure from at least two organic farms in their daily meal preparations and must ban all use of pesticides in outside areas.

Hotspot 5: excessive solid waste, and poorly managed waste disposal

Tourist accommodations create large amounts of solid waste. If poorly managed, solid waste can end up in strained landfills. The EU Ecolabel aims to reduce the amount of waste generated in tourist accommodations by encouraging the reuse or recycling of waste by optimizing waste management. For example, hotels and camping grounds cannot use any single dose packages for nonperishable food items (such as disposable toiletries) unless they are requested by guests. Disposable food service items can only be used if the tourist accommodations have an agreement with a recycler. Disposable towels and bed sheets are not allowed. Adequate containers for waste separation must be provided in each room or on all floors. Waste must be separated into specific categories (such as glass, plastic, and paper) for better recycling and disposal.

Hotspot 6: reducing transportation carbon emissions

The tourism industry often generates a large amount of carbon emissions due to the transportation of guests and supplies. EU Ecolabel encourages accommodations to reduce these emissions through the use of environmentally preferable means of transport, such as electric vehicles, bikes, and public transportation. Special agreements with transport agencies which could potentially offer eco-friendly transportation can be arranged. Tourist accommodations are encouraged to use non-combustion motor vehicles in their ground maintenance. Finally, hotels and camping sites should provide at least two locally sourced and in-season food products at each meal to reduce food transportation emissions.

Hotspot 7: excessive food waste

The tourist accommodation industry is a big player in generating food waste. The EU Ecolabel limits food waste by requiring that tourist accommodations follow a documented 'food waste reduction plan', including food waste monitoring linked to an action program focused on optimizing both food and packaging waste.

It should be noted that, similar to many hotel certification programs, the EU Ecolabel is very limited in requirements related to social engagement, building community capacity, and the protection of natural areas. This tool is primarily designed for supply chain partnerships as well as internal operations that save resources for businesses.

Communicating your success

The EU Ecolabel also provides applicants with valuable information about publicizing their sustainability accomplishments through social media. Specific social media links, hashtags, Facebook pages, and Twitter influencers that should accompany communication messages include:

- #EUEcolabel
- #SustainableTourism
- #EcologicalHolidays
- #EUEcolabelTouristAccommodations
- #SustainableTourism
- #CircularEconomy
- #SustainableChoices
- Book different Twitter
- EU Ecolabel Facebook
- Book different Facebook: @bookdifferent
- Zero Waste LinkedIn
- @Green_Hotelier
- @greentravel
- @ReunionTourisme
- @Eco_TourismNews
- @bookdifferent

Remember that there may be more region-specific social media posts that may be more appropriate for your business.

Conclusion

Certification is important for highlighting sustainability accomplishments. This chapter has explained the role of certification in attracting sustainable-minded customers and developing a sustainable supply chain. The process of developing a reliable, trustworthy, and transparent certification is to ensure separation between the funding, awarding, and verifying bodies. It must also take into account the needs and motivations of the tourism market and the tourists' needs. Recognizing the difference between green marketing and green management safeguards the reputation of a certification and helps an organization avoid the greenwashing sins. The tool in this chapter provides some concrete sustainability practices that have been prioritized by the European Union.

CASE STUDY 10.1 AUDUBON CERTIFIED GOLF RESORTS: GREEN TOURISM OR GREENWASHING?

SUSAN L. SLOCUM

Introduction

Golf courses require extensive resource use, and the construction and maintenance of golf courses are recognized as generally unsustainable. Golf courses use a vast amount of water, pesticides, and other chemicals, as well as convert natural landscapes into large-scale housing and recreational development sites (fairways, clubs, restaurants, and housing). The building of golf resorts includes the removal of trees and topsoil, causing increased erosion. Specific concerns include the pumping of ground water to support water features, resulting in saline intrusion into groundwater, and pesticides, herbicides, and fertilizers that are used to maintain a lush grassy surface free of weeds and insects. Much of this poison runs into natural waterways, killing fish and the birds that feed on fish. Pesticides, in particular, kill native insects that act as pollinators for agriculture and other plant life. Often the natural forest is destroyed and replaced with imitation forests that consist of non-native species in order to create a scenic environment for residents. Lastly, golf balls contain lead, which is also contaminating waterways and poisoning wildlife. Adler (2007) writes, "These artificial monstrosities consume on average 150 acres of land that could be put to some more useful purpose" (n.p.).

Audubon International

The Audubon Society of New York State was started over 100 years ago by Theodore Roosevelt, Frank Chapman, and John Burroughs, who are known as pioneers in the modern conservation movement. In 1996, it changed its name to Audubon International in a move to better represent its focus and began a 501(c)(3) charity incorporated in New York. Not to be confused with the Audubon Society, a well-recognized bird conservation organization, Audubon International's mission is to "deliver high-quality environmental education to facilitate the sustainable management of land, water, wildlife, and other natural resources in all places people live, work, and play" (Audubon International, 2019, n.p.). It provides technical assistance to organizations that seek to learn about environmental management practice, and the organization has received numerous conservation awards globally.

One of the largest, and most visible, programs is the Audubon certification designed to support conservation initiatives for golf courses, cemeteries, ski areas, housing developments, hotels, and communities. In particular, the *Audubon Cooperative Sanctuary Program for Golf Courses* has been endorsed by the United States Golf Association, which has resulted in the provision of over $2 million in financial support to offset the fees associated with administering the certification. The certification applies to private clubs, public and municipal courses, PGA sites, 9-hole facilities, resort courses, and golf residential communities. The goal of the certification is to "help golf courses protect the environment, preserve the natural heritage of the game of golf, and gain recognition for their efforts (Audubon International, 2018, p. 1). Barton (2008) claims that over 75% of Audubon International's clients are golf courses.

Image 10.4 Primland 18-hole Audubon-certified golf course, Meadows of Dan, Virginia
Source: Kenan Kitchen on Unsplash

The program offers information to help improve overall golf course operations and helps managers assess their environmental resources and any potential liabilities, as well as to develop a plan that fits their unique setting, goals, staff, budget, and time. The six key environmental components include:

- Environmental planning;
- Wildlife and habitat management;
- Chemical use reduction and safety;
- Water conservation;
- Water quality management;
- Outreach and education.

The certification is then issued once the environmental standards are met. The cost of the application is US$300 for properties located in the United States and US$350 for properties in other countries, although there are other expenses related to meeting certification requirements. The entire process can take one to three years to complete, and there are over 2,000 certified golf courses internationally.

The reality

In a study by Keogh, Mallen, Chard, and Hyatt (2014), the actual conservation activities at Audubon International certified golf courses in Ontario, Canada were analyzed. The most common practice was recycling, followed by water conservation. Water conservation was achieved through the use of soil moisture meters, rain-collection reservoirs used for irrigation, and low-flow toilets and fixtures in bathrooms, locker rooms, and kitchens. Moreover, buffer zones along creeks and rivers were used to prevent water contamination. The third most common practice was the conservation of electricity, specifically the use of LED bulbs and some motion sensors for indoor and outdoor lighting. However, in spite of these efforts, inefficient windows and outdated electrical systems were common, resulting in extensive electrical use. The removal of native trees was used to ventilate the grass, supporting fewer turf maintenance costs. Employee training programs centered on recycling and turning off lights. Moreover, the study found that golf patrons had low interest in and knowledge of sustainability. Their primary interest was in having a desirable playing surface. The study concluded that cost savings were the main motivator for environmental practices at these golf resorts.

Bale and Knudson (2015) claim that "Audubon International has certified as environmentally friendly more than a dozen golf courses that have killed nuisance birds. Those golf courses, mostly in California, have killed nearly 4,000 birds from 2011 through 2013, according to data from the Fish and Wildlife Service" (n.p.). While further evidence related to certified golf courses could not be uncovered, the golf industry's practice of poisoning or shooting nuisance birds (birds that cause damage or whose waste has an unpleasant odor or accumulate in large quantities) is well documented. While in the US, The Migratory Bird Treaty and Endangered Species Act prohibits trapping or killing of most birds, eggs, or nests without a permit, permits are relatively easy to come by.

As a side note, Audubon International is funded by DuPont (one of the world's largest chemical companies and producer of pesticides), cement maker LaFarge, Disney, and the US Golf Association (Selcraig, 2012). Other sponsors include turf management companies and the individual golf courses that pay for information and training services.

Reflective questions

1. Do you feel that Audubon Internal certification is adequately addressing the specific environmental impacts of the golf industry? Why or why not? If you feel they are not, which greenwashing sins are they using?

2. In 1991, a court determined that the highly respected bird conservation organization, The Audubon Society, did not have exclusive rights to the name 'Audubon'. How can the Audubon Society protect its reputation when many consumers confuse the two distinctly different organizations?

3. How can a certification balance the needs of the funding sources (the industry they are certifying and their major supply partners) with the needs of the environment and society? Is this a conflict of interest? Why or why not?

References

Adler, B. (2007). The case against golf. *Guardian*, 14 June.

Audubon International (2018). Fact sheet. Retrieved from https://auduboninternational.org/wp-content/uploads/2019/03/ACSP-Golf-Fact-Sheet-2018.pdf.

Audubon International (2019). Retrieved from https://auduboninternational.org.

Bale, R. & Knudson, T. (2015). The other Audubon: the one that allows golf courses to kill birds. *Reveal*, 14 May. Retrieved from www.revealnews.org/article/the-other-audubon-the-one-that-allows-golf-courses-to-kill-birds/.

Barton, J. (2008). How green is golf? Beyond pesticides. *Golf Digest*, May.

Keogh, C., Mallen, C., Chard, C., & Hyatt, C. (2014). Greener golf operations: a comparative case study of Ontario golf courses engaged in environmental sustainability initiatives. *Management and Organizational Studies*, 1(2), 100–121.

Selcraig, B. (2012). Greenwashing golf. The Sierra Club. Retrieved from http://vault.sierraclub.org/sierra/201207/grapple-greenwashing-golf-232.aspx.

CASE STUDY 10.2 HOTEL SECTOR'S SUSTAINABLE PRACTICES MAY BE GREENWASHING

SCOTT M. TURNER

The hotel sector is highly consumptive, and therefore it has an incentive to adopt sustainable practices that can save them money. However, a lot of the hotel industry's marketing around their sustainable practices may actually be greenwashing. Greenwashing is when a company creates a public relations or marketing campaign promoting a perception that their product or service has a strictly environmental benefit when, in fact, the company gains financial benefit that is not passed along to the consumer. There is a fine line between 'doing the right thing' and greenwashing, and often the distinction lies in the organization's motivation and messaging. If you have visited a hotel anytime since the 1990s, you have probably noticed a sign in your room requesting you reuse your towels and linens. The sign says something to the effect of:

> *Please help us save our planet. Every day millions of gallons of water are used to wash towels that have only been used once. You make the choice: A towel on the rack means, "I will use again". A towel on the floor means, "Please replace". Thank you for helping us conserve the Earth's vital resources.*

Prior to about 1986, hotel guests' expectations were that all towels and linens would be replaced with clean ones on a daily basis. Environmentalist Jay Westerveld noticed the new signage in a hotel and coined the term "greenwashing" because, while there certainly is a significant environmental benefit to reducing the amount of laundry on a daily basis, there is a financial benefit to the hotel that is not passed along to the consumer for engaging in this behavior (Watson, 2016). Westerveld thought the ploy to save money, while spinning the reason as an environmental cause, was a version of whitewashing, and he coined the new term "greenwashing" to describe the practice.

The hotel industry started saving so much money in reduced laundry services that they hired psychologists to study how they could increase towel reuse rates among their customers, known as adoption rates (Goldstein, 2008). Various messaging methods were compared including simply requesting towel reuse versus the environmental message stated above. They discovered the environmental message increases adoption compared to just requesting reuse. Interestingly, they also found that stating other customers reused their towels further increased adoption rates, and when they used verbiage that compared others who had stayed in that same room, adoption rates increased even further. It seems the social cues of others participating in an act have a positive impact on people's behavior, at least when it comes to reusing towels.

The hotel industry is also having a negative impact with regard to its sustainability efforts. Take, for example, personal care products. Many hotels provide single-use containers of bath soap, shampoo, and conditioner for their customers to use during their stay. People often use and take these products home, which adds up to a substantial cost to the hotel. There is also significant environmental impact in producing so many little plastic bottles that end up as waste. Increasingly, we are seeing hoteliers shifting to providing such products in dispenser form to reduce both the amount of product loss as well as the container cost. Similar to towel reuse, it can be difficult to distinguish where the line between eco-awareness and greenwashing exists in this shift, particularly when hotel chains choose to highlight this change for the sake of the environment, sidestepping discussions on the financial benefit that is not passed along to the consumer.

Hotels are generally extremely resource consumptive and wasteful. However, in this age of enhanced ecological and environmental awareness, some hotels are seeking ways to align their services with more environmentally sensitive practices. Some even go so far as to call themselves 'ecohotels'. While this may be little more than greenwashing, other hotels actually experience a negative financial impact when 'doing the right thing' for the environment. One example is the offering of sustainably raised and locally grown organic food options for complimentary meals like breakfasts, which often cost more than conventional options. Another is using biodegradable and environmentally friendly personal care and room cleaning products that also tend to cost more than their non-environmentally friendly counterparts. While a growing segment of the tourist population seek out such establishments, and may even be willing to pay a premium for such considerations, more often customers do not know about, nor value, these options, reducing the overall value to the hotelier from a strictly financial perspective. So, one challenge ecohotels face is to increase the value their customers perceive with eco-friendly offerings in order to justify charging rates that allow for competitive profit margin as compared to conventional, less eco-conscious hoteliers. These eco-friendly hotels are early adopters and demonstrate practices that could become industry standards. As customer expectations shift due to increasing awareness of our environmental challenges combined with the price reduction of sustainable products resulting from the growth of their demand, these practices may become more mainstream.

A new eco-conscious hotel in Barcelona, Spain has identified many initiatives they intend to roll out, but have yet to fully implement for a variety of reasons: initial start-up expense; employee buy-in; and consumer valuation versus additional cost. One initiative they are considering is the addition of grey-water systems, which could drastically reduce overall water consumption, but can be very expensive to install. One such system gaining traction has the hand-washing basin feed directly into the toilet tank so the water used to wash your hands is then used to flush the toilet. Other grey water systems feed non-toilet water into irrigation and other non-potable systems throughout the hotel. In-room recycling and composting is another initiative they are attempting to roll out. Challenges include both customer and custodial staff participation, reducing the quality of sorting, and overall impact. Biodegradable and earth-friendly cleaning products are typically more expensive and show little to no financial return due to lack of consumer interest in such matters (Cometa, 2012). Nonetheless, the hotel continues to evaluate and roll out more environmentally friendly policies as finances and social attitudes allow.

Reflective questions

1. Describe other ways hotels can attempt to become more sustainable, efficient, and less resource consumptive.
2. What messaging might hotels use to increase adoption of the various sustainability initiatives you thought of and how could you prevent them from appearing to be greenwashing?
3. What challenges might hotels face in their efforts to become more sustainable and how might we overcome those?

References

Cometa, L. (2012). Consumer beliefs about green hotels (Doctoral dissertation, Kent State University).

Goldstein, N. (2008). Changing minds and changing towels. *Psychology Today*. Retrieved from www.psychologytoday.com/us/blog/yes/200808/changing-minds-and-changing-towels.

Watson, B. (2016). History of greenwashing. *Guardian*. Retrieved from www.theguardian.com/sustainable-business/2016/aug/20/greenwashing-environmentalism-lies-companies.

STUDY QUESTIONS

1. Research a local sustainable tourism certification. What standards do they use and how could they be improved?
2. You are asked to verify an applicant's sustainability practices. What would you look for and how could you find information that may not be readily visible during an inspection?
3. Develop a set of best practices for sustainable tourism that can be used to communicate to potential applicants. Make sure you explain not only what needs to be done, but also how to do it.
4. What are the obvious signs of greenwashing? How can we inform tourists of these signs?
5. Research five certified tourism businesses or destinations. What are the primary motivations for their choice of certification?

DEFINITIONS

Accreditation   officially recognizing another as being qualified to perform a particular activity

Altruism   the belief in or practice of disinterested and selfless concern for the well-being of others

Awarding body   the agency that sets the standards for the award and promotes it to the public

Certification a type of label indicating that compliance with standards has been verified by an outside agency

Criteria   the standards established for a certification to be awarded to a business

Funding body   the organization that pays to develop and run a certification program

Green management   the actual practice of employing sustainability production techniques

Green marketing   the communication of sustainable practices to consumers, whether these practices are real or not

Greenwashing   the act of misleading consumers regarding the environmental practices of a company or the environmental benefits of a product or service

Standard   a technical specification or other precise criteria to be used consistently as rules, guidelines, or definitions, to ensure that materials, products, processes, and services are complying with best practice

Verifying body   enforces certification criteria and checks on the performance of applicants

Chapter **11**

Human capital management

Overview

This chapter provides an introduction to sustainable human capital management. The focus is particularly on how its principles can be applied within tourism, although they are generally not specific to any one industry or sector. Topics covered in this chapter relate to the ability of an organization to recruit, hire, and retain top talent, which is closely tied to an organization's reputation in the industry (and in the community) as a great place to work. This chapter provides practical guidance on setting up internal practices that nurture the kind of culture that enables people to thrive, bringing their best selves to work every day, satisfying the tourists' expectations. Building a culture that supports sustainability is also covered.

CHAPTER OBJECTIVES

At the completion of the chapter, students will be able to:

- Discuss why employees should be viewed as human capital;
- Discuss the significance of mission/vision and values;
- Articulate the challenges in recruiting, hiring, and training staff;
- Consider what motivates employees to do great work;
- Explain the value of training and development for retention and growth; and
- Identify ways to improve a company's culture in relation to sustainability.

Introduction

Management policies and human resource management practices have evolved over time as a means for organizations to adapt to external market forces and the changing expectations of workers. For example, during the industrial revolution, when factories were being built and industries needed labor to perform routine, manual tasks, employees were seen as highly expendable. The high unemployment rates at that time led workers to accept very poor working conditions in order to receive a paycheck. Fast forward to today and, unless you are working on a production line, jobs are most likely defined as service workers or knowledge workers. A **service worker** is a worker whose primary task is the serving of customer needs (Donavan, Brown, & Mowen, 2004). Since tourism is an experiential industry, most tourism workers can be classified as service workers. The term knowledge worker was first coined by Peter Drucker in his 1959 book, *The Landmarks of Tomorrow*. Drucker defined **knowledge workers** as high-level workers who apply theoretical and analytical knowledge, acquired through formal training, to develop products and services. Drucker's work brought a new profound respect for workers, who he believed were assets, rather than liabilities. This shift in thinking recognizes employees as forms of **human capital**, or a stock of knowledge, habits, social and personality attributes, including creativity that can produce economic value for an organization.

According to McKinney (n.d.), "Human capital management is a process of directing, investing in, and developing an organization's workforce" (n.p.). **Human capital management** is

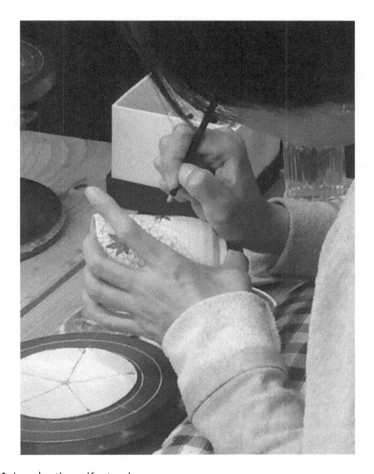

Image 11.1 Local artisan, Kyoto, Japan

Source: Susan L. Slocum

defined as the process of acquiring, training, managing, and retaining employees, whereas **human resource management** (HRM) is a term that is used to describe the management and professional development of employees within an organization. Companies today recognize the need to invest in their employees, whose knowledge and experience are highly valuable and not so easily replaced. **Institutional knowledge** is the collection of historical knowledge and wisdom that is retained by employees, and the analytical skills necessary for its effective use within the organization. The longer an employee works for an organization, the more experiences they acquire and challenges they overcome, the higher their institutional knowledge. The process of human capital management is not quite as simple as it may seem at first. There are many important factors that go into the process of valuing employees as assets, and this chapter is dedicated to considering how human capital management can be implemented in the sustainable tourism industry.

The significance of mission, vision, and values

The first step to creating a work environment where employees are regarded as human capital is in the development of an organizational culture that embraces human values and employee empowerment. This can begin with a well-thought-out mission statement. A **mission statement** is a written statement of a company's purpose and values, which communicates the company's decision-making process to both members of the company and the external community. The mission statement can differentiate an organization from its competitors, and influence the public's perception of the company's reputation. A **vision statement** is a future-based narrative meant to inspire and give direction to employees of the company rather than customers (See Chapter 1). The combination of mission and vision statements can heavily influence the culture of the work environment. According to Coleman (2013), "a company's values are the core of its culture. While a vision articulates a company's purpose, values offer a set of guidelines on the behaviors and mindsets needed to achieve that vision" (p. 2). Moreover, "A company's culture can be viewed as the glue that keeps companies together" (Hassell, 2014, n.p.).

According to Schoemaker, Nijhof, and Jonker (2006, p. 455), creating a sustainably-minded mission statement requires asking the following types of questions:

- What is our role in society?
- What are our values?
- How can we incorporate and strengthen our values in our operations?

When an organization has a clear understanding of who they are, what they are trying to achieve, and the type of culture and opportunities that they want to create so that employees can do great work, the process of recruiting, hiring, and retaining great talent becomes much easier. Companies with established values know who they are looking for and the types of personalities and talents that will help them to grow their business. Since the culture and the values of a company are codified in the mission statement, consider what the following examples say about these companies' sustainable values:

> *Alaska Airlines – "It is important to us that we achieve our objective as a socially responsible company that values not just our performance, but also our people, our community, and our environment".*

> *Sustainable Travel International – "Making a better world the destination".*

Malta Ministry for Tourism – "Our mission is to establish and execute a tourism policy which is based on the principles of sustainable tourism development to contribute to economic growth whilst respecting the heritage and environment of the Maltese islands".

Recruiting and hiring great talent

Hiring decisions are one of the most important determinants of a company's success. Not only is it crucial to hire people with the right skills for the job, they must also be a good fit for the culture that the company is consciously attempting to create. The cost of hiring the wrong person can have more than monetary consequences – the costs can extend to include the impact on existing employees through a reduction in morale, a lack of teamwork, a breakdown in communication, and an overall reduction in productivity. According to Frey (2017), "if you make a bad hire, there is a ripple effect among all who work for you, your product, and your product quality" (n.p.). So, in addition to hiring the right people, it is imperative that you take steps to coach those workers who are underperforming, or who are not demonstrating behaviors that are in line with the company's values. If coaching fails to result in immediate change, the employee must be let go (fired).

Recruiting to find the best applicants

One of the first things that an organization must do to ensure they are able to attract the right talent is to write a good job description. A formal job description is succinct but also provides enough clarity about the company and the position that a potential employee is attracted to apply. The job description should include not just the tactical details of the work, but also the manner in which the company expects the employee to perform the job, which is a way for potential employees to understand the company's core values.

For the purposes of recruiting, the best job descriptions begin with a description of the company itself and articulate why someone would want to work there (as opposed to somewhere else). The mission statement of the organization is often included up front, followed by a brief description of the culture of the organization and the type of candidates they are hoping to attract. It is important to accurately describe the role and responsibilities for the position, giving as much information about 'a day in the life' so that applicants can get a realistic impression of the job. Any minimum requirements should be listed (such as relevant education or experience, physical requirements, etc.), and desired skills and abilities. Identifying the salary/wage range and associated benefits (medical, paid time off, or other perks of the job) is another good way to attract applicants.

Organizations wishing to hire and retain top talent who are invested in the success of the company should give careful consideration to the pay and benefits offered with the job. According to Cascio (2006), "stingy pay and benefits don't necessarily translate into lower costs in the long run" (n.p.). Employee turnover is expensive. The **employee turnover rate** is the percentage of employees who leave an organization over a certain period of time (typically, one year). In skilled and semi-skilled jobs, the total cost of replacing a worker who leaves (excluding lost productivity) is calculated at 1.5 to 2.5 times the worker's annual salary (Cascio, 2006). So, looking to hire at the lowest possible wage or salary is not only unfair to workers, it sets the company up for a long-term struggle to retain talent. When employees are new to the job or if they feel like their job security is uncertain, they are either unable or unmotivated to provide exceptional customer service.

While not all companies can offer costly benefits, such as health insurance subsidies or retirement matching, there are other benefits that can (and should) be considered. These might include flexible schedules, subsidized employee meals, recognition programs, subsidized public transportation, and childcare. When hiring locally, paid time off for family sick leave may also be an important benefit, especially in developing countries where poor nutrition, malaria, or other poverty-induced illness are more prevalent.

There are many reasons for an organization to consider hiring locally, as opposed to augmenting staff by recruiting people from other locations to fill open positions. Most notably, the local economy benefits. Every employee spends the majority of their paycheck locally (the induced impact) – on rent, food, clothing, and entertainment, which can enhance a destination, reduce poverty, and bring small business opportunities to the community. Moreover, local tourism workers have specific knowledge about the local attractions, events, culture, and the environment, which can enhance the customer experience. Lastly, hiring locally shows a commitment to the values and mission statements and validates the company's pledge to sustainability. Therefore, it is financially beneficial to both a company and the local community to recruit locally, whenever possible (Fortanier & Van Wijk, 2010).

Consideration should be given to where the job posting itself is displayed. If a company is seeking to attract talent from within a population that is technology-savvy, such as urban areas or university towns, options abound. There are a multitude of online websites dedicated to sharing employment opportunities. However, if the role is designed to attract local applicants

Image 11.2 Cossack performers, Ukraine

Source: Susan L. Slocum

who may be computer illiterate (because that is not a requirement of the job, or because the area does not have reliable internet service), efforts should be made to post the job description in alternative locations where those potential candidates can be reached. That may include bulletin boards at community centers or churches, or hosting a job fair to announce the open positions at a central marketplace or school facilities.

The hiring process

Once the recruitment of potential candidates has been performed, evaluation of the credentials of each applicant is considered. When reviewing applications, it is important to recognize that everyone has preconceived notions and unconscious biases that must be actively overcome during the selection process. **Unconscious bias** is the inclination for humans to form social stereotypes that lump people together unfairly based on their past experiences. They are unconscious feelings of inclination or prejudice towards other people that can influence the way a potential employee is evaluated. All people have some levels of unconscious bias (Raymond, 2013), and everyone must consciously work to overcome these preconceived opinions.

It is imperative that during the hiring process, each applicant is given a fair and impartial opportunity for selection. For example, if an individual were interviewing for a job, one unconscious bias on the part of the interviewer could be that assumptions are made about the tattoo peeking from the interviewee sleeve. If the interviewer decided not to consider this applicant based on these assumptions, that would be discrimination in hiring and could lead to legal liability in some countries. However, avoiding this type of discrimination requires that hiring managers actively work to remain aware of their own potential for bias. Unconscious bias can lead to overlooking qualified candidates who may be the right fit for the position (Messner, Wänke, & Weibel, 2011).

Interviewing applicants is a time-consuming process, so organizations should make the most out of the experience by being prepared and creating a good impression for the candidates. Employees may need to take time off from another job, so flexibility in scheduling interviews is important. Remember: the job seeker is evaluating the organization just as much as the organization is evaluating the candidate.

At the interview itself, each candidate must be assessed not just for their work history and credentials, but also for their ability to embrace the mission and values of the organization. Thoughtful questioning during the interview process can uncover the candidate's values and their approach toward how they get their work done. For example, asking open-ended questions that require the applicant to tell a story is helpful.

- Tell me about a time when you had to make a difficult decision on the job. What did you do?
- Tell me about a time when you tried to do something and you were not successful. How did you handle that?
- Give me some examples of your best ideas for increasing the sustainability of our operation. What would you suggest?
- Tell me about a time you had to deal with a difficult customer. What happened?

Having three or more interviewers is considered helpful at removing bias in the hiring process because multiple perspectives and perceptions (otherwise known as diversity and inclusion) makes for better decision-making. **Diversity** is recognizing that each individual is unique and appreciating those unique perspectives. Differences can include race, ethnicity, gender, sexual orientation, socioeconomic status, age, physical abilities, religious beliefs, political beliefs, past experiences, education, and hopes and dreams.

One might ask, can a business be diverse and yet not inclusive? The answer is absolutely, yes. **Inclusion** is the act of harnessing diversity for the benefit of improved decision-making. Creating an inclusive environment requires a conscious effort to seek out, engage with, and listen to those individuals who are different from oneself. While human beings may have a natural tendency to associate with others who share similar tastes, experiences, values, and lifestyles (Hakim, 2000), it is important that this tendency is overcome during the hiring process and that diverse perspectives are included in decision-making. For example, while hiring locally has many benefits to a sustainable organization, allowing local hires to have a say in management decisions, embracing cultural differences within the work place and within the community-at-large, and creating an environment that empowers locals to facilitate change is all part of creating an inclusive workplace.

Retaining talent

It is often said that employees do not quit their job, they quit their boss. **Employee engagement** is the emotional commitment that employees demonstrate towards upholding the mission and values of the organization. As shown in Figure 11.1, to create an environment where employees are engaged, they need to feel that their contributions are valued and appreciated, and they also need to see how their efforts are making a difference. Motivated employees know how their work is contributing to the greater good of the organization, community, customers, and to the world.

Employee retention and engagement can be improved by ensuring that workers are paid fairly, that they are treated justly, and that all supervisors have the skills to succeed at managing people. Not only is a manager responsible for the tactical work of employee scheduling, performance evaluation, coaching, and discipline, their role should clearly be understood as helping their employees thrive. This requires curiosity, listening skills, communication, mentoring, appreciation, and inspiring their team members on a continual basis. The days of top-down, hierarchical decision-making will, hopefully, soon be over. The role of a true leader is to set the strategic vision and direction, motivate and align employees toward accomplishing that vision, empower employees to learn and grow, and see that people are recognized and rewarded for doing good work. Employees are now being encouraged to demonstrate leadership at all levels of an organization, and companies are better for it (Ofori, 2009). Decision-making that occurs on the front-lines – where the people who are doing the work have the most insight into how things can be improved – is the result of empowering people. Service workers, in particular, may have access to information that is not readily apparent to managers. For example, janitorial staff at an attraction or housekeepers in a hotel may notice waste streams in operations and

Figure 11.1 Employee engagement

may have solutions to reduce waste. Tour guides often see tourist behaviors that are unsustainable. By encouraging solutions and empowering employees to facilitate change, not only can the organization fulfill its commitment to ethical business operations, but also employees will feel valued and motivated to meet or exceed sustainability expectations. Respecting the perspective of all employees and treating them as experts in their particular role can go a long way in retaining valuable employees.

One important responsibility of a people manager is creating high-performing teams that are based on a foundation of trust and mutual respect. A **team** is a group of people united by a common business goal or the achievement of common objectives. A team of people can accomplish far more than the sum of the total of the individuals, therefore creating an environment that supports team-building and team work can increase productivity, enhance working relationships, and support innovation (Wesley, Jackson, & Lee, 2017). The technology giant Google (2015) performed a two-year, multi-million-dollar study to understand what makes a high performing team. They discovered (quite unsurprisingly) that the key to successful team-building is something they termed 'psychological safety'. The simple definition of how psychological safety is created is: kindness. In a work environment that is hostile, uncaring, vindictive, cold, or otherwise psychologically unsafe, teamwork cannot take root and employees become siloed and unproductive. Therefore, it is important that managers and supervisors, at all levels of the management hierarchy, treat employees kindly and with respect.

Companies should continually look for creative ways to stimulate a vibrant workplace. One way of collecting information about how well an organization is doing is through the use of anonymous employee feedback surveys. When they are conducted on an annual

Image 11.3 Cooking tajine in Morocco

Source: Susan L. Slocum

basis (or better still, a quarterly basis), this can be a good way to learn how engaged employees are feeling and what they would like to see the company do differently that would make them happier and more committed to the company and its mission. However, if the company does not act upon the feedback given in these anonymous employee feedback surveys, the morale of employees is likely to decline, increasing employee dissatisfaction and turnover.

Training

The first 30, 60, and 90 days of a new hire's tenure with an organization are important to their long-term retention. All companies should have an **onboarding plan**, which establishes employment goals and enables new employees to learn how to be successful in their role. Table 11.1 provides a sample onboarding and orientation schedule.

Table 11.1 Onboarding and orientation schedule

Timeline	Goals	Tasks
30 days	Learn the tools	Introduction to and practice with computer systems and other tools used on the job
		Overview of inventory management procedures
		Supervised practice with tourist interaction procedures
	Become comfortable with organizational culture	Introductions with staff in all departments
		Attend company value training
	Achieve success	Complete a small project
		Recognize a small success
60 days	Expand on the tools	Introduction and solo practice with more complex tools
		Increase customer service interactions and problem-solving
	Expand on the organizational culture	Work with other departments on projects
		Attend regular meetings
	Expand on success	Complete larger project
		Work independently on small projects
90 days	Master tools	Allow input into tool management systems and areas for improvements
		Allow input into operations systems and areas for improvement
	Master successes	Complete larger projects independently
		Provide feedback of performance metrics

The employee's direct supervisor is responsible for continuous goal setting and evaluation of the employee's progress toward meeting those goals, and an employee's goals should consist of a combination of both performance objectives and their personal/professional goals. **Performance objectives** are those that seek to improve the employee's ability to excel at their current job. **Professional goals** are those that seek to further the employee's career advancement. To retain talent, employees must come to believe that the company is invested in their career growth and will foster their development in a direction that benefits both the company and the individual (Donavan, Brown, & Mowen, 2004). According to Ilgaz (2015, n.p.), professional development can help retain employees because:

- It increases their skills – When prospective and current employees know there is the potential to raise their skill and compensation levels, an organization is much more likely to draw in and retain top candidates;
- It builds their confidence – Professional development builds employees' confidence by providing a stronger understanding of their job responsibilities and industry trends. When workers know they are competent, they become assertive leaders and great assets to an organization;
- It makes them happy – Granting employees access to professional development programs shows them they are a valued part of an organization. It also creates a positive and supportive workplace atmosphere. Both of these factors contribute greatly to employees' overall happiness; and
- It shows that an organization cares about its employees – While these training programs directly develop employees' work skills, they indirectly develop their personal lives by helping them qualify for promotions and, therefore, higher salaries.

Most formal training programs recognize the **70–20–10 rule**. That means, employers must understand that approximately 70% of an employee's growth comes from on-the-job training, 20% comes through mentoring and coaching, and 10% comes through formal training classes (Clardy, 2018). While there is a need for formal training, the subject matter must be timely and relevant to the employee, and it should be followed by actively practicing the skills and behaviors learned, otherwise they will be forgotten. Knowing that mentorship and coaching plays an even more significant role than formal training in an employee's learning curve, effort must be made to facilitate and encourage mentorship roles and 'buddies' within the organization. New hires should be paired up with a coach who can help answer their questions quickly and point them in the right direction. Finally, employees must be given opportunities to learn and grow in their roles. Providing leadership opportunities for employees demonstrates that the company trusts them and empowers them to stretch beyond their comfort zone, which leads to growth. It is important to remember that failure will happen – and that is a good thing. Failures are learning opportunities – learning what not to do again. So, when giving employees opportunity for leadership, companies that thrive must embrace the concept of failure, reflection, learning from the mistake, and then moving forward again with renewed confidence.

Reputation and goodwill

According to the Institute for Public Relations (Schreiber, 2011), all organizations have two basic responsibilities:

- Economic responsibility – this is the basic need of all organizations. For-profit companies must make a profit, and not-for-profit organizations must secure adequate financial support; and

- Legal responsibility – all organizations are expected to operate within the applicable country, state, and local laws.

Companies seeking to establish better reputations typically see two additional responsibilities:

- Ethical responsibility – to do the right thing and avoid harm, if possible; and
- Social responsibility – to be a positive contributor to society and the community.

In addition to ensuring the economic, legal, ethical, and social prosperity of a company, good leaders consider their reputation on a daily basis. Reflection is an important quality of a leader. By consistently reviewing behaviors and decision-making, and being humble enough to admit shortcomings and make course corrections, anyone can become a good leader. Good leaders generate goodwill, amongst employees, peers, and the community.

Human capital in tourism

Because tourism sells experiences, finding employees that can enhance the tourism product is vital to the success of any organization. Specific job skills can be taught once employees are hired, but personality, specifically a love of people and social interactions, cannot be easily imparted. Not all tourists want the same thing, so facilitating processes that allow for flexibility and creativity can support employee growth and the success of an organization. Providing autonomy for employees to get to know each visitor, their interests, and their expectations, as well as allowing employees to customize the experience requires trust on the part of managers. Moreover, while sustainability practices can also be encouraged on the job, a passion for sustainability may be a hard trait to find in a potential employee. Again, empowering them to take action to improve sustainability performance can be risky, but also rewarding. Sustainable tourism employment is a multi-faceted career path and finding and keeping the right people is often a challenge. The wage and benefits structure, hiring practices, employee development programs, and active social and environmental responsibility are key to the success of any company's ability to attract and retain great talent, garner lifelong customers, and earn and maintain a reputation for responsible, ethical, and fair decision-making. And remember, the employee is part of the tourist experience, therefore, s/he is part of the tourism product.

SUSTAINABILITY TOOL: BUILDING WORKPLACE CULTURE

Building an organizational culture that embraces sustainability can be a difficult process as not all people fully understand the concept of sustainability or may prioritize different aspects of the triple bottom line. Moreover, ensuring that sustainability remains a top priority when there is a change in leadership can also be challenging. The Network for Business Sustainability provides a valuable tool to support managers entitled *Embedding Sustainability in an Organization's Culture* (Bertels, Papania, & Papania, 2010). Figure 11.2 provides a general overview of the portfolio of tools that are needed to establish a long-term business culture around sustainability.

The vertical axis in Figure 11.2 is determined by what the organization is trying to accomplish. *Fulfillment* concentrates on current sustainability commitments or implementing sustainability initiatives. This process should focus on discussions about what the organization 'should do' in relation to compliance and operational excellence, or reinforcing and refining what the organization is already doing in relation to sustainability. *Innovation* is finding ways to do things

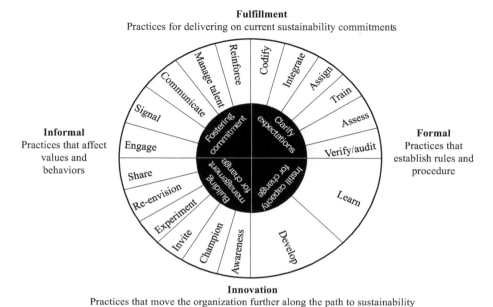

Figure 11.2 A portfolio approach to embedding sustainability

Source: Adapted from Bertels, Papania, and Papania (2010)

differently or better. These practices involve discussions of what the organization 'could do' and require experimentation, learning, and trying new things.

The horizontal axis determines the best way to meet the goals through *informal* and *formal* processes. There is an ongoing interplay between these two approaches and both can have relevance for organizational culture. Managers should be aware of the existence and impact of both 'soft' and 'hard' approaches to building culture. Informal approaches target people's values and the social norms of an organization. A **social norm** is an informal understanding that governs the behavior of members of a society or business. Informal approaches aim to establish and reinforce social norms through establishing shared values and shared ways of doing things that align with sustainability. This can be accomplished through discussion and by modelling desired behaviors. Formal approaches involve establishing rules, systems, and procedures that dictate behavior. The idea is to codify and organize values and behaviors that have developed informally through codes of conduct, procedures, systems, training materials, and the process of implementing programs.

The four quadrants in Figure 11.2, and the practices within each, characterize different systems that can be used to embed sustainability into organizational culture. Within each quadrant, there are a number of tools for managers to use to foster a culture of sustainability and corporate social responsibility. The following list provides an overview of each practice (Bertels, Papania, & Papania, 2010).

The practice of *fostering commitment* is aimed at building and reinforcing the importance of sustainability for the organization and includes engaging, signaling, communicating, managing talent, and reinforcement. It can also support and encourage those who are making efforts to embed sustainability into the operations of an organization. Specific activities that can foster commitment include:

- Raising the level of awareness and understanding of sustainability through the provision of information in informal ways:
  - Including sustainability information in company newsletters, on bulletin boards, or in memos;
  - Bringing in speakers to talk about sustainability issues;
  - Hosting internal workshops, conferences, or trade shows; and
  - Organizing sustainability competitions between business units or regional units to motivate sustainability performance or use internal competitions as a means to generate and identify new ideas.
- Encouraging employees to bring their personal sustainability behaviors into the workplace and to carry the organizational sustainability message into their communities;
- Making it easier for employees to make sustainability decisions at work and in their personal lives, such as transit pass programs, ride-sharing, and secure bicycle parking;
- Providing small grants or time off for sustainability projects launched by employees;
- Providing company time to meet about conceiving and launching sustainability initiatives; and
- Publicly recognizing employees at staff meetings, creating sustainability awards, or holding celebrations.

The practice in *clarifying expectations* is designed to integrate sustainability into the core of the organization's strategies and processes and includes codifying, integrating, assigning responsibility, training, assessing, and verifying/auditing. In this quadrant, equipping and encouraging employees via training and incentives, as well as measuring, tracking, and reporting the organization's progress, occurs. There are a number of specific activities that can clarify expectations.

- Setting explicit organizational goals for sustainability:
  - Setting sustainability goals at the business unit and departmental levels;
  - Including sustainability in personal goal setting;
  - Encouraging individuals to set their own targets for sustainability;
  - Building sustainability goals into scorecards; and
  - Ensuring that the goal progress can be measured.
- Increasing the level of priority for sustainability among the organization's values;
- Developing environmental policies, health and safety policies, ethics policies, and climate change policies;
- Developing procedures and standards related to sustainability by providing employees with sustainability performance policies or procurement policies;
- Implementing sustainability codes of conduct and translating abstract sustainability objectives into everyday work practices;
- Integrating different management systems by establishing a sustainability framework and directly integrating sustainability goals and deadlines into individual units' business plans; and

- Identifying all forms of relevant sustainability data to be monitored and collected by conducting regular internal audits of systems and processes and creating audit committees that include representatives from different departments.

Building *momentum for change* includes awareness raising: championing, inviting, experimenting, re-envisioning, and sharing. Practices in this quadrant aim to support a culture of sustainable innovation by developing the new ideas that help an organization achieve its long-term sustainability goals. These practices inspire and reassure employees so that they can experiment, try new things, take risks, and build on each other's ideas. Practices include:

- Disrupting the status quo by:
  - Interrupting people's patterns by pointing to the negative implications of current behaviors;
  - Making use of visual displays to demonstrate the implications of current behaviors; and
  - Providing opportunities for employees to experience the implications of currently unsustainable behaviors first-hand.
- Framing sustainability in everyday business language as innovation, cutting edge, and 'the right thing to do';
- Setting sustainability as urgent, and centering it around good publicity, contributing to reputation, and quality;
- Avoiding emotional language;
- Building coalitions around sustainability and encouraging knowledge-sharing across different functional areas;
- Encouraging dialogue and questions, holding staff meetings to generate ideas on sustainability, and requesting feedback from internal and external stakeholders;
- Asking employees if they are proud of their organization;
- Listening more and talking less; and
- Providing autonomy to workers and managers to develop new solutions to sustainability challenges and allowing self-started projects to germinate.

Instilling *capacity for change* includes creating opportunities for employees to learn and develop. The goal is to create structures that form the foundation for future changes in the organization. Practices include:

- Recognizing the value in external information:
  - Encouraging employees to attend industry and environmental conferences or join a sustainability organization where members share information and best practices;
  - Observing competitors' sustainability activity by scanning multiple sources habitually;
  - Researching stakeholder needs and values;
  - Scanning for changes in legislation and upcoming regulatory requirements; and
  - Using focus groups and surveys to garner customer opinions on sustainability issues.
- Selecting organizational sustainability metrics that are used by others to facilitate benchmarking;
- Welcoming proposals and suggestions that originated at the grassroots level and following through by allocating resources to pilot the best ideas;

- Taking advantage of failures and seeing them as opportunities for significant transformational and sustainable change; and
- Dedicating resources to investigating failures and then developing a process for making recommendations for improvement.

Organizational culture plays a fundamental part in the shift toward sustainability. As Bertels, Papania, and Papania (2010) write, "despite a multitude of corporate sustainability reports that describe sustainability as 'the way we do business', most business leaders lack a clear understanding of how to embed sustainability in their day-to-day decisions and processes" (p. 8). This section has provided a first step to creating an organizational culture that embraces sustainability. While not all of these tools are appropriate for all tourism organizations, they provide examples of ways to empower employees to contribute to the mission and vision of a company that wishes to increase its sustainable operations.

Conclusion

Sustainable human capital management is a human resource management approach that demonstrates concern towards the people the company employs. Hiring the right people for the job requires an effective recruitment strategy and an assessment of personal bias inherent in the selection process. By building both a diverse and inclusive team and ensuring employee engagement, managers can reduce the costs associated with employee turnover. Human capital management should provide a welcoming onboarding experience, ensure the employee's physical and psychological safety on the job, offer a living wage and appropriate benefits, and guarantee opportunities for personal and professional growth. Once the best employee has been found, providing educational opportunities, mentoring, and following the 70–20–10 rule can help support the engagement and commitment needed for long-term success. A tool has been presented that highlights the business practices necessary for building and maintain a culture of sustainability. Empowered employees can contribute to the company's sustainable values, enhance the tourist experience, and reinforce the reputation and goodwill of an organization.

CASE STUDY 11.1 GENDER AND TOURISM IN ZAMBIA'S CONSERVATION WORKFORCE

E'LISHA VICTORIA FOGLE

Background

Located in southern Africa and similar to many of its neighboring countries, Zambia is dominated by nature-based tourism. Community-based, wildlife, and ecotourism have each played essential roles in an industry that has become one of the country's major economic generators. In 2015, Zambia recorded a total of 931,000 international tourists, of which 25% came for leisure purposes. Most of these tourists came to visit the national parks or to view what locals recognize as Mosi-oa-Tunya or 'The Smoke that Thunders', but to many she is Victoria Falls – one of the Seven Natural Wonders of the World (Republic of Zambia, 2015).

Here, tourism and conservation are often combined in an effort to promote sustainability for the environment as well as the people. Zambia hosts 20 national parks and more than 30 game management areas, requiring a large number of wildlife officers

Image 11.4 Victoria Falls, Zambia

Source: E'lisha Vitoria Fogle

to protect the country's vast natural resources and manage, sometimes dangerous, human–wildlife conflicts that impact local communities and tourists. Though the role of a wildlife officer has traditionally been held by men, the inclusion of women in these positions has been shown to improve community relations, create safer and less destructive solutions to conservation, and reduce poverty and improve food security (Black, 2001). In addition, the country's present-day culture has been influenced by a colonial past, in which patriarchy, and in some cases religion, have largely impacted gender relations in the workplace. As a social system, patriarchy gives unequal authority to men where they maintain predominate control over political, economic, and social systems – disadvantaging women from access to education, healthcare, and other basic human rights (McClintock, 2013).

Scenario

As a child, Salifyanji (Saly-fee-ahn-jee) grew up watching the National Geographic Channel – growing her interest in animals, their behaviors, and their interactions with humans. Her family, unlike many of her female peers, encouraged her to do well in school so she could attend university. When the time arrived, she pursued a Wildlife Management degree from a prominent institution in Zambia, with the hope of one day becoming a wildlife officer. As a student, she realized very few of her fellow pupils were female, but that did not deter her from performing well and achieving the 'Best student' award from her program. Upon graduation, she gained experience working with several research groups studying elephants, lions, and other wildlife. Over the coming years, she volunteered at several national parks and the Department of National Parks and Wildlife to prepare for her future dream job.

When the national application period opened for new officer recruits, she felt her educational background and field experiences would help her shine as a top candidate. Over 600 applicants applied that year, 200 were advanced and only five were women – Salifyanji included. However, the successful completion of the physical and first aid training were required, where men and women were obligated to perform at the same standard for all calisthenics, regardless of gender. To the surprise of her colleagues and instruction officers, she passed the physical training and was deployed to a national park for localized wildlife preparation – the final step to becoming a wildlife officer.

Salifyanji was proud that she had achieved what so many women had not and had made it to the final stage of the application. After reporting to her post, she and her fellow trainees were instructed to meet the Park Director for orientation. Following introductions, the Park Director excused the male trainees and asked Salifyanji to stay behind. He explained that while she had performed well in training and had the credentials to make a suitable wildlife officer, she would be unable to complete the six-month long wildlife preparation because only male barracks and toilets were available, and no accommodations could be made for a female trainee.

Reflective questions

1. As a manager, what changes would you suggest to improve equal opportunities for women employed in tourism-related sectors in lesser economically developed countries, such as Zambia? What conflict could potentially arise?

2. How do social structures, such as patriarchy, influence management decisions in the workplace? How can a manager change institutional culture to be more inclusive?

3. Investigate how African women are getting involved in conservation and describe some ways it may provide empowerment for them and their communities.

References

Black, P.D.R. (2001). Women in natural resource management: finding a more balanced perspective. *Society & Natural Resources*, 14(8), 645–656.

McClintock, A. (2013). *Imperial Leather: Race, Gender, and Sexuality in the Colonial Contest*. London, Routledge.

Republic of Zambia (2015). *2015 Tourism Statistical Digest*. Ministry of Tourism and Arts.

CASE STUDY 11.2 A WILD RIDE TO TOURISM GROWTH

TRISH WRIGHT

There is a small town nestled in Southwest Idaho that relies heavily on tourism as a major source of capital and employment for the residents. Athol is located 25 miles north of Coeur d'Alene, about 40 miles east of Spokane, Washington. According to the US Census Bureau (2010), Athol's population was 692 people. Until recently, it was home to just a gas station/convenience store, a bar, and a breakfast diner. Not a stop light anywhere, even today.

Athol is also the site of the Henley Aerodrome. This private airstrip, measuring just over 250 acres, was about to change the landscape of northern Idaho. Clayton "Clay" Henley bought the land in 1973 so he could have a place for his planes. He began to do airshows on the weekends – Snoopy vs. The Red Barron. After Henley died in 1977, Gary Norton bought the property, outbidding the Walt Disney Company, and became the proud new owner of a 1918 steam locomotive. After restoring it, he built a track around the property. Since every train needs a station, a small 'town' was built including a restaurant, a gift shop, and an old-fashioned candy store. It includes immaculate

Image 11.5 Silverwood
Theme Park, Athol, Idaho

Source: Trish Wright

landscaping, clean and well-manicured grounds, and beautiful flowers and gardens. The official opening of Silverwood Theme Park occurred in 1988.

Today this 219-acre theme park includes high intensity rides, kiddie rides, a water park, a full-service sit-down restaurant, and of course many shops and concessions. The steam train is still one of the biggest attractions, with characters and a 'robbery' where the bandits 'hold up' the train. People can donate to the bandits and the money is all given to the Children's Village in Coeur d'Alene, which is an organization that helps at-risk youth. The owners match the donations given by the guests who are 'robbed'.

During peak months between Memorial Day and Labor Day, the average guest count per day can be anywhere from 3,000 when things are gearing up, to 15,000 per day when the season is in full swing. Most visitors are from the Pacific and Inland Northwest and Western Canada. However, they are seeing more foreign non-English speaking tourists. They have interpreters for most languages, including American Sign Language so hearing-impaired persons can enjoy the shows. They host special days for people with disabilities and their care givers and have STEM (Science, Technology, Engineering, and Math) school students come out to conduct experiments and calculations with the rides. The goal in to include everyone.

Silverwood Theme Park is one of Idaho's largest seasonal employers from April to October, with over 1,200 staff hired each summer (Kraner, 2017). There are also year-round staff that do landscaping, marketing, and maintenance. Silverwood is a large employer of youth in the state. Between April and October, the sleepy little town grows exponentially, and the small businesses around the park are benefactors of this influx of visitors.

The Nortons wish to create a family atmosphere, and trainees are treated as such to encourage them to spread that hospitality to the guests. Their goal is to subtly direct guests to not only enjoy themselves in a welcoming atmosphere, but behave themselves as well. For instance, while the park serves alcohol, there is a three-drink limit per person, and one hour before the park closes for the night, no alcohol is served. Bartenders and employees are all trained to recognize the signs of inebriation and instructed on how to gently and properly handle the situation as unobtrusively as possible.

The owners recognize that for many of their hires, this is their first introduction to the work force, so Silverwood provides coaching to help young employees do their best. Training is provided in things like cash handling, guest relations, horticulture, maintenance, security, and how they are expected to behave while 'on stage', as they call it. Workers also receive special perks. For every 30 hours worked, they get a free pass for a friend or family member, discounts on food and merchandise, and are also eligible for scholarships. They have bi-monthly events just for employees and guests, such as movies on the lawn, karaoke night, and game night to enhance the camaraderie of employees and let them feel appreciated for their efforts. Because of these positive programs, these youth are sought after by local employers in the area during the off season. In many ways, by providing introductory job skills, the youth of Athol are better able to prepare for their future professions. In a small remote town, these skills have greatly enhanced the opportunity for youth and the community at large.

During months of full operations, nearby small businesses and restaurants fill with tourists, and much of their annual income is made in these few months. Recently, a new

Super One grocery store with an Ace Hardware attached to it has been built. This is a benefit for both the locals and the tourists, as the nearest full-service grocery store was ten miles away.

Reflective questions

1. Since this successful park is only able to operate during months without snow, what could be done to create more capital in the winter months and keep more people employed year-round?

2. While this rural area is growing quickly, what are your thoughts on how to balance small town quaintness with convenience, without creating a feeling of homogenization?

3. While there are a few RV parks in the area, the nearest hotel is ten miles away. Local residents are resisting hotel development, stating that it would create more traffic. How would you go about changing their mind on this, or not?

References

Kraner, B. (2017). Silverwood Theme Park raises wage to keep pace with competitive labor market. *The Spokesman Review*. Retrieved from www.spokesman.com/stories/2017/mar/07/silverwood-theme-park-raises-wage-to-keep-pace-wit/.

US Census Bureau (2010). Retrieved from www.census.gov/programs-surveys/decennial-census/decade.2010.html.

STUDY QUESTIONS

1. Find a job advertisement for a tourism position. List, in order, the attributes that attract you to the position. What information is missing that could determine if you would apply for the job?

2. Develop a set of interview questions for a front desk supervisor position. Develop a set of questions for a special events coordinator position. How are they similar and how are they different?

3. You are the food court supervisor at a large theme park. You have hired a new employee. What training elements would you include for their first day on the job? What new training would you add on their 30th day of work? Why did you select that particular training at that time?

4. You have an employee that has a strong track record of service for your organization, but after three years on the job they are becoming demotivated. How would you address the problem?

5. Develop a set of best practices that encourage a corporate culture of sustainability. How would you implement them?

DEFINITIONS

70–20–10 rule   approximately 70% of an employee's growth comes from on-the-job training, 20% comes through mentoring and coaching, and 10% comes through formal training classes

Diversity   recognizing that each individual is unique and appreciating those differences

Employee engagement   the emotional commitment that employees demonstrate towards upholding the mission and values of the company

Employee turnover rate   the percentage of employees who leave an organization over a certain period of time (typically, one year)

Human capital   the stock of knowledge, habits, social and personality attributes, including creativity, embodied in the ability to perform labor so as to produce economic value

Human capital management the process of acquiring, training, managing, and retaining employees

Human resource management the management and professional development of employees within an organization

Inclusion the act of harnessing diversity for the benefit of improving decision-making and growth

Institutional knowledge the collection of historical knowledge and wisdom that is retained by employees and the analytical skills necessary for its effective use within the organization

Knowledge worker workers who apply theoretical and analytical knowledge, acquired through formal training, to develop products and services

Mission statement a written statement of a company's purpose and values, which informs the company's decision-making and trade-off to both members of the company and the external community

Onboarding plan a plan that establishes employment goals and enables new employees to learn how to be successful in their role

Performance objective a goal that seeks to improve the employee's ability to excel at their current job

Professional goal a goal that seeks to further the employee's career advancement

Service worker a worker whose primary task is the serving of customer needs

Social norm an informal understanding that governs the behavior of members of a society or business

Team a group of people united by a common business goal or achieving common objectives

Unconscious bias the inclination for humans to form social stereotypes that lump people together unfairly based on their past experiences

Chapter **12**

Visitor management

Overview

A leading cause of negative impacts within a destination results from visitor behavior. Therefore, managing the visitor can promote sustainability as well as add value to the tourism product. This chapter explains the pros and cons of managing visitor numbers, using carrying capacity limits, as well as the advantages and disadvantages of adapting resources to mitigate visitor impacts. Sustainability requires long-term, permanent changes in behaviors, and a commitment to encouraging visitors to alter their behavior in the future. Tools such as communication, interpretation, and education can support this goal. The Mindfulness model is explained as a way to encourage interactive and entertaining forms of interpretation.

CHAPTER OBJECTIVES

At the completion of the chapter, students will be able to:

- Discuss visitor management strategies as they relate to the sustainable use of tourism resources;
- Define the different types of carrying capacity;
- Explain ways to adapt a resource through substitutions, site hardening, and visitor/ operator qualifications;
- Articulate the importance of communication, interpretation, and education in the conservation of tourism resources; and
- Implement the Mindfulness model to enhance the visitor experience while communicating the need for sustainable behavior.

Introduction

While a sustainable business may be able to mitigate some of the negative influence of tourism through the supply chain (see Chapter 9), it is also important to minimize the negative impacts incurred through tourist visitation. Because tourism is simultaneously created and consumed, the tourist often creates numerous side effects that are detrimental to the environment or the society they are visiting. **Visitor management** involves the management tools and interventions that regulate the movement and behavior of visitors in a destination, natural area, or attraction (Albrecht, 2017). The best way to control visitor impacts is to manage the visitor experience. Most visitors want a managed experience because they may only visit a site once in their lifetime and want to make sure they get the most out of the experience (du Cros & McKercher, 2015). Visitor management can include the oversight of tourism facilities, transportation routes, visitor flows, guiding, and interpretive signage. Not only can visitor management plans reduce some of the harmful effects of tourism, they can enhance the tourist experience and increase levels of satisfaction through educational opportunities that promote sustainable behaviors in an interesting and interactive way.

There are three primary strategies used in visitor management: controlling visitor numbers; adapting a resource to prevent negative impacts (such as the use of fencing, pathways, or lighting); and modifying visitor behavior. Visitor management varies depending on the destination, attraction type, management style and community needs, and like many other sustainability management tools, visitor management strategies should be appropriate to the resource under threat. Moreover, tourism should develop a long-term, quality-oriented strategy to counteract future challenges the destination may face. It is important to address visitor expectations by recognizing visitor motivations and fostering creative ways to communicate appropriate behavioral messages to tourists. As Figure 12.1 shows, when people access natural and cultural resources, they can better comprehend the meaning and inherent value of conserving them, which in turn creates enjoyment and a reason why people want to visit them (du Cros & McKercher, 2015). The goal is to educate the tourist while enhancing the experience, and to ensure long-term behavioral changes in the visitors.

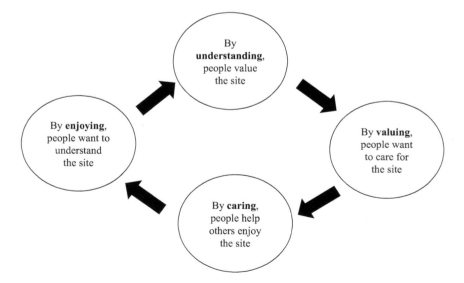

Figure 12.1 Establishing inherent value through tourism visitation

Controlling visitor numbers

The United Nations Educational, Scientific, and Cultural Organisation (UNESCO) recognizes that blocking access to tourism sites is an effective, yet crude, way to manage visitor impacts. In fact, visitors do not have a 'right' to visit many sites, especially when the protection of natural or cultural resources takes precedence over the interests of tourists. Moreover, local residents may place restrictions on the number of visitors allowed in a destination if tourism begins to affect the quality of, or access to, natural resources. According to LaGrave (2016), Santorini, an island in Greece, has restricted cruise ship visitation to 8,000 visitors per day in an effort to reduce overcrowding. Likewise, the country of Bhutan requires visitors to book with a licensed Bhutanese tour operator and pay a fee of $200 to $250 per day to support free education, health care, and poverty alleviation for local residents (this fee includes accommodations, meals, in-country transportation, and guide services). Koh Tachai, part of Similan National Park in Thailand, was closed indefinitely "due to ecological damage caused by mass tourism, [as] the environment is unable to restore itself" (Mu Ko Similan National Park of Thailand, 2018). These are just a few examples of destinations using visitation restrictions to limit tourism growth. Table 12.1 provides a list of possible strategies for high use areas and options for managing visitor numbers.

Demarketing is a form of advertising used to decrease demand for a certain product or experience. Demarketing is not the opposite of marketing, but an integral part of general marketing and is used to reduce or shift demand. General demarketing is used when the goal is to reduce total demand, and selective demarketing is used to reduce demand of a

Table 12.1 Strategies and tactics for managing high levels of use

Strategy	Management tactics and techniques
Reduce use of the entire protected area	• Limit number of visitors in the entire protected area • Limit length of stay • Encourage use of other areas • Require certain skills and/or equipment • Charge a flat visitor fee • Make access more difficult
Reduce use of problem areas	• Inform about problem areas and alternative areas • Discourage or prohibit use of problem area • Limit number of visitors in problem areas • Encourage/require a stay limit in problem areas • Make access harder/easier to areas • Eliminate facilities/attractions in problem areas, improve facilities/attractions in alternative areas • Encourage travel to a similar attraction • Establish different skill/equipment requirements • Charge differential visitor fees

Table 12.1 continued

Strategy	Management tactics and techniques
Modify the location of use within problem areas	• Discourage/prohibit certain uses
	• Encourage/permit certain uses in certain areas
	• Locate facilities on durable sites
	• Concentrate use through facility design or information
	• Segregate different types of visitors
Modify the timing of use	• Encourage use outside of peak use periods
	• Discourage/ban use when impact potential is high
	• Fees in periods of high use/high impact potential
Modify type of use and visitor behavior	• Discourage/ban damaging practices/equipment
	• Encourage/require behavior, skills, equipment
	• Teach a wilderness/cultural ethic
	• Encourage/require a party size and/or limit on number of visitors
	• Discourage/prohibit overnight use
Modify visitor expectations	• Inform visitors about appropriate uses
	• Inform about potential conditions
Increase the resistance of the resource	• Shield the site from impact
	• Strengthen the site
Maintain/rehabilitate resource	• Remove problems
	• Maintain/rehabilitate impacted locations

Source: Adapted from Eagles, McCool, Haynes, and Phillips (2002)

certain customer group (Kotler & Levy, 1971). The use of demarketing can be effective in sustainable tourism when demand for a certain aspect of a resource is too high, therefore it can involve redistributing visitation to other areas or to different time periods in order to protect a resource. It can also be used to discourage specific types of visitors if these visitors are disruptive. Demarketing is most effective when used at the point of sale rather than at the point of consumption. In other words, tourists should be influenced and managed before they actually decide to visit (Clements, 1989). Demarketing involves a four-step process (Table 12.2).

Carrying capacity

In order to determine the appropriate number of visitors, managers attempt to determine an area's carrying capacity. As discussed in Chapter 7, **carrying capacity** considers the amount of use any given land or environment can endure over time without degrading its suitability for that use (Fennel, 2015, p. 175). **Carrying capacity in tourism** refers to the maximum number of people that may visit a tourist destination at the same time, without causing destruction of

Table 12.2 Four-step demarketing process

The demarketing process	
Marketing objective	Develop a set of clear objectives
Tourist insights	Perform research on current tourist behaviors
Demarketing strategy	Based on objectives and insights, design a demarketing strategy
Implementation and revision	Implement the strategy in line with objectives. Re-evaluate strategy periodically to alter and improve outcomes

the physical, economic, and socio-cultural environment and an unacceptable decrease in the quality of visitors' satisfaction (Liu, 2003).

In tourism, there are generally three types of carrying capacity. The **physical capacity** is the maximum number of tourists that an area is actually able to support and is generally used in natural areas, such as national coastal parks. It can be calculated as:

Physical capacity per day = area (in meters) × visitors per meter × daily duration of stay

The **economic capacity** is the level of acceptable change within the local economy of a tourist destination and is described as the point at which the increased revenue brought by tourism development is overtaken by the inflation caused by tourism (O'Reilly, 1986). Economic capacity is generally used in destination management. **Social capacity** relates to the negative socio-cultural impacts related to tourism development. Reduced visitor enjoyment and increased crime are indicators that the social carrying capacity of a destination has been exceeded.

Other ways to minimize visitor impacts include spreading visitors more evenly across the destination, selling advance-purchase tickets, or increasing the entrance prices. By broadening the selection of activities and experiences, or by encouraging visitors to arrive at less pressured moments in the day, week, month, or year, the number of visitors at any given time can be reduced. However, the spreading of tourist visits results in the same number of visitors, just dispersed more evenly. Spreading can increase visitor enjoyment, but may not reduce the overall impacts to a resource. The advance sale of entrance tickets allows a business or organization to meet carrying capacity guidelines, and visitors may perceive the site as more authentic or as a 'once in a lifetime' attraction. One of the most common ways to control visitor numbers is through an increase in entrance fees. While high prices for tourism services is an effective way to reduce visitation, it can exclude lower income populations, especially local residents, who may want to visit their hometown attractions. Instead, many attractions may consider **congestion-related pricing systems** by offering low-priced tickets for periods of slow visitation and more expensive prices during peak periods, or **dual pricing systems**, where tourists pay a higher price than local residents. Keep in mind that customers may get frustrated if they do not know to plan ahead, so it is important to make sure visitors know where to purchase tickets, when to visit, and how much the entrance fees will be. Visitors need real-time information in order to plan their visit appropriately.

The home of Wanampi

After Minyma Kuniya defeated Wati Liru, her spirit combined with her nephew's and together they became Wanampi (water snake). Wanampi lives here today and has the power to control the source of this precious water.

Kapi is sacred

This is the most reliable kapi (water) around the base of Uluru. In traditional times Anangu would sing out 'Kuka kuka' and Wanampi would release the kapi and let it flow into the waterhole.

Listen to country

This is a good place to listen to country. Take a minute to sit down, close your eyes and breathe deeply. Enjoy this moment. Listen to the birds. Can you hear water trickling? Concentrate on the wind. Can you hear it? Feel it? Kuniya is a strong woman, this place has a strong feeling.

As with all water sources in the desert, this waterhole is a place of great respect and treated as sacred. Swimming, polluting, or scaring the animals away would threaten the survival of our people. Today, wildlife still depend upon it for survival.

Please do not swim or disturb this special place in any way.

Image 12.1 Interpretation for a sacred site at Uluru, Northern Territory, Australia

Source: Susan L. Slocum

Adapting a resource

Changing a tourist resource allows for reduced or centralized impacts. Brunson and Shelby (1993) suggest that substitutability can help managers find less impactful alternatives that also meet visitor expectations. **Substitutability** in tourism refers to the interchangeability of activities and experiences by varying one or more of the following: the timing of the experience, the means of gaining access to the experience, the setting, and the activity. For example, motor boats can cause pollution in rivers and lakes, their noise can disturb wildlife, and often they conflict with other activities, such as swimming and fishing, which causes conflicts between visitors with different expectations. By allowing only non-motorized boats (such as canoes and kayaks), many of these problems can be eliminated. Other forms of substitutability include site hardening, requiring visitor and/or operational qualifications, and the construction of physical barriers. Studies have shown that by changing how people use a resource or by changing their access to the resource, visitors learn to find less intrusive substitutes that can be just as satisfying (Manning, 1999). However, it is important to understand what the visitors' expectations are before adapting a resource.

Site hardening involves constructing facilities, paved trails, or roads to reduce the impacts of visitors on sensitive soils and vegetation and to help meet the visitors' needs for usable access (Spenceley et al., 2015). In a way, site hardening sacrifices certain areas in order to preserve other, more sensitive areas. Paving a pathway encourages visitors to stay within the confines of the trail and protects the native vegetation nearby. Many national parks will have 'developed' areas, where accommodations and visitor services are centralized, requiring more exertion to reach the pristine areas. Some of these areas may only be accessible by walking many miles and may require camping or backpacking as a way to reduce visitor numbers. One downside of site hardening is that once an area is developed and easily accessible, visitation to that area increases, putting pressure to add more amenities and grow the hardened area.

Another method of adapting a resource is commonly referred to as **visitor and/or operator qualifications** and means limiting entry only to those possessing certain required qualifications. Examples include scuba divers who must be qualified to use a marine protected area; tour leaders that must have a certificate of competence; and users of the protected area who must be accompanied by a qualified local guide (Eagles, McCool, Haynes, & Phillips, 2002). From a sustainability perspective, requiring licensed guides provides employment opportunities for local residents who often possess historic or traditional knowledge about the resource being visited. The certification process also provides an opportunity to train visitors or tour operators on sustainability issues and teaches visitors behavioral best practices.

Lastly, for highly endangered resources, physical barriers may be built to ensure visitors cannot destroy valuable resources. As is common in museums, creating an environment where visitors can see, but not touch, has been shown to effectively discourage both unintended impacts and intentional destruction (such as graffiti). Common examples include roping off archeological remains or valuable artwork, showcasing miniature displays to provide aerial views of an attraction, or making copies or replicas where visitor damage is too extensive.

Image 12.2 Statue of Liberty replica, Las Vegas, NV

Source: Susan L. Slocum

Modifying visitor behavior

The goal of modifying visitor behavior is to get visitors to consider their behavior in relationship to the resources they are enjoying. Tourism managers must balance revenue management with communication, interpretation, and education. First, general information about the visitors' motivations and expectations must be gathered before appropriate marketing, promotion, revenue management, and codes of conduct can be developed to suit the needs of the market and the business. In sustainability, the goal is to have visitors understand the negative impacts that result from tourism, to learn new ways of behaving in order to be better stewards of natural and cultural attractions, and ultimately retain this information so that their behavior is permanently changed as they visit other sites and destinations.

Communication is the process of conveying information or evoking understanding. Communication tools include signage, pamphlets, or audio messages that list expected behaviors. Unfortunately, most communication messages are lists of forbidden activities (e.g. no alcohol on site, dogs must be on leash, or children must be accompanied by an adult), and are often ignored by visitors. One of the more effective ways to communicate is through the use of guides who can orally explain appropriate behaviors and provide the reasoning behind certain restrictions.

Interpretation is an educational activity, which aims to reveal meanings and relationships through the use of original objects, first-hand experience, and illustrative media, rather than simply communicating factual information. Interpretation can offer a connection between whatever is being viewed and the visitor by providing detailed information about a resource's use, meaning, or historical significance. **Education** is a form of learning in which the knowledge, skills, and habits of a group of people are transferred from one generation to the next through teaching, training, or research. Education implies transformation in the visitors as they learn new things and change the way they perceive the world around them. According to Tan and Law (2016), "Unlike direct visitor management strategies, education and persuasive communication do not impose overt enforcements or controls. Visitors are instead encouraged to engage voluntarily in sustainable behavior through positive messages, self-discovery, and experiential learning" (p. 135). Interpretation is often the tool used to educate visitors.

Managing interpretation

On-site interpretation is designed to encourage visitors to discover new ways of thinking about their surroundings and can assist in protecting natural and cultural resources. Just like interpreters who translate one language into another, tourism interpreters "translate artifacts, collections, and physical resources into a language that helps visitors make meaning of these resources" (Bacher et al., 2007, p. 2). Effective interpretation provides visitor orientation, information, and inspiration in the right amounts and at the right times so that visitors will have a more enjoyable, meaningful, and complete experience. Ham (1992) recognizes four qualities that distinguish interpretation from other forms of communication. Interpretation should be pleasurable, relevant, organized, and it should possess a theme that can be easily followed by the audience. It should also connect the visitor's life experiences to the resource being visited to describe deeper meanings and truths (Beck & Cable, 1998). According to the US National Park Service (NPS), effective interpretation answers the question, "Why should I care?"

Interpretation can enhance the authenticity of a site. However, it is important to evaluate whose authenticity is being communicated. In relation to heritage sites, du Cros and McKercher

Appropriate communication technologies

Figure 12.2 Elements of interpretation

Source: Adapted from Bacher et al. (2007, p. 10)

(2015) write, "As much as some people would like to believe absolute history exists, in reality multiple, contested histories often share the same physical locale" (p. 41). Moreover, authenticity is different from reality. For example, pollution, poverty, poor sanitation, and oppression might not be the appropriate message to communicate when attempting to enhance the visitor experience in an impoverished area. As discussed in many chapters throughout this book, negotiating the aspects that stakeholders want to communicate and providing an experience that tourists can put into a context they understand is part of the challenges of interpretation. As Fennell (2015) writes, interpretation is both "an art and a science" (p. 115).

An easy way to remember the important elements of interpretation is to use the acronym ART. **ART** stands for audience, resource, and technology as shown in Figure 12.2 (Bacher et al., 2007, p. 10). The better the interpreter's knowledge of the resource and audience, and the more appropriate their techniques for presenting their knowledge to that audience, the more likely the visitors will form their own personal connections with the resource.

Interpretation can be delivered in two ways, through personal services or through technology. Personal services include informal contacts, talks, guided walks, living history, and demonstrations. Effective interpreters should possess the following skill sets (Bacher et al., 2007, p. 1):

- Understand their role to facilitate connections between resource meanings and audience interests;
- Understand, recognize, and create opportunities for audiences to make their own intellectual and emotional connections to resource meanings;
- Understand, recognize, and cohesively develop an idea or ideas in interpretive products and activities;
- Understand the roles and relationships of resource knowledge, audience knowledge, and interpretive techniques in interpretive products and activities; and
- Purposefully reflect on interpretive philosophies and best practices, deepen their understandings, and apply these philosophies and best practices to all interpretive competencies.

In order for personal services to be effective, guides should make eye contact with their audience, possess confidence in the subject material, and be organized so that the narrative is easy

Image 12.3 Christchurch Botanic Gardens, New Zealand

Source: Susan L. Slocum

to follow and tells a compelling story. According to the US National Park Service (2007), only 22% of visitors in the US national parks received interpretation through personal services.

Lastly, it is important to tell a story through interpretation. The story should include a plot or storyline that has a linear flow from the introduction, to the central part in which actions take place, and finally the end. The end should include either a revelation or a resolution. Visitors are more interested in hearing about people than about things, so adding a human element or characters to the storyline can further engage visitors. Using active language is also helpful in grabbing and maintaining attention. In other words, get straight to the point by making clear who is performing the action. For example:

- Passive language: These plants are used by indigenous people for medicine;
- Active language: Indigenous people use these plants for medicine.

Text-based interpretation is generally a passive form of communication, so using technology can help to engage the visitor. Technology allows for a multisensory experience that is a "proactive form of communication that may act to draw visitors in and shape messages to suit personal contexts" (Hughes & Morrison-Saunders, 2005, p. 161). **Interpretation intensity** is a comparison of quantity and type of interpretation between sites. It is more than just the number of signs or displays available, it includes the intensity of the visitors' interactions through social connections with the site.

One of the primary goals of interpretation is the development of mindfulness. **Mindfulness** is caring about the world around us, and the **Mindfulness model** is the process of developing mindful visitors (Moscardo, 1996). Before beginning to develop interpretation, it is important to establish the one overall message that you would like to get across to your visitors. As a sustainable organization, that message may be the natural or cultural importance of a resource, or how the existence of a resource impacts the world as a whole. Remember, the overall message must be interesting and should resonate with tourists so that the message is retained in the long-term.

In designing a technology-based interpretive program, the Mindfulness model (Table 12.3) highlights the ingredients needed to engage visitors in the communication process. However, it is important to avoid sensory overload by overwhelming the visitor with too much information or too many bells and whistles that distract from the messages (Roggenbuck, 1992). Howard (1998) recognizes that there are some experiences that require little interpretation, such as a sunset over the ocean or an animal encounter in the wild. From a sustainability perspective, the goal is to enhance the visitor experience while simultaneously communicating information, facilitating appropriate behavior, and instilling a long-term value for the resource. Therefore, appropriate types and intensity of interpretation should be considered. Additionally, interpretation should consider the following aspects:

- **Knowledge and understanding:** What kind of information (facts, messages, ideas) will visitors receive and take away? How does the information help visitors make sense of complex situations?
- **Skills:** Following a visit, what kind of skills might people have developed as part of their visit? Are visitors encouraged to try and do new things?
- **Attitudes and values:** What kind of attitudes, perceptions, and opinions do we want visitors to develop about the subject or organization? How will people feel during their visit?
- **Enjoyment, inspiration, and creativity:** What do we do to help our visitors think creatively and express their creativity? How much fun is this project? Do we surprise and challenge our visitors?
- **Activity, behavior, and progression:** How do we want people to behave during their visit? What would we like our visitors to do (differently) as a result of their visit?

Interpretation technologies

Different communication tools have advantages and disadvantages. Pamphlets, fliers, and other printed material can be read anytime and retained for use at a later date. They are also considered less obtrusive over permanent signs, but can create a waste trail when they are discarded after use. However, permanent signage provides information at a specific location of interest (Moscardo et al., 2004). All printed materials should be visually appealing and engaging to the visitor. Otherwise, they may miss out on important information if it has not grabbed their attention. Moreover, these traditional forms of communication do not require specific technological knowledge.

Other, more high-tech communication tools include MP3 players, GPS tracking devices, mobile services, and interactive displays. Audio-visual devices require the least amount of effort for consuming interpretive information and will increase the number of visitors who listen to (versus reading) the interpretive messages (Davidson, Lee, & George, 1991). Simple audio-visual technologies include pre-recorded narratives that either play continuously as visitors walk

Table 12.3 Elements of the Mindfulness model

Communication factors	Cognitive advantages
Variety and change	Using a variety of techniques to engage the visitor is important as individuals learn in different ways
Multisensory media	The multisensory, audio-visual, and dynamic interpretive techniques are good ways to enhance visitor attention and learning
Novelty/conflict/surprise	The surprise, conflict, or novelty factor is important to keep the interest of visitors and to prevent tiredness and boredom
Use of questions	Questions increase visitors' learning. They are how mindful visitors recall the knowledge that they have learned while wandering at the site
Visitor control/interactive exhibits	Interactive material is useful to catch and keep visitors' attention as well as to improve their learning and interest
Connection to visitors	Effective interpretation can relate the present experience to the prior experience of visitors. It is best to connect the story of the site with the visitor's story
Good physical orientation	Visitors who can easily find their way inside an attraction are more mindful than those who do not

Source: Adapted from Moscardo (1996)

through a site, can be started by pushing a button (such as at a display) to receive more information, or are GPS-triggered when a person enters a specific space and the recording starts. Researchers have found mixed results with pre-recorded interpretive tools. Positives include ease of finding interesting displays or remote tour stops, although some people may feel a loss of control with automatically triggered messages. These types of technologies appear to work best with cultural sites, as nature-based tourists may find them intrusive when looking for an escape from their at-home technology dependence (Wolf, Stricker, & Hagenloh, 2013). There is evidence that interactive displays provide autonomy for the visitor to choose the information they receive and can be the most engaging type of technology (Rademaker, 2008). Interactive displays can incorporate storytelling, quizzes, video, and computer graphics and have been shown to increase visitors' attention span (Tubb, 2003).

Evaluating interpretation

Finding a balance between what information is being delivered and the way that information is received can be challenging. The goal of interpretation is to facilitate education, so ensuring this is achieved requires feedback and constant evaluation. This can be done through surveys or short interviews of tourists to confirm they have received the intended message. However, it is also important that the lessons being learned are appropriate to the stakeholders within a community. As communities evolve, so must the interpretive messaging. Just imagine what would be said about the role of women or the ethnic diversity in your community 50 years ago. Most likely, that information would be outdated today. Make sure that all stakeholders are regularly invited to hear the interpretation message, including the community, natural resource experts, indigenous groups, tourism businesses, and tourists. By using ongoing feedback, the message stays relevant.

Conclusion

Sustainable tourism involves providing a quality experience for the visitor, while improving the quality of life for the host community and protecting the quality of the natural and cultural environment. This chapter has shown ways to manage tourism behavior to ensure sustainability initiatives are successful while enhancing the tourist experience through learning and interpretation. Education can lead to life-long changes that not only protect local resources, but lead to long-term changes in behavior by helping tourists to better understand their role in sustainable tourism. Education can also create competitive advantage if it forms a personal connection between the visitor and the resource. Interpretation is a valuable tool for education and should include aspects of storytelling, technology, and skill enhancement. The goal is to create mindful tourists that support long-term changes in behavior that will be remembered when they visit other sites.

CASE STUDY 12.1 DEMARKETING: THE CASE OF BLUE MOUNTAINS NATIONAL PARK, AUSTRALIA

SUSAN L. SLOCUM

Introduction

Blue Mountains National Park comprises 247,000 hectares in New South Wales (NSW) and borders the western suburban fringe of Sydney, 63 kilometers away. In 2000, it was listed on the UNESCO World Heritage List, along with seven other protected areas now known as the Greater Blue Mountains World Heritage Area, based on its outstanding natural value. Its sandstone landscape, Aboriginal sites, and historic features are a major attraction for both domestic and international tourists. With approximately 4.1 million visitors in 2018, Blue Mountains National Park is one of the top visitor attractions in Australia (NSW Government and Destination NSW, 2019). The area is used for both passive natural activities, such as picnicking, as well as high-adventure activities, such as bushwalking and rock climbing.

Armstrong and Kern (2011) highlight a number of demarketing strategies used by the New South Wales National Park and Wildlife Service (NPWS). While the authors claim that "the demarketing measures employed are not consciously used as demarketing" (p. 28), they recognize that the NPWS does use promotion and marketing to manage visitation and environmental impacts in sensitive areas and in parks that receive a large numbers of visitors. Specifically, they claim that "they are not employed across the whole park or for all user groups, but are adopted for certain experiences in very specific contexts and circumstances" (p. 28). These strategies are explained in relation to the marketing mix elements of the park: product, distribution, price, and promotion strategies.

Product strategies

The most common product demarketing strategy was limiting the number of participants in any specific activity through zoning. The fours zones include (Blue Mountains City Council, 2013):

- Nature reserves and national parks – Equivalent to regional open space and national parks where recreational use is permitted without consent, and basic visitor facilities (trails, toilets) are provided;

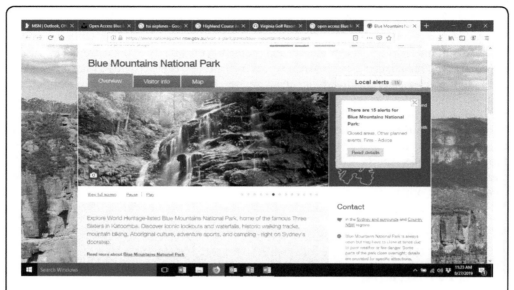

Image 12.4 Closures listed on the website of Blue Mountains National Park, Australia

Source: State of New South Wales and Department of Planning, Industry, and Environment

- Environmental conservation – Equivalent to recreation environmental protection where recreational use is permitted, and intermediate visitor service (roads, parking) are provided, banning the construction of hotels, multi-dwelling houses, and other buildings (retail, service stations) related to visitor services;
- Environmental management – Equivalent to bushland conservation where full-service tourist facilities are provided, except full-time living facilities; and
- Environmental living – Equivalent to residential bushland conservation and residential investigation where all community-living facilities are allowed (dwelling house, churches, and hospitals), except service stations.

Other product strategies include a limit on the number of camping nights permitted and limited vehicle access to popular areas. Temporary closure of specific areas occurs, usually due to fire danger, bushfire incidents, landslides, rock falls, flooding, and drought. Armstrong and Kern (2011) acknowledge that closures are rarely accompanied by information directing visitors to other sites, which could have a negative impact on visitor satisfaction.

Distribution strategies

Although there are no overall restrictions on visitor numbers, the *Park Management Plan* does provide certain tools to limit total visitor numbers for specific activities or sites in the park, when necessary. The park uses a booking system to cap the number of visitors camping in specific areas. Reservations require the guest to agree to general and park-specific camping regulations as a way to promote sustainable environmental behavior. Group size is restricted for certain activities including cycling, vehicle touring, and rock climbing. The park also limits signage or does not provide signs for highly sensitive areas or areas needing repair around the park. Lastly, all commercial guides are required to obtain licenses in order to control specific types of actions and the quality of recreational users' experiences.

Pricing strategies

All visitors are required to pay AUS$8 per vehicle to enter the park and the entrance gates are closed in the evening to limit access. While entrance fees appear to be quite low, prior to charging for admittance, there had been extensive problems with vandalism and trash accumulation. Once gates were installed and fees charged, "the visitor demographics changed completely and [the area] became a family destination" (Armstrong & Kern, 2011, p. 31).

Promotional strategies

Three types of promotional demarketing are used by Blue Mountains National Park. The first is providing messages about temporary or permanent visitor restrictions in their brochures and on the website. The second strategy is the use of marketing messages that emphasize appropriate environmental behavior. Efforts to educate visitors before their visit include agreeing to codes of conduct and reviewing regulation before a guest can purchase park services (entrance fee or camp ground reservation). While visiting the park, signage is used to remind tourists of appropriate behavior and to reinforce conservation messages. The third is the non-promotion of certain sensitive areas or experiences by "the deliberate omission of certain areas, sites, or experiences in promotional material" (p. 32).

Conclusion

While the demarketing strategies used in Blue Mountains National Park are not necessarily intentionally designed to reduce visitor numbers – rather they are ways to ensure the protection of valuable pristine assets – they have ultimately influenced overall visitor numbers. In 2018, the park saw only a 0.6% increase in visitor numbers over 2017, though visitor spending increased 14.8% (NSW Government and Destination NSW, 2019). These statistics show that managing visitor numbers does not necessarily mean a decline in economic impact. Demarketing has resulted in attracting a more environmentally conscious tourist to the Blue Mountains National Park.

Reflective questions

1. Do you think demarketing strategies in natural areas conflict with conservation efforts? Why or why not? What more can be done to encourage support for conservation?

2. Which of the demarketing strategies used by Blue Mountains National Park are the most effective at achieving visitor management? Why? What strategies do you think are the least effective? Why?

3. What can be done to encourage a more strategic approach to visitor management at Blue Mountains National Park? How could you encourage staff to become more engaged and deliberate in the demarketing process?

References

Armstrong, E.K. & Kern, C.L. (2011). Demarketing manages visitor demand in the Blue Mountains National Park. *Journal of Ecotourism*, 10(1), 21–37.

Blue Mountains City Council (2013). Fact sheet 14, Environmental zones. Retrieved from BMCC_Fact_Sheet_14_Environmental_Zones.pdf.

NSW Government and Destination NSW (2019). Travel to Blue Mountains tourism region, year ended December 2018. Retrieved from www.destinationnsw.com.au/tourism/facts-and-figures/regional-tourism-statistics/blue-mountains.

CASE STUDY 12.2 CULTURAL IMMERSION FACILITATORS AS HUMAN CAPITAL IN SLOVENIA

SUSAN L. SLOCUM

Introduction

The fall of communism has had a substantial impact on the livelihood of many Eastern Europeans, especially tour guiding professionals. The former soviet economic structures organized the economy as a state-run system of enterprises, where tourism businesses were owned and managed by the government. Prices were set by the government, and travel was restricted within the borders of Soviet-bloc countries. Foreign visitation was highly restricted. In 1989, with the fall of the Soviet Union, many countries embraced a market economy, where free trade set market prices, and tourism in Eastern Europe was exposed to the forces of competition from Western European destinations.

The former Yugoslavia faced additional hardships during this transition as the country divided into seven new countries, each ethnically and culturally diverse. These ethnic differences resulted in a number of civil wars that raged throughout the 1990s. One country to emerge was Slovenia, which received its independence in 1991 and was admitted to the European Union in 2004.

The transition process from communism to capitalism has been difficult as governments privatized tourism businesses and encouraged entrepreneurship among residents. However, many former soviet workers had no experience with customer service skills, brand identity, or interpretation. By recognizing that tourism in emerging economies is particularly important, not only as an avenue to create jobs, but also as a means of producing favorable images of the countries within political circles (Horáková, 2010), Slovenia was faced with the challenge of becoming competitive in the global tourism economy.

While visitation to Slovenia is still low, in 2016 *National Geographic Traveler's Magazine* declared Slovenia a country with the world's most sustainable tourism sector (Christ, 2017). Slovenia boasts extensive natural resources with access to the Alps and the Mediterranean Sea, and over 50% of its land is covered by forests. It is well-known for its ski resorts and has 40 natural parks and reserves. Only 2.6 million people visited in 2018, and Slovenia is anticipating an expected growth rate of 6% in 2019 (Total Slovenian News, 2019).

G-Guides

Ratiu and Oroian (2012) recognize that the education and training systems in former Soviet-bloc countries are experiencing rapid change as these countries move towards

Image 12.5 A church in rural Slovenia

Source: Luke Stackpoole on Unsplash

a knowledge-based economy. Developing knowledge workers must be a priority if sustainable tourism development is to be a success and human capital goals realized. While in Slovenia, tour guides are required to hold a license, there is no mandatory training to obtain a national license. Language competency is determined by the highest level of high school completed and no further verification is required. Therefore, establishing a system of training to support a sustainable path towards tourism development has been an important investment for tourism in Slovenia.

Čampelj (2020) believes that well-trained tour guides can support a cultural immersion experience for visitors and can redefine the image of the country. While often viewed as a mass tourism activity, tour guiding is a powerful tool in the construction of tourist experiences. Rather than utilizing 'path finding' or leading tourists through the maze of attractions, tour guides can be facilitators of local knowledge and situate the attractions within a story of history, identity, and knowledge. This role of cultural immersion facilitator requires a revised assessment of the tour guiding profession.

G-Guides is a private research institute in Slovenia that has developed a certification curriculum for tour guides. The training modules focus on sustainable development, responsible tourism, communicating sustainability to the tourists, and intercultural communication, including a cultural immersion component. Čampelj (2020) highlights that "the key to its success has been the ability to bring the tourism stakeholders on-board in the region and to encourage their cooperation in the training process of regional tour guides" (p. 150).

The training is divided into three parts. Part 1 focuses on developing basic knowledge levels related to tour guiding responsibilities and best practice in sustainable tourism. Table 12.4 shows the modules and content covered in Part 1 of the training.

Table 12.4 G-Guide's tourist guides' training modules

Module	Content
1. Sustainable and Responsible Tourism – Basics	• Basics of sustainable development • Definitions and terminology • History of sustainable tourism development • Triple bottom line approach in tourism • Sustainable development goals
2. Responsible Tourist Guiding	• Acceleration of responsible tourism, local development and circular economy with tourist guiding
3. Development of Sustainable Destinations	• Levels of sustainable development of destination • Tourists' expectations from sustainable destination • Sustainable and responsible tourism products • Acceleration of responsible consumption on a destination
4. Work and Responsibilities of Tourist Guides	• Cooperation with other stakeholders • Responsibilities of a tourist guide professional • Positive impacts of responsible work of tourist guides • Negative impacts of the irresponsible work of tourist guides
5. Sustainability as Unique Selling Propositions (USP)	• Elements of sustainability turned into USP • Sustainable development and circular economy as a key opportunity for destinations

Module	Content
6. Code of Conduct for Sustainable Tourist Guides	• Code of conduct for responsible tourist guides
7. Collaboration and Cooperation of Local Stakeholders	• Cooperation between tourist guides and other stakeholders • Including local stakeholders into our story • Creating authentic experience with the cooperation of local stakeholders and engaging storytelling
8. Types of Modern Tourists and their Expectations	• Motives for travelling • Expectations of modern tourists • Influence of digital technology on the work of tourist guides • Types of modern tourists • Intercultural differences • Segmentation of modern tourists
9. Best Case Examples	• Case studies of responsible tourist guiding practices
10. Communicating Sustainability	• How to communicate sustainability • Examples • How to avoid negative connotative meanings of sustainability • Encouraging responsible behaviour and consumption
11. Practicum	• Practical use of the knowledge • Guiding with all the principles of sustainable tourist guiding • Improvement tips and suggestions

Source: Adapted from Čampelj (2020)

The second part of the training is designed to improve the communication skills of the tour guides and to formulate positive attitudes towards visitors. In this stage, the learning modules cover basic communication skills, communication competencies, intercultural communication tools, rhetoric, crisis management, complaint management, group management, and how to handle questions. These skill sets are designed to instill the knowledge and attitudes required for professional competences that support a safe and enjoyable tourist experience and a more intensive cultural immersion. The third part of the training focuses on creating and redefining the image of the country and includes modules on marketing and branding, creating and managing destination image, communicating unique selling propositions, communicating brand values in the service sector, and storytelling for tour guides.

By building human capital and supporting the development of knowledge-based workers, G-Guides is encouraging not only a more sustainable tourism sector for Slovenia but is also enhancing the tourist experience. By building brand recognition and promoting positive images of the country, G-Guides is helping Slovenia harness success as a sustainable and enjoyable destination.

Reflective questions

1. Do you feel former communist countries are at an advantage or disadvantage because of their delay in developing international tourism? Do you think this delay can enhance or discourage sustainability?

2. Would this type of training be advantageous in your home country? Why or why not?

3. How can you improve this training to ensure that graduates embrace sustainability values and communicate those values to visitors?

References

Čampelj, M. (2020). From tourist guides to cultural immersion facilitators: sustainable tourism and redefining destination image in Slovenia. In Slocum, S.L. and Klitsounova, V. (Eds), *Tourism Development in Post-Soviet Nations: From Communism to Capitalism* (pp. 143–154), Basingstoke, UK, Palgrave Macmillan.

Christ, C. (2017). This is the world's most sustainable country. National Geographic Society. Retrieved from www.nationalgeographic.com/travel/destinations/europe/slovenia/worlds-most-sustainable-eco-green-country/.

Horáková, H. (2010). Post-communist transformation of tourism in Czech rural areas: new dilemmas. *Anthropological Notebooks*, 16(1), 63–81.

Ratiu, R.F. & Oroian, M. (2012). Continuous professional training: the condition for the Romanian tourism survival. *Procedia – Social and Behavioral Sciences*, 46, 5626–5630.

Total Slovenian News (2019). Strong first half for Slovenian tourism in 2019. Retrieved from www.total-slovenia-news.com/travel/4215-strong-first-half-for-slovenian-tourism-in-2019.

STUDY QUESTIONS

1. Which type of visitor management strategies are being used in the following scenarios? Do you think they are effective, why or why not?
- A walkway built through a natural area;
- Free guided tours;
- The rental of an MP3 player with recorded information;
- A museum that closes two days each week;
- A policy that requires children under 15 to be accompanied by an adult;
- Doubling the price of admission;
- Hiring security to ensure visitors do not touch artifacts;
- Distributing fliers that explain appropriate behaviors;
- Requiring visitors to hire local guides.

2. You have been tasked with determining the carrying capacity of a museum. Which types of carrying capacity would you use and what data would you need? Why?

3. When organizing tours to a remote indigenous village, what visitor qualifications would you require? What operator qualifications would you require? Why?

4. Develop a script that tells the story of an event in your hometown. What is the underlying message you want the visitor to take away with them?

5. Before taking a group of senior citizens on a two-week trip to Hong Kong, you are asked to educate your guests on sustainable travel behaviors. Using the Mindfulness model, what elements would you use to promote sustainable travel?

DEFINITIONS

ART   stands for audience, resource, and technology as a way to provide effective interpretation

Carrying capacity   the amount of use any given land or environment can endure over time without degrading its suitability for that use

Carrying capacity in tourism   the maximum number of people that may visit a tourist destination at the same time, without causing destruction of the physical, economic, socio-cultural environment and an unacceptable decrease in the quality of visitors' satisfaction

Communication   conveying information or evoking understanding

Congestion-related pricing system   a system of offering cheaper prices for periods of low visitation and more expensive ones for peak periods

Demarketing   a way to decrease demand for a certain product or experience

Dual pricing system   a pricing system where tourists pay a higher price than locals

Economic capacity   the level of acceptable change within the local economy of a tourist destination that is described as the point at which the increased revenue brought by tourism development is overtaken by the inflation caused by tourism

Education   a form of learning in which the knowledge, skills, and habits of a group of people are transferred from one generation to the next through teaching, training, or research

Interpretation   an educational activity which aims to reveal meanings and relationships through the use of original objects, by first-hand experience, and by illustrative media, rather than simply communicate factual information

Interpretation intensity   a comparison of quantity and type of interpretation between sites

Mindfulness   caring about the world around us

Mindfulness model   the process of developing mindful visitors

Operator qualification   limiting entry only to those possessing required qualifications

Physical capacity   the maximum number of individuals that an area is able to support

Site hardening   constructing facilities and locating trails and roads to reduce the impacts of visitors on sensitive soils and vegetation, and to help meet the visitors' needs for usable access

Social capacity   the maximum level of visitation an area can sustain before visitor enjoyment is reduced and increased social ills result

Substitutability   the interchangeability of activities and experiences by varying one or more of the following: the timing of the experience, the means of gaining access to the experience, the setting, and the activity

Visitor management   the management tools and interventions that regulate the movement and behavior of visitors in a destination, natural area, or attraction

13

The future of sustainable tourism

Overview

This chapter highlights emerging trends in both tourism and sustainability. It provides an overview on the changing economic situations that are leading to the emergence of new destinations and new travel segments, as well as economic challenges, including: increased poverty, rural-to-urban migration, and human resource needs within the industry. Environmental challenges, including climate change, renewable energy, and waste management are discussed. Economic developments have directly led to social trends, including the rise of secularism, nationalism, and xenophobia. Emerging consumer trends are also described.

CHAPTER OBJECTIVES

At the completion of the chapter, students will be able to:

• Explain futures studies, megatrends, and their relevance to sustainable tourism;
• List global economic, environmental, and social trends and how they impact tourism;
• Describe appropriate responses to current trends from a sustainable tourism perspective; and
• Evaluate emergent consumer trends and their influence on the future of tourism.

Introduction

Tourism, as a major global industry, is relatively new compared to other industries, such as manufacturing and agriculture, although it is growing at an unprecedented rate. Major breakthroughs in transportation, banking (the advent of the credit card), communications (satellite communications as well as marketing reach), and construction have fueled the growth of tourism (Dator & Yeoman, 2015). Predicting new innovations, future challenges, and social and environmental conditions, and the impact they may have on tourism, is not a precise science. However, many researchers have drawn conclusions based on historic trends and scientific observations in order to forecast the future. **Futures studies** (colloquially called "futures") is the formal and systematic study of possible, probable, and preferable futures, and the methods of foresight development for individuals, groups, and human society. Most strategic planning, such as the development of operational plans with a one- to three-year time horizon, are not considered a part of futures studies (Benckendorff, 2008). Specifically, futures studies attempt to gain a holistic or systemic view based on insights from a range of different disciplines in order to theorize on trends and predict outcomes.

This chapter will focus on megatrends rather than local influences, which can vary from destination to destination. **Megatrends** are significant, globally relevant, social, economic, political, environmental, and technological changes over the long-term. They typically have decades-long impacts and, therefore, have the potential to fundamentally alter and upset industries around the world, including the global tourism sector. The Organization for Economic Co-operation and Development (2018) lists the following influences that will have a direct impact on tourism in the future:

- The complexity of tourism policy development due to its cross-cutting, multi-level, and fragmented nature, and competing policy priorities and budgetary constraints;
- The impact of external factors on tourism, including macro-economic conditions, exchange rates, safety and security, and natural disasters;
- The global shift to a resource-efficient economy; and
- The continued transformation of tourism services linked with emerging technologies and digitalization of the economy.

Industry reports show that the number one trend in tourism is an increase in sustainable travel options (Organization for Economic Co-operation and Development, 2018). From a sustainable tourism perspective, there are trends that will influence sustainability, and there are trends that will affect tourism. These trends come from changing needs in relation to the economy, environment, and society, as well as the travel consumer. Often it is the awareness of economic, environmental, and social challenges that directly influence consumer trends (Williams & Ponsford, 2009). Most importantly, sustained development of the tourism sector, and the success of individual tourism enterprises, will depend on tourism's ability to adapt to these emerging trends. This chapter will look at current challenges to sustainability, and how tourism businesses can prepare to remain competitive over the course of time.

Economic trends

The world economy has been shifting. Since the Industrial Revolution, exponential growth has occurred in western countries, such as European countries, the United States, Canada, Australia, and New Zealand. It is estimated that the fastest growing economies are now located in the south and east, economies like China, India, and some countries in sub-Saharan Africa (specifically South Africa). These areas are experiencing a growing middle-class, which is leading to an increase in outbound tourism (Wallace & Riley, 2015). They are also experiencing growth in tourism infrastructure, resulting in new emerging destinations, and intensifying competition in the tourism industry. Traditional destinations are "in an extremely intense competitive race

Image 13.1 Capilano Suspension Bridge, BC, Canada

Source: Susan L. Slocum

for the global tourism dollar" (Wallace & Riley, 2015, p. 54). Webster and Ivanov (2015) term this trend as "the fall of the American empire" (p. 58) which implies a change in global leadership within the tourism economy. They foresee a change in the international language away from English, and destinations will need a wider variety of language proficiencies to include

Table 13.1 Top 10 countries in terms of tourist arrivals and tourist revenue

Country and its world region	Total tourist arrivals (million)	Visitors' country of origin	Total tourist revenue (US$ billion)
China (Asia-Pacific)	4,530	US	1,030
India (Asia-Pacific)	1,540	China	680
US (America)	1,250	Germany	380
Japan (Asia-Pacific)	320	UK	250
France (Europe)	280	Japan	230
Indonesia (Asia-Pacific)	260	France	200
Spain (Europe)	200	Indonesia	190
Brazil (America)	180	Italy	170
Germany (Europe)	170	Mexico	140
UK (Europe)	160	Spain	130

Source: Adapted from Rui (2018)

Mandarin, Hindi, and Russian. Moreover, tourism business conglomerates are likely to come from these emerging economies, changing the industrial culture of tourism. Table 13.1 highlights the global leaders in tourist arrivals, the primary visitors' country of origin, and tourism revenue earned in 2017 (Rui, 2018).

While many developing countries are seeing a growth in the middle class, there is a growing disparity between the highest income earners and the lowest, meaning that people who are at the lowest socioeconomic level will find it harder to earn enough money for basic necessities, such as food, housing, health care, and education. Alam and Paramati (2016) claim that tourism has both positive and negative effects on income levels. Tourism can increase local economic activity but also causes inflation and a rise in housing prices, further isolating the poor. The market dominance of multinational corporations can create tough barriers to entry for small businesses. Therefore, tourism businesses will need to focus on **pro-poor tourism** initiatives, defined as tourism that generates net benefits for the poor, as a means to reduce poverty in tourism areas and ensure destination attractiveness. They write that pro-poor tourism should be "viewed as a tool to create enhanced opportunities, generate mass employment and benefits to the most vulnerable groups of the society by making them involved in the production of tourism goods and services" (p. 112).

Recent population booms, tied to a global response to overcome infant and childhood illnesses, are also occurring, and as of 2011, approximately 30% of the world's population was under 18 years of age (US Central Intelligence Agency, 2017). As these young people seek employment opportunities in industrial areas through rural-to-urban migration, tourism destinations have the potential to receive extensive inward migration. **Rural-to-urban migration** occurs when people seek employment and income opportunities in industrialized areas, which can include mass tourism destinations. In 2010, for the first time in human history, more people lived in urban areas than in rural areas as a result of rural-to-urban migration. Rural-to-urban migration can increase poverty in both rural and urban areas. Rural areas often lose young, educated members of the community, resulting in an aging population, a lack of small business investment, reduced tax income, and fewer social services. It can also be challenging for industrialized areas, as there are not always enough housing or jobs for those moving into these cities. Government policies that support rural development have been shown to reduce rural-to-urban migration, including investment in traditional industries, such as agriculture, which can also reinforce rural tourism development (see Chapter 7) (Slocum & Curtis, 2017). Since many tourism jobs require low education levels, such as housekeeping, landscape maintenance, and cooking, tourism destinations often receive inward migration of people with few job skills outside of agriculture or other traditional rural industries. Therefore, developing human capital to support the local community will be increasingly necessary to counter a potential increase in poverty within the destination. Moreover, partnerships with rural communities, such as local sourcing or organizing tours to rural areas, can support pro-poor tourism growth and reduce rural-to-urban migration.

Technology needs within tourism are also changing, and tourism will need to reassess its hiring practices and pay scales. Tourism has started to change from a labor-intensive industry into a capital-intensive and technology-intensive industry (Rui, 2018). Therefore, human capital equipped with higher-level skills, such as critical-thinking, management and business talents, and technology-based problem-solving, will be required. The World Travel and Tourism Council (2015) estimates that the employee turnover rate in the tourism industry is an average of 18%, with the turnover rates of the non-technical workers, salespersons, and customer service staff the highest. Moreover, tourism is competing for talent with STEM disciplines (Science, Technology, Engineering, and Mathematics) where pay and benefits exceed tourism compensation. Investing in human capital and paying a fair wage will be an ongoing challenge for the tourism industry.

Environmental trends

One of the most pressing environmental issues today is global climate change. While many politicians debate the cause of climate change, 97% of scientists are united in recognizing climate change as a predominately human-caused phenomenon (US National Aeronautics and Space Administration, 2018). **Climate change** is a change in the statistical distribution of extreme weather patterns when that change lasts for an extended period of time. While changes in the earth's climate have occurred naturally over hundreds of thousands of years, the rapid change over the past 200 years is a direct result of greenhouse gas emissions, specifically carbon dioxide and other gases (Chapter 8) released into the atmosphere from the burning of fossil fuels (coal, natural gas, and oil). These gases trap the heat from the sun, which would normally dissipate into space, warming the earth's atmosphere. Table 13.2 highlights the primary evidence to support climate change. These gases can also cause **acid rain**, or rainfall made sufficiently acidic by atmospheric pollution, which results in environmental harm, typically to forests and lakes, but also to man-made structures and ancient historical artifacts. Acid rain has taken its toll on numerous cultural attractions, including the Washington Mall in Washington, DC, the Acropolis in Athens, the Leshan Giant Buddha at Mount Emei in China, the Taj Mahal in India, and the Dampier Rock Art Complex in Australia (United Nations Educational, Scientific, and Cultural Organization, 2018).

Not only does the warming of the earth's surface cause environmental changes, the overuse or destruction of natural resources has had an alarming effect on ecosystems. An **endangered species** is a type of organism that is threatened by extinction. Species become endangered for two main reasons: loss of habitat and loss of genetic variation (National Geographic Society,

Table 13.2 Evidence of climate change

Rise in planetary surface temperature	The planet's average surface temperature has risen about 1.62 degrees Fahrenheit (0.9 degrees Celsius) since the late 19th century
	• Most of the warming occurred in the past 35 years, with the five warmest years on record taking place since 2010
	• 2016 was the warmest year on record, and eight of the 12 months that make up the year – from January through September, with the exception of June – were the warmest on record for those respective month
Warming oceans	The oceans have absorbed much of this increased heat
	• The top 700 meters (about 2,300 feet) of ocean has warmed more than 0.4 degrees Fahrenheit since 1969
Shrinking ice sheets	The Greenland and Antarctic ice sheets have decreased in mass
	• Greenland lost an average of 281 billion tons of ice per year between 1993 and 2016
	• Antarctica lost about 119 billion tons during the same time period. The rate of Antarctica ice mass loss has tripled in the last decade
	• Glaciers are retreating almost everywhere around the world – including in the Alps, Himalayas, Andes, Rockies, Alaska and Africa
Decreased snow cover	Satellite observations reveal that the amount of spring snow cover in the Northern Hemisphere has decreased over the past five decades and that the snow is melting earlier
Sea level rise	Global sea level rose about 8 inches in the last century. The rate in the last two decades, however, is nearly double that of the last century and is accelerating slightly every year
Declining Arctic sea ice	Both the extent and thickness of Arctic sea ice has declined rapidly over the last several decades
Extreme weather events	Storms are becoming more severe
	• Tropical cyclones are expected to increase in frequency and intensity in both the Atlantic and Pacific oceans
	• Tornado activity in the United States has become more variable, with a decrease in the number of days per year with tornadoes and an increase in the number of tornadoes on these days
Ocean acidification	The acidity of surface ocean waters has increased by about 30 percent
	• The amount of carbon dioxide absorbed by the upper layer of the oceans is increasing by about 2 billion tons per year

Source: United States National Aeronautics and Space Administration (2018)

2018). Loss of habitat occurs when trees or native vegetation are cleared to develop housing, agriculture, or other industrial development. Once the habitat is removed, many species may die off or relocate to areas that are less hospitable, negatively impacting their ability to find food or reproduce. Hotel construction, especially in ecologically sensitive areas, can increase habitat loss. **Genetic variation** is the diversity found within a species. When organisms have trouble finding a mate, because of habitat loss or a sudden reduction in the population, inbreeding results. Disease is much more common, and deadlier, among inbred groups, and fewer off-spring survive to maturity (National Geographic Society, 2018). Overhunting and overfishing have also contributed to a decrease in genetic variation, as often the largest and strongest of a population are sought after.

There are strong connections between increases in poverty and escalations in illegal hunting, called **poaching**. The black rhino and northern white rhinos have recently gone extinct in the wild due to excessive poaching and habitat loss (World Wildlife Fund, 2018) and poaching (specifically for ivory) is impacting African elephants and the communities that depend on revenue from safari travelers. While many countries have outlawed the trade of ivory, the price of black market ivory has increased drastically, making ivory poaching a very profitable businesses for impoverished communities (Clark & Fears, 2014).

This book has explained how tourism is dependent on natural and cultural resources as a means to attract visitors and maintain competitive advantage. Environmental degradation is having a profound impact on tourism resources. For example, the International Coral Reef Initiative (2013) estimates that, "9% of the earth's coral reefs have already been seriously degraded or lost, and greater than 60% are under immediate and direct threat" (p. 3). Not only do one million species of fish, invertebrates, and algae live in and around the world's reefs, millions of tourists are drawn to destinations for snorkeling, fishing, and scuba diving. Lastly, pollutants, such as plastics, pesticides, and heavy metals have taken their toll on many species. Ecosystems depend on the food chain and when one species in the chain, say insects, are exposed to poisons, they infect the species that depend on them for food. Many marine animals and birds eat plastic unknowingly and die of starvation.

All tourism businesses and destinations will need to adapt in order to minimize risks and capitalize on any new opportunities in a sustainable way. As a tourism business, it is important to support the monitoring of environmental changes, including both natural and cultural resources, as a first step in protecting the resource. Supporting local conservation efforts is becoming more vital. Moreover, recognizing social costs and ensuring that tourists pay for the damage they cause through greenhouse gas emissions from transportation, vegetation loss from recreational uses, and excessive use of water and energy, will be required in the future. Using fewer resources, generating less waste, and using environmentally friendly energy sources is also becoming increasingly important.

It is expected that tourism businesses will need to embrace the use of renewable energy sources as a means to reduce climate change. **Renewable energy** is energy that is collected from renewable resources, which are naturally replenished on a human timescale, such as sunlight, wind, rain, tides, waves, and geothermal heat. In the past 10 years, the cost of solar power has declined by approximately 80%, and the cost of wind power has dropped by approximately 40% (Ralon, Taylor, Ilas, Diaz-Bone, & Kairies, 2017). Renewable electricity transmission, mostly in the form of hydroelectric power, is around 22% globally. One of the barriers to renewable energy use is the high cost of converting infrastructure, specifically converting already existing power plants that use coal or oil. New development projects may find that renewable energy sources are less expensive, but existing businesses may struggle with funding these capital projects. Since the

Image 13.2 Releasing sea turtles into the wild, Cabo San Lucas, Mexico
Source: Susan L. Slocum

Paris Climate Agreement, signed in 2016, financial support for sustainable energy is on the rise. Many countries now provide grants, tax incentives, and subsidies for businesses converting to renewable energy, and these programs are expected to increase (Michalena & Hills, 2013).

Social trends

Many of the economic trends discussed above are leading to social challenges, which can affect the success of tourism destinations. Humans have always been social creatures who identify with certain social groups. These social groups have developed **social norms**, or informal understandings that govern the behavior of members of a society or business. Social norms dictate appropriate behaviors by members of a community or society. As social norms change from generation to generation, social conflict ensues. Keenan (2008) notes that globalization has had intense influences on social norms, specifically:

- Individuals in a globalizing community typically suffer from significant disruptions in relationships, and the community's ability to regulate itself is eroded;
- Globalization can distort the process of creating and enforcing social norms by allowing individuals to immunize themselves from the sanctions typically employed to enforce norms; and
- Globalization makes it possible for individuals to engage in an activity that carries social sanctions in a place where they are immune to the real effects of those sanctions.

Byproducts of globalization include secularism and nationalism. **Secularism** is the principle of separating the state from religious institutions and resulted from the creation of civil laws that were not tied to scripture during the Age of Enlightenment in eighteenth-century Europe. As the influence of religion in society declined, nationalism rose in response (Bieber, 2018). **Nationalism** is the identification with one's own nation and support for its interests, especially to the exclusion or detriment of the interests of other nations. The rise in secularism and nationalism have fueled feelings of **xenophobia**, the fear and hatred of strangers, foreigners, or of anything that is strange or foreign. Globalization has generated a global society and has promoted western values and social norms that often conflict with traditional norms.

While clashes between cultures is not a new phenomenon, the interconnectedness of economies and societies, and the domination of western values inherent in both, have marginalized many ethnic and religious groups. In an era of instant news, social media, and international communication technologies, western values, such as individualism and consumerism, are creating local strife and fueling xenophobia. As people feel increasingly marginalized and globalization begins to impact social norms, such as gender roles or religious rites, conflict and civil unrest results. In relation to tourism, news stories of civil conflict can have a large impact on tourist visitation (Webster, 2017). Le (2017) writes, "insecurity and instability would only fan the flame for terrorism and further jeopardize the tourism industry" (p. 9). Moreover, tourists are often victims in terrorists' attacks or local violence, as their presence is seen as a factor of globalization. They are easy targets that can be blamed for social unrest, especially if they represent the imposition of western values.

Cyber-attacks are also used to disrupt the global system, and like terrorist attacks, can be devastating to the tourism industry. A **cyber-attack** is any attempt to expose, alter, disable, destroy, steal, or gain unauthorized access to, or make unauthorized use of, computers and computer networks. Cyber-attacks have increased exponentially in recent years, as shown in Figure 13.1 (World Economic Forum, 2017). Tourism is especially prone to cyber-attacks because of the complicated supply chain and the large number of small businesses in the industry. Tourism businesses not only have names, addresses, and credit cards for their guests, but may also have

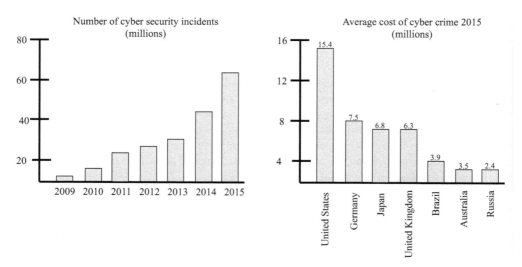

Figure 13.1 Cyber-attacks (2009–2015)

Source: World Economic Forum (2017)

Image 13.3 Hiroshima, Japan

Source: Susan L. Slocum

passport information. With the rise in bank transfers to pay for expensive tours, this data can also be stolen.

Having safety and security plans in place will increasingly become expected in tourism. A **safety plan** includes actions and procedures designed to avoid dangerous situations. Safety plans protect tourists from medical emergencies, such as building barriers along cliffsides to prevent injury. They may also include weather-related evacuation plans. A **security plan** is a document that defines roles and responsibilities, policies and procedures in the event of security incidents. Security plans include plans to respond to robbery, kidnapping, or natural disasters.

Consumer trends

Many of the global trends mentioned above have given rise to new consumer trends. Awareness of global poverty, climate change, and civil unrest is changing the expectations of consumers of tourism. Primarily, the rise in **overtourism**, which occurs when there are too many visitors to a particular destination, is fueling poverty, environmental degradation, and social displacement in traditional tourism destinations (Goodwin, 2017). Overtourism "describes destinations where hosts or guests, locals or visitors, feel that there are too many visitors and that the quality of life in the area or the quality of the experience has deteriorated unacceptably" (Goodwin, 2017, p. 1).

Overcrowding in destinations is pushing travelers further from traditional sites, spreading both the positive and negative impacts of tourism to more rural and remote areas. **Last chance tourism** is when tourists increasingly seek to experience the world's most endangered sites before they vanish or are permanently transformed (Lemelin, Dawson, Stewart, Maher, & Lueck, 2010). Last chance tourism is spurring overtourism in some of the world's most at-risk locations, such as the Amazon, Machu Pichu, the Antarctic, and the Maldives. World Heritage Sites are also seeing a substantial increase in visitation, causing destruction to ancient monuments and traditional religious sites. As destinations absorb more tourism, authenticity is threatened, therefore tourists are seeking more local interactions with 'exotic' ethnic groups (Groulx, Lemieux, Dawson, Stewart, & Yudina, 2016). These trends have the potential to further spread economic, environmental, and social impacts, such as increases in income disparities, inflation, habitat loss, and social conflict.

Other consumer trends, such as sustainable consumption, food tourism, and localism were discussed in detail in Chapter 5, however the changing demographics of travelers is also leading to new areas for innovation. The increase in tourists from the south and east is resulting in changes to customer expectations. Examples include a rise in the need for specialized food, such as Halal (food prepared according to Muslim law) and vegetarian food (specifically for Hindus and Buddhists). Multigenerational trips could become more common, as emerging tourist segments (specifically the Chinese) prefer to travel with children, parents, and grandparents. Another trend is the rise in travel options for same-sex couples. Lastly, there is an increase in travel by people with disabilities, leading to an increased need for inclusive tourism. **Inclusive tourism** refers to the capacity of a tourism destination or attraction to enable all persons, regardless of physical or mental ability, to participate in, and benefit from, tourism activity. Ensuring that these new markets have a variety of travel options, in a safe and welcoming environment, will be increasingly important.

SUSTAINABILITY TOOL: TREND FORECASTING

Trend forecasting is a complicated but useful way to look at past sales or market growth, determine possible trends from that data, and use the information to infer what could happen in the future. Managers typically use trend forecasting to help determine future areas of sales growth or to estimate the success of new products or services. In destination management, if an area does not have the businesses to attract interested tourists, they may need to encourage start-up businesses before engaging in a trend. Not all trends occur in all areas at the same time, so tracking trends in the area where you do business is a good place to start. Keep in mind that visitors may expect that certain trends have been reached in the areas they travel, only to be disappointed. Therefore, tracking emerging trends before there is substantial market pressure is also important.

Tracking global trends

First, a manager must know what trends to look for in order to collect the appropriate data. This information can be found in news articles, industry reports, and from the multinational policy organizations, such as the United Nations World Tourism Organization. Social media is also a good place for following trends. For example, the Ontario Culinary Tourism Alliance (2015) reports that tourists share millions of photos of food tourism activities on social media. This report directly influenced Intrepid, an international tour operator, to begin offering food tourism trips to Asia. They now offer food-related travel to over 20 destinations (Parmar, 2016).

Market segmentation can help determine where to look for trends. When using a geographic segmentation strategy, say promoting products to the Chinese market, it is important to follow trends in China. This can provide a good overview of where Chinese tourists are going and how much they are spending. However, there may be a report on psychographic traits that could inform geographic segmentation trends. For example, McKinsey and Company (2018) has reported the rise in Chinese backpacking tourism, which may not be noted in general reports on Chinese tourism. Other examples include trends related to demographic traits, such as changes in family travel, women traveling solo, or the changing travel preferences of millennials (those born between 1980 and 1996).

Tracking local trends

Local trends may include activities that a community or destination is offering, or they could be trends that visiting tourists are expecting when they arrive at a destination. Specific tools for data collection are discussed in Chapter 5, but once the data is collected, a manager must decide how to analyze it. While many statistical methods are quite complex, there are some easier methods that can be very effective at evaluating trends.

Time series analysis

Time series forecasting is a quantitative forecasting method, meaning it is based on tangible, concrete numbers from the past. **Time series data** is data where the numerical value is known over different points in time. Typically, this numerical data is plotted on a graph, with the horizontal x-axis being used to plot time, such as the month or year, and the vertical y-data being used to plot the information you are trying to predict, such as sales amounts, number of people engaged in an activity, or requests about a certain interest. There are several different types of patterns that tend to appear on a time-series graph (Figure 13.2).

A **constant pattern** occurs when there is no net increase or decrease over time. There may be an increase or decrease at specific dates, but the overall average stays the same. However, even if the average results are the same within a year, there still can be seasonal changes. For example, sales of craft beer tours may be consistently greater in the summer and lower in the winter, although the average is the same over the entire year.

A **linear pattern** is a steady increase or decrease in numbers over time. On a graph, this appears as a straight line angled diagonally up or down. If someone looked at the sales of circus tickets, they might see a diagonal line angled downward. One may conclude that the media attention

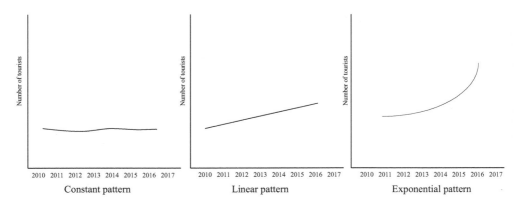

Figure 13.2 Time series trend patterns

related to the poor treatment of animals has caused a downward trend in circus visitation. If you manage an aquarium, this data may be useful to predict a decline in visitation, giving you ample time to address the change in social values.

An **exponential pattern** indicates that data is rising at an increasing rate over time, rather than a steady change. Instead of a straight line pointing diagonally up, this graph shows a curved line (similar to a hockey stick) where the last point in later years is dramatically higher than the first year, if the rate is increasing. For example, travel to Antarctica has increased exponentially in tourism numbers. According to the International Association of Antarctica Tour Operators (2018), in 2015 there were 27,200 visitors and in 2016 there were 30,300, representing an annual growth rate of 12%. In 2017, there were 36,900 visitors, representing an annual growth rate of 22%. While tourism is growing in Antarctica, the pace of growth is also increasing.

One key disadvantage to time series analysis is the assumption that what has happened in the past in going to happen in the future. Using the Antarctic example above, if we had looked at the visitation in 2014, we would see that it was 37,400, meaning that 2015 saw an actual decrease in visitation. Expectations about recent trends are generally more accurate in the short term, but when used in long-term forecasting, can cause problems. A **turning point** is when a swing in one direction ends and a swing in another direction begins. While there are complex statistical methods to calculate turning points, these tools are generally beyond the scope of most managers (Wan & Song, 2018).

Scenario writing

Scenario writing is the process of creating alternative hypothetical futures relating to particular circumstances that could alter demand in the future. Not only can it be used to predict the future, but it can also clarify the issues behind changes in consumer demand. For scenario writing to be effective, there must be a clear understanding of where demand is currently. Once a baseline is established, then an analysis of different situations is applied. Generally, a worst-case, a best-case, and a middle alternative is developed. The process of determining what each case would look like can be very helpful in assessing strengths and weakness in a business model (see SWOT analysis, Chapter 8). For example, climate change may cause droughts in certain areas. Assessing current water usage and forecasting reductions in rainfall, can help a business plan for future water shortages and find ways to reduce water usage in the present. Important questions to ask include understanding how visitors use water, how a company or destination uses water, how water usage affects customer satisfaction, and how competition for limited water between other community members may impact local relationships. Once a set of scenarios is developed, a strategy forward should be developed for each case.

Conclusion

Predicting the future is not an exact science, but there are signs that new trends are on the horizon. Being prepared to diversify the tourism product and encompass emerging markets is becoming more important to the success of tourism businesses and destinations. However, ensuring the long-term survival of the tourism industry, specifically the natural and cultural experiences tourists seek, is a primary focus of sustainable tourism. Tourism should be beneficial not only to the visitors, but to the people, the environments, the cultures, and the artifacts of the world. The status quo is no longer working. Therefore, understanding the challenges to sustainability and to tourism are important parts of successful management. Ethics will remain the primary challenge of tourism's future leaders, like yourself.

CASE STUDY 13.1 CLIMATE CHANGE AND THREATS TO PARADISE: THE CASE OF THE MALDIVES

SUSAN L. SLOCUM

Introduction

Changes in the earth's temperature, resulting from increased greenhouse gas emissions, have had wide-ranging impacts across the globe. While some countries may benefit from warmer temperatures, most regions will incur devastating effects from changing weather patterns. Using independent sources from research stations, weather stations, satellites, ocean buoys, and tide gauges, The National Climate Assessment (2014), concludes that "precipitation patterns are changing, sea level is rising, the oceans are becoming more acidic, and the frequency and intensity of some extreme weather events are increasing" (n.p.).

The Maldives is a country in the Indian Ocean that is comprised of over 1,000 low-lying coral atolls, with an average elevation of 1.5 meters (4 feet, 11 in) above sea level, making it the world's lowest and flattest country. The population of 447,000 inhabitants live on 138 islands, leaving the remainder as island paradises used primarily for agriculture and tourism. The Maldives are especially prone to the effects of climate change, as Nachmany et al. (2015, p. 2) write:

> Over 80% of inhabited land is less than 1m above sea level. While the territory is protected against most oceanic storms by an expansive coral reef, rising sea levels may literally wipe out the island's dry land through regular tidal flooding. In the past six years, more than 90% of the inhabited islands have reported being flooded annually, with 37% of the islands reporting flooding as a recurring event. Furthermore, 97% of the islands also report shoreline erosion, and 45% of the tourist resorts also report severe erosion issues.

The Maldives is a sun, surf, and sea (3S) travel destination, and most visitors travel to enjoy the white sandy beaches and extensive coral reefs. In 2017, over 1.4 million tourists visited the Maldives, accounting for 28% of the GDP and more than 60% of the Maldives' foreign exchange receipts (Mohamed & Shaha, 2019). Over 90% of government tax revenue comes from import duties and tourism related taxes. As a country dependent on tourism revenue, not only is climate change threatening the livelihood of local residents, it could have profound impacts on the success of 3S tourism.

Image 13.4 Malé, the Maldives

Source: @seefromthesky on Unsplash

The communities that reside in the Maldives have a number of colloquial sayings that highlight their knowledge of the environmental challenges of island living. The local proverb "Rashuge eh faraay girenyaa aneh faraay vodeyne" ("If one side of the island erodes, sand accretion will occur on the other side") demonstrates the knowledge individuals have of island erosion. Conversely, the proverb "Rahkaave thibiyyaa dhathuru" ("If one is prepared one can travel safely") indicates the importance of preparedness for risk reduction (Shakeela & Becken, 2015, p. 69).

While the government has developed a number of policies to combat the effects of climate change and has invested extensive resources in bringing its concerns to the global stage, in reality economic development has taken priority. In 2010, the Maldives announced it would switch to 100% renewable energy by the year 2020 as a means to become carbon neutral (United Nations Framework Convention on Climate Change, 2010). However, discussions on climate change could potentially reduce international investment in new resort construction, and climate change regulation increases operational costs for tourism (Shakeela & Becken, 2015).Therefore, in 2017, the new President, Abdulla Yameen, changed political direction, stating that investments in mega resorts, not renewable energy, is the best way to finance climate change mitigation (Vidal, 2017). His vision includes a 'smart' country with a new capital city, high-tech centers, economic free zones, foreign universities, six-star hotels, high-end housing, and several new airports to attract the global elite. Moreover, there are plans to abandon nearly one-third of the populated islands by relocating thousands of people to larger islands that can provide better schools, health clinics, fresh water, and waste facilities. It still remains to be seen if these abandoned islands will be converted into the promised mega resorts.

Climate change could potentially destroy valuable tourism resources. Research shows that almost 80% of tourists visit the Maldives primarily for exotic beach holidays and 35% visit to dive the coral reefs (Ministry of Environment and Energy, 2015). The bleaching of coral reefs and beach erosion is threatening the competitiveness of the Maldives as a tourism destination. Moreover, increasing ambient air temperatures could make the Maldives too hot for an enjoyable holiday. A shorter rainy season brings less fresh water to the islands, limiting water resources for tourism establishments. Population density increases vector-borne diseases, such as dengue fever, chikungunya, and the zika virus transmitted by mosquitos in tropical areas. A lack of waste treatment can have negative impacts on the limited clean water resources, human health, and on the heath of the coral reefs.

As resources become scarcer, competition between the tourism industry and the residents of the Maldives could become heated. Moreover, if the Maldives pursues a tourism marketing campaign that encourages elite visitors from the highest income bracket, social disparities may become more pronounced, resulting in civil unrest. Governance that instills resilience for communities and involves all stakeholders, including climate change specialists, should establish policies that balance the economic needs of the Maldives with the environmental and social challenges resulting from climate change. However, there must be political will to address these inherent challenges.

Reflective questions

1. Climate change mitigation is an expensive endeavor as it requires extensive investment in new technologies. Do you feel increasing tourism can solve some of the climate change issues? Why or why not?

2. Knowing the threats facing the Maldives, would you invest in future tourism development projects there? Do you think they would be profitable investments? Why or why not?

3. What are some additional solutions that could help the Maldives combat the negative impacts of climate change? How would you implement them?

References

Ministry of Environment and Energy (2015). Maldives: fifth national report to the United Nations Convention on Biological Diversity. Retrieved from www.cbd.int/doc/world/mv/mv-nr-05-en.pdf.

Mohamed, A. & Shaha, M. (2019). November statistics show Maldives close to 1.5m tourist arrival target. Hotelier Maldives, January 4. Retrieved from www.hoteliermaldives.com/statistics-maldives-1-5m-tourist-target/.

Nachmany, M., Fankhauser, S., Davidová, J., Kingsmill, N., Landesman, T., Roppongi, H., Schleifer, P., Setzer, J., Sharman, A., Singleton, C.S., Sundaresan, J., & Townshend, T. (2015). Climate change legislation in Maldives: an excerpt from the 2015 global climate legislation study: a review of climate change legislation in 99 countries. Grantham Research Institute.

The National Climate Assessment (2014). Our changing climate. Retrieved from https://nca2014.globalchange.gov/report/our-changing-climate.

Shakeela, A. & Becken, S. (2015). Understanding tourism leaders' perceptions of risks from climate change: an assessment of policy-making processes in the Maldives using the social amplification of risk framework (SARF). *Journal of Sustainable Tourism*, 23(1), 65–84.

United Nations Framework Convention on Climate Change. (2010). *National Economic Environment Development Studies*. Malé: Ministry of Housing and Environment.

Vidal, J. (2017). "We need development": Maldives switches focus from climate threat to mass tourism. *Guardian*, March 3.

CASE STUDY 13.2 SOCIAL UNREST IN SOUTH AFRICA AND TOURISM AS COLONIZATION

SUSAN L. SLOCUM

Introduction

South Africa has emerged as the leading tourism destination in Sub-Sahara Africa primarily because of its varied landscapes and diverse people. It is home to Kruger National Park (home to the Big 5: lion, leopard, rhinoceros, elephant, and Cape buffalo), the infamous Stellenbosch wine region, the Cape of Good Hope (and the African penguins that live there), and sun-soaked coastlines of Durbin and KwaZulu-Natal. With over 57 million people, South Africa is a melting pot of cultures, languages, and traditions. Moreover, solid economic development has boosted the tourism industry, with direct flights from every continent and a wide range of travel options.

South Africa is a country that has faced more than its fair share of trials and tribulations. The original inhabitants, collectively known as the Khoisan, were almost completely decimated or absorbed during the Bantu expansion (approximately 1,000 BC) when large groups from west and central Africa migrated to the area. By the thirteenth century, white Europeans settled the region to support trade routes between Asia and Europe. When slavery was abolished by the British in 1838, many white farmers moved further inland, spreading white influence and colonization to more remote areas around southern Africa. During the early 1800s, another mass inward migration occurred, when Boers (later to be known as Afrikaners) arrived from the Netherlands and another wave of English arrive to mine gold and diamonds in South Africa. After the Boer Wars in 1902, South Africa became a part of the British empire.

While the British had outlawed slavery, racial discrimination towards black Africans was deeply rooted in legislation and social life. The 'pass system' was implemented, and black Africans could not work in agriculture, mining, or industry without a pass. Excessive taxes and a lack of jobs pushed the native people deeper into poverty. In May 1961, the Republic of South Africa was granted sovereignty and became an independent country, ruled by the white Afrikaners. Racial segregation and white minority rule, known officially as apartheid, included the evictions of thousands of African people from urban centers to 'reserves', now known as townships, as a means to separate the races. Interracial marriage was banned and having friends outside your racial group was frowned upon.

In 1991, apartheid officially ended, and majority rule was complete in 1994 when the first black president (Nelson Mandela) was elected. In fear of retaliation, many white

Image 13.5 Riots in South Africa

Source: Pawel Janiak on Unsplash

Afrikaners left South Africa, resulting in an exodus of skilled labor. Moreover, the country was deep in debt, and over 5 million South Africans had contracted the HIV virus, leaving over 2 million children orphaned (Gibson, 2015). Today, South Africa is still one of the most unequal countries in the world with around 47% of South Africans (mostly black) living in poverty. Crush (2006) claims that as a result of apartheid, South Africa has the highest level of xenophobia in the world, specifically aimed at refugees, asylum seekers, migrants, and host communities.

Theorists recognize tourism as a continued form of colonization, which disempowers local residents and creates conflict, sometimes violence, against visitors and tourism establishments. Devine and Ojeda (2017, p. 606) write:

> Instead of narrating multiple, co-existing, and contentious histories, identities and relations that define place, tourism's spatial fetishism paints an imaginary picture that reflects the ideals and desires of their creators and marketing agencies . . . (the industry) obscures the constitutive violence that produces paradise, found in multi-million dollar advertising campaigns, privatized man-made beaches, whale watching, and slum tours.

They claim that the process of developing tourism frequently includes the commodification of local culture, land dispossession to create tourism sites, the removal of community (as in the development of nature reserves), and the marginalization of local peoples. Tourism services that separate visitors from communities, and the excessive luxury often found in these areas, can often mirror colonial practices. Moreover, poverty tourism, known as township tourism in sub-Saharan Africa, celebrates many of the subversive apartheid practices because "these peripheral black settlements offer tourists a glimpse of what is touted as 'real life' in South Africa" (Hikido, 2018, p. 2581). The future success of township tourism requires the maintenance of poverty and underdevelopment.

Political instability can have negative effects on GDP growth, private investment, inflation, total productivity, as well as physical and human capital accumulations (Ferreira & Perks, 2016). Continued political tension, corruption, as well as social and labor unrest in South Africa has received negative media attention and impacted the success of tourism. Moreover, the xenophobic culture has led to violence against visitors to South Africa, which in turn has reduced visitor numbers and international investment in the tourism industry. Specifically, the highly publicized rate of rape and murder in South Africa, occasionally aimed at tourists, as well as the corruption inherent in the political arena, resulted in the issuance of travel warnings by China, Australia, and the United Kingdom in 2015.

It takes time for communities to overcome centuries of racism, violence, and marginalization. Yet, sustainable tourism may be an avenue through which healing can occur. As Devine and Ojeda (2017) note, "the tight linkages between tourism and capital accumulation, tourism and colonialism, tourism and sexism, and tourism and militarization . . . are historically and geographically situated and contingent, and thus, they can be unmade. That is the challenge" (p. 614).

Reflective questions

1. As a tourism professional in South Africa, how can you support the healing process and make a positive impact on South African society?

2. What steps can you take to keep tourists safe without isolating the tourists from South African culture and local communities?

3. Do you agree with the assessment that tourism is another form of colonization? Why or why not?

References

Crush, J. (2006). *The Perfect Storm: Realities of Xenophobia in Contemporary South Africa*, Southern African Migration Project (Eds). University of Cape Town and Queen's University, Canada.

Devine, J. & Ojeda, D. (2017). Violence and dispossession in tourism development: a critical geographical approach. *Journal of Sustainable Tourism*, 25(5), 605–617.

Ferreira, D. & Perks, S. (2016). The influence of the political climate on South Africa's tourism industry. The 2016 International Academic Research Conference, London–Zurich.

Gibson, J.L. (2015). Apartheid's long shadow: how racial divides distort South Africa's democracy. *Foreign Affairs*, March/April.

Hikido, A. (2018). Entrepreneurship in South African township tourism: the impact of interracial social capital. *Ethnic and Racial Studies*, 41(14), 2580–2598.

STUDY QUESTIONS

1. Classify the following scenarios as economic, environmental, or social trends and explain your choice. What could you do to enhance (or counteract) these trends?
- An increase in active tourism experiences, such as hiking and bicycling trips;
- You advertise an entry-level position earning minimum wage and no one applies for the job;
- There is an increase in petty crime around your resort;
- The local government issues a smog alert and recommends people stay indoors;
- Tourists complain about long lines at your local museum;
- An increase in fuel costs results in higher airline prices and a reduction in visitation;
- The local government official is accused of embezzlement and the local community holds a series of demonstrations;
- You notice an increase in visitors from Korea who do not speak the local language.

2. Research the current trends that could affect the tourism industry in your hometown. Prioritize them and explain why they are important or unimportant.

3. Develop a tourism product or experience that takes into account the economic, environmental, and social global trends. Explain why you developed it the way you did.

4. Using the consumer trends discussed in Chapter 5, explain why you think these trends have emerged based on the megatrends discussed in this chapter.

5. You run trekking and animal viewing tours through a local nature area. Develop a best-case and worst-case scenario as they relate to climate change.

DEFINITIONS

Acid rain   rainfall made sufficiently acidic by atmospheric pollution that it causes environmental harm

Climate change   a change in the statistical distribution of extreme weather patterns when that change lasts for an extended period of time

Constant pattern a graphical pattern that occurs when there is no net increase or decrease over time

Cyber-attack any attempt to expose, alter, disable, destroy, steal, or gain unauthorized access to or make unauthorized use of computers and computer networks

Endangered species a type of organism that is threatened by extinction

Exponential pattern a graphical pattern that indicates that data is rising at an increasing rate over time

Futures studies ("futures") the formal and systematic study of possible, probable, and preferable futures, and of methods of foresight development for individuals, groups, and human society

Genetic variation the diversity found within a species

Inclusive tourism travel designed for people with disabilities

Last chance tourism when tourists increasingly seek to experience the world's most endangered sites before they vanish or are permanently transformed

Linear pattern a graphical pattern that occurs when there is a steady increase or decrease in numbers over time

Megatrends a significant, globally relevant, social, economic, political, environmental, and technological change over the long-term

Nationalism the identification with one's own nation and support for its interests, especially to the exclusion or detriment of the interests of other nations

Overtourism too many visitors to a particular destination

Poaching illegal hunting

Pro-poor tourism tourism that generates net benefits for the poor

Renewable energy energy that is collected from renewable resources, which are naturally replenished on a human timescale, such as sunlight, wind, rain, tides, waves, and geothermal heat

Rural-to-urban migration when people seek employment and income opportunities in industrialized areas

Safety plan actions and procedures designed to avoid dangerous situations

Scenario writing the process of creating alternative hypothetical futures relating to particular circumstances that could alter demand in the future

Secularism the principle of separation of the state from religious institutions

Security plan a document that defines roles and responsibilities, policies and procedures in the event of security incidents

Social norm an informal understanding that governs the behavior of members of a society or business

Time series data where the numerical value of data is known over different points in time

Turning point when a swing in one direction ends and a swing in another direction begins

Xenophobia the fear and hatred of strangers, foreigners, or of anything that is strange or foreign

Glossary

3S destinations   sun, sea, and sand destinations

70–20–10 rule   approximately 70% of an employee's growth comes from on-the-job training, 20% comes through mentoring and coaching, and 10% comes through formal training classes

Accreditation   officially recognizing another as being qualified to perform a particular activity

Acid rain   rainfall made sufficiently acidic by atmospheric pollution that it causes environmental harm

Adaptancy platform   promotes low-impact tourism development that can reduce negative impacts

Advocacy platform   sees tourism as a good thing and celebrates tourism's positive impacts on the economy and cross-cultural understandings

Airbnb   a website that allows travelers to find low-budget informal accommodation in the prospective destination

Alternative development   development that emanates from, and is guided by, the needs of individual societies

Alternative tourism   tourism that is appropriate to the local environment, social, and cultural values, and that optimizes local decision-making, enhances the local economy, and promotes meaningful encounters between tourists and the local community

Alternative tourist   a visitor who generally enjoys meeting new people, expects to learn something new when they travel, appreciates a wide range of activities, seeks out challenges, is concerned with social issues, and embraces change

Altruism   the belief in or practice of disinterested and selfless concern for the well-being of others

Anthropocentrism   the philosophy that humans are the sole bearers of intrinsic environmental value, and all other living things are there to sustain humanity's existence

ART   stands for audience, resource, and technology as a way to provide effective interpretation

Attribute   a descriptive quality that a visitor believes a destination or business has, such as physical characteristics, like beaches, nightclubs, or outstanding food choices

Awarding body   the agency that sets the standards for the award and promotes it to the public

Backward linkage   a channel through which information, material, and money flow between a company and its suppliers

Balance sheet   contains an organization's assets, liabilities, and owners' equity

Behavioral segmentation   splits consumers into groups according to their observed behaviors

Benchmarking   the process of comparing a business's process and performance metrics to industry best practices from other companies; it can be used to track performance over time

Benefit   the personal values each visitor attaches to each attribute

Bonding social capital   social networks made up of homogeneous groups of people

Brand   a unique name, term, sign, symbol, design, or combination of these that identifies the good or services of one seller or group of sellers and differentiates them from the competition

Brexit vote   the vote by the United Kingdom to leave the European Union

Bridging social capital   social networks made up of socially heterogeneous groups that include people with different backgrounds

Built capital   any pre-existing or planned formation that is constructed or retrofitted to suit community needs

Business marketing   marketing the actual products, services, or experiences that a single business entity offers

Capacity building   a process that supports only the initial stages of building or creating capacities and assumes that there are no existing capacities at the start

Capacity development   the process through which individuals, organizations, and societies obtain, strengthen, and maintain the capabilities to set and achieve their own development objectives over time

Capital   factors of production that generate wealth through investment

Capitalism   an economic and political system in which a country's trade and industry are controlled by private owners for profit, rather than by the state

Carrying capacity   the amount of use any given land or environment can endure over time without degrading its suitability for that use

Carrying capacity in tourism   the maximum number of people that may visit a tourist destination at the same time, without causing destruction of the physical, economic, socio-cultural environment and an unacceptable decrease in the quality of visitors' satisfaction

Cash flow statement   shows how changes in balance sheet and income affect cash and cash equivalents, and breaks the analysis down to operating, investing, and financing activities

Cautionary platform   views tourism as a bad thing because of its negative impacts

Certification   a type of label indicating that compliance with standards has been verified by an outside agency

Climate change   a change in the statistical distribution of extreme weather patterns when that change lasts for an extended period of time

Colonization   action of appropriating a place or domain for one's own use and establishing control over the indigenous people of an area

Commodification   the transformation of goods, services, ideas, and people into commodities, or objects of trade

Communication   conveying information or evoking understanding

Community development   a process where community members come together to take collective action and generate solutions to common problems

Community-based tourism   a collaborative approach to tourism in which community members exercise control through active participation in the appraisal, development, management, and/or ownership of enterprises that delivers net socio-economic benefits to community members, conserves natural and cultural resources, and adds value to the experiences of local and foreign visitors

Comparative advantage when countries specialize in the production and export of the goods which they can produce relatively less expensively than other countries because they possess specific resources, such as labor, capital, and land

Competition-oriented pricing the practice of setting prices based on the prices of other comparable businesses

Congestion-related pricing system a system of offering cheaper prices for periods of low visitation and more expensive ones for peak periods

Conservation the principle that the environment and its resources should be used by humans and managed in a responsible manner

Consortium an association of two or more companies with the objective of pooling their resources to achieve a common goal

Constant pattern a graphical pattern that occurs when there is no net increase or decrease over time

Cost-based pricing price is determined by calculating the cost of production plus a per-unit profit margin on each item sold

Cost–benefit analysis a technique used to determine the desirability of proposed projects by quantifying and calculating their relevant costs and benefits

Criteria the standards established for a certification to be awarded to a business

Crowd sourcing a financial model in which individuals or organizations solicit investment from a large, relatively open, and often rapidly-evolving, group of internet users

Crowding when visitors perceive too many people in an area, spoiling the atmosphere, ambiance, or user experience

Cultural capital the stock of values, arts, crafts, cultural knowledge, performance, social practices, and access to heritage resources

Cultural heritage the legacy of physical artefacts and intangible attributes of a group or society that are inherited from past generations, maintained in the present, and bestowed for the benefit of future generations

Cultural tourism a traveler's engagement with a country or region's culture, specifically the lifestyle of the people in those geographical areas, the history of those people, their art, architecture, religion(s), and other elements that helped shape their way of life

Customer satisfaction generated by providing an experience (tourism product) that meets or exceeds the customer's expectations

Cyber-attack any attempt to expose, alter, disable, destroy, steal, or gain unauthorized access to or make unauthorized use of computers and computer networks

Demand-oriented pricing price is based on consumers' willingness to pay

Demarketing a way to decrease demand for a certain product or experience

Demographic segmentation divides consumers into categories such as age, income, race, family size, and socioeconomic status

Destination marketing marketing for a specific location that generally includes all activities, sights, and tourism businesses in a destination

Destination marketing and management organization (DMO) an organization that represents destinations and helps to develop long-term travel and tourism strategies

Direct effect a change in local economic activity resulting from businesses selling directly to tourists

Discount rate the rate of return used to discount future cash flows

Distribution channel the chain of businesses or intermediaries through which a good or service passes until it reaches the end consumer

Diversity recognizing that each individual is unique and appreciating those differences

Downstream activities all selling activities such as tour operators and concessionaires

Dual pricing system a pricing system where tourists pay a higher price than locals

Ecocentrism   the philosophy that there is inherent worth to all living things regardless of their usefulness to humans

Economic capacity   the level of acceptable change within the local economy of a tourist destination that is described as the point at which the increased revenue brought by tourism development is overtaken by the inflation caused by tourism

Economic dependency   an unending situation in which economies and economic agents rely on one aspect or thing in order to be successful

Economic development   the process by which a nation improves the economic, political, and social well-being of its people

Economic growth   the increase in value of goods and services produced per person, or at an aggregate level, by an economy from one year to another

Economic leakage   revenue, in the form of payments to tour companies and hotels that does not stay in the economy where visitation occurs

Economies of scale   a proportionate saving in costs gained by an increased level of production

Ecotourism   low impact nature-based tourism which contributes to the maintenance of species and habitats either directly through a contribution to conservation and/or indirectly by providing enough revenue to the local community for local people to value, and therefore protect their wildlife heritage area as a source of income

Education   a form of learning in which the knowledge, skills, and habits of a group of people are transferred from one generation to the next through teaching, training, or research

Employee engagement   the emotional commitment that employees demonstrate towards upholding the mission and values of the company

Employee turnover rate   the percentage of employees who leave an organization over a certain period of time (typically, one year)

Empowerment   the process of becoming stronger and more confident, especially in controlling one's life and claiming one's rights

Endangered species   a type of organism that is threatened by extinction

Environmental capital   includes natural capital, other natural assets, such as weather, and built capital

Environmental scanning   the process of monitoring the external environment

Environmentalism   a social movement that is based on political and ethical views of the environment

Excursionist (also known as a day-tripper)   a traveler that lives in close proximity to a destination and only stays for a short visit

Expectations   strong beliefs that something will happen which are derived from the need to fulfill a goal that has some intrinsic value or attractiveness

Exponential pattern   a graphical pattern that indicates that data is rising at an increasing rate over time

External cost   a cost to society, regardless of who pays for it

Factors of production   the inputs that are used in the production of goods or services in order to make an economic profit. The factors of production include land, labor, capital, and entrepreneurship

Fair pricing   ensuring that the revenue earned from the product or service is equitably shared between the producer, the supply chain, and the end seller

Financial capital   financial wealth that is used to start or maintain a business

Focal companies   companies in the supply chain, with direct contact to end customers, and having bargain power over other actors in the supply chain

Focus group   a group of two or more people who are answering the interview questions simultaneously

Food tourism   the desire to experience a particular type of food or the produce of a specific region while traveling

Foreign exchange   the money earned from the export of goods or services and the receipt of foreign currency

Free trade   policies that seek to eliminate government-imposed barriers to trade

Funding body   the organization that pays to develop and run a certification program

Futures studies ("futures")   the formal and systematic study of possible, probable, and preferable futures, and of methods of foresight development for individuals, groups, and human society

Gateway community   a community neighboring a national park or nature area

Genetic variation   the diversity found within a species

Geographic segmentation   separates markets according to physical location criteria

Global village   the world characterized by instant communication, the proliferation of transnational corporations, and the pervasive influence of mass media and popular cultural trends from the West

Globalization   the process by which people and goods move easily across borders

Globalization from below   globalization that is regulated by the local governance institutions

Glocalization   the practice of conducting business according to both local and global considerations

Goal   an envisioned future state that people commit to achieving

Governance   the ways in which society allocates, controls, and coordinates resources

Green economy   an economy that results in improved human well-being and social equity, while significantly reducing environmental risks and ecological scarcities

Green management   the actual practice of employing sustainability production techniques

Green marketing   the communication of sustainable practices to consumers, whether these practices are real or not

Greenhouse gas   a gas that enters the earth's atmosphere and traps heat, causing a warming of the atmosphere

Greening   the act of becoming more aware and attempting to mitigate the environmental consequences of economic activities

Greenwashing   the act of misleading consumers regarding the environmental practices of a company or the environmental benefits of a product or service

Horizontal collaboration   collaboration between firms in the same level of the tourism supply chain

Human capital   the stock of knowledge, habits, social and personality attributes, including creativity, embodied in the ability to perform labor so as to produce economic value

Human capital management   the process of acquiring, training, managing, and retaining employees

Human resource management (HRM)   the management and professional development of employees within an organization

Human resources   the people who make up the workforce of an organization, business sector, or economy

Imperialism   a policy of extending a country's power and influence through diplomacy or military force

Inclusion   the act of harnessing diversity for the benefit of improving decision-making and growth

Inclusive tourism   travel designed for people with disabilities

Income statement   shows the net return of a business, its revenue minus its expenses, or its profit

Indirect effect   a change in sales, income, or employment within a region in industries supplying goods and services to tourism businesses

Induced effect   a change in expenditures within a region as a result of household spending of the income earned in tourism and supporting industries

Institutional knowledge   the collection of historical knowledge and wisdom that is retained by employees and the analytical skills necessary for its effective use within the organization

Intangible culture   the practices and representations of artifacts, objects, and cultural spaces

Integrated waste management plan   a working document that outlines the process of managing waste that is created, implementing disposal methods that reduce harm to the environment, and waste reduction methods, such as reusing, recycling, and composting

Interpretation   an educational activity, which aims to reveal meanings and relationships through the use of original objects, by first-hand experience, and by illustrative media, rather than simply communicate factual information

Interpretation intensity   a comparison of quantity and type of interpretation between sites

Isolationism   a national policy of avoiding political or economic entanglements with other countries

Knowledge worker   workers who apply theoretical and analytical knowledge, acquired through formal training, to develop products and services

Knowledge-based platform   views tourism from a holistic perspective, through the critical analysis of the underlying structures of tourism rather than just its impacts

Last chance tourism   when tourists increasingly seek to experience the world's most endangered sites before they vanish or are permanently transformed

Laws   the system of rules designed to regulate behavior

Leakage   when consumer goods and services are imported from abroad or when tourism revenue leaves an economy

Linear pattern   a graphical pattern that occurs when there is a steady increase or decrease in numbers over time

Lobbying   the process of trying to persuade elected officials to take particular actions or change certain laws

Localism   the belief in and expression of the unique character of localities

Locavist   a person that travels closer to home and invests locally in their communities with money, time, and personal energy

Locavore   a person whose diet consists only or principally of locally grown or produced food

Logrolling   the practice whereby two or more legislators agree to trade votes for bills that they each would like to see passed

LOHAS (Lifestyles of Health and Sustainability)   a social and economic movement that reflects a marketplace of goods and services that is immersed in meaningful person values of self as well as the social and natural world

Market segmentation   the activity of dividing a broad consumer base, normally consisting of existing and potential customers, into sub-groups of consumers (known as segments) based on some type of shared characteristics

Marketing   the activities of a company associated with buying and selling a product or service, which include advertising, selling, and delivering products to people

Marketing mix   a combination of factors that can be controlled by a company to influence consumers to purchase its products which consists of four primary elements: product, distribution, price, and promotion

Mass tourism   the aggressive development of standardized travel packages that result in tens of thousands of visitors going to the same destination

Materiality   determines which topics, or significant impacts, are relevant and important

Megatrend   a significant, globally relevant, social, economic, political, environmental, and technological change over the long-term

Micro finance   the lending of small amounts of money at low interest to new businesses, generally but not exclusively, in the developing world. Also known as micro credit

Microbrewery   a brewery that produces a volume of less than 15,000 barrels of beer, and sells at least 70% of it to locations off-site

Mindfulness   caring about the world around us

Mindfulness model   the process of developing mindful visitors

Mission statement   a written statement of a company's purpose and values, which informs the company's decision-making and trade-off to both members of the company and the external community

Motivation   the desire or willingness to do something or go somewhere to fulfill specific needs

Multilateral agreement   a treaty between three or more sovereign states that stipulates established guidelines that participating nations mutually agreed upon

Multinational company   a company whose base of operation is found in a specific country, but who has subsidiaries in two or more other countries

Nationalism   the identification with one's own nation and support for its interests, especially to the exclusion or detriment of the interests of other nations

Natural capital   the world's stock of natural resources, which includes geology, soils, air, water, and all living organisms

Nature-based tourism   any tourism activities that involve the use of natural areas

Neolocalism (new localism)   a renewed interest in preserving and promoting the identity of a community and restoring aspects that make it culturally unique

Net present value   a measure of discounted future cash inflows and outflows in present day monetary terms

Niche tourism   specific tourism products that are tailored to meet the needs of a particular audience or market segment

Non-renewable resources   resources that take millions of years to form and cannot be renewed in a human lifetime

Objective   the measurable step taken to achieve a goal

Onboarding plan   a plan that establishes employment goals and enables new employees to learn how to be successful in their role

Opportunity cost   the loss of potential gain from other alternatives when one alternative is chosen

Overtourism   too many visitors to a particular destination

Paradigm   a system of concepts, values, perceptions, and practices shared by a society, which forms a particular vision of reality or a worldview

Parity pricing   setting the price equal to the competition

Penetration pricing   setting the price lower than the competition

Performance objective   a goal that seeks to improve the employee's ability to excel at their current job

Physical capacity   the maximum number of individuals that an area is able to support

Poaching   illegal hunting

Policy   a definitive course of action that determines present and future decisions

Political capital   the ability to use power in support of political or economic positions

Politics   the process of making decisions that apply to members of a group

Premium pricing   setting the price higher than the competition

Preservation   the principle that lands and their natural resources should not be consumed by humans and should instead be maintained in their pristine form

Primary data   data collected to address specific problems, or to investigate specific tourism trends

Private cost   the cost the firm pays to purchase capital equipment, hire labor, and buy materials or other inputs

Private sector   the part of an economy that invests in profit-making businesses, such as hotel accommodations, restaurants, and entertainment (private industries)

Professional goal   a goal that seeks to further the employee's career advancement

Pro-poor tourism   tourism that generates net benefits for the poor

Protectionism   the policy of protecting domestic industries against foreign competition through the use of quotas, subsidies, and tariffs

Psychographic segmentation   separates consumers by lifestyle choices, including their activities, interests, and opinions

Public sector   the part of an economy that is under government control, financed through tax revenue, and provides services for all members of society (public services)

Regulation   a policy tool that governs how laws are enforced and the penalties for violation

Renewable energy   energy that is collected from renewable resources, which are naturally replenished on a human timescale, such as sunlight, wind, rain, tides, waves, and geothermal heat

Renewable resources   resources that are replenished naturally and can be used repeatedly

Reverse logistics   the process of transporting goods and services backward along the supply chain, such as returned or defective products, or the disposal of waste

Rural tourism   a country experience which encompasses a wide range of attractions and activities that take place in agricultural or non-urban areas

Rural-to-urban migration   when people seek employment and income opportunities in industrialized areas

Safety plan   actions and procedures designed to avoid dangerous situations

Satisfaction   providing an experience (tourism product) that meets or exceeds the customer's expectations

Saturation   when interviewees are repeating information uncovered in previous interviews and when no new knowledge is being acquired

Scenario writing   the process of creating alternative hypothetical futures relating to particular circumstances that could alter demand in the future

Secondary data   data collected, analyzed, and presented to answer different questions or to solve different problems than those the data was originally collected to investigate

Secularism   the principle of separation of the state from religious institutions

Security plan   a document that defines roles and responsibilities, policies and procedures in the event of security incidents

Sense of place   what sets a place (destination) apart from others, and invokes strong feelings in people who live there or travel there as tourists

Service worker   a worker whose primary task is the serving of customer needs

Silk Road   a network of routes linking regions of Asia and Europe in the ancient world that was established by the Han Dynasty of China

Site hardening   constructing facilities and locating trails and roads to reduce the impacts of visitors on sensitive soils and vegetation, and to help meet the visitors' needs for usable access

Slow cities   a development strategy that promotes the slow philosophy to urban living by providing a political agenda of local distinctiveness within urban development

Slow tourism   a philosophy of travelling that allows visitors to experience the authentic side of a destination by spending an extended amount of time in one area

Social capacity   the maximum level of visitation an area can sustain before visitor enjoyment is reduced and increased social ills result

Social capital   the links, shared values, and understandings that enable individuals and groups in a society to trust one another and so work together

Social cost   the combination of private costs and external costs of production

Social indicator   a direct and valid statistical measure which monitors levels and changes over time in a fundamental social concern

Social norm   an informal understanding that governs the behavior of members of a society or business

Stakeholder   an entity or individual that can reasonably be expected to be significantly affected by the organization's activities, products, or services

Standard   a technical specification or other precise criteria to be used consistently as rules, guidelines, or definitions, to ensure that materials, products, processes, and services are complying with best practice

Stated data   data that reflect what respondents say they will do, which may or may not be what they actually do

Strong sustainability   the idea that the existing stock of natural capital must be maintained and enhanced because the functions it performs cannot be duplicated through technological advancements

Substitutability   the interchangeability of activities and experiences by varying one or more of the following: the timing of the experience, the means of gaining access to the experience, the setting, and the activity

Sustainable consumption   the use of goods and related products which bring a better quality of life to those who produce them, while minimizing the use of natural resources, toxic materials, waste, and pollutants over the product life cycle, so as not to jeopardize the needs of future generations

Sustainable development   meeting current human development goals while at the same time supporting the ability of natural systems to provide the natural resources and ecosystem services on which future generations will depend

Sustainable mass tourism   a type of mass tourism which promotes economic, environmental, and socio-cultural enhancements within a destination

Sustainable tourism   tourism development that meets the needs of present tourists and host regions while protecting and enhancing opportunities for the future

SWOT analysis   the strengths, weaknesses, opportunities, and threats related to business competition

System   an interdependent series of elements that interact in order to achieve some end result

Tangible culture   physical cultural and historical artifacts, such as architecture or other built heritage

Team   a group of people united by a common business goal or achieving common objectives

Time series data   where the numerical value of data is known over different points in time

Topic boundary   a description of where impacts occur for each material topic, and in which ways the organization is involved with those impacts

Total economic impact   the sum of the direct, indirect, and induced effects

Tourism   the temporary movement of people to destinations outside their normal places of work and residence, the activities undertaken during their stay in those destinations, and the facilities created to cater to their needs

Tourism supply chain (TSC)   a network of tourism organizations involved in a series of diverse activities, including the provision of an entire spectrum of components of tourism products/services, such as flights and accommodation, ending with the sale of tourism products in the tourism region

Tourism trade balance   the difference between inbound tourism expenditure and outbound tourism expenditure

Tourism typology   a classification of tourists based on psychological characteristics

Travel   the physical process of moving from one area to another

Triple bottom line   an accounting framework that considers impacts to the economy, the environment, and the society

Turning point   when a swing in one direction ends and a swing in another direction begins

Unconscious bias   the inclination for humans to form social stereotypes that lump people together unfairly based on their past experiences

Upstream activities   the inputs that a company buys to make or sell its product and includes suppliers, purchases, and production lines

Value added tax   sales tax collected in pieces along the production chain

Value chain   a system which describes how private businesses in collaboration with governments and civil society receive or access resources as inputs, add value through various processes (planning, development, financing, marketing, distribution, pricing, positioning, among others), and sell the resulting products to visitors

Verifying body   enforces certification criteria and checks on the performance of applicants

Vertical collaboration   collaborations between a firm at different levels within the supply chain, such as inputs, or the partners to which they sell their final products

Vision statement   a future-based narrative meant to inspire and give direction to employees of the company rather than customers

Visitor/operator qualification   limiting entry only to those possessing required qualifications

Visitor management   the management tools and interventions that regulate the movement and behavior of visitors in a destination, natural area, or attraction

Voluntourism   tourism that provides opportunities for people to do volunteer work while also participating in tourism as a way to 'do good' or 'give back' to a community

Weak sustainability   the philosophy that man-made capital is more important than natural capital

Willingness to pay   the maximum price at or below which a consumer will definitely buy one unit of a product

Xenophobia   the fear and hatred of strangers, foreigners, or of anything that is strange or foreign

References

Aidoo, A.A. (2010). A critical assessment of tourism as a development strategy in Ghana: with particular emphasis on the opportunities and dilemmas of ecotourism and cultural tourism. Unpublished dissertation, University of Delaware.

Alam, M.S. & Paramati, S.R. (2016). The impact of tourism on income inequality in developing economies: does Kuznets curve hypothesis exist. *Annals of Tourism Research*, 61, 111–126.

Albrecht, D. (2014). *Rethinking Rural: Global Community and Economic Development in the Small Town West*. Pullman, WA, Washington State University Press.

Albrecht, J.N. (Ed.) (2017). *Visitor Management in Tourist Destinations*, Volume 3. Wallingford, UK, CABI.

Ali-Knight, J.M. (2011). The role of niche tourism products in destination development. Retrieved from www.napier.ac.uk/~/media/worktribe/output-209366/fullthesispdf.pdf.

Allen, C. & Clouth, S. (2012). *A Guidebook to the Green Economy. Issue 1: Green Economy, Green Growth, and Low Carbon Development – History, Definitions and a Guide to Recent Publications*. UN Division for Sustainable Development, New York, Department of Economic and Social Affairs (UN-DESA).

Alves, I.M. (2009). Green spin everywhere: how greenwashing reveals the limits of the CSR Paradigm. *Journal of Global Change & Governance*, 2(1), 1–26.

Archibugi, D. & Pietrobelli, C. (2003). The globalisation of technology and its implications for developing countries: windows of opportunity or further burden? *Technological Forecasting and Social Change*, 70(9), 861–883.

Ashworth, G.J. & Tunbridge, J.E. (2004). Whose tourist-historic city? Localizing the global and globalizing the local. In Lew, A.A., Hall, C.M., & Williams, A.M. (Eds), *A Companion to Tourism*, Malden, MA, Blackwell Publishing.

Bacher, K., Balthrus, A., Barrie, B., Bliss, K., Cardea, D., Chandler, L., & Lacome, B. (2007). *Foundations of Interpretation Curriculum Content Narrative*. Interpretive Development Program, National Park Service, Department of the Interior.

Bahamas Ministry of Tourism (2020). Vision and mission. Retrieved from www.tourismtoday.com/about-us/vision-mission.

Barr, S., Shaw, G., Coles, T., & Prillwitz, J. (2010). 'A holiday is a holiday': practicing sustainability, home and away. *Journal of Transport Geography*, 18(3), 474–481.

Baumann, P. & Sinha, S. (2001). Linking development with democratic processes in India: political capital and sustainable livelihoods analysis. London, Overseas Development Institute.

Beck, L. & Cable, T. (1998). *Interpretation for the 21st Century*. Champaign, IL, Sagamore Publishing.

Becken, S. (2007). Tourists' perception of international air travel's impact on the global climate and potential climate change policies. *Journal of Sustainable Tourism*, 15(4), 351–368.

Benckendorff, P. (2008). Envisioning sustainable tourism futures: an evaluation of the futures wheel method. *Tourism and Hospitality Research*, 8(1), 25–36.

Beni, M.C. (2001). *Análise Estrutural do Turismo*, 4th edition. Senac-são Paulo, são Paulo, Brazil.

Bertels, S., Papania, L., & Papania, D. (2010). Embedding sustainability in organizational culture: a systematic review of the body of knowledge. *Network for Business Sustainability*, 25, 1–74.

Bieber, F. (2018). Is nationalism on the rise? Assessing global trends. *Ethnopolitics*, 17(5), 519–540.

Black, R. & Crabtree, A. (Eds) (2007). *Quality Assurance and Certification in Ecotourism*, Vol. 5. Wallingford, UK, CABI.

Blue River Resort and Hot Springs, Costa Rica (2018). Our mission, vision, and values. Retrieved from www.blueriverresort.com/env_missions/our-mission-vision-and-values/.

Boley, B.B. & Nickerson, N.P. (2013). Profiling geotravelers: an a priori segmentation identifying and defining sustainable travelers using the Geotraveler Tendency Scale (GTS). *Journal of Sustainable Tourism*, 21(2), 314–330.

Boxill, I. (2004). Towards an alternative tourism for Jamaica. *International Journal of Contemporary Hospitality Management*, 16, 269–272.

Bramwell, B. (2004). Mass tourism, diversification, and sustainability in southern coastal regions. In Bramwell, B. (Ed.), *Coastal Mass Tourism* (pp. 1–31), Clevedon, UK, Channel View.

Bramwell, B. & Alletorp, L. (2001). Attitudes in the Danish tourism industry to the roles of business and government in sustainable tourism. *International Journal of Tourism Research*, 3(2), 91–103.

Bramwell, B. & Lane, B. (2011). Critical research on the governance of tourism and sustainability. *Journal of Sustainable Tourism*, 19(4–5), 411–421.

Brewers Association (Ed.). (n.d.). Craft beer industry market segments. Retrieved from www.brewersassociation.org/statistics/market-segments.

Brida, J.G. & Zapata, S. (2009). Cruise tourism: economic, socio-cultural and environmental impacts. *International Journal of Leisure and Tourism Marketing*, 1(3), 205–226.

Brohman, J. (1996). New directions in tourism for third world development. *Annals of Tourism Research*, 23(1), 568–590.

Brunson, M. & Shelby, B. (1993). Recreation substitutability: a research agenda. *Leisure Sciences*, 15, 67–74.

Buhalis, D. (2000). Marketing the competitive destination of the future. *Tourism Management*, 21, 97–116.

Burchett, K. (2014). Anthropocentrism and nature: an attempt at reconciliation. *Teoria-Rivista di Filosofia*, 34(2), 119–137.

Burgoon, B., Oliver, T., & Trubowitz, P. (2017). Globalization, domestic politics, and transatlantic relations. *International Politics*, 54(4), 420–433.

Butler, R. (1980). The concept of a tourist area cycle of evolution: implications for management of resources. *Canadian Geographer*, 24, 5–12.

Caribbean Tourism Organization (n.d.). *Good Practices in Community-based Tourism in the Caribbean*. Carl Bro Intelligent Solutions.

Cascio, W. (2006). The high cost of low wages. *Harvard Business Review*, December.

Center for Responsible Politics (2018). Issue profile: travel and tourism. Retrieved from www.opensecrets.org/federal-lobbying/issues/summary?cycle=2018&id=TOU&year=2018.

Chang, T.C. (1999). Local uniqueness in the global village: heritage tourism in Singapore. *Professional Geographer*, 51(1), 91–103.

China Tourism Commission (2018). Tourism performance. Retrieved from www.tourism.gov.hk/english/statistics/statistics_perform.html.

Clardy, A. (2018). 70–20–10 and the dominance of informal learning: a fact in search of evidence. *Human Resource Development Review*, 17(2), 153–178.

Clark, P. & Fears, D. (2014). The horn and ivory trade. *Washington Post*, August 10.

Clements, M.A. (1989). Selecting tourist traffic by demarketing. *Tourism Management*, 10(2), 89–94.

Coffey, R. (2014). The eight forms of community wealth, Part 1: Built capital. Michigan State University Extension. Retrieved from http://msue.anr.msu.edu/news/the_eight_forms_of_community_wealth_part_1_built_capital.

Coleman, J. (1988). Social capital in the creation of human capital. *American Journal of Sociology*, 94, 95–120.

Coleman, J. (2013). Six components of a great corporate culture. *Harvard Business Review*, May, 2016.

Cooke, P. (Ed.) (1989). *Localities: The Changing Face of Urban Britain*. London, Unwin Hyman.

Coyle, D. (2016). Was Brexit a vote against globalization? Retrieved from www.weforum.org/agenda/2016/08/was-brexit-a-vote-against-globalization.

Cross, J.E. (2001). *What is Sense of Place?* Fort Collin, CO, Colorado State University Libraries.

Cruise Lines International Association, Inc. (2017). 2018 Cruise industry outlook, December. Retrieved from www.cruising.org/docs/default-source/research/clia-2018-state-of-the-industry.pdf?sfvrsn=0.

Dator, J. & Yeoman, I. (2015). Tourism in Hawaii 1776–2076: futurist Jim Dator talks with Ian Yeoman. *Journal of Tourism Futures*, 1(1), 36–45.

Davidson, B., Lee, C., & George, H.E. (1991). Increased exhibit accessibility through multisensory interaction. *Curator*, 34, 273–290.

Delmendo, L.C. (2017). Hong Kong's red-hot property market. *Global Property Guide*, 18 May. Retrieved from www.globalpropertyguide.com/Asia/Hong-Kong/Price-History.

Dodds, R. & Joppe, M. (2005). *CSR in the Tourism Industry? The Status of and Potential for Certification, Codes of Conduct and Guidelines*. IFC.

Donavan, D.T., Brown, T.J., & Mowen, J.C. (2004). Internal benefits of service-worker customer orientation: job satisfaction, commitment, and organizational citizenship behaviors. *Journal of Marketing*, 68(1), 128–146.

Drucker, P.F. (1959). *The Landmarks of Tomorrow*. New York, Harper & Row.

du Cros, H. & McKercher, B. (2015). *Cultural Tourism*. Oxon, UK, Routledge.

Duffield, J., Neher, C., & Patterson, D. (2006). *Wolves and People in Yellowstone: Impacts on the Regional Economy*. University of Montana, Final Report for Yellowstone Park Foundation.

Dwyer, L. (2015). Globalization of tourism: drivers and outcomes. *Tourism Recreation Research*, 40(3), 326–339.

Eadington, W.R. & Smith, V.L. (1992). Introduction: the emergence of alternative forms of tourism. In Smith, V.L. & Eadington, W.R. (Eds), *Tourism Alternatives: Potentials and Problems in the Development of Tourism* (pp. 1–12). Philadelphia, PA, University of Pennsylvania Press.

Eagles, P.F., McCool, S.F., Haynes, C.D., & Phillips, A. (2002). *Sustainable Tourism in Protected Areas: Guidelines for Planning and Management* (Vol. 8). Gland, Switzerland, IUCN.

Edgell, D.L. & Swanson, J.R. (2013). *Tourism Policy and Planning Yesterday, Today, and Tomorrow*. London, Routledge.

Emerich, M.M. (2011). *The Gospel of Sustainability: Media, Market and LOHAS*. Urbana, IL, University of Illinois Press.

Emirates Group (2017). Emirates Group announces 2016–17 results. Retrieved from www.emirates.com/media-centre/ek-newsroom-emirates-group-announces-2016-17-results#.

European Union Ecolabel (2018). EU ecolabel network toolkit, May 2018, Tourist accommodations. Retrieved from http://ec.europa.eu/environment/ecolabel/digital_toolkit.html.

Evans, M., Marsh, D., & Stoker, G. (2013). Understanding localism. *Policy Studies*, 34(4), 401–407.

Everett, S. & Slocum, S.L. (2013). Food and tourism, an effective partnership? A UK-based review. *Journal of Sustainable Tourism*, 21(7), 789–809.

Farmaki, A., Altinay, L., Botterill, D., & Hilke, S. (2015). Politics and sustainable tourism: the case of Cyprus. *Tourism Management*, 47, 178–190.

Fennel, D.A. (2015). *Ecotourism*, 4th edition. Oxon, Routledge.

Ferdussy, S. & Rahman, M.S. (2009). Impact of multinational corporations on developing countries. *The Chittagong University Journal of Business Administration*, 24, 111–137.

Flack, W. (1997). American microbreweries and neolocalism: ale-ing for a sense of place. *Journal of Cultural Geography*, 16(2), 37–53.

Flora, C.B. & Flora, J.L. (2013). *Rural Communities: Legacy and Change*, 4th edition. Boulder, CO, Westview Press.

Font, X. (2002). Environmental certification in tourism and hospitality: progress, process and progress. *Tourism Management*, 23(3), 197–205.

Font, X. & Buckley, R. (Eds) (2001). *Tourism Ecolabelling: Certification and Promotion of Sustainable Management*. Wallingford, UK, CABI.

Font, X., Walmsley, A., Cogotti, S., McCombes, L., & Hausler, N. (2012). Corporate social responsibility: the disclosure–performance gap. *Tourism Management*, 33, 1544–1553.

Fortanier, F. & Van Wijk, J. (2010). Sustainable tourism industry development in sub-Saharan Africa: consequences of foreign hotels for local employment. *International Business Review*, 19(2), 191–205.

Frey, L. (2017). The cost of a bad hire can be astronomical. Retrieved from www.shrm.org/resourcesandtools/hr-topics/employee-relations/pages/cost-of-bad-hires.aspx.

Friedman, T.L. (2000). *The Lexus and the Olive Tree: Understanding Globalization*. New York, Farrar, Straus and Giroux.

Fullagar, S., Markwell, K., & Wilson, E. (Eds) (2012). *Slow Tourism: Experiences and Mobilities*. Bristol, UK, Channel View Publications.

Fyall, A. & Garrod, B. (1997). Sustainable tourism: towards a methodology for implementing the concept. In Stabler, M. (Ed.) *Tourism and Sustainability: Principles to Practice* (pp. 51–68). Oxon, CABI.

García-Cabrera, A.M., Suárez-Ortega, S.M., & Durán-Herrera, J.J. (2016). Multinational corporations, co-evolution, and sustainable tourism in Africa. *European Journal of Tourism Research*, 13, 23–42.

George, E.W., Mair, H., & Reid, D.G. (2009). *Rural Tourism Development: Localism and Cultural Change*. Bristol, UK, Channel View Publications.

German Federal Ministry for Economic Cooperation and Development (GFMECD) (2014). *Tourism Planning in Development Cooperation: A Handbook*. Retrieved from www.giz.de/expertise/downloads/giz2014-en-tourism-handbook.pdf.

Global Sustainability Standards Board (GSSB) (2016). GRI 101: foundation. Retrieved from www.globalreporting.org/standards/media/1036/gri-101-foundation-2016.pdf.

Goldin, C. (2016). *Human Capital: Handbook of Cliometrics*. Verlag Berlin Heidelberg, Springer.

Goldman, G.E., Nakazawa, A., & Taylor, D. (1994). *Cost–benefit Analysis of Local Tourism Development*. Western Rural Development Center, Oregon State University.

Goodwin, H. (1995). Tourism and the environment. *Biologist*, 42(3), 129–133.

Goodwin, H. (2017). *The Challenge of Overtourism*. Responsible Tourism Partnership Working Paper 4.

Google (2015). The five keys to a successful Google team. Retrieved from https://rework.withgoogle.com/blog/five-keys-to-a-successful-google-team/.

Gössling, S. & Hall, C.M. (2013). Sustainable culinary systems: an introduction. In Hall, C.M. & Gössling, S. (Eds), *Sustainable Culinary Systems: Local Food, Innovation, Tourism, and Hospitality* (pp. 3–44). London and New York, Routledge.

Graefe, D., Mowen, A., & Graefe, A. (2018). Craft beer enthusiasts' support for neolocalism and environmental causes. In Slocum, S.L., Kline, C., & Cavaliere, C. (Eds), *Craft Beverages and Tourism, Volume 2 – Environmental, Societal, and Marketing Implications* (pp. 27–48). Basingstoke, UK, Palgrave Macmillan.

Gray, A. (2017). What is globalization anyway? Retrieved from www.weforumorg/agenda/2017/what-is-globalization-explainer/.

Greenwood, D.J. (1989). Culture by the pound: an anthropological perspective on tourism as cultural commodification. In Smith, V. (Ed.), *Hosts and Guests: The Anthropology of Tourism*, 2nd edition (pp. 171–185). Philadelphia, PA, University of Pennsylvania Press.

Groulx, M., Lemieux, C., Dawson, J., Stewart, E., & Yudina, O. (2016). Motivations to engage in last chance tourism in the Churchill Wildlife Management Area and Wapusk National Park: the role of place identity and nature relatedness. *Journal of Sustainable Tourism*, 24(11), 1523–1540.

Gruca, T.S. & Rego, L.L. (2005). Customer satisfaction, cash flow, and shareholder value. *Journal of Marketing*, 69(3), 115–113.

Guyette, S.M. (2013). *Sustainable Cultural Tourism: Small-scale Solutions*. Santa Fe, NM, Bear Path Press.

Hakim, C. (2000). *Work-lifestyle Choices in the 21st Century: Preference Theory*. Oxford, Oxford University Press.

Hall, C.M. (2011). A typology of governance and its implications for tourism policy analysis. *Journal of Sustainable Tourism*, 19(4–5), 437–457.

Hall, C.M. & Sharples, E. (Eds) (2008). *Food and Wine Festivals and Events around the World: Development, Management and Markets*. Oxford, Butterworth Heinemann.

Hall, K. (2014). Create a sense of belonging. *Psychology Today*. Retrieved from www.psychology-today.com/blog/pieces-mind/201403/create-sense-belonging.

Ham, S. (1992). *Environmental Interpretation: A Practical Guide for People with Big Ideas and Small Budgets*. Golden, CO, North American Press.

Hamin, E.M. (2001). The US National Park Service's partnership parks: collaborative responses to middle landscapes. *Land Use Policy*, 18, 123–135.

Hammitt, W.E. & Cole, D.C. (1987). *Wildland Recreation: Ecology and Management*. New York, John Wiley.

Han, H. & Hyun, S.S. (2018). College youth travelers' eco-purchase behavior and recycling activity while traveling: an examination of gender difference. *Journal of Travel & Tourism Marketing*, 35(6), 740–754.

Hassell, D. (2014). How investing in employees ensures your organization's success. Columbia Business School. Retrieved from www.inc.com/young-entrepreneur-council/how-investing-in-employees-ensures-your-organization-s-success.html.

Heckhausen, H. (1989). *Motivation and Action*, 2nd edition (P.K. Leppmann, trans.). Berlin, Springer-Verlag.

Heim, J. (2011). *LOHAS or the Consumption of Sustainability*. Freiburg, University of Freiburg.

Heitmann, S., Robinson, P., & Povey, G. (2011). Slow food, slow cities and slow tourism. In Robinson, P., Heitmann, S., & Dieke, P. (Eds), *Research Themes for Tourism* (pp. 114–127). Wallingford, UK, CABI.

Hollenhorst, S.J., Houge-Mackenzie, S., & Ostergren, D.M. (2014). The trouble with tourism. *Tourism Recreation Research*, 39(3), 305–319.

Holtkamp, C., Shelton, T., Daly, G., Hiner, C.C., & Hagelman, R.R. (2016). Assessing neolocalism in microbreweries. *Applied Geography*, 2(1), 66–78.

Howard, J. (1998). Environmental education and interpretation: developing an affective difference. *Australian Journal of Environmental Education*, 14, 65–69.

Hudson, S. & Hudson, L. (2017). *Marketing for Tourism, Hospitality and Events: A Global and Digital Approach*. London, Sage.

Hughes, M. & Morrison-Saunders, A. (2005). Influence of on-site interpretation intensity on visitors to natural areas. *Journal of Ecotourism*, 4(3), 161–177.

Ilbery, B. & Kneafsey, M. (1998). Product and place: promoting quality products and services in the lagging rural regions of the European Union. *European Urban and Regional Studies*, 5(4), 329–341.

Ilgaz, Z. (2015). The best employees stay with companies that help them to get better. *Entrepreneur*. Retrieved from www.entrepreneur.com/article/249490.

International Association of Antarctica Tour Operators (2018). IAATO reports latest Antarctic tourism figures ahead of responsible tourism conference. Retrieved from https://iaato.org/documents/10157/2305849/IAATO+News+Release+-+annual+meeting+opens+2018+FINAL.pdf/b3d9e66a-1974-4db9-b410-18250bd434fb.

International Coral Reef Initiative (2013). A continuing call to action. Retrieved from www.icriforum.org/sites/default/files/ICRI_BOOKLET_2014_UPRIGHT.pdf.

International Monetary Fund (2002). Globalization: threat or opportunity? www.imf.org/external/np/exr/ib/2000/041200to.htm.

Irshad, H. (2010). *Rural Tourism: An Overview*. Rural Development Division, Government of Alberta, Canada.

Jacobs, C. (2011). *Community Capitals: Built Capital*. Department of Agriculture and Biological Sciences, South Dakota State University, Paper 523.

Jafari, J. (1990). Research and scholarship: the basis of tourism education. *Journal of Tourism Studies*, 1, 33–41.

Jenkins, C.L. (1982). The use of investment incentives for tourism projects in developing countries. *Tourism Management*, 3(2), 91–97.

Jones, P., Hillier, D., & Comfort, D. (2016). Sustainability in the hospitality industry: some personal reflections on corporate challenges and research agendas. *International Journal of Contemporary Hospitality Management*, 28(1), 36–67.

Jonker, J. & de Witte, M. (2006). *Management Models for Corporate Social Responsibility*. Heidelberg, Springer-Verlag.

Kang, M. & Moscardo, G. (2006). Exploring cross-cultural differences in attitudes towards responsible tourist behaviour: a comparison of Korean, British and Australian tourists. *Asia Pacific Journal of Tourism Research*, 11(4), 303–320.

Keeble, B.R. (1988). The Brundtland report: 'Our common future'. *Medicine and War*, 4(1), 17–25.

Keeley, B.R. (2007). *Human Capital: How What You Know Shapes Your Life*. Paris, OECD Publishing.

Keenan, P.J. (2008). Do norms still matter: the corrosive effects of globalization on the vitality of norms. *Vand. J. Transnat'l L.*, 41, 327.

Keller, K.L. (1993). Conceptualizing, measuring, and managing customer-based branding equity. *Journal of Marketing*, 57(1), 1–22.

Khan, N. & Trivedi, P. (2015). Gender differences and sustainable consumption behavior. *British Journal of Marketing Studies*, 3(3), 29–35.

Kogut, B. (2001). Multinational corporations. *International Encyclopedia of the Social & Behavioral Sciences*, 10197–10204.

Kotler, P. & Levy, S. (1971). Demarketing, yes, demarketing. *Harvard Business Review*, November–December, 74–80.

Koutra, C. (2008). Financial capital for tourism development and wealth creation. Retrieved from https://core.ac.uk/download/pdf/133026.pdf.

LaGrave, K. (2016). 15 places telling tourists to stay home. *Traveler*. Retrieved from www.cntraveler.com/galleries/2015-06-19/barcelona-bhutan-places-that-limit-tourist-numbers.

Lane, B. (2009). Thirty years of sustainable tourism: drivers, progress, problems – and the future. In Gossling, S., Hall, C.M., & Weaver, D.B. (Eds) *Thirty Years of Sustainable Tourism* (pp. 19–31). London, Routledge.

Laurance, W.F. (1999). Gaia's Lungs: are rainforests inhaling Earth's excess carbon dioxide? *Natural History*, 108(2), 96–96.

Le, A.V. (2017). Trump's presidency: the future of American tourism industry. *Journal of Tourism Futures*, 3(1), 8–12.

Lee, S. & Slocum, S.L. (2015). Understanding the role of local food in the meeting industry: an exploratory study of meeting planners' perception of local food in sustainable meeting planning. *Journal of Convention & Event Tourism*, 6(1), 45–60.

Lee, S., Jeon, S., & Kim, D. (2011). The impact of tour quality and tourist satisfaction on tourist loyalty: the case of Chinese tourists in Korea. *Tourism Management*, 32(5), 1115–1124.

Lee, Y., Chang, C.H., & Chen, Y.S. (2013). The influence of novelty, flexibility, and synergy of package tours on tourist satisfaction: an analysis of structural equation modeling (SEM). *Quality & Quantity*, 47(4), 1869–1882.

Lele, S. (1991). Sustainable development: a critical view. *World Development*, 19(6), 607–621.

Lemelin, H., Dawson, J., Stewart, E.J., Maher, P., & Lueck, M. (2010). Last-chance tourism: the boom, doom, and gloom of visiting vanishing destinations. *Current Issues in Tourism*, 13(5), 477–493.

Leslie, D. (2000). Holistic approach. In Jafari, J. (Ed.), *Encyclopedia of Tourism* (p. 281). London and New York, Routledge.

Lester, M. & dela Rama, M. (2018). Neo-protectionism in the age of Brexit and Trump: what does Australia do with its powerful friends? In Oberoi, R. & Halsall, J.P. (Eds), *Revisiting Globalization: From a Borderless to a Gated Globe* (pp. 91–119). Cham, Switzerland, Springer.

Liburd, J.J. (2012). Tourism research 2.0. *Annals of Tourism Research*, 39(2), 883–907.

Liu, Z. (2003) Sustainable tourism development: a critique. *Journal of Sustainable Tourism*, 11(6), 459–475.

Lohmann, G. & Netto, A.P. (2016). *Tourism Theory: Concepts, Models and Systems*. Oxon, CABI.

López-Sánchez, Y. & Pulido-Fernández, J.I. (2016). In search of the pro-sustainable tourist: a segmentation based on the tourist 'sustainable intelligence'. *Tourism Management Perspectives*, 17, 59–71.

Lowe, P. (1989). The rural idyllic defended: from preservation to conservation. In Mingay, G.E. (Ed.), *The Rural Idyllic* (pp. 133–130). Oxon, Routledge.

Luo, X. & Bhattacharya, C.B. (2006). Corporate social responsibility, customer satisfaction, and market value. *Journal of Marketing*, 70(4), 1–18.

Luo, Y. & Deng, J. (2008). The new environmental paradigm and nature-based tourism motivation. *Journal of Travel Research*, 46(4), 392–402.

Lyon, S. (2006). Evaluating fair trade consumption: politics, defetishization and producer participation. *International Journal of Consumer Studies*, 30(5), 452–464.

Mair, J. & Laing, J.H. (2013). Encouraging pro-environmental behaviour: the role of sustainability-focused events. *Journal of Sustainable Tourism*, 21(8), 1113–1128.

Makower, J. (2009). *Strategies for the Green Economy: Opportunities and Challenges in the New World of Business*. New York, McGraw Hill.

Manning, R. (1999). *Studies in Outdoor Recreation: Search and Research for Satisfaction*. Corvallis, Oregon State University Press.

Mark, J.J. (2018). Silk Road. Retrieved from www.ancient.eu/Silk_Road/.

Mathieson, A. & Wall, G. (1982). *Tourism: Economic, Physical and Social Impacts*. Harlow, UK, Longman.

Mattos, D. (2015). Community capitals framework as a measure of community development. Cornhusker Economics September 2, 2015. Retrieved from https://pdfs.semanticscholar.org/f599/531cf5fb0210d14becbb0633766091dee8eb.pdf.

McDonald, S., Oates, C.J., Thyne, M., Alevizou, P.J., & McMorland, L.A. (2009). Comparing sustainable consumption patterns across product sectors. *International Journal of Consumer Studies*, 33(2), 137–145.

McGehee, N.G., Lee, S., O'Bannon, T., & Perdue, R. (2010). Tourism-related social capital and its relationship with other forms of capital: An exploratory study. *Journal of Travel Research*, 49, 486–500.

McKercher, B. & du Cros, H. (2002). *Cultural Tourism: The Partnership Between Tourism and Cultural Heritage Management*. New York, Haworth.

McKercher, B., Ho, P.S., & du Cros, H. (2004). Attributes of popular cultural attractions in Hong Kong. *Annals of Tourism Research*, 31(2), 393–407.

McKinney, P. (n.d.). What is human capital in management? Definition and value. Retrieved from https://study.com/academy/lesson/what-is-human-capital-in-management-definition-value-quiz.html.

McKinsey and Company (2018). Chinese tourists: dispelling the myths. An in-depth look at China's outbound tourist market. Retrieved from www.mckinsey.com/~/media/mckinsey/industries/travel%20transport%20and%20logistics/our%20insights/huanying%20to%20the%20new%20chinese%20traveler/chinese-tourists-dispelling-the-myths.ashx.

Mehmetoglu, M. (2010). Factors influencing the willingness to behave environmentally friendly at home and holiday settings. *Scandinavian Journal of Hospitality and Tourism*, 10(4), 430–447.

Messner, C., Wänke, M., & Weibel, C. (2011). Unconscious personnel selection. *Social Cognition*, 29(6), 699–710.

Michalena, E. & Hills, J.M. (2013). Renewable energy governance. In Michalena, E. & Hills, J.M. (Eds), *Renewable Energy* (pp. 3–8). London, Springer-Verlag.

Montanari, A. & Staniscia, B. (2009). Culinary tourism as a tool for regional re-equilibrium. *European Planning Studies*, 17(10), 1463–1483.

Montgomery, J. & Inkles, A. (2001). *Social Capital as a Policy Resource*. Dordrecht, Kluwer Academy Publishers.

Moscardo, G. (1996). Mindful visitors: heritage and tourism. *Annals of Tourism Research*, 23(2), 376–397.

Moscardo, G. (2012). Building social capital to enhance the quality-of-life of destination residents. In Uysal, M., Perdue, R., & Sirgy, M.J. (Eds) *Handbook of Tourism and Quality-of-Life Research* (pp. 403–421). Dordrecht, Springer.

Moscardo, G., Woods, B., & Saltzer, R. (2004). *The Role of Interpretation in Wildlife Tourism*. Research Park, Champaign, IL, Common Ground Publishing.

Mosley, L. & Uno, S. (2007). Racing to the bottom or climbing to the top? Economic globalization and collective labor rights. *Comparative Political Studies*, 40(8), 923–948.

Mowforth, M. & Munt, I. (2009). *Tourism and Sustainability: Development, Globalization and New Tourism*, 3rd edition. Abingdon, Routledge.

Mu Ko Similan National Park of Thailand (2018). Koh Tachai Island. Retrieved from https://similan-islands.com/koh-tachai/.

National Geographic Society (2018). National Geographic education resource library. Retrieved from www.nationalgeographic.org/education/resource-library/?q=&page=1&per_page=25.

Newton, A.C. (2015). Defining the green economy and the potential role of green tourism. In Reddy, V. and Wilkes, K. (Eds) *Tourism in the Green Economy* (pp. 32–45). London, Routledge.

Nitzan, J. & Bichler, S. (2009). *Capital as Power: A Study of Order and Creorder*. London, Routledge.

Ocean Park Corporation (2005). Vision and mission. Retrieved from www.oceanpark.com.hk/en/corporate-information/vision-and-mission.

Ofori, G. (2009). Ethical leadership: examining the relationships with full range leadership model, employee outcomes, and organizational culture. *Journal of Business Ethics*, 90(4), 533.

Oh, J.Y. & Schuett, M.A. (2010). Exploring expenditure-based segmentation for rural tourism: overnight stay visitors versus excursionists to fee-fishing sites. *Journal of Travel & Tourism Marketing*, 27(1), 31–50.

Ontario Culinary Tourism Alliance (2015). The rise of food tourism. Retrieved from https://skift.com/2015/02/17/new-free-skift-report-the-rise-of-food-tourism/.

O'Reilly, A.M. (1986). Tourism carrying capacity: concept and issues. *Tourism Management*, 7(4), 254–258.

Organization for Economic Co-operation and Development (2018). *OECD Tourism Trends and Policies 2018*. Paris, OECD Publishing.

Parmar, P. (2016). How culinary tourism is becoming a growing trend in travel. Retrieved from www.huffingtonpost.ca/parmjit-parmar/the-rise-of-culinary-tourism_b_7596704.html.

Passafaro, P., Cini, F., Boi, L., D'Angelo, M., Heering, M.S., Luchetti, L., . . . & Sassu, F. (2015). The "sustainable tourist": values, attitudes, and personality traits. *Tourism and Hospitality Research*, 15(4), 225–239.

Peeters, P. (2012). A clear path towards sustainable mass tourism? Rejoinder to the paper "Organic, incremental and induced paths to sustainable mass tourism convergence" by D.B. Weaver. *Tourism Management*, 33, 1038–1041.

Pettypiece, S. (2018). Trump to tell Davos that "America First" is good for globalism. Retrieved from www.bloomberg.com/news/articles/2018-01-25/trump-to-tell-davos-that-america-first-is-good-for-globalism.

Plüss, C., Zotz, A., Monshausen, A., & Kühhas, C. (2016). Sustainability in tourism: a guide through the label jungle. Global Sustainable Tourism Council. Retrieved from https://destinet.eu/who-who/civil-society-ngos/ecotrans/publications/guide-through-label-jungle-1/.

Pomering, A., Noble, G., & Johnson, L.W. (2011) Conceptualising a contemporary marketing mix for sustainable tourism. *Journal of Sustainable Tourism*, 19(8), 953–969.

Pongsathornwiwat, N., Huynh, V.N., & Jeenanunta, C. (2017). Developing evaluation criteria for partner selection in tourism supply chain networks. *International Journal of Knowledge and Systems Science (IJKSS)*, 8(1), 39–52.

Prest, A. & Turvey, R. (1965). Cost–benefit analysis: a survey. *The Economic Journal*, 75(300), 683–735.

Prince, S. & Ioannides, D. (2017). Contextualizing the complexities of managing alternative tourism at the community-level: a case study of a Nordic eco-village. *Tourism Management*, 60, 348–356.

Rademaker, L.G. (2008). *Interpretive Technology in Parks: A Study of Visitor Experiences with Portable Multimedia Devices*. Missoula, MT, University of Montana.

Ralon, P., Taylor, M., Ilas, A., Diaz-Bone, H., & Kairies, K.P. (2017). Electricity storage and renewables: costs and markets to 2030. Abu Dhabi, International Renewable Energy Agency.

Ray, P.H. & Anderson, S.R. (2000). *The Cultural Creatives: How 50 Million People are Changing the World*. New York, Harmony Books.

Raymond, J. (2013). Sexist attitudes: most of us are biased. *Nature*, 495(7439), 33.

Reid, N. & Gatrell, J.D. (2017). Craft breweries and economic development: local geographies of beer. *Polymath: An Interdisciplinary Arts and Sciences Journal*, 7(2), 90–110.

Reid, R.D. & Bojanic, D.C. (2009). *Hospitality Marketing Management*. Hoboken, NJ, John Wiley and Sons.

Riker, M.S. (2016). Despite being one of Hawaii's most iconic beaches, many visitors don't know Waikiki Beach is actually an engineered beach that has been filled with imported sand for decades. *US News and World Report*, March 2, Associated Press.

Rivera, J. (2002). Assessing a voluntary environmental initiative in the developing world: the Costa Rican certification for sustainable tourism. *Policy Sciences*, 35(4), 333–360.

Rixen, C. & Rolando, A. (Eds) (2013). *The Impacts of Skiing and Related Winter Recreational Activities on Mountain Environments*. Oak Park, IL, Bentham Science Publishers.

Robinson, P., Heitmann, S., & Dieke, P.U. (Eds) (2011). *Research Themes for Tourism*. Wallingford, UK, CABI.

Roggenbuck, J. (1992) Use of persuasion to reduce resource impacts and visitor conflicts. In Manfredo, M. (Ed.) *Influencing Human Behaviour* (pp. 149–208). Champaign, IL, Sagamore Publishing Company.

Rosser, M., Rosser, V., & Barkley, J. (2003). *Comparative Economics in a Transforming World Economy*. Cambridge, MA, MIT Press.

Rui, S. (2018). Report on world tourism economy trends (2018). Tourism Research Center, Chinese Academy of Social Sciences, March 7, 2018, Berlin.

Salazar, N. (2012). Community-based cultural tourism: issues, threats and opportunities. *Journal of Sustainable Tourism*, 20(1), 9–22.

Salzmann, O., Ionescu-Somers, A., & Steger, U. (2005). The business case for corporate sustainability: literature review and research options. *European Management Journal*, 23(1), 27–36.

Sarkis, J. (2012). A boundaries and flows perspective of green supply chain management. *Supply Chain Management*, 17(2), 202–216.

Scheyvens, R. (2002). *Tourism for Development: Empowering Communities*. Essex, UK, Pearson Education Limited.

Schnell, S.M. (2011). The local traveler: farming, food, and place in state and provincial tourism guides, 1993–2008. *Journal of Cultural Geography*, 28(2), 281–309.

Schnell, S.M. (2013). Deliberate identities: becoming local in America in a global age. *Journal of Cultural Geography*, 30(1), 55–89.

Schoemaker, M., Nijhof, A., & Jonker, J. (2006). Human value management: the influence of the contemporary developments of corporate social responsibility and social capital on HRM. *Management Revue*, 448–465.

Schreiber, E. (2011). Reputation. Institute for Public Relations. Retrieved from https://instituteforpr.org/reputation/.

Seuring, S., Müller, M., Westhaus, M., & Morana, R. (2005). Conducting a literature review: the example of sustainability in supply chains. In: Kotzab, H., Seuring, S., Muller, M., & Reiner, G. (Eds), *Conducting a Literature Review: The Example of Sustainability in Supply Chains* (pp. 91–106). Heidelberg, Physica-Verlag.

Seyfang, G. (2008). Avoiding Asda? Exploring consumer motivations in local organic food networks. *Local Environment*, 13(3), 187–201.

Shangquan, G. (2000). Economic globalization: trends, risks and risk prevention. *Economic & Social Affairs, CDP Background Paper*, 1.

Sharpley, R. (2009). *Tourism Development and the Environment: Beyond Sustainability?* London, Earthscan.

Sheller, M. & Urry, J. (2004). Places to stay, places to play. In Sheller, M. & Urry, J. (Eds) *Tourism Mobilities: Places to Play, Places in Play* (pp. 1–10). London, Routledge.

Shepherd, R. (2002). Commodification, culture and tourism. *Tourist Studies*, 2(2), 183–201.

Sigala, M. (2008). A supply chain management approach for investigating the role of tour operators on sustainable tourism: the case of TUI. *Journal of Cleaner Production*, 16(15), 1589–1599.

Simmons, D.G. (1994). Community participation in tourism planning. *Tourism Management*, 15(2), 98–108.

Skanavis, C. & Sakellari, M. (2008). Gender and sustainable tourism: women's participation in the environmental decision-making process. *European Journal of Tourism Research*, 1(2).

Škapa, R. (2014). Reverse logistics as sustainable tool in tourism industry: scope and motivation. *European Journal of Tourism, Hospitality and Recreation*, 5(1), 1.

Slocum, S.L. & Curtis, K.R. (2016). Assessing sustainable food behaviours of national park visitors: domestic/on vocation linkages, and their implications for park policies. *Journal of Sustainable Tourism*, 24(1), 153–167.

Slocum, S.L. & Curtis, K.R. (2017). *Food and Agricultural Tourism: Theory and Best Practice*. Abingdon, Routledge.

Slocum, S.L. & Everett, S. (2010). Food tourism initiatives: resistance on the ground. In C. Brebbia (Ed.), *The Sustainable World* (pp. 745–758). Southampton, UK, WIT Press.

Sohn, E. & Yuan, J. (2013). Who are the culinary tourists? An observation at a food and wine festival. *International Journal of Culture, Tourism and Hospitality Research*, 7(2), 118–131.

Spenceley, A., Kohl, J., McArthur, S., Myles, P., Notarianni, M., Paleczny, D., Pickering, C., & Worboys, G.L. (2015). Visitor management. In Worboys, G.L., Lockwood, M., Kothari, A., Feary S., & Pulsford, I. (Eds), *Protected Area Governance and Management* (pp. 715–750). Canberra, ANU Press.

Sustainable Events Alliance (2010). About the Sustainable Event Alliance. Retrieved from https://sustainable-event-alliance.org/about-2/.

Swarbrooke, J. (1999). *Sustainable Tourism Management*. Wallingford, UK, CABI.

Szakály, Z., Popp, J., Kontor, E., Kovács, S., Pető, K., & Jasák, H. (2017). Attitudes of the life-style of health and sustainability segment in Hungary. *Sustainability*, 9(10), 1763.

Szpilko, D. (2017). Tourism supply chain: overview of selected literature. *Procedia Engineering*, 182, 687–693.

Tan, E. & Law, R. (2016). Learning as a softer visitor management approach for sustainable tourism. *Journal of Sustainable Tourism*, 24(1), 132–152.

Tanzi, V. (2017, April). Corruption, complexity and tax evasion. Tax and Corruption Symposium. *eJournal of Tax Research*, 15(2), December, 1–25.

Teo, P. (2002). Striking a balance for sustainable tourism: implications of the discourse on globalisation. *Journal of Sustainable Tourism*, 10(6), 459–474.

Thompson, D. (2010). How does a "value added tax" work, anyway? Retrieved from www.theatlantic.com/business/archive/2010/03/how-does-a-value-added-tax-work-anyway/36834/.

Timothy, D. (2011). *Cultural Heritage and Tourism: An Introduction*. Bristol, UK, Channel View Publications.

Torell, E. (2002). From past to present: the historical context of environmental and coastal management in Tanzania. *Development Southern Africa*, 19(2), 273–288.

Tosun, C. (2000). Limits to community participation in the tourism development process in developing countries. *Tourism Management*, 21(6), 613–633.

Tourism Concern (n.d.). How does tourism affect the demand for water? Retrieved from www.tourismconcern.org.uk/wp-content/uploads/2014/09/Unit2-Resource-A-1.pdf.

Tubb, K.N. (2003). An evaluation of the effectiveness of interpretation within Dartmoor National Park in reaching the goals of sustainable tourism development. *Journal of Sustainable Tourism*, 11, 476–498.

United Kingdom Department for Environment, Food and Rural Affairs (DEFRA) (2008). *A Framework for Pro-environmental Behaviours*. London, Department for Environment, Food and Rural Affairs.

United Kingdom Department for International Development (1999). Tourism and poverty elimination: untapped potential. London, DFID.

United Nations (2001). Global registry of voluntary commitments and multi-stakeholder partnerships. Retrieved from https://sustainabledevelopment.un.org/partnership/?p=1495.

United Nations (2015). Transforming our world: The 2030 agenda for sustainable development. *Resolution adopted by the General Assembly*.

United Nations Development Programme (2009). *Capacity Development: A UNDP Primer*. New York, UNDP.

United Nations Educational, Scientific and Cultural Organization (2003). Identification and documentation of modern heritage. World Heritage Papers Number 5, Paris, UNESCO World Heritage Centre.

United Nations Educational, Scientific, and Cultural Organization (2015). World Heritage sustainable tourism toolkit. Retrieved from http://whc.unesco.org/sustainabletourismtoolkit/guides/guide-4-engaging-local-communities-and-businesses.

United Nations Educational, Scientific, and Cultural Organization (2018). List of world heritage in danger. Retrieved from https://whc.unesco.org/en/danger/.

United Nations Environment Programme (UNEP) & United Nations World Tourism Organization (UNWTO) (2007). *Climate Change and Tourism: Responding to Global Challenges*. UNEP and UNWTO.

United Nations Environment Programme (2011). Towards a green economy: pathways to sustainable development and poverty eradication. UNEP: Geneva. Retrieved from https://sustainabledevelopment.un.org/content/documents/126GER_synthesis_en.pdf.

United Nations World Tourism Organization (UNWTO) (1985). Tourism bill of rights and tourist code. Sofia, Bulgaria, UNWTO.

United Nations World Tourism Organization (1999). Global code of ethics for tourism. Retrieved from http://ethics.unwto.org/content/global-code-ethics-tourism.

United Nations World Tourism Organization (2005). Tourism, micro-finance and poverty alleviation. International year of micro-credit. Madrid, UNWTO.

United Nations World Tourism Organization (2014). *World Tourism Barometer and Statistical Annex*, 12(5). World Tourism Organization, Madrid.

United Nations World Tourism Organization (2017). *Yearbook of Tourism Statistics, 2017 Edition*. World Tourism Organization, Madrid.

United Nations World Tourism Organization (2019a). Who we are. Retrieved from http://www2.unwto.org/content/who-we-are-0.

United Nations World Tourism Organization (2019b). History. Retrieved from http://www2.unwto.org/content/history-0.

United Nations World Tourism Organization (n.d.). FAQ: climate change and tourism. Retrieved from http://sdt.unwto.org/content/faq-climate-change-and-tourism.

United States Central Intelligence Agency (2017). *The CIA World Factbook 2016*. Washington, DC, Central Intelligence Agency.

United States Environmental Protection Agency (2018). Overview of greenhouse gases. Retrieved from www.epa.gov/ghgemissions/overview-greenhouse-gases.

United States Federal Highway Administration (2016). Annual vehicle miles traveled in the US. Retrieved from www.afdc.energy.gov/data/.

United States National Aeronautics and Space Administration (2018). Scientific consensus: earth's climate is warming. Retrieved from https://climate.nasa.gov/scientific-consensus/.

United States National Park Service (2007). Foundations of interpretation curriculum content narrative. Retrieved from www.nps.gov/idp/interp/101/foundationscurriculum.pdf.

United States Trade Representative (2018). Northern American Free Trade Agreement. Retrieved from https://ustr.gov/trade-agreements/free-trade-agreements/north-american-free-trade-agreement-nafta.

Urh, B. (2015). Lifestyle of health and sustainability: the importance of health consciousness impact on LOHAS market growth in ecotourism. *Quaestus*, 6(1), 167–177.

Virginia Restaurant, Lodging, and Travel Association (2019). Government affairs updates. Retrieved from www.vrlta.org/page/GeneralAssembly.

Wallace, G.N. & Pierce, S.M. (1996). An evaluation of ecotourism in the Amazon, Brazil. *Annals of Tourism Research*, 23(4), 843–873.

Wallace, S. & Riley, S. (2015). Tourism 2025: an industry perspective. *Journal of Tourism Futures*, 1(1), 53–57.

Wallach, L.M. (2001). Accountable governance in the era of globalization: the WTO, NAFTA, and international harmonization of standards. *University of Kansas Law Review*, 50, 823.

Wan, S.K. & Song, H. (2018). Forecasting turning points in tourism growth. *Annals of Tourism Research*, 72, 156–167.

Weaver, D.B. & Lawton, L. (2014). *Tourism Management*. Milton, Queensland, John Wiley & Sons.

Weaver, D.B. (2000). A broad context model of destination development scenarios. *Tourism Management*, 21(3), 217–224.

Weaver, D.B. (2009). Reflections on sustainable tourism and paradigm changes. In Gössling, S., Hall, C.M., & Weaver, D. (Eds), *Sustainable Tourism Futures: Perspectives on Systems, Restructuring and Innovations* (pp. 32–42). London, Routledge.

Weaver, D.B. (2010). Indigenous tourism stages and their implications for sustainability. *Journal of Sustainable Tourism*, 18(1), 43–60.

Weaver, D.B. (2012). Organic, incremental and induced paths to sustainable mass tourism convergence. *Tourism Management*, 33, 1030–1037.

Weaver, L.C. & Petersen, T. (2008). Namibia communal area conservancies. *Best practices in Sustainable Hunting*, 1, 48–52.

Webster, C. (2017). Political turbulence and business as usual: tourism's future. *Journal of Tourism Futures*, 3(1), 4–7.

Webster, C. & Ivanov, S. (2015). Geopolitical drivers of future tourist flows. *Journal of Tourism Futures*, 1(1), 58–68.

Wesley, S.C., Jackson, V.P., & Lee, M. (2017). The perceived importance of core soft skills between retailing and tourism management students, faculty and businesses. *Employee Relations*, 39(1), 79–99.

Williams, P.W. & Ponsford, I.F. (2009). Confronting tourism's environmental paradox: transitioning for sustainable tourism. *Futures*, 41(6), 396–404.

Wilson, S., Fesenmaier, D., Fesenmaier, J., & Van Es, J. (2001). Factors for success in rural tourism development. *Journal of Travel Research*, 40, 132–138.

Wolf, I.D., Stricker, H.K., & Hagenloh, G. (2013). Interpretive media that attract park visitors and enhance their experiences: a comparison of modern and traditional tools using GPS tracking and GIS technology. *Tourism Management Perspectives*, 7, 59–72.

World Economic Forum (2017). *Tourism and Job Creation: Advancing the 2030 Development Agenda.* Geneva, World Economic Forum.

World Summit on Sustainable Tourism (2015). The world charter for sustainable tourism +20. Retrieved from www.institutoturismoresponsable.com/events/sustainabletourismcharter 2015/the-world-charter-for-sustainable-tourism/index.html.

World Travel and Tourism Council (2015). Governing national tourism policy. Retrieved from www.wttc.org/publications/other/governing-national-tourism-policy/.

World Travel and Tourism Council (2016). *Travel and Tourism Economic Impact 2016 World.* London, WTTC.

World Travel and Tourism Council (2019). About WTTC. Retrieved from www.wttc.org/about/.

World Wildlife Fund (2018). Facts. Retrieved from www.worldwildlife.org/species/rhino.

Yamamoto, D. & Gill, A.M. (1999). Emerging trends in Japanese package tourism. *Journal of Travel Research*, 38(2), 134–143.

Yasarata, M., Altinay, L., Burns, P., & Okumus, F. (2010). Politics and sustainable tourism development: can they co-exist? Voices from North Cyprus. *Tourism Management*, 31(3), 345–356.

Zahra, A. & McGehee, N.G. (2013). Volunteer tourism: a host community capital perspective. *Annals of Tourism Research*, 42, 22–45.

Zakaria, S. & Yusoff, W.F.W. (2011). Transforming human resources into human capital. *Information Management and Business Review*, 2(2), 48–54.

Zekeri, A.A. (2013). Community capital and local economic development efforts. *Professional Agricultural Workers Journal*, 1(1), 7.

Zhang, X., Song, H., & Huang, G.Q. (2009). Tourism supply chain management: a new research agenda. *Tourism Management*, 30(3), 345–358.

Index

Page numbers in **bold** indicate references to tables or figures. Page numbers in *italics* indicate references in case studies.